ISAIAH
THE
GOSPEL PROPHET

By
M. L. Andreasen

TEACH Services, Inc.
Brushton, New York

**PRINTED IN
THE UNITED STATES OF AMERICA**

World rights reserved. This book or any portion thereof may not be copied or reproduced in any form or manner whatever, except as provided by law, without the written permission of the publisher, except by a reviewer who may quote brief passages in a review.

The author assumes full responsibility for the accuracy
of all facts and quotations as cited in this book.

Facsimile Reproduction

As this book played a formative role in the development of Christian thought and the publisher feels that this book, with its candor and depth, still holds significance for the church today. Therefore the publisher has chosen to reproduce this historical classic from an original copy. Frequent variations in the quality of the print are unavoidable due to the condition of the original. Thus the print may look darker or lighter or appear to be missing detail, more in some places than in others.

2006 07 08 09 10 11 12 · 5 4 3 2 1

Copyright © 2001 TEACH Services, Inc.
ISBN-13: 978-1-57258-183-8
ISBN-10: 1-57258-183-2
Library of Congress Control Number: 2001092187

Published by

TEACH Services, Inc.
www.TEACHServices.com

Isaiah, the Gospel Prophet

A Preacher of Righteousness

Index to volumes

Isaiah, The Gospel Prophet, Volume 1 3

Sabbath School Quarterly, 3rd. Quarter, 1928 95

Isaiah, The Gospel Prophet, Volume 2 135

Sabbath School Quarterly, 4th Quarter, 1928 224

Isaiah, The Gospel Prophet, Volume 3 263

Sabbath School Quarterly, 1st. Quarter, 1929 359

"His name shall be called Wonderful, Counselor, The mighty God, The everlasting Father, The Prince of Peace." Isa. 9:6

Isaiah, the Gospel Prophet

A Preacher of Righteousness

Lesson Notes and Helps

By M. L. ANDREASEN

Volume 1

"Wash you, make you clean; put away the evil of your doings from before Mine eyes; cease to do evil; learn to do well; seek judgment, relieve the oppressed, judge the fatherless, plead for the widow.

"Come now, and let us reason together, saith the Lord: though your sins be as scarlet, they shall be as white as snow; though they be red like crimson, they shall be as wool." Isa. 1: 16-18.

It is peace that you need,— Heaven's forgiveness and peace and love in the soul. Money cannot buy it, intellect cannot procure it, wisdom cannot attain to it; you can never hope, by your own effort, to secure it. But God offers it to you as a gift, "without money and without price." It is yours, if you will but reach out your hand and grasp it. The Lord says, "Though your sins be as scarlet, they shall be as white as snow; though they be red like crimson, they shall be as wool." "A new heart also will I give you, and a new spirit will I put within you."

You have confessed your sins, and in heart put them away. You have resolved to give yourself to God. Now go to Him, and ask that He will wash away your sins, and give you a new heart. Then believe that He does this because He has promised. —"Steps to Christ," p. 53.

Contents

	Lessons From the Book of Isaiah	7
I.	The Times of Isaiah: Spiritual Conditions	13
II.	Results of Israel's Rebellion	19
III.	The Call to the House of Jacob	24
IV.	The Vineyard; The Six Woes; Messianic Prophecies; The Remnant	30
V.	A Song of Praise; The Earth Destroyed; The Fall of Satan	37
VI.	The Trials and Triumphs of God's People	43
VII.	The Vineyard; False Security	49
VIII.	Events Connected With the Coming of the Lord	56
IX.	The Judgment and the Time of Trouble	62
X.	The Destruction of the Earth; The New Earth	69
XI.	Invasion of Judah by Assyria; God Delivers His People	75
XII.	Hezekiah's Prayer Answered; His Pride Rebuked	82
XIII.	Warnings and Reproofs; An Unheeded Call to Repentance	87

Lessons From the Book of Isaiah
Introduction

ISAIAH, whose name signifies "Jehovah is salvation," is one of the four so-called major prophets. He lived in Jerusalem, and was closely connected with the court, probably court preacher. He was of royal blood, and tradition makes him the cousin of King Uzziah. His father, Amoz, of whom we know nothing beyond his name, should not be confused with the prophet Amos, to whom he was not related.

Very little is known of Isaiah's early life. The schools of the prophets were in existence in his day, and he may have attended them, but of this nothing certain is known. That he had a good education, whether he received it in the prophetic schools or in Jerusalem, is testified to abundantly by his writings, which show not only a profound grasp of spiritual values, but also reveal a literary culture that places him in the very front rank of Old Testament writers. He was married and had two sons, to whom he gave symbolic names: Shear-jashub, "a remnant shall return" (Isa. 7:3); and Maher-shalal-hash-baz, "hastening to the spoil! hurrying to the prey!" Isa. 8:2, 3.

Isaiah prophesied during the reigns of Uzziah, Jotham, Ahaz, and Hezekiah, kings of Judah. Isa. 1:1. Uzziah, also called Azariah (2 Kings 14:21), reigned fifty-two years, and died about 740 B. C. 2 Chron. 26:3. His son, Jotham, was associated with him on the throne after Uzziah was stricken with leprosy (2 Chron. 26:21), and reigned sixteen years. Jotham was followed by Ahaz, who also is said to have reigned sixteen years. 2 Chron. 28:1. He in turn was followed by Hezekiah, who reigned twenty-nine years. 2 Chron. 29:1. There is good reason for believing that these reigns overlapped. Manasseh, who followed Hezekiah, began to reign early in the seventh century, about 699 B. C., and reigned fifty-five years. 2 Chron. 33:1. It was during his reign that Isaiah died, being, according to tradition, placed between two planks and sawed asunder. To this there may be a reference in Hebrews 11:36-38.

Isaiah was a prophet of righteousness, of holiness, of justice. He was a prophet of faith, of courage, of consecration. His was a ministry of great earnestness and boldness coupled with deep spirituality and profound reverence. His hatred of sin was deep, intense, uncompromising; his conception of God, lofty, reverential, awesome. Injustice, covetousness, pride, hypocrisy, he denounced in unmeasured terms. Isa. 1:10-23; 2:11-17; 3:9-15; 5:7-25; 28:7-15. With Isaiah outward formalities counted little; sacrifices were worthless, attendance at public worship also was worthless. Isa. 1:11-13. Nothing has any real value in the sight of God that is not grounded in purity of life and heart, in true humility, in obedience. Isa. 1:19. Other prophets and teachers have had special characteristics that identified them. Micah is thus the prophet of justice; Hosea, of love. Elijah was the man of faith and courage; John the Baptist, the fearless denouncer of sin. John the beloved was deeply spiritual, a teacher of true holiness. James stands forth as a contemner of hypocrisy and sham. All these traits, found separately in these men, were united in Isaiah. Hence he has been called "the king of prophets," "the evangelical prophet;" "the St. John of the Old Testament," "the St. Paul of the Old Testament." He is all of that, and more. In all the characteristics of a true prophet he is pre-eminently great.

Isaiah lived in a time that called for courage as well as conviction, for action as well as faith. He was not only prophet, but statesman. Four definite invasions of the land by Assyria took place during Isaiah's active ministry: the first by Tiglath-Pileser III, in 734-732 B. C.; the second by Shalmaneser IV and Sargon II, in 725-720, at which time Samaria fell; the third by Sargon, in 712-710; and the fourth by Sennacherib, in 701. In each of these political crises Isaiah bore a prominent part, and his sound advice, unflinching courage, clear vision, and abounding faith proved no small factor in saving Judah, at least for a century more, from the fate that overtook the northern kingdom — Israel.

The outstanding political fact during Isaiah's life was these Assyrian invasions. The two kingdoms, Israel and Judah, were both threatened, together with the other small kingdoms that stood in the way of the Assyrian advance. The easiest way to avoid extinction seemed to buy off the conquerors, as did Menahem and Hezekiah (2 Kings 15:19; 18:13-16); or as did Ahaz, to make an alliance with the enemy, which also involved the payment of money. 2 Kings 16:8. Isaiah knew that such was but a temporary expedient, that it would only reveal to Assyria that there were treasures in Judah which could be had for the taking. The king had only exposed his kingdom to the cupidity of Assyria, had "made Judah naked," and it "helped him not" and "strengthened him not." 2 Chron. 28:19-21.

Against such shortsighted policies Isaiah made his protests. He was against alliances of all kinds. His message was one of trust

Lessons From the Book of Isaiah

in the Lord. "Be not afraid," he told Hezekiah. 2 Kings 19:6. This message of faith he bore in every crisis. The Lord only could help. If king and people would but turn to Him and confess and abjure their sins, God would work mightily for them. This was abundantly demonstrated in the time of Hezekiah, when the people humbled themselves and sought forgiveness. The Lord wrought mightily for them and delivered them. 2 Kings 19:6, 7, 32-35. Isaiah saw clearly that departure from God was the real cause of Israel's political calamities, and that a turning to God was the only permanent remedy. This view guided Isaiah in all his messages.

Even as Isaiah is one of the greatest prophets, so his book is one of the most important of Old Testament volumes. "This book is justly placed in the Hebrew Bible at the head of the prophetic writings," says Harman. "Isaiah is the most sublime, versatile, and comprehensive of all the prophets."—"*Introduction to the Book of Isaiah,*" *p. 330.*

Ewald, one of the critics, speaking of the literary value of the book, says: "In Isaiah we see prophetic authorship reaching its culminating point. Everything conspired to raise him to an elevation to which no prophet, either before or after, could as a writer attain."—"*Isaiah,*" *Vol. I, p. xii.*

Different writers speak of the lofty and majestic calmness, the energy and liveliness, of the style of Isaiah. He is called an expert in the use of images, of epigrams and metaphors. His descriptions are vivid with a wonderful variety of style. His Hebrew is of the purest and best, his vocabulary larger than that of any other book of the Bible.

Few of the books of the Bible have been under the fire of higher criticism as has Isaiah. In this it shares honors with the Pentateuch. Aben Ezra, a Spanish rabbi of the twelfth century, was the first to question the authorship of the book. He rejected chapters 40-66 as not having been written by Isaiah or in his time. Not until the nineteenth century do we hear any further criticism, but then a perfect avalanche began. Not only were chapters 40-66 questioned, but every part of the book was closely scrutinized. Each chapter and each verse was minutely examined with the critics' magnifying glass, and the dissection went on apace. One of the critics, Eichhorn, went so far as to divide the book into eighty-five oracles, or fragments, which he attributed to different authors and times. Ewald, however, believes there are only seven authors, a considerable reduction. As these critics rejected Isaiah as the author of chapters 40-66, they were hard put to it to find who had written them. It must have been one as great as Isaiah, for the language of chapters 40-66 is as lofty and sublime as that of other parts of the book. And how could such a one remain unknown? Cheyne, a learned critic, is frankly perplexed, as are the others, over this matter. He says that whoever wrote the chapters imitated the style of Isaiah and knew his prophecies by heart. (See "The Prophecies of Isaiah," Vol. II, p. 232.) Having found no suitable person to father the book, critics agreed to call the author the "Great Unnamed."

But this hardly settles the matter. The "Great Unnamed" was supposed to have lived at the time of the return from the Babylonian captivity, a contemporary of Ezra. But how would it be possible for the "Great Unnamed" to produce such a marvelous piece of literature, and yet remain unknown to his contemporaries? And more than that, how could he deceive Ezra to such a degree that when the collection of canonical books was made, Ezra could be persuaded to include these chapters in the canon when they had never been heard of before? And still more, would Ezra attribute these chapters to Isaiah, as he does, if the contemporaries of Ezra had not believed them to be the work of the prophet? It is inconceivable that Ezra and his coworkers should come upon such a valuable treasure as chapters 40-66, and never raise a question as to their authenticity, but calmly include them in the canon as the work of Isaiah. Would not the orthodox Jews, who are so very careful in their transcription of the Scriptures as even to count every word, have raised a question in regard to these hitherto unknown chapters? But history records no such event. Even though we should admit the contention of the critics that Ezra did not make the compilation of the Scriptures, yet the fact remains that the canon was made up by some one at that time, and the argument holds good. It would seem that the evidence is overwhelmingly in favor of the belief that when these chapters were included in the canon, they had been in existence for some time, and were believed to be the work of Isaiah. On no other hypothesis can their admittance to the canon be explained.

It is not the plan here to attempt a defense of the unity of Isaiah, to prove that all the chapters of the book are the work of the man whose name it bears. A few further observations, however, may be in place:

The Septuagint, a Greek translation of the Hebrew Scriptures made about 250 B. C., ascribes the entire book to Isaiah. Jesus, the son of Sirach, who lived about 180 B. C., distinctly says that chapters 40-66 were the work of Isaiah, a contemporary of Hezekiah. The New Testament writers definitely accept Isaiah as the author of the later chapters. (See Matt. 3:3; Mark 1:2, R. V.; Luke 3: 4-6; John 12:38; Rom. 10:16-21.) Josephus does likewise. (See " Antiquities," book XI, chap. 1.)

When we turn to the book itself, we find abundant evidence of its unity. Throughout Isaiah there is a similarity of language and constructions, of thoughts and images, of characteristic expressions. The book is one in respect to language, subject matter, and treatment. Of this, abundant evidence could be produced. One interesting instance may be cited: The name, " the Holy One of Israel," is peculiar to Isaiah. It is used elsewhere in the Old Testament only six times, but in Isaiah twenty-five times, twelve times in chapters 1-39 and thirteen times in chapters 40-66. " The presence of this divine name in all the different portions of the book is of more value in identifying Isaiah as the author of these prophecies than as though his name had been inscribed at the beginning of every chapter."—*Robinson's " Isaiah," p. 14.* The fact that this name is used practically only by Isaiah, and that it is used nearly the same number of times in the last part of the book as in the first part, " interlocks inseparably all the various portions with one another, and stamps them with the personal imprimatur of him who saw the vision of the majestic God seated on His throne high and lifted up " — *Ibid.*

Than Isaiah no other prophet had a clearer vision of the results both of sin and of righteousness. He was unsparing in his denunciation of those who tried to cover their lack of true religion with a cloak of zeal for outward ceremonies. When enemies were at the gate, he knew that the real enemy to be feared was sin in the heart.

Isaiah was patriotic, but his patriotism did not lead him to condone wrong or oppression. He was as ready to denounce sin in Israel as sin in Moab. He spared neither king nor peasant, priest nor people. Sin in the nation or sin in the individual would lead to the same result — separation from God, and defeat. Throughout the book this is pointed out, clearly and distinctly.

But even as Isaiah denounced sin, so he also lifted up Him who alone can save from sin. He was essentially a preacher of righteousness. He believed in the ultimate triumph of right. He was optimistic, but not with the kind of optimism that refuses squarely to face the facts. He knew men and how to deal with them. He also knew God and how to prevail with Him. And only he who knows both God and man can be an effective preacher. Isaiah was that kind of man.

The prophets of the Old Testament were more than mere foretellers. In fact, predicting future events is not necessarily a part of the work of a prophet. John the Baptist was a great prophet, but we have no record of any prediction by him. A prophet is a forth-teller rather than a foreteller. He speaks forth that which God gives him. He is God's mouthpiece. Deut. 18:18. When Moses complained that he could not speak well, God gave him Aaron. "Thou shalt speak unto him, and put words in his mouth;" and "Aaron thy brother shall be thy prophet." Ex. 4:15; 7:1. Aaron was Moses' prophet, that is, he spoke for Moses.

The prophets were the conscience of the nation. They were men who saw the evil of their times, but who also saw God. They were not vague dreamers, but men who interpreted God's message for the time. Such men and such messages are needed to-day. We are nearing the harbor, and if the world ever needed a pilot, it needs one now. We should all pray for prophetic insight and vision, for courage and conviction. And when the Lord speaks, let us not be silent. "The Lord God hath spoken, who can but prophesy?" Amos 3:8.

CHAPTER I

The Times of Isaiah: Spiritual Conditions

The Call of Isaiah

UZZIAH, also called Azariah, king of Judah, began his reign early in the eighth century B. C., and continued for fifty-two years. 2 Kings 14: 21; 15: 1, 2. A considerable portion of this time Jeroboam II of Israel reigned contemporaneously with him. Both reigns were long, and marked by great temporal prosperity. For centuries before this the kingdom of Israel had exhausted itself in unsuccessful wars abroad, and rebellion and civil wars at home. King after king had been assassinated, only to make room for a worse one to follow. Spirituality not merely declined, but became almost extinct. All the abominations of the heathen, against which Israel had been faithfully warned, gradually became common in the land. Heathen altars were erected, on which human sacrifices were offered, and the custom of burning little children as an offering to Moloch was prevalent. The licentious rites of Baal worship were carried on under every green tree, and Jerusalem was the scene of bloody orgies and filthy, degrading practices.

With all this, however, Israel did not give up the form of their regular worship of Jehovah. They were faithful in attendance at the temple services and regularly brought their offerings. That, in fact, was one of the complaints of the Lord, that the people would come right from their abominable Baal worship to the temple as if the two were compatible. "They have committed adultery, and blood is in their hands," says the Lord. Yet in that condition, "when they had slain their children to their idols, then they came the same day into My sanctuary." Eze. 23: 37-39. No wonder the Lord said: "I will hide Mine eyes from you: yea, when ye make many prayers, I will not hear: your hands are full of blood." Isa. 1: 15. "They feared the Lord, and served their own gods," says the writer of Kings. 2 Kings 17: 33.

These conditions had gradually grown worse in spite of all the messages the Lord had sent them. Hosea and Amos had faithfully sounded the warning, but apparently to no purpose. Israel was "bent to backsliding." Hosea 11: 7. Calamities of many kinds had overtaken them, but they did not seek the only source from which help could come. They had "deeply corrupted themselves," and God was about to give them up. Hosea 9:9. But before visiting final judgment upon Israel, God gave them a little time of prosperity. This was during the time of Jeroboam II. God had punished His people, but they did not repent. Now He would give prosperity and success. Would that effect what adversity had not? "Why should ye be stricken any more?" says God, "ye will revolt more and more." Isa. 1:5. But this time of Israel's "Indian summer," as it has been called, only aggravated conditions. With prosperity came vice blacker and worse than ever. When success against their old enemy Damascus attended their arms, Israel took it as an evidence of God's favor, and closed their eyes to existing evils. Riches in spoil and tribute poured in, and as always, with riches and luxury came corruption. The continual wars of the last centuries had driven many of the farmers from the soil to the protection of the cities, and the prosperous, independent middle classes were gradually disappearing. In their stead came the very rich and the very poor.

Oppression, corruption, and injustice were the order of the day. The rich "sold the righteous for silver, and the poor for a pair of shoes." Amos 2:6. Moral conditions were worse than ever. Prosperity as well as adversity had failed to bring God's people to their senses. The Lord could do nothing to save them. Destruction was determined. "I will smite the winter house with the summer house; and the houses of ivory shall perish," said the Lord. Amos 3:15. They "that lie upon beds of ivory, . . . and eat the lambs out of the flock; . . . that drink wine in bowls, . . . but they are not grieved for the affliction of Joseph: . . . now shall they go captive with the first that go captive, and the banquet of them that stretched themselves shall be removed." "Because I will do this unto thee, prepare to meet thy God, O Israel." Amos 6:4-7; 4:12.

The situation was not much better in Judah. There was outward prosperity, as in Israel; but prosperity led to the same result. God had "marvelously helped" Uzziah, and "as long as he sought the Lord, God made him to prosper." 2 Chron. 26:15, 5. "But when he was strong, his heart was lifted up to his destruction: for he transgressed against the Lord his God, and went into the temple of the Lord to burn incense upon the altar of incense." Verse 16. This was against the Lord's plain command, and the king was smitten with that dread disease, leprosy. Being thus shut off from contact with the people, he associated with him on the throne Jotham,

The Times of Isaiah

his son, and together they ruled eleven years, when Uzziah died and Jotham became sole ruler.

It was during this time that Isaiah began his prophetic ministry. He knew the conditions in northern Israel, and the messages that had been sent through Amos and Hosea. He saw that the same conditions prevailed in Judah that had brought the northern kingdom to the brink of ruin, and he well knew that Judah could not escape the fate that threatened Israel unless there was deep repentance and a genuine revival of godliness. To him the case seemed almost hopeless. What could he, a young man, do? The rich were grinding "the faces of the poor," they were joining "house to house" and "field to field," drinking and carousing; the women were interested only in finery and apparel; the whole land was "full of idols." Isa. 3:15; 5:8, 11, 12; 3:16-24; 2:8. The king, Jotham, though good compared to some others, was a weakling, under the influence of his harem; and even the judges were corrupt. Isa. 3:12; 10:1, 2. Uzziah had been a restraining influence, but he was now a leper, and apparently unrepentant, as the leprosy still clung to him. And furthermore, it was reported that he could not live long. What would then happen?

It was "in the year that King Uzziah died" (Isa. 6:1) that Isaiah had his first vision. It was a time of great discouragement and dark forebodings. Isaiah shrank from the task before him, for it seemed so utterly hopeless. Judah was fast following in the footsteps of Israel, and who could stop them? If Hosea and Amos had not been able to hold Israel in check, how could anything be done to save Judah? Probably also a presentiment of his rejection by king and people came to Isaiah, and he would most certainly know that his messages would not be accepted by the priests any more than were those of Amos. Amos 7:10-13. What Judah needed was a prophet that would stir the conscience of the people and rouse them from their lethargy, preparing them for the crisis before them. And Isaiah was very doubtful that he was the man. In fact, he felt that he was not. He was "undone." Isa. 6:5.

It was with thoughts such as these that the great vision came to him. He had evidently gone up to worship, when suddenly the vision rises before him. The Lord is seen sitting on a throne, high and lifted up, and His train fills the temple. The seraphim, a high order of angels, cry, "Holy, holy, holy." The foundations of the threshold shake at the voice of the angels, and the house is filled with the smoke of incense. At the sight of this, Isaiah cries out in anguish: "Woe is me! for I am undone; because I am a man of unclean lips, and I dwell in the midst of a people of unclean lips: for mine eyes have seen the King, the Lord of hosts." Isa. 6: 5.

This vision was the great decisive event in Isaiah's history. It settled his career, his destiny. Henceforth men could not intimidate him. He had seen the Lord. His lips had been touched with coals from off the altar. From now on they were to be dedicated wholly to the Lord. " Holy, holy, holy," would ever ring in the prophet's ears. He had " seen the King, the Lord of hosts."

As the live coal was laid on Isaiah's mouth, the wonderful words were spoken: " Lo, this hath touched thy lips; and thine iniquity is taken away, and thy sin purged." Verse 7. For the first time Isaiah now hears the Lord's voice as He asks: " Whom shall I send, and who will go for us?" With exalted joy as well as deep humility Isaiah answers, " Here am I," and then prays, " Send me." The answer comes back immediately, " Go." Verses 8, 9.

Before this vision, Isaiah had shrunk from the responsibility that would be his should he accept the call to be the Lord's messenger. After he had seen the Lord, he willingly offered himself for service. The Lord now instructs him what to say to the people, plainly telling him that they will neither understand nor accept his message. As Isaiah doubtless is wondering as to the use of preaching to such a people and how long he should continue, the Lord tells him to persevere as long as there are any people left, until the land is " utterly desolate." Verse 11. His work was not to be entirely fruitless. There shall be left " a tenth " (verse 13), which should be as the stump of a sturdy oak that still retains its life and will survive. Those that were thus left were to be called the " holy seed."

It is interesting to note how Isaiah all through his ministry clings to the thought of the remnant who shall survive. His work was not to be a complete failure. God Himself had said there would be a remnant. This thought buoyed him up, and he reverts to it again and again all through his book.

Lessons for To-day

Isaiah 6: 1. " The year that king Uzziah died." The experience which Isaiah had that day in the temple left such a deep impression upon him that it was ever fresh in his mind. The year that king Uzziah died was not an ordinary year to Isaiah. It was *the* year. It is well for us to remember God's mercy and recall His blessings. " Would it not be well for us to observe holidays unto God, when we could revive in our minds the memory of His dealing with us? Would it not be well to consider His past blessings, to remember the impressive warnings that have come home to our souls, so that we shall not forget God?"—"*Counsels to Teachers,*" *p. 343.*

"I saw also the Lord." When Isaiah saw the Lord, it was more than His form or appearance. He saw His holiness, His character, and he received cleansing as well as forgiveness, a commission as well as a vision. We too should thus see the Lord.

Verse 2. "Covered his face." Reverence is fast disappearing from the hearts of men. Reverence for holy things, for the Sabbath, for the house of God, for those in authority in the church and in the state, for virtue, for the word of God, for the law — how little of it is found to-day! Yet, true religion must be founded on reverence, or it is not religion.

Verse 3. "Holy, holy, holy." In its original derivation the Hebrew word "holy" means "separate, apart from, distinct." Holiness is the central virtue in God's character, that includes all others. God is love, light, goodness, and all His other separate characteristics, but the one inclusive trait is "holiness." And without holiness no man can see Him. Stainless holiness, perfect purity, utter and eternal hostility to every shade and taint of sin,— that is God's character.

Verse 5. "Woe is me." The immediate effect upon Isaiah of seeing God was a profound sense of his own unfitness. "Woe is me," he cried. He that has seen God has also seen himself; and he that has not seen himself has not seen God. Whoever trusts his own righteousness thereby proclaims to the world that he has seen neither God nor himself — that he is blind.

Verse 5. "Unclean lips." Unclean lips reveal an unclean heart. Cleanse the heart, and the lips will be clean. May God keep us from suggestive, slangy phrases, indelicate stories, ribald songs, unseemly jokes, undue familiarity! "Be ye clean, that bear the vessels of the Lord." Isa. 52: 11.

Verse 7. "Thine iniquity is taken away, and thy sin purged." Here fire is used as the cleansing agency. Num. 31:23. It is possible, then, to come in contact with the fire of divine holiness, and live. Isa. 33:14. But would Isaiah have lived had he not accepted the cleansing?

Verse 8. "Whom shall I send?" The Lord did not directly ask Isaiah to go. He asked a question that gave Isaiah a chance to volunteer. That is the way of the Lord. Had He said: "Isaiah,

18   *Isaiah, the Gospel Prophet*

will you go?" the privilege of offering himself would not have been so complete and free. How considerate the Lord is! "Who will go for us?" Not, "Who will go?" but, "Who will go *for us?*" Some may offer to go for the adventure, or for the glory, or for the pay. "Who will go for us"—for the Lord?

Verse 10. "Ears heavy." It is a sad fact that the rejection of truth renders the mental, moral, and spiritual conditions of those who reject it worse than before. Those who accept the truth rejoice in it. But the same truth will make harder the heart of those who reject it, and cause them to shut their eyes and close their ears.

Verse 11. "Lord, how long?" What is the use of preaching if men do not accept? May we not consider the work finished when we have gone over the ground once and men have "rejected" the truth? It is well to remember that sometimes when we think men have rejected the truth, they have not really rejected it, but only our presentation of it. Such may later accept it when presented with more spiritual power. "How long?" Never give up. As long as there is an inhabitant left, keep on working. It may seem that the results are meager, but God has a remnant.

Verse 13. "A tenth." Even as the tithe belongs to the Lord, so the Lord has a "holy seed." Do not conclude from this that just "a tenth" will be saved. Even if so, "a tenth" of what? The stress is rather on the fact that the Lord has a remnant, and that they are holy as the tithe is holy.

CHAPTER II
Results of Israel's Rebellion
Lesson Scripture: Isaiah 1

THE first chapter of Isaiah is really a summary of Isaiah's teachings. Its five leading ideas — the separation between God and His people, which sin has caused; the inadequacy of outward ceremonies as a substitute for true heart worship; the call of God to repent and turn to Him; the surety of the judgment to come; and the remnant — form the ground and basis of Isaiah's teaching throughout the book.

The chapter is divided into two main sections, verses 2-20 and 21-31. The first division deals with the Lord's controversy with His people.

Isaiah 1:2-9. God has brought up children, and they have rebelled against Him. He calls heaven and earth to witness this astounding situation. Even the dumb creatures know their owner, but Israel does not know or consider. They have provoked God and "gone away backward." God has tried both kindness and punishment. It is of no use to strike them any more; they only rebel the more. Calamities have come upon them, and had it not been for "the remnant," all would have been destroyed, as were Sodom and Gomorrah.

Verses 10-17. When these disasters came upon the people and the land, Israel became very zealous for the outward observance of the forms of religion. Sacrifices were brought in abundance. New moons, sabbaths, and solemn meetings were observed. Many prayers were said. But all these were an insult to Jehovah. Did Israel think that these outward forms could satisfy God? Rather, they were an "abomination" to Him. He was "weary" of them. Israel had completely misunderstood the nature of religion. What God wants is heart transformation, a putting away of evil, a learning to do well. If that change takes place in the life, it will show itself, not merely in a punctual observance of the mechanical aspects of religion, but in relieving the oppressed and helping such as have no natural protectors — the orphan and the widow.

Verses 18-20. God now appeals to their reason. Though their sins may be of the deepest dye, they may be forgiven. But they must be willing and obedient. If they do not accept this gracious offer, judgment will come.

The second division (verses 21-31) deals principally with the judgment.

Verses 21-23. Jerusalem has fallen from her high estate. The princes are the leaders in backsliding. They are rebellious, and accept bribes, and do not care for the oppressed.

Verses 24-31. There shall come a change, however. The prophet looks forward to the time when "the destruction of the transgressors and of the sinners shall be together, and they that forsake the Lord shall be consumed." That, of course, is the final judgment. Then Jerusalem, the New Jerusalem, shall be called "The city of righteousness, the faithful city."

Notes

Isaiah 1:7. It is not known for a certainty to what time this refers. It must, of course, have been at the time of one of the invasions of Judah, either by the Assyrians or the allied Syrians and Ephraimites. Isaiah's prophecies are not always in chronological order, and this chapter was probably not first in order of time.

Verse 8. "Cottage" is "booth" in the A. R. V. Thieving was common in those days, and it was necessary to watch the crop very closely when it was ripening, to protect it from thieves and perhaps from wild animals. A little booth or lodge, consisting of four sticks set in the ground with a bit of canvas for a roof, would be erected in the midst of the garden, and there the lonely watcher would sit. This is the picture here used to portray the situation of God's people — alone and forsaken.

Verse 10. The "rulers of Sodom," really the judges. God here likens Israel to Sodom and Gomorrah. They had fallen so low that this designation was just.

Verses 11-15. The priests ministered in the sanctuary, and were vitally interested in the sacrificial system. With some exceptions a certain portion of each offering belonged to them. The skin of the burnt offerings was given to the priest that offered it. Lev. 7:8. The flour and the oil of the meal (A. R. V.) offering were divided equally among the sons of Aaron. Lev. 7:9, 10; 6:14-18; 2:3. The breast and the shoulder were also given to them. Lev. 10:12-15.

It is easily seen that these offerings constituted no small revenue, especially when it is remembered that at the great yearly feasts as many as a million people were in Jerusalem, each one of whom would bring some offering. The hides alone would bring a large sum. Supposing the people should listen to the prophetic messages and really stop sinning; what would become of the offerings? There would indeed still be praise and thank offerings, but trespass and sin offerings, which constituted by far the larger part of the individual offerings, would cease. Heb. 10:2. And that would vitally affect the income of the priests.

As the priests became corrupted, they were more and more zealous for the observance of the sacrificial law. They would "feed on the sin" of the people, "and set their heart on their iniquity." Hosea 4:8, A. R. V. Instead of teaching the people to stop sinning, they would emphasize the virtue of sacrifices, for the more sin, the more sacrifice.

It was not long before the people came to look upon sacrifices as a kind of payment for sin. They reasoned that it was probably better not to sin, but that God was willing to accept a payment instead of obedience. It was in effect the idea that sin cost a certain amount of money. Later the Roman Catholic Church tolerated the same doctrine.

Against this pernicious belief the prophets took a definite stand from the beginning. "To obey is better than sacrifice," was always the prophetic message. 1 Sam. 15:22. (See also Amos 5:21-23; Micah 6:7.) This kind of message brought the prophets into direct conflict with the corrupt priesthood, and was often the cause of their persecution and death. Amos 7:10-13; Jer. 20:1, 2; 26:8. The careful student of the Old Testament would do well to keep this conflict between the prophets and the priests in mind. It constitutes, in fact, the real background of God's work for the healing of His people. The prophetic message was that of obedience, of spiritual service, of conversion, of holiness. That is the message of Isaiah in the verses under consideration. And that also is the message of Christ.

Verse 17. Throughout the whole book of Isaiah the word "judgment" should be translated "justice," as in the American Revised Version.

Lessons for To-day

Isaiah 1:2. Few burdens are harder to bear than those caused by an unthankful child. God knows what it means. He has brought up children that have rebelled against Him. In 2 Timothy 3:2 the apostle gives unthankful children as one of the signs of the last days. Are we as thankful as we should be? This has reference to both old and young. (On "rebellion," see 1 Sam. 15:23.)

Verse 3. How often we say, "I didn't think"! That is one complaint God has against His people. They do "not consider," do not think, do not weigh the matter carefully. The ox and the ass know their crib, know where to go to get their feed. Do we know the hand that feeds us, and are we thankful? Or do we simply accept God's gifts and do "not consider"? The possession of a mind is one great distinction between man and beast. Do we use as we ought that which distinguishes us from the brutes?

Verse 4. "Children that are corrupters"—"that deal corruptly," A. R. V. "Corrupt" is a strong word, and means that which is in a state of decomposition; tainted; putrid; of a perverted character; given to bribery; dishonest; depraved.

"The Holy One of Israel." This is Isaiah's favorite name for God. After he had seen God in vision and heard the angels sing, "Holy, holy, holy," the Lord became to him "the Holy One of Israel."

Verse 6. "From the sole of the foot." This verse contains a dreadful picture of man. There is "no soundness" anywhere. Sin has done thorough work.

As complete, however, as is sin's devastation, equally complete is God's work of healing. "Arise, and be baptized, and wash away thy sins," were the words spoken to Paul. Acts 22:16. The work of grace symbolized by baptism is a complete work. That is why sprinkling can never be a satisfying form of baptism. We are full of sin, from head to foot. The cleansing element must be co-extensive with the sin. Hence grace must penetrate to the deepest recesses of the heart. And the symbol of that grace—baptism, the washing away of sin—must be a complete immersion. It is not the head or the feet only that are sinful; it is the whole man. Hence the whole man must be baptized, not a part of him.

Verse 9. There shall be "a very small remnant" left. But these few are the salt of the earth. Had it not been for them, the earth would ere this have been destroyed, as were Sodom and Gomorrah.

Verse 10. "Give ear unto the law." This expression is appropriate and timely in this day of lawlessness.

Verses 16, 17. "Cease to do evil; learn to do well." To abstain from evil is well, but is only half of what God requires. It is at best a negative virtue. In the judgment it is not enough to say that we did not commit this or that sin. It is not merely a question of what we did *not* do, but of what we *did* do. If a man falls overboard and drowns, it is no justification to say that we had no part in the matter, that we did not push him off the boat. The question would rather be, why we did not throw out a life preserver and thus save him.

Verse 18. "Let us reason together." Instead of passing sentence, God extends pardon. Israel had certainly done enough evil to merit any judgment which God might mete out; but instead He reasons with man, offering him pardon full and free.

"Let us." Who are the "us"? God and man. It is God and *you*. He wants to reason with you, and cause you to see what a glorious salvation He has provided.

Verse 19. "Willing and obedient." God accepts no forced service. There must be a willing mind. And the actions must correspond to the mind. When the mind and the life are thus in harmony, all God's promises are ours.

Verse 23. "Companions of thieves." We are known by the company we keep. We ourselves may not steal, but may associate with them that do. We may not take God's name in vain, we may not run to the excess in sin that some do; but if we take pleasure in the company of worldlings, if we unite with them in their pleasures and sports, God may put us down in His book as "companions of thieves" or companions of pleasure lovers. It is better not to yoke ourselves up with ungodly associates.

Verse 25. "Take away all thy tin." God will "purely purge away thy dross." He will take away all that is of lesser worth. Tin is not worthless, but it is of less value than gold or silver. In character building only the best is good enough for God's people. Everything in our character that is not pure gold God will take away.

Verse 27. "Zion shall be redeemed with justice," A. R. V. The thought here is not that a person will be redeemed because he does justice, that is, that he is saved by works; but rather that God's plan of redemption is in accordance with justice and righteousness, that He does not do away with law in order to save man.

Verse 31. "The strong shall be as tow." Tow is very inflammable material. A spark will ignite it. "The maker of it," rather "his work" (A. R. V.), shall be the spark. Thus the man and his work shall burn together.

CHAPTER III
The Call to the House of Jacob
Lesson Scripture: Isaiah 2; 3; 4

ISAIAH 2: 1-9. These verses contain the call of the people to "go up to the mountain of the Lord." The parallel scripture is found in Micah 4: 1-3.

At first sight this scripture seems to teach a turning of the nations to the Lord, and the beginning of the millennium when men shall learn war no more. A more careful view, however, makes us hesitate to accept any such conclusion. Some of the reasons for our not accepting the popular interpretation are:

1. Joel presents a message exactly the opposite of this. Instead of beating their swords into plowshares, Joel is commanded to tell the people to beat their plowshares into swords. The message in Joel is God's command to the prophet. The opposite statement in Isaiah is what "many people" say. Hence as between what God says and what "many people" say, we accept God's word.

2. Mountains are doubtless symbolic of political powers. In Revelation 17: 9, 10, the seven mountains are seven kings, or kingdoms, on which the woman sits. In Daniel 2: 35 we are told that the kingdoms of this world are broken to pieces by the stone cut out without hands. The kingdom of God destroys earthly kingdoms. Here in Isaiah we find "the mountain of the Lord's house" "at the head of the mountains" (A. R. V., margin). It is not here destroying the kingdoms of the world, but heading them up, "established in the top of the mountains." Instead of this being God's people, the description rather seems to fit the apostate church spoken of in Revelation 17, who shall sit on the seven mountains. Verse 9.

3. "The house of Jacob" (A. R. V.) as a name for God's people, has a suspicious sound as here used. God has forsaken the house, or children, of Jacob (verse 6), or rather "rejected" them, as the original indicates. The reason for the rejection is that they are "replenished from the east," they are "soothsayers," they "please themselves in" or "strike hands with" (A. R. V.), that is, make alliances with strangers. Also, their land is full of idols and they worship them. From this it seems clear that the house of Jacob here mentioned is not the true people of God, but the false.

The Call to the House of Jacob

We therefore conclude that this prophecy of Isaiah refers to a false movement in the last days. The apostate power shall accept the leadership of the nations, shall "rebuke," "arbitrate for," "will decide concerning" (verse 4, A. R. V., margin), the nations, and "many people," in fact, "all nations shall flow unto it."

Verses 10-22. Events of the day of the Lord. When the day of the Lord shall come, "the lofty looks of man shall be humbled." It will be a dreadful day. Men will crawl into the holes of the rocks when the earth shakes under the majesty of the Lord's presence. "The Lord alone shall be exalted in that day."

Isaiah 3:1-15. God's controversy with Judah and Jerusalem.

God is about to punish His people. He will take away their stay of bread and water. Children will rule over them, and general anarchy and ruin will result. This is because "their tongue and their doings are against the Lord." In this time of trouble God will not forget His own. "The Lord standeth up to plead" for them. They have been beaten to pieces and ground down (verse 15), but in the end it will be well with them. Verse 10.

Isaiah 3: 16 to 4: 1. God's controversy with the daughters of Zion.

As long as the women of a nation retain their virtue and integrity, the nation will survive. When women succumb to the vices and practices of men, the nation is doomed. Every child born into the world is given into the charge of some woman who has the first chance to mold and train the little one. As long as women discharge this responsibility in the fear of God, there is hope. When the womanhood of a nation goes wrong, when outward adornment becomes of greater interest to them than inward piety, where shall help be found?

The women here mentioned are not heathen. They are the daughters of Zion, professed Christians. They wish to bear the name of Christ, but will neither dress themselves nor live to please Him. Isa. 4: 1. Instead of Christ's robe of righteousness, they will wear their own apparel. Instead of accepting Him, the bread that came down from heaven (John 6: 33), they want to eat their own bread.

Isaiah 4: 26. God's true church in the last days.

These verses deal with the purified church as the latter rain is poured upon them, and with conditions after probation ceases, just before the Lord comes. The remnant, those that "are escaped," that are "left," are "beautiful and glorious," for God will have purged away "the filth of the daughters of Zion." This will be done by the "spirit of judgment" and of "burning." "Our God is a consuming fire" (Heb. 12:29), and His presence in the church will consume away the dross.

Verses 5 and 6 speak of the last year before the Lord comes, the year of the seven last plagues, when God will shield His people as they have sought refuge in solitary places. Over every little group of believers will be seen the cloud by day and the shining of a flaming fire by night, as when God brought His people out of Egypt. When the plagues fall, there will be a place of refuge and a covert from the storm and rain.

Notes

Isaiah 2:5. The "house of Jacob" may here have a special significance. Jacob was the name of a son of Isaac before his conversion. After that his name was Israel. The power here mentioned is the house of Jacob, not Israel. While this point should perhaps not be pressed too far, it is worthy of notice that when God's people are mentioned later on, it is as Israel. Chap. 4:2, 3.

Verse 6. "Soothsayers." We do not know what particular form of divination is here meant. Some translate the word "cloud compellers," that is, rain makers.

Verse 19. "To shake terribly," literally "to terrify the earth." This without doubt is at the time of the great earthquake. Rev. 16:18.

Isaiah 3:16. "Mincing as they go, and making a tinkling." The "tinkling" (verse 18) was caused by the "ankle chains" (verse 20, A. R. V.), a short chain uniting the feet, which also caused the "mincing."

Verses 18-24. We do not know what all these ornaments were. Different times give different names to prevailing styles and customs. Among others we find in the A. R. V. the following familiar names: "pendants" instead of "chains;" "sashes" and "perfume boxes" instead of "headbands" and "tablets" (verses 19, 20); "shawls" and "satchels" instead of "wimples" and "crisping pins" (verse 22); "hand mirrors" instead of "glasses" (verse 23). "Well-set hair," of verse 24, literally means "turner's work," artificial curls. Instead of "burning" read "branding," a symbol of slavery.

The Call to the House of Jacob

Lessons for To-day

Isaiah 2:3. Carefulness is needed in reading the word. We should not attribute to God that which the people say, but should rightly divide the word of truth. 2 Tim. 2:15.

Verses 3, 4. We should not lightly pass by these verses, thinking that they contain only what the people say. While that is true, yet they are a part of the Bible, and will be just as literally fulfilled as any other part. In the last days the people will say exactly what is here said. The apostate church will regain temporal power, and will take the leadership of nations, and they will flow into it. The whole world will wonder after the beast. Rev. 13:3. And the politico-religious church will arbitrate among the nations and judge them.

Verse 7. " Neither is there any end of their treasures." (See James 5.)

Verse 8. " Worship the work of their own hands." That is true of idols, and it is equally true of science. Men are so infatuated with their own discoveries that they literally worship science.

Verses 10-17. Man's pride shall be brought down. Note upon whom the day of the Lord will come. There are ten " upons." All of them have reference to some kind of pride. Men worship the work of their own hands. Delving into the secrets of nature, men have found a few grains from the marvelous storehouse of God's wisdom. These they exhibit with pride, and almost think themselves gods. And yet the wisest of men are but as children by the seashore, thinking to empty the ocean with a spoon.

Verse 21. To fear the Lord and to have fear of the Lord are two different experiences. Those who fear the Lord now need have no fear of Him when He comes.

Isaiah 3:9. Some men can hide their emotions, but none can hide their lives. Their countenances will witness against them. The sins of Sodom will be revealed in their looks. Nature cannot be cheated. And it will surely be " woe unto their soul." They that sin against their body " have rewarded evil unto themselves."

Verses 10, 11. Notice that both the righteous and the wicked merely receive the reward of their doings.

Verse 12. " They which lead thee cause thee to err." What a responsibility it is to be a leader!

Verse 14. God notices every act of oppression, by whomever done.

Verses 16-24. Many of the things here mentioned are in themselves perfectly lawful to use and wear. But when anything is worn or used for display, to attract attention, it becomes questionable, though in itself it may serve a useful purpose. We would not, however, recommend that the men spend too much time discussing women's foibles. Let each one look to his own shortcomings.

Isaiah 4:1. Seven women, one man. Seven is the complete number. "Women" represents a church (Rev. 12:1, 2; 17:3), but in this case not the true or pure church, for there is a reproach. How true it is to-day that the churches will not accept the bread that came down from heaven, but rather eat their own food — the traditions of men. They want the name, but reject the garment which Christ provides, and hence will be found at last without the wedding garment.

Verse 2. "In that day." Note how often this phrase is repeated in Isaiah.

"The branch of the Lord," the true people of God. John 15:5.

"Them that are escaped"— the remnant. The last church will have the wedding garment rejected by others. This is what makes the church "beautiful and glorious."

Verse 3. "He that is left," "he that remaineth,"— the remnant. It is he that remains that will be saved; the rest are shaken out.

"Among the living." In the early church God took an active part in keeping the church above reproach. Ananias and Sapphira tried to deceive, and they were carried out dead. Acts 5:1-11. Apostolic power for which we pray presupposes apostolic purity. In the days of the apostles "great fear came upon all the church" when they heard about Ananias and Sapphira, and "of the rest durst no man join himself to them." Verses 11, 13. It was dangerous in those days for a sinner to belong to the church. Even so in the last days, those that remain, those that are among the living, "shall be called holy, even every one." When God purifies His church, when the Holy Spirit is poured out, it will not be well with the sinners in Zion.

Verse 4. "Washed away the filth." It is not enough that sin be repented of and pardoned; it must be washed away. It is one thing to cover over, to forgive; it is another thing to wash away, to cleanse. The one is righteousness by faith, the other is holiness. God will not only "forgive us our sins," but will also "cleanse." 1 John 1:9.

"Spirit of burning." This is none other but God, who as a consuming fire "shall suddenly come to His temple." There "He shall sit as a refiner and purifier," for "He is like a refiner's fire, and like fullers' soap." He "shall . . . purge them as gold and silver." Mal. 3: 1-3. The great question in that day will be, "Who may abide the day of His coming? and who shall stand when He appeareth?" When God has finished His work, Zion will be "the perfection of beauty." God being in Zion (the church), and having purified it, it will be true that "*out* of Zion . . . God hath shined." Ps. 50: 2.

Verse 5. "Every dwelling place of Mount Zion." In the last year of probation God's people will be scattered all over the earth, many in desolate places and among the mountains. But wherever a small group may be, there the visible sign of God's presence is. What a wonderful time that must be, in spite of the trials and deprivations! We will apparently be permitted to gather in small groups as we flee to the mountains. Men and governments may wish us ill, and starvation and even death may stare us in the face; but with a little group — such as we have learned to love and trust — what precious seasons together may we not even then enjoy, knowing that the pillar of cloud and of fire is with us! (See "The Great Controversy," chapter "The Time of Trouble.")

"Upon all the glory." God's people are here meant. They are "beautiful and glorious." Verse 2.

Verse 6. God will not leave His own. "In the time of trouble He shall hide me in His pavillon: in the secret of His tabernacle shall He hide me." Ps. 27: 5.

CHAPTER IV

The Vineyard; The Six Woes; Messianic Prophecies; The Remnant

Lesson Scripture: Isaiah 5; 7; 10; 11

ISAIAH 5: 1-7. Isaiah's parable of the vineyard bears a close resemblance to the one spoken by the Lord on the same subject, as recorded in Matthew 21: 33-41; Mark 12: 1-9; Luke 20: 9-16. Both deal with God's care for His people and with their ingratitude, but Christ's parable definitely states that the vineyard will be given to others, while Isaiah's merely prophesies the rejection of the Jews without suggesting anything concerning the Gentiles.

God had done everything possible for His vineyard. The hill was fruitful, it was fenced, and the stones were gathered out. The vine itself was of the choicest, and the outlook was so promising that God did not wait for the harvest, but immediately erected a tower and a wine press. Great therefore was the disappointment when the vineyard brought forth wild grapes. "What could have been done more to My vineyard, that I have not done in it?" asks God, appealing to the people to give their judgment in the matter. When Christ in the parable asks a question of like portent, the answer is given: "He will miserably destroy those wicked men, and will let out His vineyard unto other husbandmen." Matt. 21: 41. In like manner Isaiah appeals to those whom he addresses to commit themselves, and though no record of their answer is given, it was doubtless of the same nature as that given when Christ asked, What will the Lord of the vineyard do to those wicked husbandmen?

The record next states what God will do to the vineyard. It shall be trodden down, the wall removed, no rain shall fall, and briers and thorns shall flourish.

Verses 8-30. Six woes are pronounced against evil-doers. God had a right to expect good fruit from His vineyard. The six woes recount the kind of fruit He did get, namely, "wild grapes."

The first woe condemns covetousness and selfishness. Joining house to house and laying field to field, is the charge. The punishment is made to fit the crime. The vineyard that would ordinarily yield four thousand gallons shall yield only eight gallons; the cornfield shall return only one tenth of the seed sown.

The second woe is directed against drunkenness and dissipation, with all the vices that usually follow when men have been "inflamed" with wine. "The harp, and the viol, the tabret, and pipe, and wine" are not a combination that makes for peace and purity.

The third woe condemns scoffers and mocking skeptics. They challenge God to make His judgments come. They are braggarts who will be on their knees begging for mercy when God does reveal Himself.

The fourth woe is spoken against those who turn things upside down, calling good evil and light darkness.

The fifth woe condemns those who are self-conceited —"wise in their own eyes."

The sixth woe concerns the leaders, the judges, who permit their judgment to become affected by strong drink, so that they will "justify the wicked for a bribe." A. R. V. "They have cast away the law of the Lord of hosts, and despised the word of the Holy One of Israel."

Verses 26-30. Here is set forth the sure destruction approaching. It is the army of the Lord that is coming. Who that army is we are not told. In some respects the description is like that in Joel 2: 2-11.

Isaiah 7: 1-16. Here is portrayed what we may call the crisis of 735 B. C. The Assyrian king, Tiglath-Pileser IV, had long threatened the independence of the small states of Palestine. Pekah, king of northern Israel, and Rezin, king of Syria, made an alliance to resist the expected advance. They invited Ahaz, king of Judah, to join this alliance, and when he refused, they decided to make war upon Ahaz, dethrone him, and set up another king who would assist them. When Ahaz heard this, "his heart was moved," and both he and his people were afraid. At this juncture the Lord tells Isaiah to go to the king and tell him not to fear or be faint-hearted. The kings of Israel and Syria are only "the two tails of these smoking firebrands;" they are weak, and need not be feared. Make no entangling alliances, Isaiah counseled. Trust in God. He will give you a sign if you desire it.

Ahaz, as appears from 2 Kings 16: 7, had probably already made up his mind to ally himself with Assyria, hence he refuses to seek any sign, giving a very pious answer: "I will not ask, neither will I tempt the Lord." (See also Deut. 6: 16.) Isaiah, however, sees through the plan of Ahaz, and is indignant that the king should refuse God's proffered sign. It may be praiseworthy not to ask a sign of God, but when God offers a sign, it is as much an insult not to accept His offer as to refuse to take an outstretched hand. So Isaiah tells him plainly that he is wearying God, and that God will give him a sign whether he asks for it or not." " Behold, a virgin shall conceive, and bear a son," and before that child shall be old enough to know the difference between good and evil, " the land that thou abhorrest shall be forsaken of both her kings." According to this statement, only a few years would elapse before the enemies whom Ahaz now feared should be destroyed. Rezin died in the third year of Ahaz (2 Kings 16:9); and Pekah in the fourth year. 2 Kings 15:27, 30; 16:1.

Few texts of Scripture have been discussed more than verses 14-16 of this chapter. Some commentators hold that the prophecy refers only to the time of Isaiah, and has no Messianic importance. Others hold that it has reference only to Christ, and has no local application whatever. Still others hold that it has a double application and fulfillment. We agree with the last view.

Double prophecies are not uncommon, as witness the account in Matthew 24. The prophecies of the fall of Jerusalem and of the end of the world are there woven into one story, yet there need be no confusion in separating them. So here. It would seem strange for God to give Ahaz a sign that would not be fulfilled for more than seven hundred years. It would certainly be no sign to Ahaz. How much more likely that God would give him a sign, such as we believe He did, that but a few years would pass before the land should be forsaken of both her kings — a sign that was fulfilled.

On the other hand, there are reasons which compel us to believe that we here deal with a definite Messianic prophecy. The original reads " the " virgin, not " a " virgin, and would therefore point to some definite virgin. The sign was given to " the house of David," though it was addressed to Ahaz. Hence it has a much wider significance than if given to Ahaz alone. " Immanuel," God with us, is another distinguishing characteristic. But the most conclusive is the fact that Matthew quotes verse 14 and applies it to Christ and Mary. Matt. 1:22, 23. That proof is sufficient and final.

As noted above, however, no Messianic application of the prophecy can explain verse 16, hence we conclude this prophecy to have a double bearing and fulfillment. Thus interpreted, there is no vagueness or uncertainty.

Isaiah 9:6, 7. " Unto us a child is born." Immanuel is His name, but not His only one. He is also Counselor, God, Father,

The Vineyard; The Six Woes

and Prince of Peace. There shall be no end to the increase of His government and peace.

Isaiah 11:1-9. While He is God, He is also man, for He shall come from "the stem of Jesse." Verse 1. A sevenfold measure of the spirit shall rest upon Him. Verse 2. This will enable Him to judge motives, and not be guided merely by what He sees or hears. Verse 3. He will at last exterminate all the wicked from the earth. Verse 4. Then shall begin that blessed reign of righteousness when even the animal creation shall be at peace and the little child shall be safe. Verses 6-8. There shall be none left to hurt or destroy, and the earth shall be full of the knowledge of the Lord. Verse 9.

Isaiah 10:20-23. It will, however, only be a "remnant" that will have part in this. Literal Israel may be as many as the sands of the sea, but only a remnant among them shall return.

Isaiah 11:10-16. This remnant shall not come from any one country, but from the four corners of the earth. Verses 11, 12. This, however, will not cause any national feeling. One shall not vex another, and there shall be no envy. Verse 13. They shall stand together as they attack their common enemies. Verse 14. God will open the way for them as in olden times He parted the Red Sea. Verses 15, 16.

Notes

Isaiah 5:1, 2. The "fruitful hill" is Jerusalem; the "fence," or wall, is the law of God; the "tower" is the temple.

Isaiah 7:2. Ephraim is another name for Israel. Israel and Judah should always be kept distinct. They were two separate kingdoms.

"As the trees of the wood are moved." There are many beautiful literary gems like this.

Verse 3. "Shear-jashub" means the remnant shall return. Isaiah was so interested in the remnant that he named one of his sons after it.

"Conduit." In case of a siege it was important that a water supply be secured for Jerusalem. There was a pool near one of the gates, and the king had gone out to inspect it, probably with a view of making sure of a sufficient supply of water should there be a siege. This pool is also mentioned in 2 Kings 18:17.

Verse 8. "Threescore and five years." Usher's explanation of this date, though not entirely satisfactory, is probably the best we have. He says that sixty-five years later, about 669 B. C., Asshur-

Isaiah, the Gospel Prophet

banipal — the Osnapper of Ezra 4:2, 10 — sent from Babylon the foreign colonists who occupied Samaria, and entirely destroyed those who were left of Israel who had been carried into captivity 721 B. C.

Isaiah 9:6. "The government shall be upon His shoulders." This is prophetic of the great authority given the Son in the work of bringing this revolted world back into allegiance to the Father. (Compare 1 Cor. 15:24-28 with Isa. 9:7.)

Isaiah 11:15. "The tongue of the Egyptian Sea" is the place where Israel crossed the Red Sea.

Lessons for To-day

Isaiah 5:1-7. Note the careful approach of Isaiah. He did not condemn the people immediately. He first told them a story, and tried to get them to commit themselves as to its meaning. "Judge, I pray you, betwixt me and my vineyard," he said. Christ used the same method, and in their answer the people condemned themselves. Matt. 21:40, 41. Nathan also told David a story enlisting his sympathy, and David condemned himself. 2 Sam. 12:1-10. The secret of right approach is worth learning. While we cannot always avoid antagonism, our duty is to study the best methods — Christ's methods — of work.

Verse 2. He "made a wine press." God could have waited to see how matters would come out before making the wine press. Knowing the end from the beginning, God would sometimes not need to do all He does to save a man when that man will be lost eventually. But God always arranges His plans as if He expects the man to be saved. He gives the man every opportunity, going ahead with His program as if He expected nothing but success. Thus Christ treated Judas, and He nearly won him. Faith in a man is a wonderful stimulus for that man to go right. God showed faith even in Judah. He did not look for or expect failure. He "looked for judgment," for righteousness in one for whom He had paid such a price.

Verses 8-24. "Another book was opened, wherein were recorded the sins of those who profess the truth. Under the general heading of selfishness came every other sin. There were also headings over every column, and underneath these, opposite each name, were recorded, in their respective columns, the lesser sins. Under covetousness came falsehood, theft, robbery, fraud, and avarice; under ambition came pride and extravagance; jealousy stood at the head of malice, envy, and hatred; and intemperance headed a long list of fearful crimes, such as lasciviousness, adultery, indulgence of animal passions, etc."—"*Testimonies,*" *Vol. IV, pp. 384, 385.*

Verse 12. "They regard not, . . . neither consider;" that is, they do not think. This is one of the great complaints God has against the people. Why do they not think, why do they not consider? It is a marvel to God that men will not use their reason. God has made that complaint before in this book: He will use it again. Why do not men see in nature "the operation of His hands"? They would, did they but think. They would see "the work of the Lord" if they looked for it.

Verse 19. The attitude of scoffers. 2 Peter 3:3, 4, is explanatory of this verse.

Isaiah 7:12. Ahaz has been called the king of "no faith." He would not commit himself. His kingdom was in danger. God offered to help him, and even condescended to give him a sign. But, as we have seen, Ahaz gave a polite and pious reason for not accepting God's help. He felt that he could get along without God. Isaiah told him that such an attitude was wearisome to God as well as to men.

There are some things that make God weary. Isa. 1:14. To do nothing in a crisis is high treason. The careless, listless, though polite attitude is one that even God cannot tolerate.

Isaiah 9:7. "The throne of David." The throne on which Christ sits is called the throne of David. Christ is God and man, so while God is His Father, so also is David. Luke 1:32. This great honor came to David because of his intense desire to build a house for the Lord, a thing which God had hoped some one would think of without being told. God, as well as man, appreciates spontaneous, willing service, and He was so pleased that David thought of what he might do for God that He gave David the blessed promise: "Thy throne shall stand forever." (See 2 Sam. 7:1-17.)

Here is a lesson for all. We are not to do merely what we are asked to do, that and no more. Rather, having accomplished our work, we are gladly to ask, Lord, is there anything else I can do for Thee? Blessed is the man that does not have to be told everything he must do. Twice blessed is the man who can find work to do, and having found it and done it, asks for more. He is a man after God's own heart.

Isaiah 9:2. The Spirit of the Lord is many-sided. It is not confined to any one activity. The completely Spirit-filled man will have the fear of the Lord in his heart, as well as knowledge, understanding, wisdom, counsel, and might. Let none having one of these characteristics think lightly of one having another.

Isaiah 10:20. "In that day," the day of the Lord. Note how often this phrase occurs. We are dealing with present truth.

Isaiah 11:10, 12. An ensign is a banner. Christ is here spoken of as an ensign, a rallying point. In verse 12 Christ sets up an ensign to rally His people. The enemies also have their banner. Ps. 74:7. They have "done wickedly in the sanctuary," they have "burned up all the synagogues of God in the land," and said, "Let us destroy them together." Verses 3, 8. On the banner of the remnant is inscribed: "Here is the patience of the saints: here are they that keep the commandments of God, and the faith of Jesus." Rev. 14:12. (See "Testimonies," Vol. VII, p. 150.) "Christ is our example. The determination of Antichrist to carry out the rebellion he began in heaven will continue to work in the children of disobedience. Their envy and hatred against those who obey the fourth commandment, will wax more and more bitter. But the people of God are not to hide their banner. They are not to ignore the commandments of God, and, in order to have an easy time, go with the multitude to do evil."—"*Testimonies," Vol. IX, p. 230.*

Verse 13. Envy is no part of Christianity. Rather we are told to rejoice in the prosperity of others.

To vex is to provoke by inflicting small irritations; to annoy; to irritate. It may be one of the "small foxes," but it is a very annoying and unworthy one. Not having the courage to attack boldly, the coward will resort to small vexations. Of such beware.

CHAPTER V

A Song of Praise; The Earth Destroyed; The Fall of Satan

Lesson Scripture: Isaiah 12; 13; 24; 14

THE twelfth chapter of Isaiah is a song of praise and thanksgiving, and records an experience, as do all worth-while hymns. "That day" refers to the day of the Lord. Isa. 2: 11, 12. God has been angry with His people, but His anger is turned away and He now comforts them. God's anger would perhaps be better described by the terms "displeasure" or "righteous indignation." Of the Saviour it is recorded that on one occasion He "looked round about on them with anger, being grieved for the hardness of their hearts." Mark 3: 5. The people of whom Isaiah writes in this place have put their trust wholly in the Lord, and are drinking freely from the wells of salvation. The original reads "because" instead of "though" in verse 1, and from this it appears that His people are even thanking God for the discipline they have experienced.

It was the custom of Israel to sing songs of praise upon important occasions. Of this kind is the song of Moses recorded in Exodus 15: 1-19 after the deliverance of Israel from Egypt. As Isaiah has just recorded another deliverance where God "the second time" (Isa. 11: 11) delivers His people, it is very fitting that there should be another song of triumph. As this whole experience finds its application at this time, and as the people of God will sing the song of Moses and the song of the Lamb (Rev. 15: 3), this chapter in Isaiah should claim our special study. It is the advent song of praise and deliverance.

Isaiah 13: 1-9. The prophet has been occupied with God's people, their experiences and final triumph. He now returns to consider what fate awaits the wicked when the day of the Lord comes to them. The subject of the chapter is "the burden of Babylon," and it deals with the punishment and destruction of Babylon.

God has called His "sanctified ones" and His "mighty ones" — the angels — to perform the work in hand. Verse 3. (Cf. Joel 3: 11.) The "kingdoms of nations" are there, and men are gathered from "the end of heaven." Verses 4, 5. It is the day of the

Lord, and the destruction shall come from the Almighty. Verse 6. Men will be completely overwhelmed with fear and agony, as one in the pangs of childbirth; they shall look in horror on each other, and their faces shall be as the faces of flames. Verses 7, 8. The reason for this is that the day of the Lord has come and that sinners shall be destroyed. Verse 9.

Verses 10-13. One of the signs of the day of the Lord is the darkening of the sun and the moon. The heavens also shall be shaken and the earth removed out of her place. It is the day of the Lord's fierce anger.

Isaiah 24: 1-4. There can hardly be conceived any picture of destruction more complete than that pictured in these verses. God makes the earth empty and waste, turns it upside down, and scatters the people. The metaphor is peculiarly expressive, the words being "those which were used for cleaning a dirty dish."— *G. A. Smith*. The earth shall be utterly emptied and spoiled. It is in the same condition it was after the flood. Gen. 6: 11.

Verses 5, 6. The reason for this terrible calamity lies in the attitude of the people. " They have transgressed the laws, changed the ordinance, broken the everlasting covenant." When God has finished with the earth, there are but " few men left."

Verses 7-12. These verses are a description of the earth as the plagues fall and the final destruction comes. Utter confusion reigns. Men are crying in the streets for wine in which to drown their terror. Cities crash and become a desolation. Nothing but destruction is seen.

Verses 13-16. How will God's people, who will be upon the earth during the falling of the plagues, fare at this time? The remnant will be few as when an olive tree is shaken and only a few olives remain. But when destruction is raging and a thousand fall at their side, " they shall lift up their voice, they shall sing for the majesty of the Lord." From the east and from the west, from the isles and from the uttermost parts of the earth, songs of praise ascend to God. In the midst of the fearful description of the destruction of the earth as given in this chapter, these few verses are put in to assure us that God has not forgotten His own. Knowing that the righteous will be on the earth at that time, and knowing that we would all be interested in their welfare, God inserts a few lines to tell us that all is well.

Verses 17-20. The prophet now returns to the subject of the desolate earth, and finishes the picture. The wicked are fleeing for their lives. As one falls into a pit and barely escapes, he is taken

A Song of Praise

in the snare. There is no hope. "The windows from on high are open," and God is pouring out His wrath. "The earth is rent asunder, the earth is shaken violently." A. R. V. It staggers like a drunken man, it sways "to and fro like a hammock;" at last it falls, and shall not rise again.

Verses 21-23. God is now about to punish the transgressors. "The host of the high ones that are on high," the wicked angels, as well as the kings on earth, are "gathered together, as prisoners are gathered in the pit." Even Satan himself is bound. Rev. 20: 1, 2. "After many days"—a thousand years—"shall they be visited."

Isaiah 14: 12-14. Before his fall, Satan was known as Lucifer, which means "light bearer." Self-exaltation was the cause of his fall. He sought to exalt himself above the stars (angels) of God; he aspired to sit upon the mount of the congregation in the sides of the north, the place that belongs to God (Ps. 48: 2); he would be like the Most High.

Ezekiel 28: 12-19. Under the symbol of the king of Tyre, the history of Satan and his fall is here given. His heart was lifted up, and he said, "I am God." Verses 2, 9. He was wiser than Daniel (verse 3); but because he had set his heart "as the heart of God," he would be brought down to the pit. Verses 6, 8. Lucifer had been in Eden, the garden of God. At that time he was "full of wisdom, and perfect in beauty." Verse 12. He was the anointed cherub that covered, and God had appointed him to that office—"I have set thee so." Verse 14. From the day he was created he was perfect until he became disaffected. Because of his sins, God will cast him out as profane. His beauty was his undoing, and he corrupted his wisdom by reason of his brightness. He will at last be destroyed, and become ashes on the earth, "and never shalt thou be any more." Verse 19.

Notes

Isaiah 12: 1. For "though," read "because."

Verse 2. "Lord Jehovah." This combination is found in only one other place, Isaiah 26: 4.

Verse 6. "Inhabitant" ("inhabitress," margin), Zion being personified as a woman.

Isaiah 13: 1. "Burden," rather "oracle" or "utterance," used only when the message is of a denunciatory or disapproving nature.

Verse 2. "Lift ye up a banner," "exalt the voice," "shake the hand"—all are means of signaling, of calling together to battle.

Verse 3. "My sanctified ones," "My mighty ones." Commentators generally explain these to be men of war, perhaps the Medes and Persians. While it is true that God often uses one nation to punish another, and that thus a nation may be spoken of as being consecrated to carry out God's will, we believe the evidence here to be in favor of the view that the "sanctified ones" are the angels. In past times one nation has been used by God to punish another, and that may even to a certain extent be true in the last war culminating in Armageddon; but it cannot be entirely true, for in that war *all* nations are to be punished and exterminated; hence God Himself must be overruling events. (See Rev. 19: 11-16.)

Verse 5. "The whole land," read "the whole earth." Also read "earth" for "land" in verse 9.

Verse 10. "Constellations" is the same word as "Orion" in Amos 5:8 and Job 9:9. As it is in the plural here, it denotes Orion and other constellations.

"In his going forth," or "at his rising."

Verse 11. "Punish the world." Critics have tried to confine the disasters spoken of in this chapter to Palestine, hence have insisted on using "land" instead of "earth," as in verses 5, 9. Here, however, the world, not Palestine, is mentioned. All must admit that this speaks of a universal catastrophe.

Verse 12. Gold from Ophir was considered specially pure. The locality of Ophir is not known with certainty. 1 Kings 9:28.

Verse 13. When God says He "will shake the heavens," and that "the earth shall remove out of her place," we do not take these to be figurative expressions. We believe they will be literally fulfilled.

Isaiah 24:1. "Turneth it upside down." If this is a literal happening, as we believe it is, it may explain how the sun will appear at midnight, "shining in its strength." (See "The Great Controversy," p. 636.)

Verse 3. For "land" read "earth," as in verses 1, 4, etc.

Verse 5. "Transgressed the laws." God holds mankind amenable to moral law as written in the ten commandments, or if that is not known, to the same "law written in their hearts." Rom. 2:15. These are one and the same law. The heathen or uninformed Christians who do not as yet know the written law, are held responsible for such light as they have.

"Changed the ordinance"—"violated the statutes." A. R. V.

Verse 6. "Are desolate"—"found guilty." A. R. V.

Verse 15. "Glorify ye the Lord in the fires." While the reading here is somewhat doubtful, to a believer in the third angel's message the translation is satisfactory. The fires of the last day are coming. God Himself, who is a devouring fire, will appear. In the midst of the scenes of the last days will be God's people. Why should they not glorify Him in the fires? Dan. 3: 19-21. Why should they not sing? Isa. 24: 16.

Verses 17, 18. God here uses the terms of the hunter. The prevailing idea is that there is no escape.

Verse 22. "The pit "—" the bottomless pit" of Revelation 20: 1. "Many days "—" a thousand years." Rev. 20: 3. (See "The Great Controversy," p. 661.)

Ezekiel 28:12. "King of Tyrus," symbolic of Satan. For other instances of Satan being addressed through another, see Genesis 3: 15; Matthew 16: 22, 23.

Verse 14. "Anointed cherub." Cherubim are the highest order of angels. Lucifer was " anointed," that is, ordained or consecrated to that office.

"That covereth." There were two cherubim on the ark that covered "the mercy seat with their wings." Ex. 25: 20. Apparently, Lucifer was one of these.

"Thou wast upon the holy mountain of God "— in the immediate presence of God, as is also shown by the expression "stones of fire."

Verse 16. "Abundance of thy traffic" (A. R. V.), instead of "multitude of thy merchandise."

Lessons for To-day

Isaiah 12: 1. We should thank God for adversity as well as prosperity. Rain and dark days as well as sunshine are needed for the maturing of the grain.

Verse 3. The water in the wells of salvation is deep and clear. But it must be drawn. Every prayerful study of the word, every quiet meditation, every communion with God or Christian service to man, is drawing water out of the wells of salvation. But this drawing must be "with joy," willingly, not as a matter of duty or in order to reach a goal or to make a record.

Verse 4. Not "call upon the Lord," but "call upon His name." Not "the Lord is exalted," but "His name is exalted." God is in His name, and His name expresses His character. It is therefore the character of God that is here meant and which is to be proclaimed. The best way to proclaim it is to have it woven into our own characters, and then we shall live it. Rev. 14: 1.

Isaiah 13:4. "Jehovah of hosts is mustering the host for the battle." A. R. V. God has charge. Armageddon has come. They that have taken the sword shall perish with the sword. Rev. 13:10. Let not the church of God take the sword, lest it perish by it.

Verse 12. The value of a man, of a soul, who can compute it? We do not value as we should a human soul. "What shall it profit a man, if he shall gain the whole world, and lose his own soul?" or the souls of his children? Mark 8:36. Yet "the precious sons of Zion, comparable to fine gold, how are they esteemed as earthen pitchers!" "The daughter of My people is become cruel, like the ostriches in the wilderness." Lam. 4:2, 3. These large birds lay their eggs in sand to be hatched by the sun, forgetting "that the foot may crush them, or that the wild beast may break them. She is hardened against her young ones, as though they were not hers." Job 39:15, 16.

Isaiah 24:11. "All joy is darkened, the mirth of the land is gone." Every conceivable source of amusement is now being sought. The world is pleasure-mad. But it will all have an end. And then there will come corresponding sorrow. It is better to joy in the Lord than in wine; in His word than in worldly wisdom; in hymns of praise than in cheap songs; in His blessings than in the world's approval. "He addeth no sorrow with it." Prov. 10:22.

Verses 13, 14. The world will not be saved, but a few will be saved out of the world. One with God is a majority. We need to learn to stand alone, and to praise God in the midst of difficulties. Even amid the fires of the last day we may glorify God.

Isaiah 14:13, 14. Five times "I" is used in these two verses. It is well for us not to follow the example of Lucifer even in our speech.

Ezekiel 28:13. We have no record of any other angel's being decked with jewels. The Septuagint says: "Thou hast bound upon thee every precious stone," that is, Lucifer hung every ornament upon him that he could. One way in which Lucifer showed his pride was in his apparel. Christians should not imitate him.

Verse 17. Beauty is often a source of pride. There is always a tendency to spend time on outward adornment rather than on inward beauty. A polished exterior, a vacant mind, and an impoverished soul too often go together. Yet it need not and should not be so. God Himself is a lover of the beautiful. Only let us see to it that more time and effort are used on the culture of mind and heart than on dress and appearance.

CHAPTER VI
The Trials and Triumphs of God's People
Lesson Scripture: Isaiah 25; 26

Isaiah 25. A song of praise and deliverance.

Verses 1-5. Thanksgiving is offered for deliverance. The prophet, speaking for the people, is thanking God for the "wonderful things" He has done. In the preceding chapter the final scenes of earth's history have been depicted. Through all the plagues and calamities God has protected His own, and they are now giving Him thanks. The "counsels of old," the prophecies and warnings given by prophets in olden times, have all been fulfilled in the destruction of the earth and in the saving of God's people, and are found to be "faithfulness and truth." The people can now testify to the statement: "Like as the Lord of hosts thought to do unto us, according to our ways, and according to our doings, so hath He dealt with us." Zech. 1:6.

The cities have been broken down, and "the city of ungodly men shall not be built forever." Verse 2, Septuagint. "Strong people" and "terrible nations" shall fear God. Verse 3. This finds its fulfillment at the time of the plagues. The "terrible ones," mentioned in verses 3-5, the bitter enemies of God, shall let loose a tremendous "blast" against the saints, but God will protect them. He will be "a strength to the poor, a strength to the needy in his distress, a refuge from the storm, a shadow from the heat." Verse 4. The "blast" will spend itself "as a storm against the wall," harmless as the rain beating against solid masonry. As the wicked thus see their efforts against the saints thwarted, they will conclude that it is not men, but God against whom they are fighting, and they will "fear" Him. As a cloud tempers the heat, so God has intervened and been "a shadow from the heat" to the saints during the fourth plague. (See Psalms 91; Revelation 16.)

Verses 6-8. The banquet of the Lord. This section speaks of that glorious time when the redeemed shall meet at the feast of the Lord, the "marriage supper" (Matt. 22:2-14), or the "marriage supper of the Lamb." Rev. 19:7-9. It will be "a feast of fat things, ... full of marrow, of wines on the lees well refined." All gross conceptions must, of course, be banished. At that time also will be destroyed "the covering cast over all people, and the veil that is spread over all nations." We shall not then see darkly, but face to face. Death will be swallowed up in victory, "and the Lord God will wipe away tears from off all faces." The rebuke, the taunts and revilings, which God's people have suffered, shall be no more. "The Lord hath spoken it."

Verses 9-12. "A hymn of praise in view of deliverance from Moab." What a wonderful shout that will be when God's people see Him for whom they have waited appear in the clouds of heaven! Satan, as his crowning deception, has tried to impersonate Christ, and almost the whole world has been deceived. Now the true Christ appears, and the cry is raised, "Lo, this is our God."

Moab here stands as representative of the enemies of God. It was Moab who hired Balaam to curse Israel, and thus hinder them from entering the Promised Land. Num. 22:6. It was Moab who enticed Israel at Baal-Peor. Numbers 25. Moab, the son of an incestuous union (Gen. 19:37), was one of the bitterest enemies of God and His people. 2 Kings 24:2; Eze. 25:8-11. He is now to meet his doom. He shall be "trodden down" ("threshed," margin). Verse 10.

Isaiah 26. The song of the saved; a meditation.

"That day" is the day of the Lord. Probation is past, but the redeemed have not yet entered the city. Their thoughts are upon the events that have just taken place, both trials and triumphs, and upon the immediate future. The saints are meditating on the ways of God with men. Experiences and reflections follow one after another. The result is a wonderfully interesting and instructive chapter — meat in due season.

Verses 1-4. A song of praise to God for His salvation and strength. The city of God is "a strong city." Its gates will open to those who keep "the truth." He who keeps his mind stayed on God will have "perfect peace." Jehovah is the "rock of ages," therefore trust in Him.

Verses 5-11. Reflection on God's way with the wicked and with the just. God will bring the proud to the ground, "even to the dust;" but the way of the righteous is "a right way" (A. R. V., margin), for God directs him. He waits for God, and his desire is to God's name and to His memorial. Both in the night and in the morning He seeks the Lord. The wicked, however, will not learn. God's goodness he misinterprets, and though he were placed

The Trials and Triumphs of God's People

in most favorable surroundings, he would still deal unjustly. The difficulty with the wicked is that "they will not see."

Verses 12-19. Prayer, confession, and prophecy. Whatever good we may have done, God should have the praise, for He has done "all our works for us" (margin). We have formerly had other gods who ruled over us, but that time is past. Let even the memory thereof perish. We have been in pain as she that is to be delivered of a child; but when we see what has been accomplished by our labor, we have brought forth only wind. "We have not wrought any deliverance in the earth; neither have inhabitants of the world been born." A. R. V., margin. In spite of all that has been done, the world is not saved. God's purpose, however, will not be frustrated. The dead shall rise. It will be but a little while till the indignation be overpast. Hide until then.

It seems probable that it is during the "little moment" mentioned in verse 20 that the experiences of this chapter take place.

Notes

Isaiah 25:6. "All people." Among the saved every nationality will be represented.

"Feast of fat things," "wines on the lees well refined." An Oriental figure, denoting the best of everything, a banquet. (See Ps. 36:8; 63:5.)

Verse 7. "The covering." Now we see through a glass darkly. Few have a right view of life. Many things here appear dark and incomprehensible. There is a covering, a veil, over so many things. The time will come when it shall be taken away.

Verse 8. "Swallow up death in victory"—"death forever." A. R. V.

Verse 11. Kay, one of the learned commentators, has an interesting note on this verse. He maintains that the pronoun in "He shall spread" and "He shall bring" in both cases refers to the Lord Jesus. Speaking of spreading forth the hands as he that swims, he says that this is a remarkable figure, used elsewhere of prayer, entreaty, or agonizing lamentation. Isa. 1:15; 65:2; Jer. 4:31.

Continuing, he says: "Can it be conceived then that any victory was ever gained by a divine Person over the archenemy — over death and sin — in which the conqueror 'spread out His hands' as 'one that swimmeth' amidst deep waters, or as one who prays, entreats, or suffers agony might 'spread forth his hands'? What Christian can hesitate for an answer? It was while Jesus 'stretched forth His hands' (cf. John 21:18) on the cross that He 'triumphed' over principalities and powers. Col. 2:14, 15."

Isaiah 26:2. "Keepeth the truth," or fidelity; maintaining loyalty of faith toward God.

Verse 4. "Everlasting strength"—"the rock of ages," margin.

Verse 7. "Weight," "level," as the scales are kept level and straight. The A. R. V. has "direct the path of the just."

Verse 8. "Remembrance;" rather, "memorial."

Verse 15. "Thou hast increased the nation," the "righteous nation" of verse 2.

"Thou art glorified," through their keeping "the truth."

Verse 2. "Thou hadst removed it;" rather, "Thou hast enlarged all the borders of the land." A. R. V.

Verse 18. Instead of "fallen," read "been born." A. R. V., margin.

Verse 20. "Enter thou into thy chambers, and shut thy doors about thee. Hide thyself." Some of God's people of the last generation will be "taken away from the evil to come." They will "enter into peace," resting "in their beds." Isa. 57:1, 2.

The greater part, however, will live through the time of the plagues. God will hide them "in His pavilion: in the secret of His tabernacle shall He hide me." Ps. 27:5. God will provide a tabernacle, a place of refuge, where they will be safe. When we pray, we are to enter our closet and shut the door. Matt. 6:6. God here invites the people to enter their chambers and shut the door. The time of trouble will be a time of prayer.

Verse 21. "The earth also shall disclose her blood." Uncovered blood calls for vengeance. Gen. 4:11; Eze. 24:7, 8.

"No more cover her slain." The earth as well as the sea shall give back her dead. Rev. 20:13.

Lessons for To-day

Isaiah 25:1. A song of praise. Prayer is often emphasized as a Christian privilege and duty. So also are faith, study of the Scriptures, meditation, working for souls. These are all important. But praise is no less so. We thank God too little, we do not praise Him enough. Let the next prayer meeting be a praise meeting. God has done "wonderful things."

Verse 4. "The poor" and "the needy." These refer not to some one else, but to me. If I do not feel either poor or needy, may God pity me and open my eyes.

Verse 6. "Fat things full of marrow." When God spreads a feast of good things for His people, there will be real nourishment — not husks. Do not press the figure too far, but retain the essential elements. The wine is "well refined"— no human impurity added to the word. Isa. 55: 1.

Verse 8. "Swallow up death in victory." In the resurrection this will be fulfilled, and still more in the translation of the saints. Then and there the last enemy will be vanquished. 1 Cor. 15: 51-57. If sin is the sting of death, then if we are to escape death, we must get rid of the sting.

Verse 9. Waiting for the Lord. Is any one doing that? Or are we merely hurrying, getting ready to meet Him? Only he that is dressed, all ready to go, can be said to be waiting. Are we waiting for the Lord, or is He waiting for us?

Isaiah 26:2. "Keepeth the truth." Rev. 22:14. Truth is a word full of meaning. It includes life as well as belief. Truth is the password without which none can "enter in."

Verse 3. "Perfect peace." No worry, no anxiety — what a blessed condition! How well it would be if our minds were "stayed on" God! But our minds wander, and oftentimes our hearts wander with our minds. Lord, stay our minds!

Verse 4. "The Rock of ages" (margin). Christ, "He is the Rock." Deut. 32:4; Isa. 32:2. Unmoved and unmovable is our Rock. We need not fear. He is our fortress.

Verse 8. God's people do not merely wait for Him, they wait for Him "in the way of Thy judgments;" that is, "have stood by the way along which we expected and desired Jehovah to appear in judgment."— *Cambridge Bible*.

Verse 9. "I will seek Thee early "— the morning watch.

Verse 10. Favorable circumstances may be a help at times, but stanch Christian character does not depend upon circumstances. The wicked man will do wickedly in the best of environments — "in the land of uprightness," heaven. Some people have been brought up very carefully and have always been shielded from evil. That does not necessarily make them better. Lack of opportunity to do evil — like the man behind prison bars — does not of itself make sturdy Christians. Contact with the problems of sin, the doing of positive good, the resisting of temptation, the hand-to-hand fight with the powers of evil,— these make for healthy Christian experience, for the development of spiritual resistance. Environment or heredity, neither will save.

Verse 11. "They will not see: but they shall see." None is so blind as he that will not see. "But they shall see." The day will come, and the day is here, when men will see. And seeing will for many mean condemnation.

Verse 12. If God has "wrought all our works for us" (margin), He should have all the praise. Let men therefore see your good works and glorify the Father. Matt. 5:16. If any should glorify you, beware; you are taking glory belonging to God, and that is dangerous. Herod did that, and died. Acts 12:23. Or if you are in the habit of glorifying any one, beware also. "Fear God, and give glory to Him." Rev. 14:7.

Verse 16. "In trouble have they visited Thee." It is well to seek God when we are in trouble. But sometimes we wonder, with Luther, why we should seek God only or even principally when we are in distress.

Verse 18. Sometimes we do our best, but it seems that little is accomplished. In such cases we need not be overanxious. If we do what we can in sowing and watering, we may leave the matter of increase with God. 1 Cor. 3:6. Having put the seed in the ground and having watered it, the virtue needed is patience, not worry. James 5:7.

Verse 20. "Shut thy doors about thee; hide thyself." In this time of hurry and bustle, every one needs a door that he can shut, a place where he can hide himself. That need not be a literal door, but some place where one can hide himself for a moment, where he can be alone. It may be a chamber, or it may be a hayloft, or a quiet place in a grove. The kind of place is not important, but it is vital to every one to find some place where he can commune with himself and with His God.

CHAPTER VII

The Vineyard; False Security

Lesson Scripture: Isaiah 27; 28

ISAIAH 27:1. God's judgments on the world are symbolically represented by the destruction of three great monsters,— the "piercing serpent," the "crooked serpent," and the "dragon." The dragon and the serpent have always stood for Satan. Rev. 20:2. These three monsters are therefore three evil powers, probably the same as the three mentioned in Revelation 16:13, the dragon, the beast, and the false prophet.

Verses 2-6. God's "vineyard." While God is punishing the world, He will see to it that no harm comes to His people. Speaking of the church under the symbol of a vineyard, the Lord announces Himself as its keeper. Night and day will He watch it, "lest any hurt it."

"Fury is not in Me," God says; that is, He is not angry with His vineyard, as in a former parable. Isa. 5:4-7. But if "briers and thorns," the enemies of God and His vineyard, should array themselves in battle against God, He would "go through them," "He would burn them together." If, however, these enemies should decide to surrender to God, He would graciously accept them, and they might make their peace with Him. Returning to the figure of the vineyard, God would plant them, and they would "take root," and, thus becoming a part of Israel, would "blossom and bud, and fill the face of the world with fruit."

Verses 7-11. A call to repentance and reformation. This is a difficult section, of which we may barely touch the outlines. God has not punished Israel as He has punished the nations "that smote him." Verse 7. "In measure" only have the backslidings of His people been punished, and God has stayed "His rough wind in the day of the east wind." Verse 8. On condition that Israel will tear down their heathen altars and crush them as chalkstones, so that the groves "and the sun images shall rise no more" (A. R. V.), God will forgive their iniquity. Verse 9. Yet Jerusalem cannot be saved; it shall for a time become a desolation. Verse 10. By a sudden change of metaphor, Israel now becomes a tree. As the boughs wither, they are broken off. Rom. 11:17. The people have "no understanding." Though God has made them, He will not have mercy upon them if they continue in sin, nor will He show them special favor. Verse 11.

Verses 12, 13. Isaiah usually adds a word of cheer and encouragement even to his gloomiest prophecies. So he does here. "The Lord shall beat off," as the olive tree is beaten to obtain the fruit (Deut. 24: 20), or as the grain is beaten on the threshing floor (Ruth 2: 17); that is, the Lord shall gather a harvest, though it may not be so bountiful, from "the channel of the river unto the stream of Egypt," from the Euphrates to the southern border of Palestine. This takes in the territory occupied by the Jews, and this part of the prophecy applies specifically to them. They shall be gathered, not as a nation, but "one by one." Verse 12. More than these, however, shall be saved. The great trumpet shall be blown, and from Assyria and Egypt — here representing the Gentile nations — shall the redeemed come to "worship the Lord in the holy mount," even the New Jerusalem. Verse 13.

Isaiah 28: 1-4. A warning to Ephraim. Samaria was the chief city of the northern kingdom, here called Ephraim. It was a rival of Jerusalem, and was of "glorious beauty," situated on a hill, having white terraced streets, and was at the head of "the fat valley." But Ephraim had departed from God. Pride and excess had done their work, and it was now as a "fading flower." Verse 1. Punishment is about to come. God has a "strong one" (Assyria), which shall come "as a tempest of hail and a destroying storm," and cast Samaria "down to the earth." Verse 2. "Ephraim shall be trodden under feet" (verse 3), and shall be swallowed up (margin) by Assyria as one swallows the first-ripe figs, which were considered a delicacy. Verse 4, A. R. V. This prophecy was given sometime before the fall of Samaria, which took place in 721 B. C.

Verses 5, 6. The prophet now suddenly turns from the destruction of Samaria to the fate of the remnant in "that day." To them the Lord shall be "a crown of glory" and "a diadem of beauty." Verse 5. To them that sit "in judgment," that is, to the leaders of His people, He will give the "spirit of judgment." In the many difficult questions that come before them for judgment, God will give wisdom. He will also give "strength to them that turn back the battle at the gate." Verse 6, A. R. V.

Verses 7, 8. Conditions in Judah. Israel has sinned, as recorded in verses 1-4, but Judah is not faultless. He also has come short. "Strong drink" has caused both priest and prophet even in Judah to "stumble in judgment" and "err in vision." Verse 7.

Verses 9-13. From among the many conflicting interpretations

The Vineyard; False Security

of these verses we offer the following as the most consistent with the instruction given this people:

God is addressing the professed people of God, not indeed the remnant mentioned in verses 5, 6, but popular Christians. Their priests and prophets have gone astray. These would naturally be the ones upon whom the Lord would depend for teaching the people; but not being able to use them, "whom shall He teach?" Verse 9. Children, "drawn from the breasts"? The Lord is compelled to use such as offer themselves, and as the message must after all be given in a very simple way, "precept upon precept; line upon line" (verse 10), God can and does use "stammering lips" and men of "another tongue." Verse 11. To these He gives the message of "refreshing," that they may cause "the weary to rest." Verse 12. This message is to be taught the people, and repeated again and again. It is a decisive message, for those who do not accept will "fall backward, and be broken." Verse 13.

This whole section finds its completion in Matthew 11: 25-30. Christ thanks the Father that "these things" are hid from the wise and prudent, and revealed "unto babes." "Even so, Father: for so it seemed good in Thy sight." Then follows the message of rest: "Come unto Me, all ye that labor and are heavy laden, and I will give you rest."

God would gladly use "the wise and prudent," but priest and prophet have both failed Him, and He has now given the vineyard to others who, though comparatively inexperienced, will bring to Him the fruits thereof.

Verses 14-22. God rebukes the scoffers that rule in Jerusalem. In the last days shall come some that shall ridicule the idea of Christ's second coming. 2 Peter 3: 3. They do not believe in the signs of His coming. Of this kind are evidently those mentioned in verse 15, who "have made a covenant with death" and are "at agreement" with hell. Their refuge of lies, however, will not stand the test. There is only one sure foundation. It is "a tried stone, a precious corner stone." "He that believes on Him shall by no means be ashamed." Verse 16, Septuagint. God, who is the master workman, will use both line and plummet. His work will stand the test; but the refuge of lies shall be swept away. Verse 17. All their supposed agreements with hell and death shall be disannulled, and they shall not escape the scourge which will overtake them every time it passes through. Verses 18, 19. That which they have depended upon for a covering and a refuge is insufficient. Verse 20. The work which the Lord is about to do is a "strange

work." His nature being love and mercy, to Him the infliction of punishment is a "strange act." Do not mock at this. It will only make your guilt and your punishment greater. Verses 21, 22.
Verses 23-29. A lesson from the field. The plowman plows all day, not merely for the purpose of plowing, but to get the ground ready for sowing. Verse 24. When the soil is prepared, he scatters the seed. Verse 25. Then comes the harvest and threshing. Each kind of grain is threshed according to its nature. The common way of driving over the grain an oxcart with a great number of sharp-edged wheels, would not do for the more tender kinds. It would completely crush and bruise the kernels. Hence a staff or rod is used. Verses 27, 28. The same method is used by God in dealing with people, "making a difference" of some. Jude 22.

Notes

Isaiah 27: 1. It is not known what animal is indicated by "leviathan." Its root meaning being "that which is coiled or twisted," it has been applied as in the present instance to serpents. The description in Job 41, however, does not seem to fit any creature now living.

Verse 9. "Groves and images." Groves were used for idolatrous worship. "Images"—"sun images." A. R. V.

Verse 12. "The river"—Euphrates. Deut. 11:24.

"The stream of Egypt" is not the Nile, but the Wady el Arish, which forms the southwestern frontier of Palestine.

Verse 13. "Great trumpet," the same as the trumpet or trump in Matthew 24:31; 1 Corinthians 15:52; 1 Thessalonians 4:16.

Isaiah 28:1. Samaria, situated on a low hill, with white terraced streets running all around it and with a profusion of trees of all kinds, was not unlike a flower when looked at from a distance. It was now a fading flower.

Verse 4. "Hasty fruit"—"first-ripe figs." A. R. V. The early figs, which were found in the latter part of June, were considered a great delicacy. Jer. 24:2. The ordinary fig season came in August.

Verse 14. Scoffers represent the last degree of ungodliness, open contempt. A person may be an unbeliever, and yet a decent respect for the opinions of others may restrain him from scoffing. When that last restraint is gone, little more can be done to help the person. Some scoffers, however, are not out-and-out unbelievers. They retain the Christian name, but have the scoffing spirit. These are no better than the others.

The Vineyard; False Security

Verse 15. "Covenant with death." Anything which claims to mitigate the fear of death and is not based on the gospel, is a vain covenant. Any one who says that he has made provision for the future and is not afraid of death, cherishes a vain hope, unless his provision is based upon a living faith in God.

Verse 17. Line and plummet. The "line" is used to make sure that the work is level; the "plummet," that it is vertical, straight up and down, not leaning to one side or the other.

Verse 18. "Overflowing scourge"— any calamity or punishment sent by God, here specifically the seven last plagues. Revelation 16.

Verse 21. Perazim, Gibeon. At Perazim, David defeated the Philistines. 1 Chron. 14: 11-16. God at that time fought for His people; now He fights against them. This is part of "His strange work."

Verse 22. "Consumption"—"a decree of destruction." A. R. V.

Verse 25. Fitches, cummin, wheat, barley, rye — different kinds of grain.

Verse 27. "Threshing instruments." "Three methods of threshing are here alluded to: (a) Beating with a rod or flail (see Ruth 2: 17); (b) treading with the feet of cattle (Deut. 25: 4; Micah 4: 13); (c) drawing over the grain a heavy wooden sledge, with sharp stones or iron spikes fixed in its under surface, or a wagon with a great number of sharp-edged wheels. The point of the illustration is that the method suitable to one kind of grain would be ruinous to another (verse 27); and that even the rougher methods are applied with moderation (verse 28)."— *Cambridge Bible.*

Verse 28. In the A. R. V., margin, this verse is translated: "Is bread grain crushed? Nay, he will not ever be threshing it, and driving his cart wheels and his horses over it; he doth not crush it."

Lessons for To-day

Isaiah 27: 2, 3. "In that day sing." We need never fear. The terrible monsters mentioned in verse 1 might have a tendency to make us afraid; but the Lord watches "lest any hurt" His people.

Verses 4-6. "Briers and thorns"— God's enemies. But even these He invites, and they make peace with Him. God will cause them to bear fruit, as well as blossom and bud. If God has not given up hope for such as may truly be designated "briers and thorns," neither should we. Sharp, disagreeable, hurtful cumberers of the ground they may seem, but God still invites them. So should we.

Verse 8. "In measure." All God's doings are "in measure," with moderation. He will stay the "rough wind in the day of the east wind." To be moderate in all things is a Christian virtue. Phil. 4: 5. Extreme tendencies should be avoided. It is possible to be so straight as to lean backward.

Verse 9. "Beaten in sunder." God will take away sin upon condition that we tear down our altars of wickedness and "beat in sunder" the stones thereof. Not a particle must be left. We are to hate "even the garment spotted by the flesh." Jude 23. When we tear down the altar but leave the stones, we are apt to build another altar with them.

Verse 11. "Show them no favor." Equal opportunities for all, special favors for none. There is no respect of persons with God. Acts 10: 34. Neither should there be with us. James 2: 9. The parents should have no favorites, neither should the minister or teacher. And the people should show no partiality, extolling one worker above another.

Verse 12. "One by one." Men are not saved by nations or communities. One by one, is God's method. And in that all can have a part. One personal contact is worth more than many sermons. To listen to a sermon over the radio may be good. To listen to the same sermon in the church where the speaker may be seen, is better. For speaker and listener to come in personal contact is best.

Isaiah 28: 1. "Glorious beauty is a fading flower." The only beauty that continues through the years is beauty of soul. The ugliest person may have that. Youth will fade. "Glorious beauty" will vanish. But he whose mind is enriched with glorious truth, whose soul is touched with divine fire, whose heart is opened to eternal values, will abide.

Verse 6. "Spirit of judgment"— good judgment. The promise is here that the Lord will be a help to those that need Him. Weighty matters come up for decision. At such times we may know that the Lord will be to us a "spirit of judgment."

Verse 7. "Swallowed up of wine." Note the wording. It does not say that the people swallow the wine, but that the wine swallows them. This denotes an advanced stage of drinking. It is a law of nature that if we do not kill evil, evil will kill us. If we do not root out the thorns and briers of our life, they will choke us. So will any bad habit. Even of that which in itself is good we may evoke evil. As long as we control our appetite, all is well. Where it controls us, we are on dangerous ground. Money is not necessarily evil; but let money become a dominating factor in our lives, and we completely lose our perspective. As long as we control circumstances, we are men; when they control us, we are weaklings.

Verse 10. "Precept upon precept; line upon line." Many are anxious to present the whole truth at once. They need to learn that truth is a gradual unfolding, not an explosion. Also, they who think themselves in possession of all knowledge and are continually demanding something new, should remember that it is only the things we do that we really know. We may have much knowledge, but God measures our real attainment, not by what we know, but by what we do. Hence we may all need repetition of that which we theoretically know.

Verse 11. "Stammering lips." God can use the simple and the unlearned, and reveal His glory and power through them. But let no one glory in his deficiency. The truth should work wonders for any man. Our pioneers did a mighty work and laid a sure foundation, but not always with perfect grammar. God blessed them wonderfully. Let no one speak a disparaging word. But with the opportunities now offered our young men, they must not rest content with meager attainments, nor boast of their advantages. Our strength lies in our humility.

Verse 16. "He that believeth." This is New Testament doctrine in the Old Testament — faith, founded on Him who is the "sure foundation," the "tried stone," the "precious corner stone."

Verse 20. A bed that is too short and a covering that is too narrow do not make for comfort. So with many false teachings to-day. They are both too short and too narrow, and the hope they give is also too short and too narrow.

Verse 22. "Be ye not mockers." It is best never to mock. Even if we do not believe as others do, we should not mock or ridicule them. Little would be gained thereby, and much lost. Many doors have thus been closed to the presentation of truth. Ridicule is offensive, and convinces nobody.

Verses 24-28. Even as not all grain can be treated the same way, so also with people. To use stereotyped systems that cannot be varied, is not best. One person can be approached only in a certain way. Find that way. Become an expert in soul winning. Use at least the same tact and wisdom in catching men that you do in catching fish.

CHAPTER VIII

Events Connected With the Coming of the Lord

Lesson Scripture: Isaiah 29; 30

Isaiah 29: 1-12. The approaching siege of Jerusalem.

Verse 2. Under the symbolic name of Ariel, the lion of God, Jerusalem's future is revealed. God will "distress Ariel."

Verses 3, 4. The city will be besieged and taken.

Verses 5, 6. The enemy will be numerous, and the visitation of the Lord accompanied by earthquake and tempest.

Verses 7, 8. The multitude that fights against Jerusalem shall vanish, however, as a dream.

Verses 9, 10. But this wonderful deliverance the people will not understand. Both they and their prophets are as in a "deep sleep."

Verses 11, 12. The doings of the Lord are as a sealed book to them, and neither the learned nor the unlearned can read it.

Verses 13-16. Warnings against hypocrisy and plottings.

Verse 13. The people offer God lip service, but their hearts are far from Him. Their worship is guided by the precepts of men.

Verse 14. God will therefore do a marvelous work among them, and the wisdom of the wise men will perish, and the understanding of the prudent shall be hid.

Verse 15. A woe is pronounced upon those that "seek deep," whose work is "in the dark," who do not believe that God can see them or that He knows what they are doing

Verse 16. But their work is of no more worth than "potter's clay." Their conception of God is contained in the two statements: "He made me not," and, "He had no understanding."

Verses 17-24. Promises to God's people.

Verses 17-19. In a little while "Lebanon shall be turned into a fruitful field." When that day comes, the deaf shall hear and the blind shall see, the meek shall rejoice in the Lord, and the poor in the Holy One.

Verse 20. The reason for this condition is that God's enemies, the scorners and them that watch for iniquity, are cut off.

Verse 21. These are they that "make a man an offender for a word," that entrap men and turn aside justice.

Verses 22-24. God, who redeemed Abraham, has a special promise for Jacob. Some of Jacob's children shall be saved, and shall "fear the God of Israel." Even some who have "erred in spirit" and have "murmured shall learn doctrine." The meaning is that some of the least likely, some of the most hardened, shall eventually be saved.

Isaiah 30: 1-7. Warning against alliance with Egypt.

Verses 1-3. A woe is pronounced against them that counsel with others instead of with the Lord, that add sin to sin, and trust in the king instead of in the Lord.

Verses 4-7. Their experience was not satisfactory; they were ashamed of Egypt who could not help them; it was only a "land of trouble." To trust in Egypt was "vain, and to no purpose."

Isaiah 30: 8-17. Warnings to Israel.

Verses 8, 9. The prophet is now commanded to write on a tablet and to note in a book, that it may be a witness against them forever, the charge that the people are rebellious and that they disregard the law. They forbid the seers to see, and direct the prophets to speak only smooth things.

Verses 10, 11. "Get you out of the way," they cry, trouble us no more with talk of Israel's Majesty.

Verses 12-14. Because they thus despise the word of God and trust in oppression and perverseness, their iniquity shall be as a breach ready to fall, swelling out in a high wall, whose breaking comes suddenly. The destruction shall be complete, as when a pitcher is broken with hardly a piece left.

Verses 15-17. Their only hope to escape this destruction is to turn to the Lord. Thus they might be saved. But they would not. They preferred to trust to their own strength. God would therefore show them how futile their plans were. A thousand should flee at the rebuke of one, until but few were left.

Isaiah 30: 18-26. Promises to Israel.

Verses 18-21. Those that wait for the Lord are called blessed. For them will the Lord wait, and He will be gracious unto them. They shall weep no more; when they cry to God, He will hear and answer them. The Lord may let them pass through seasons of affliction, but He will not forsake them. He will guide them, and they shall hear the still small voice leading them in the right way when there is danger of going astray.

Verses 22-25. As they thus follow the Lord and throw away all idols, prosperity comes to them, and in the day of God's vengeance — the day of slaughter — they shall not suffer.

Verse 26. In that day the light of the moon shall be as that of the sun, and the light of the sun shall be sevenfold.

Isaiah 30: 27-33. The coming of the Lord.

Verses 27-29. God shall come " as a devouring fire." He is full of indignation, and He will sift the nations. The heart of God's people will be filled with gladness, and they will sing as Israel of old did when they came to the temple service at the time of the Passover.

Verses 30-33. God's voice is heard, and the wicked flee panic-stricken while the tempest rages and the hailstones fall. The place of burning, Tophet, is prepared. Satan shall there suffer in the fire prepared and kindled by the Lord.

Notes

Isaiah 29:13. " Precept of men "—" a mere tradition learned by rote."— *Moffatt.*

Isaiah 30:8. " Table," rather " tablet."

Verses 9-12. The charges against the people are that they are rebellious, do not tell the truth, refuse to hear the law, seek flattery rather than honest truth, and demand that God's messengers depart, not wishing to hear any more rebuke.

Verse 13. " The slight beginnings of transgression, its inevitable tendency to gravitate more and more from the moral perpendicular, till a critical point is reached, then the suddenness of the final catastrophe, are vividly expressed by this magnificent simile. (See Ps. 62: 3)."— *Cambridge.*

Verse 14. " Sherd," a small piece of pottery.

Verse 20. Moffatt translates: " Yet He your Teacher never leaves you now; you see your Teacher for yourselves."

Verse 26. " Light of seven days," perhaps a reference to the light as it was in the beginning, in creation week, and as it shall be again.

Verse 28. " There shall be a bridle in the jaws of the people, causing them to err." This indicates religious domination. Some one is driving the people as a horse or mule is driven. Ps. 32:9.

The Coming of the Lord

Verse 29. "Song, as in the night." The Passover feast was celebrated at night. "It is a night of watching unto Jehovah." Ex. 12:42, A. R. V., margin. The paschal hymn was Psalms 113 to 118.

Verse 33. "Tophet," a place of burning. It was located in the valley of Hinnom, south of Jerusalem. A great pit was dug in the ground, where the human sacrifices were burned. (See 2 Kings 23:10; Jer. 7:31.)

"The Lord . . . doth kindle it." "God is a consuming fire." Heb. 12:29. God Himself kindles the hell fire. When the wicked are destroyed, the fire will come down from God out of heaven, and devour them. Rev. 20:9. The fire that destroys the wicked comes from God — God's presence.

Lessons for To-day

Isaiah 29:13. "Precept of men." Due respect must always be given to those in authority, both in church and in state. God, however, is greater than any man, and our worship must never be according to the "precept of men."

Verses 14-16. "The wisdom of their wise men shall perish." We believe this prophecy is about to see its fulfillment. There has never been such widespread knowledge as to-day. In every field of science, wonderful advance has been made. And the end is not yet. The future holds yet greater things in store as men delve into the secrets of nature. We thank God as we see this, for it is a fulfillment of prophecy. Dan. 12:4.

But increase in learning has not brought a corresponding increase in godliness. Quite the reverse. Men take honor to themselves that belongs only to God. They discourse learnedly of that concerning which they have no knowledge. When men turn things "upside down" and conclude that God "made me not" and that "He had no understanding," it is about time for God to intervene. And He will do so. Men's theories will go down as God proceeds to do His "marvelous work." It is a wonderful privilege to live in a time when God will vindicate His truth. We can afford to wait and be patient. As a vessel falls to the ground and is broken into a thousand pieces, so men's carefully built hypotheses and deductions shall be broken and scattered to the four winds. And the crash is not far off.

Verse 18. Blessed day when this shall be fulfilled, spiritually and literally. The promise is not merely that the deaf shall hear, but that they shall hear "the words of the book." Some that are not literally deaf, are deaf as far as "the book" is concerned. The promise is that they shall hear. So keep on praying and working.

Verse 20. "Watch for iniquity." We generally find what we look for. He who goes to India to find tigers, will find them. He who goes there to find souls, will also find them. Those that look for faults, are apt to find them. Those that look for virtue and good works, will find them. Beware, therefore, for what you look. You may find it. Some "watch for iniquity." The vulture looks for and finds death and decay. "Look for the beautiful, look for the true."

Verse 21. "An offender for a word." "If any man offend not in word, the same is a perfect man." James 3:2. As no one seems to be exempt, how charitable we should be with one another! Also how careful we should be in our words! One little word may cause wounds that time can scarcely heal. So let all be careful in speech, also let all be charitable.

Isaiah 30:10. "Smooth things." Courtesy and politeness are valuable as far as they are an outgrowth of a kind heart and gentle disposition. When they merely cover a selfish and mean heart, they become an offense. Kind, encouraging words are a blessing; when they degenerate into flattery, they are an abomination. We should help and cheer one another; but where our words of optimism tend to obscure the truth, we need to beware. The true servant of God will be optimistic and cheerful, but that will not cause him to neglect sterner duties. Truth, however harsh and unpleasant, must be faced. He will not preach "smooth things" merely to please. He will proclaim "the word," whether men will hear or forbear.

Verse 15. "In quietness and in confidence shall be your strength." The quiet, confident man will win. Blustering conduct, hasty words, extreme expressions, do not convince.

Verse 18. "Blessed are all they that wait for Him." This blessing may be ours.

Verse 19. "Weep no more." God's people will all go through experiences that will make this promise very precious. "When He shall hear it, He will answer thee." Yet it should be remembered that the answer may not always be favorable. God answers a prayer in three ways,— Yes, No, Wait.

Verse 21. "A word behind thee." When we have turned aside from or run ahead of the Lord, He will patiently call us back. He will lead us in the right way. The word may be the voice of conscience, a message from the desk, God's word directly, or guiding circumstances. We need to be awake to hear the right word.

Verse 29. Song in the midst of calamity; gladness of heart in the midst of confusion. "In Me ye might have peace. In the world ye shall have tribulation." John 16:33. In the midst of sorrow the Christian may have a song in the heart.

CHAPTER IX

The Judgment and the Time of Trouble

Lesson Scripture: Isaiah 32; 33

Isaiah 32: 1-8. The blessings of Christ's kingdom.

Verse 1. Christ and His saints shall reign in righteousness and justice.

Verse 2. When the storm and tempest come, Christ is a hiding place and a covert; He is as a refreshing stream and as the shadow of a rock in a weary land.

Verses 3, 4. At that time men shall have restored to them true moral perceptions. They shall not see dimly, nor have ears that do not hear. The hasty and inconsiderate person who constantly "blurts out crude and ill-judged opinions," shall have understanding, and the stammerer shall speak plainly.

Verses 5-8. The vile and the churlish person shall be judged by true standards, so shall also he who is liberal.

Isaiah 32: 9-20. A message to the women that are at ease.

Verses 9, 10. They shall be troubled many days and years, for the harvest shall fail.

Verses 11, 12. The calamity is such that they will tremble and smite themselves on the breast in token of sorrow.

Verses 13, 14. Thorns and briers have come up, and the palaces are forsaken and the city a desolation.

Verses 15-17. This state of things will continue "until the Spirit be poured upon us from on high." Then all shall be changed. The wilderness becomes a fruitful field, and the fruitful field a forest. Justice and righteousness shall prevail; and their work shall be peace; and the effect quietness and assurance forever.

Verses 18, 19. The people shall be secure in quiet resting places when the hail is coming down on the forest.

Verse 20. The chapter ends with a blessing upon them that sow beside all waters.

On the whole it seems better to give verses 9-20 a spiritual interpretation, as there are vital objections to considering them literally. The desolation that shall come continues until "the

Spirit" is " poured upon us from on high." Then immediate fruitfulness ensues. This is the " latter rain."

Isaiah 33: 1-13. The time of trouble.

Verse 1. The first verse is a woe pronounced against the oppressor of God's people. He has hitherto escaped, but his time shall come.

Verse 2. It is " the time of trouble." God's people are praying to Him to be gracious to them and to be their salvation.

Verses 3, 4. When God lifted up Himself, the nations were scattered as His army ran to and fro like locusts. (See Joel 2:9.)

Verses 5, 6. The Lord is exalted; He has filled Zion with justice and righteousness. And wisdom, knowledge, and salvation, that is, a right religious attitude, is the true strength of His people at this time; the fear of the Lord is a treasure.

Verses 7-9. While God's people are thus fortified, the wicked are having a hard time. Strong men cry, ambassadors weep, and travel ceases. Men have broken the covenant. Even nature is affected. The earth mourns, Lebanon is ashamed, and Sharon is like a wilderness.

Verses 10-13. The Lord will display His power. As against Him the nations and their plans are but chaff; they shall be burned up. Those that are near and those that are afar off shall hear and acknowledge God's might.

Isaiah 33: 14-24. The King in His beauty.

Verses 14-17. There are sinners in the church. There are also hypocrites. The time will come when they shall be " surprised." The great question is: " Who among us shall dwell with the devouring fire?" that is, who shall be able to dwell with God, who is a devouring fire? Heb. 12:29. The answer is very definite. Six qualifications are given: His life must be righteous; his speech right; he must despise unjust gain; he must abhor bribes; his ears must be closed to any suggestion of sin; he must not look on that which is evil. If he fulfills these conditions, he shall " dwell on high;" God shall keep him in times of danger, " bread shall be given him," and his water " shall be sure." He " shall see the King in His beauty," and also the land that now seems " very far off," even as Moses saw the Promised Land.

Verses 18, 19. For a moment the thoughts wander back to the experiences through which God's people have passed. As they see the " goodly land," the land of " far distances," and the King in

His beauty, they wonder if it is really true or only a dream. Ps. 126:1. "Where are they who oppressed us?" "Where are the tyrant's officers, who taxed us, charged us, took our tribute? These insolent creatures you shall see no more," the answer comes back. (Moffatt's translation.)

Verse 20. Look again upon the goodly land, look upon Zion, the city of our solemnities. It shall not be taken down as a tent, no stake shall ever be removed, nor shall any cord be broken.

Verse 21. The figure now changes. "There Jehovah will be with us in majesty, a place of broad rivers and streams." A. R. V. Even as the Lord is a "hiding place" (Ps. 32:7), so also He is a place of broad rivers, that is, of refreshment and spiritual blessings, "a river never raided by a galley, sailed by no ships of war." (Moffatt.)

Verse 22. The Lord is our judge, our lawgiver, our king; He also is our Saviour.

Verse 23. Coming back to the picture of rivers and boats in verse 21, the prophet now observes that there would have been no hope for the ship Zion if God had not helped. It was in an unseaworthy condition, and could never have weathered the gale. "Thy ropes hung slack, they could not hold fast the foot of their mast, they could not spread the sail." Had not God interfered, it would have become a prey.

Verse 24. In that blessed country none shall say, "I am sick." And the reason is that they shall be forgiven their iniquity.

Notes

Isaiah 32:2. "A man." "Behold the man whose name is the Branch." Zech. 6:12. The prerogatives here mentioned as exercised by this "man" are divine. (Compare Isa. 25:4; Ps. 18:2; 31:3; 143:6.) Hence this "man" is also God, even Christ.

Moffatt translates verses 4, 5: "The hasty shall learn how to judge, and stammerers shall speak clearly; the impious shall be called no more 'your honor,' and knaves no more be ranked as noblemen."

Verse 12. The American Revised Version reads: "They shall smite upon the breasts," that is, in sorrow and despair.

Isaiah 33:1. "That spoilest"— the same word as is used in Isaiah 21:2 of Babylon.

Verse 2. "Arm every morning." The "time of trouble" is not over in a day. Hence God's people pray for help "every morning."

Verse 4. "Like . . . the caterpillar," so that all is consumed.

"As the running to and fro of locusts;" the same verb is used of the "northern army" in Joel 2:9.

Verse 6. "And abundance of salvation, wisdom, and knowledge shall be the stability of thy times." A. R. V., margin. The meaning is that stability must be built on something other than prosperity,— on Christian conduct and character.

Verse 7. "Valiant ones"—"messengers" (margin); really, "lionlike heroes," "ambassadors" of peace. 2 Cor. 5:20. God's messengers.

Verse 9. "The earth mourneth." A paraphrase of this text would translate "earth," "nature." That is, nature is in sympathy with and mourns over the distress. The places mentioned are those noted for luxuriant vegetation and natural beauty.

Verses 11, 12. Note "chaff," "stubble," "lime," "thorns,"— things that are consumed utterly and quickly.

Verse 15. "Shaketh his hands," as Paul shook off the viper. Acts 28:5.

Verse 16. "Munitions of rocks;" rather, "stronghold of rocks." The Septuagint has: "He shall dwell in a high cave of a strong rock."

Verse 17. "Land that is very far off;" Hebrew, "land of far distances."

Verse 18. "Meditate terror;" rather, "shall muse on the terror." A. R. V. That is, the mind shall revert for a moment to the experiences just passed through. Paul quotes this verse partly in 1 Corinthians 1:20. The meaning, of course, is that there will be none to oppress or persecute. A further meaning might be that some that perhaps expected to be there will not appear. A scribe is a learned man. So is the "receiver." But they will not be there when God makes up His jewels.

Verse 20. "City of our solemnities" or "festal assemblies," the place where the assemblies of the future will be held as well as those of the past. Some have thought that the New Jerusalem would be like our present cities, a place of noise and confusion. It will be "a quiet habitation."

Verse 21. "Galley," "gallant ship," vessels of war.

Verse 23. "Tacklings," in this case "ropes."

Lessons for To-day

Isaiah 32:1, 2. "Behold, a King . . . and a Man." In the Old Testament as well as in the New, the fact that Christ is divine, God as well as man, is fundamental.

Verse 2. Note the four things Christ is here said to be:
(1) "A hiding place from the wind." When the winds of affliction and sorrow blow, when the time of trouble comes, He is our refuge. Ps. 27:5. He will hide us "from the pride of man" and from the "strife of tongues." Ps. 31:20. "Rock of Ages, cleft for me, let me hide myself in Thee."
(2) "A covert from the tempest." A "covert" is defined to be "a protection; a shelter; a defense; something that covers and shelters." Christ will create for His people "a defense," "a tabernacle ... in the daytime ... for a covert." Isa. 4:6. This is more than a hiding place; it is protection, defense.
(3) "As rivers of water in a dry place." Water not only refreshes in case of thirst, but is also the source of life to land otherwise waste and useless. Water will make the parched earth bring forth and bud. Water means bread; absence of it, starvation. So Christ is the source of life. He is the well of water of John 4:14.
(4) "A shadow of a great rock." Christ is the Rock. 1 Cor. 10:4. Throughout our journey in this "weary land," He is a cooling shadow. In that shadow we may find rest, refreshment, security, protection.

Verse 4. "The rash." We are all apt to do and say rash things. How well it would be if we did not! Many heartaches would be saved, and many wounds avoided.

Verse 5. "The vile," really "the fool." A. R. V. How sad to be one or to act like one! We may well pray God to help us not to make fools of ourselves.

Verse 7. "The churl." A churl is a miser, a niggard, the opposite of "the liberal" in verse 8. It also includes the qualities of selfishness, narrow-mindedness, rudeness in manner or temper, obstinacy, sullenness. From all such may God deliver us!

Verse 11. "Be troubled, ye careless ones." Worry does no good, yet there are some things that God wishes we were troubled about. "Ye careless ones," God says, "be troubled." Think of the condition you are in, think of what is coming. Rouse yourselves, tremble.

Verses 15, 16. "Until ... then." The preceding verses portray conditions before the Spirit is poured out. Note the words rash, vile, churl, iniquity, hypocrisy, error, hungry, thirsty, wicked devices, lying words, careless, troubled, thorns, briers, forsaken. This is the condition "until the Spirit be poured upon us. ... Then" fruitful, judgment (justice), righteousness, peace, quietness, assurance, peaceable habitation, sure dwellings, quiet resting places.

The Judgment and the Time of Trouble

The first effect of the Spirit is fruitfulness. The dry, stony ground of the heart is broken up, and it begins to bear fruit — fruit in the character developed and in souls won for the kingdom of God.

Verses 16-18. Then come justice and righteousness, and the work and effect of righteousness, which are peace, quietness, and assurance or confidence. We may test our own lives according to this formula. Do we bear the fruits here mentioned? Are we for peace, and do we enjoy it as a personal experience? Have we quietness and confidence, which is another name for faith?

Verse 20. " Sow beside all waters." That means the Pacific Ocean, the China Sea, and also along the Amazon River. That means the South American Indians, the natives of Borneo, and the cultured Europeans and Americans. " Blessed are ye " if ye will do that.

Isaiah 33: 2. " Every morning " we need God.

Verse 6. " The fear of the Lord is His treasure." We may not lay up treasure here on earth. The fear of the Lord is a treasure and should be our treasure.

Verse 7. " Valiant ones." God's people may be noncombatants in wars of nations. That does not mean they are cowards. God calls them " valiant ones," " lionlike heroes." No greater courage was ever demanded of soldiers than many of our missionaries exhibit daily in their work, and that without blare of trumpets or hope of earthly honor or reward. God, however, keeps a reckoning with His " ambassadors of peace."

Verse 14. " Hypocrites." Let no one use that word of another. God alone can see the heart and know the motives. There are hypocrites in the church. The question for me is, Am I one? Am I honest in all things? or do I try to appear that which I am not? Does my home life correspond to my church life? Blessed is the man whose wife and children believe him to be a Christian. Blessed is the official whose stenographer has faith in his Christianity. Blessed is the employer whose " hired men " respect him as a servant of the Most High. Blessed is the man whose dog, or cow, or horse proclaims his master a Christian.

Verses 15, 16. Watch your walk and talk; beware of covetousness and bribes; refuse to listen to evil, and shut your eyes from seeing it. If you do this, your reward is sure. Bread and water — not an elaborate fare, but sufficient. At that time we will be thankful for it. Why not now? Why return thanks to the Lord for the food He provides as we sit at the table, and then grumble over it the next minute? If one grumbles, "saying grace" is a questionable virtue.

Verse 17. "The King in His beauty." That which seers have longed for shall be our privilege. We shall see the King. Rev. 22:4.

Verse 20. Some prefer to live in the country because it is quiet there. But the New Jerusalem is also "a quiet habitation."

Verse 23. "Thy tacklings are loosed." It is important in case of storm to have everything in order. There must be no slack ropes, no swaying mast. So in Christian life. Are you ready, or are things at loose ends? Are the sails set and hatches down? The storm is coming. There is no time to waste.

CHAPTER X

The Destruction of the Earth; The New Earth

Lesson Scripture: Isaiah 34; 35

Isaiah 34: 1-17. The divine judgment of the world.

Verses 1-3. God calls upon nations and peoples to listen, upon the earth and the fullness thereof to hear; the whole world is called upon. The Lord has indignation against all nations and wrath against all their host. He has devoted them to the slaughter. The slain shall be cast out, and the stench of their dead bodies shall come up.

Verse 4. The " host of heaven "— the heavenly bodies —" shall be dissolved," and the heavens themselves " shall be rolled together as a scroll." (See Rev. 6: 14; 2 Peter 3: 10, 11.) The stars shall fall as the leaf falls from the vine and as figs fall from the tree. (See Rev. 6: 13; Matt. 24: 29.)

Verses 5-7. In the war of old (Rev. 12:7), the sword of the Lord " drunk its fill in heaven " (Isa. 34: 5, A. R. V.) ; now it shall come down in judgment upon God's enemies, " the people of My curse." As there formerly had been great sacrifices of lambs and goats, so shall there now be a great slaughter in Bozrah, in the land of Edom. The " land shall be soaked with blood," so great shall be the slaughter.

Verses 8-10. " The day of the Lord's vengeance " upon the ungodly has come, and the " year of recompenses for the controversy of Zion." The streams shall be turned into pitch and the dust into brimstone. Day and night it shall burn, and the smoke of it goes up forever. The land shall lie waste from generation to generation, and none shall pass through it.

Verses 11-15. Some of the animals and birds will be there, however, among them the pelican, the porcupine, the owl, and the raven. The land shall be completely emptied as the line of confusion and the plummet of emptiness is stretched out upon it. Neither nobles nor princes will be there, and instead of palaces shall be nettles, and brambles where jackals shall live and ostriches hold court. There also the wild beasts shall meet with the wolves, the wild goats and the night monsters shall find a place of rest. The dart snake shall make her nest there, and the vultures shall be gathered together, every one with her mate. (See A. R. V.)

Verses 16, 17. Search the book of the Lord, and read. Not one of these things shall be missing or want of fulfillment. God has spoken through the mouth of the prophet, and the Spirit of the Lord has gathered them. He has cast lots for them, and divided it to them by line; He has given unclean creatures the land to possess it forever, from generation to generation they shall dwell therein.

Isaiah 35: 1-10. The joy of the redeemed.

Verses 1-4. The wilderness and the desert shall rejoice and blossom as the rose. It shall blossom abundantly, and be fruitful. The children of God shall see the glory and excellency of the Lord. Be of good courage, therefore, help those that are weak. Say to them that are fearful, Be not afraid. "The Lord will come, both to punish the wicked and reward the good; He will save you."

Verses 5-8. When the Lord comes, the blind shall receive their sight and the deaf shall hear, the lame leap and the dumb sing. The earth also shall be transformed, and the desert and thirsty land shall become pools of water. There shall be a highway called "the way of holiness" over which no unclean shall pass; it is reserved for the redeemed. However unlearned and simple they may be, they need not err.

There shall be no lions or other wild beasts; the redeemed only shall walk there. They shall return and come to Zion with songs, and everlasting joy shall be upon their heads. With joy and gladness are they anointed, and sorrow and sighing shall cease.

Notes

The calamities in chapter 34 are said to come on Idumea (verses 4-6), the Greek form of Edom. This name was given to Esau after he had sold his birthright to Jacob. Gen. 25: 32-34. The hatred engendered at that time seems to have been transmitted to the children, for Edom is symbolic of brother hate, absence of pity, perpetual wrath. Amos 1: 11. The Herod who killed the little children in Bethlehem was an Edomite.

That the chapter has a far wider application than merely Edom, is clear from a reading of it. It is "the earth," "the world," "all nations," that are addressed. Verses 1, 2. Yet without doubt

The Destruction of the Earth

the use of the word "Idumea" is significant. Esau and Jacob were brothers. Both had their names changed, Esau to Edom, and Jacob to Israel. The judgment in chapter 34 is upon Edom, brother to Israel, but who sold his birthright for a mess of pottage. We conclude therefore that in a special sense the judgment of chapter 34 applies, not to the heathen, but to those who have been and are closely related to Israel, who have sold their interest in eternal life for a pittance. It is often true that those who have been nearest to God's truth and have turned away from it, become the bitterest enemies of it. That may be the reason for the heavy punishment — the dreadful picture — presented in this chapter.

Isaiah 34:2. "All nations." This judgment is world wide.

Verse 5. "My sword hath drunk its fill in heaven." A. R. V. The war against Satan (Rev. 12:7) was a war against those who had known the truth and once rejoiced in it. The sword will again be used in a similar mission when it descends on Edom. What a dreadful designation, "the people of My curse"!

Verse 6. "Bozrah," a chief city of Edom.

Verse 7. "Unicorns"—"wild oxen." A. R. V.

Verse 8. "Day of . . . vengeance," "year of recompenses." Note, it is a *day* of wrath, but a *year* of reward — Isaiah's way of stating that God's mercy far outweighs His wrath.

Verse 10. "From generation to generation." The earth shall lie waste a thousand years. Rev. 20:2.

Verse 11. "Cormorant," "bittern." The American Revised Version translates these "pelican" and "porcupine."

"Line of confusion," "stones of emptiness," really "plummet of emptiness." Even as in erecting a building, line and plummet are used to see that all is level and horizontal — indicative of God's justice and righteousness; so also in tearing down, in punishment, God uses line and plummet. The punishment is according to rule, it is "on the square." (See Rev. 16:5.)

Verse 13. "Dragons," "owls." The American Revised Version has it "jackals," "ostriches."

Verse 14. "Wild beasts," "satyr," "screech owl." The American Revised Version gives "wolves," "wild goat," "night monster."

Verse 15. "Great owl"—"dart snake." A. R. V.

Verse 17. A paraphrase would read: "He [God] has allotted them [the wild beasts mentioned before] the land; He has assigned it as their home. They shall possess it forever, from generation to generation shall they dwell therein."

Isaiah 35:1. "The rose." Blossoms beautiful as the rose or narcissus shall spring from the thirsty ground.

Verse 2. "Lebanon," "Carmel," "Sharon"— places of beauty and fruitfulness.

Verse 7. "Parched ground"—"mirage." A. R. V., margin. A mirage is one of those delusive images that travelers in the desert often see. Thirsty and exhausted they look about them, and suddenly appears, but a little distance away, a beautiful oasis with palm trees and cooling water. They hasten to get there, only to find it an illusion.

Now it shall be different. No more shall there be any delusion. There shall be real water, springs of water, pools.

Verse 8. "It shall be for those"—"It shall be for the redeemed." A. R. V.

Lessons for To-day

Brotherly love is one of the most wonderful things on earth. Brotherly hate is as unlovely and deep-seated as love is beautiful and permanent. Hate among brothers is unnatural, a denial of the very wellsprings of life, a repudiation of the laws of existence. It is peculiarly hateful to God. In this chapter is given a picture of how much God hates this particular sin.

Hate among brethren is no better than hate among brothers. Let all beware lest a little root of bitterness spring up and bear fruit. Love, God's most precious gift, should be cherished as a tender plant, and not exposed to the poisonous gases of wagging tongues or the frost and withering blast of a jealous disposition.

Those among God's people who have known the truth and turned away from it will be among our bitterest enemies. We need to pray God, not merely that we remain in the truth, but in the love of it. To belong to those whom God designates as "the people of My curse" (verse 5), must be a dreadful thing.

Verse 16. "Seek ye out of the book." Here is an invitation to search "the book," with the definite statement that if we do so we shall find that "no one of these shall fail," that is, every prophecy is or will be definitely and adequately fulfilled. The statement is really a challenge. As God offered Ahaz a sign, so He offers the world a sign by which it may know the truth of the word. Prophecy is the test. The world, like Ahaz, refuses to accept the challenge.

Isaiah 35:2. "They shall see the glory of the Lord." Moses prayed that he might see the glory of the Lord. Ex. 33:18. This was granted him, and Moses discovered then that God's glory is His character. Ex. 34: 5-7. The remnant will "give glory to Him" who made heaven and earth. They will have the Father's name in their foreheads.

Verse 3. "Strengthen," "confirm." It is the privilege of the strong to help the weak. This is a distinctly Christian attitude. The heathen do not ordinarily help the weak. Most heathen tribes kill the weak infant and permit only the strong to live. The aged, the sick, the wounded, are often left to survive or perish. Christianity brought a new note into the world. "Strengthen the weak," became the watchword.

This has a literal and also a spiritual application. There are those that are weak in the faith. Do not leave them to perish. Help them, strengthen them. There are young people whose feet stumble because they are weak-kneed. Censure and criticism have probably failed to help them. Why not follow the injunction of this scripture? There is more blessing in saving one soul to the truth than in dismissing ten from the church. Let us all help the weak instead of criticizing them.

Verse 4. "Fearful heart." Some are by nature courageous, others are fearful. Condemnation will only make the faint-hearted more so. Speak words of courage. "Be strong."

Verses 3 and 4 advocate a tender regard for the weak. And this regard must not spend itself in sympathy only, beautiful as that is. It calls for words of encouragement, but it calls for more than that. Strengthen them, confirm them, is the message. Make them strong wherein they have been weak, and then establish them, confirm them, so they will remain strong. "God will come." The coming has been delayed. Do not lose heart, however. "God will come." Let that be the keynote of every message. Let there be no uncertainty about it. The King is at the door.

Verse 7. "Parched ground," in American Revised Version, margin, is "mirage." This optical illusion is common to the desert. But that is not the only place where it works harm. It is in daily life that its harm is most apparent. The experienced traveler in life looks on the gayly lighted scene of festivity where there is dancing, hilarity, and merriment, and knows he is looking on a mirage. The youth can see only joy, happiness, and a good time; but the Christian is not deceived. He knows that it is all an illusion. There is no real happiness or joy there. They are dancing with death, and hell is yawning. The inviting scene is only "parched ground," a mirage.

Verse 8. " A highway," " the way of holiness." Holiness is not a destination at which you arrive, but the road you are traveling. It is not a distant point, but a present possession. At the beginning of it is righteousness by faith, at the end is glory. It leads to heaven, to perfection, to complete sanctification. It was originally "the way of the tree of life." Gen. 3:24. Now it leads by the "new way" (Heb. 10:19, 20), through the sanctuary, to the same goal. Rev. 22:14.

"Shall not err." The way is plain, there are no "detours," and it is marked all the way, so no one need err. Keep your eyes on the road, watch the signs, proceed carefully where it is marked "danger," keep out of the ruts and on the right side of the road, and you cannot go wrong.

Verse 10. "Come to Zion." The promise includes the end óf the journey. They shall "come to Zion," not half way or to some other place, but to Zion. That has a finality about it that is reassuring. Come to Zion! the end of the journey. No wonder there shall be joy and gladness.

> "We're marching upward to Zion,
> The beautiful city of God."

CHAPTER XI
Invasion of Judah by Assyria; God Delivers His People

Lesson Scripture: Isaiah 36; 37

WITHOUT entering into a discussion of the chronological difficulties of these chapters, the story of the lesson is as follows:

Isaiah 36: 1-3. Sennacherib became king of Assyria upon the murder of his father Sargon. In the fourteenth year of Hezekiah he came up against Judah, and captured the defensed cities — forty-six in all was his boast. From Lachish, a fortress in Judah, the king sent the chief of his officers, Rabshakeh, with a great army, to Jerusalem to demand submission and tribute. From 2 Kings 18: 17 we learn that two other officers accompanied Rabshakeh, and these three envoys met a similar number appointed by Hezekiah.

Verses 4-22. Rabshakeh now proceeds to tell the Jews that their only hope is to submit to Sennacherib. It is no use to trust in Egypt. That is a broken reed. Nor is it any use to trust in God. If the Assyrian god is not stronger than the God of the Hebrews, how is it that they have already taken so many cities? he asks. They have defeated all the gods of the other nations, they have even taken Samaria. Do not " let Hezekiah make you trust in the Lord, saying, The Lord will surely deliver us: this city shall not be delivered into the hand of the king of Assyria." Rather let us make a treaty together. With this message the three envoys hastened to the king.

Isaiah 37: 1-5. Hezekiah, when he heard it, " rent his clothes," a sign of deep grief, " and went into the house of the Lord." In his great trouble the king turned to God, and sent word to Isaiah to unite with him in prayer. 2 Chron. 32: 20.

Verses 6, 7. Isaiah immediately sent word back to Hezekiah that he need not be afraid of the blasphemy of the king of Assyria. God " will send a blast upon him, and he shall hear a rumor, and return to his own land." There he shall be killed.

Verses 8-13. In the meantime Rabshakeh had returned and found that the king of Assyria had moved from Lachish to Libnah, a city not far away, and was besieging it. When he found that

Tirhakah, king of Egypt and Ethiopia, had sent an army to help Judah, he sent messengers to Hezekiah with substantially the same message as before. "Do not let God deceive you," he said; "Jerusalem cannot stand before the king of Assyria. Have you not heard what has happened to all the other nations that tried to oppose the king? They are utterly destroyed."

Verses 14-20. Upon receipt of the message, Hezekiah immediately sought the Lord. Going again to the temple, he spread the letter before the Lord, and prayed earnestly that God would incline His ear and "hear all the words of Sennacherib, which hath sent to reproach the living God." He realized the truth of the statement that the king had "laid waste all the nations, and their countries." "Now therefore, O Lord our God, save us from his hand, that all the kingdoms of the earth may know that Thou art the Lord, even Thou only."

Verses 21-25. Isaiah, who apparently had been informed of the contents of the letter, either by messenger or by revelation, now sends to Hezekiah a message of courage and prediction. God has heard his prayer (2 Kings 19:20), and tells him not to be afraid of Assyria. Instead of trembling for their safety, Israel might well despise and laugh to scorn an enemy that reproached and blasphemed the Holy One of Israel. Sennacherib had sent Rabshakeh to boast against the Lord. He proudly told how he had come to Lebanon and had cut down the tall cedars and choice fir trees. Mountains had not stopped him; neither did deserts constitute an obstacle. He had dug wells and drunk the water. Again, if rivers were in his way, he had simply dried them up.

Verses 26-30. God now reminds Assyria of a few fundamental principles. He uses one nation to punish another, and had permitted Assyria, as an agent of God, "to lay waste defensed cities." Because of this the inhabitants had not been able to resist the onslaught, but had been "dismayed and confounded." Assyria, however, instead of giving God the glory, had boasted of its great power, and had rebelled against God. The Lord therefore said, I will "put My hook in thy nose, and My bridle in thy lips," and turn Assyria back to where it came from. As an assurance that God would really do this He gives Hezekiah a sign. The first and the second year they should eat that which "groweth of itself" and "that which springeth of the same." The third year they should return to normal conditions, and sow and reap as usual.

Verses 31-35. The remnant that is escaped of Judah shall again prosper and bear fruit and take root downward. They shall go

Invasion of Judah by Assyria

forth from Jerusalem and Mount Zion. "The zeal of the Lord of hosts shall do this." Sennacherib shall not take the city, nor even besiege it. By the way that he came he shall return. God will defend Jerusalem for His own sake and for the sake of David. Verses 36-38. These comforting words were sent to Hezekiah, and God's promise was not long in fulfillment. The angel of the Lord was sent into the Assyrian camp, and according to the record 185,000 were slain. So Sennacherib returned to his own land, and took up his abode at Nineveh. One day while worshiping in the temple of his god, Nisroch, two of his sons killed him, after which they escaped into Armenia, while Esar-haddon, another son, became king.

Notes

The events mentioned in this lesson had been predicted many years before by Isaiah himself. About thirty years previously he prophesied that "the king of Assyria, and all his glory," should "pass through Judah" and "overflow and go over." This would be because God's people had refused "the waters of Shiloah." Isa. 8:6-8. Isaiah had also predicted the punishment that should come upon Assyria, because, instead of giving God the glory and recognizing himself merely as the executor of God's wrath, the king had said: "By the strength of my hand I have done it, and by my wisdom; for I am prudent." Therefore God would punish "the stout heart of the king of Assyria, and the glory of his high looks." Isa. 10:12, 13. The fulfillment of these two things — the overrunning of Judah by Assyria, and the punishment of the king for refusing to give God the glory — constitutes the lesson.

Isaiah 36:2. "Rabshakeh" is not a proper name, but a title, and means "the chief of the officers."

"Lachish" is situated about thirty-five miles southwest of Jerusalem.

Verse 5. "I have counsel and strength for war." These are the words of Hezekiah which Rabshakeh is quoting. In some way the Assyrian envoy had heard that Hezekiah had said this, and he is now repeating Hezekiah's words to show their improbability.

Verse 6. "This broken reed" is Egypt. Egypt had been a strong power, now it was only a broken reed.

Verse 8. Rabshakeh is challenging Hezekiah, and at the same time showing how weak Judah is. "I will give thee two thousand horses," he says, "if thou be able . . . to set riders upon them."

78 *Isaiah, the Gospel Prophet*

That is, Judah was so reduced that Rabshakeh felt safe in asserting that there were not left two thousand cavalry in Jerusalem.

Verse 10. Here the envoy claims to be sent by the Lord to destroy the land. "The Lord said unto me, Go up against this land, and destroy it." This was partly true. Isa. 10: 5, 6.

Verse 19. "Where are the gods of Hamath and Arphad?" These were cities of Mesopotamia which Assyria had taken.

Isaiah 37: 1. "Rent his clothes," "sackcloth." These were signs of sorrow and deep grief. Sackcloth was a coarse textile woven of hair, generally black. (See Rev. 6: 12.)

Verse 8. "Libnah," about ten miles north of Lachish.

Verse 9. "Tirhakah" was king of Egypt. Assyria had already, under Sargon, defeated Egypt, and Rabshakeh was not afraid of another attack, though he would without doubt be glad to have Jerusalem capitulate before the arrival of the Egyptian armies.

Verse 12. Gozan, and Haran, and Rezeph were cities of Mesopotamia.

Verse 16. "Between the cherubims." On the ark were two cherubim, and God was conceived of as dwelling between them because His presence appeared there in the tabernacle. This would make the mercy seat and the ark containing the ten commandments the foundation of God's throne.

Verse 22. "The virgin, the daughter of Zion." God here represents His people as a tender maiden, weak, defenseless, yet bold enough to resist the king of Assyria and bid him defiance.

"Shake the head." This was a gesture of scorn. Ps. 22:7; Matt. 27: 39.

Verse 24. "The height of the mountains," "the sides of Lebanon." This boast reminds us of Satan's words. Isa. 14: 13, 14. By "tall cedars" and "choice fir trees" are probably symbolized the leaders of the nation; "the height of his border," Jerusalem.

Verse 25. Mountains, deserts, and rivers had not stopped Sennacherib. Note his boast. If a river were in his way, he merely stepped on it and dried it up.

Verses 26-29. God now takes Assyria to task. Assyria was indeed intended by God "to lay waste defensed cities," but because of its pride God would now put a "hook" in its nose. This was a favorite way for Assyria to treat its prisoners, and God merely turns its treatment of prisoners upon itself.

Verse 30. There has been much disagreement among commentators in regard to this verse. The Hebrew word translated "such as groweth of itself" occurs only in one other place in the Bible,

Invasion of Judah by Assyria

in Leviticus 25: 11, and refers to the year of jubilee, in which year "ye shall return every man unto his possession." Verse 13. It seems likely that at this time, when Jerusalem was in danger of being taken, God calls attention to the approaching year of jubilee, the observance of which had been neglected. God would do just what He had promised (Lev. 25: 21), and this would constitute the sign.

Verses 31, 32. Note "the remnant." The courage of Isaiah in this crisis should not escape us. The enemy had overrun the land of Judah and taken forty-six cities. The northern kingdom, Israel, was destroyed. Egypt as well as the surrounding nations had been defeated. Hezekiah was "shut up like a bird in a cage, in Jerusalem, his royal city," according to Sennacherib's own inscription. There was no human help in sight; the city was despoiled of her treasures, the army reduced to a few thousand, and the people discouraged. Had God forsaken His people? The outlook was very dark indeed. It was in this crisis that Isaiah's faith and courage rose triumphant. He counseled king and people to trust in God, and the crisis was turned into a glorious victory — not by anything man did, but by God's intervening hand.

Lessons for To-day

Isaiah 36: 1. "Assyria came up against all the defensed cities of Judah, and took them." God permits calamities to come to peoples and nations because of their sins. One nation is used to punish another. Let not the one who escapes temporarily, boast against another who is defeated. God keeps a strict account with nations as with men. National pride goes before national fall.

Verses 2-8. "Rabshakeh." This man appears to have been boastful, ignorant, and contemptuous — three bad habits. His speech was not entirely without truth. When he mentioned the futility of trusting to Egypt, a "broken reed," he spoke the truth. When he quoted Hezekiah as saying that he, Hezekiah, had both counsel and strength for war, he was touching a weak point in Hezekiah's position. But when he mentioned the uselessness of trusting in God, and that Hezekiah probably had offended Jehovah by taking away the altars throughout the land, he completely missed the mark, and showed his ignorance of God's nature. Boastfulness, ignorance, and contemptuousness are a trinity to be avoided.

Verses 16, 17. "A land like your own land." Rabshakeh counseled Judah to surrender, to compromise. He would not treat them harshly. He would let them eat of their own vine and of their own fig tree and drink of their own cistern, "until I come and take you away." But even then it would only be to "a land like your own land." How fair the promises of the enemy are! Come with me, surrender, I will not do you any harm, he says. You may do as you please; and when I take you away, it will be "to a land like your own land." Let the young beware. Do not believe the enemy. Do not let any one "take you away" by fair promises. Do not surrender. Do not make compromising alliances. The land to which you go, the union that looks so innocent and harmless, will not prove satisfactory.

Rabshakeh's promises are such as the world has always offered. Jerusalem was in a state of siege. Deprivation, suffering, hunger, perhaps even death, awaited the Jews. Why not surrender? If they did, there would be plenty for them. And it was promised that the captivity would not be hard. It will be just "like your own land." So now men are tempted by Satan to compromise. "Give up your peculiar belief, and all will be well," the enemy says. "Other religions are just as good. You will starve to death if you obey God. Come with us, and we will show you a land 'like your own land.'"

Verse 21. "Answered him not a word." The power of silence is impressive. When *not* to speak is as important to learn as when to speak. "Be still, and know." Ps. 46: 10. The silent hour, the hour of meditation, is most precious. It is often when we are still that we learn to know God as we never could in any other way. When we pray, we reveal what is in our hearts and our soul's inmost desires. When we are still before God, He reveals Himself to us.

Isaiah 37: 4. "Lift up thy prayer for the remnant." Hezekiah, instead of getting the army ready for an attack, decides to seek the Lord and to ask Isaiah to pray for the remnant. So also our strength lies not in armies or worldly wisdom. Prayer can do that which neither skill nor might can accomplish. The time is soon coming when to all appearances our situation will be as hopeless as was Hezekiah's. Prayer will be our only refuge.

Verse 6. "Be not afraid of the words that thou hast heard." God can quickly change the aspect of things. The outlook *was* dark for the one who had not taken God into the reckoning; but for Isaiah, the man of faith, things looked encouraging. Isaiah's secret was this: he had had a message from the Lord. Our secret is the same: we have a message from the Lord. With the knowledge we have of how events will take place, we need not fear. Immanuel, God with us.

Verse 18. Always face the situation squarely. Do not try to evade or deny facts. Assyria had "laid waste all the nations." That, however, only made God's power seem the greater. Truth never hurt God's word.

Verse 20. Note that Hezekiah asked deliverance, not for his own sake or even for his people's, but that the knowledge of God might be spread through the earth. His aim was God's glory.

Verse 24. "By thy servants hast thou reproached the Lord." Men are responsible not only for what they themselves do, but for what their agents or servants do. This is recognized in all worldly affairs. The blame returns upon the master that empowers them. So in the affairs of God. Reproach is cast upon the Lord when His servants do not rightly represent Him. How careful we should be!

Verse 31. "Root downward," "fruit upward." God wants His people to bear fruit; He also wants them to be rooted and grounded. John 15:2; Eph. 3:17. Some may be rooted and grounded in the truth, understand it well, and be able to give a reason for their faith, and yet not bear fruit. They take no active part in the work and endeavors of the church; they bring no souls to God, nor do their part in bringing an income to the church so others can be sent out. They are rooted, but bear no fruit.

Others are very active in all endeavors. They are always ready both to speak and to do. But they are not rooted and grounded. God wants root. He also wants fruit.

CHAPTER XII

Hezekiah's Prayer Answered; His Pride Rebuked

Lesson Scripture: Isaiah 38; 39

ISAIAH 38: 1-3. The story of chapters 38 and 39 is a very simple one. Hezekiah is sick unto death. Isaiah sends word to him to prepare his house, for he will soon die. To this Hezekiah is not reconciled, but prays the Lord to prolong his life. He pleads his upright conduct, how he has walked before the Lord "in truth and with a perfect heart." He weeps "with great weeping" (margin).

Verses 4-6. Word now comes to Isaiah to tell the king that God has heard his prayer and seen his tears, and that fifteen years will be added to his life. God also promises to deliver him out of the hand of the king of Assyria and to defend Jerusalem.

Verses 7, 8. Hezekiah then asks what sign, if any, Isaiah can give that he will be healed and be able to attend service in the house of the Lord within three days. Isaiah asks him if he wants the shadow of the sundial to go backward or forward ten degrees. Hezekiah answers that it would be a light thing for the shadow to go down ten degrees, and asks that it be turned back. Isaiah asks of the Lord the sign wanted, and the shadow goes backward ten degrees. 2 Kings 20: 8-11. Isaiah then commands that a lump of figs be placed on the boil, and Hezekiah recovers. 2 Kings 20: 7; Isa. 38: 21.

Verses 9-16. Hezekiah committed to writing his meditation upon his sickness and recovery. From this it is clear that he was not at all reconciled to dying. He felt that should he die he would be "deprived of the residue" of the years that he might naturally expect to live. He rather felt like reproving God for His intent to cut him off "with pining sickness." God was like a lion who would break all his bones, and though Hezekiah should try to bear up as well as he could, it would be "in bitterness" of soul.

Verses 17-20. God, however, had delivered him and forgiven his sins, casting them behind His back. He would now praise the Lord, who had saved him and was ready to save him.

Isaiah 39: 1, 2. The sickness and recovery of Hezekiah had

Hezekiah's Prayer Answered

been reported to the king of Babylon, who sent letters and a present to the king. Hezekiah was very glad to receive these ambassadors, and showed them his house and all the precious things he had. "There was nothing in his house, nor in all his dominion, that Hezekiah showed them not."

Verses 3-7. As soon as Isaiah heard of this, he knew that the king had committed a serious indiscretion. Instead of telling the ambassadors of the great things God had done for him, he had shown them the riches of his kingdom. The ambassadors would now go home deeply impressed with the wealth of Hezekiah, rather than with a profound reverence for Hezekiah's God. Hezekiah had completely failed in the hour of opportunity.

Sternly Isaiah asks of the king the circumstances. Having learned the truth, Isaiah pronounces the doom. All this wealth which Hezekiah has so foolishly shown Babylon, shall be carried to Babylon; nothing shall be left. Also Hezekiah's sons shall be carried away captive, and become servants of the king of Babylon.

Verse 8. To this message Hezekiah bows in submission, saying, "Good is the word of the Lord." He also expresses thankfulness that this calamity is not to come in his day. 2 Chron. 32: 26.

Notes

Isaiah 38: 1. "In those days." Hezekiah reigned twenty-nine years in all. 2 Kings 18: 2. As fifteen years were added to his life as a result of his prayer, the events in this chapter must have taken place in the fourteenth year of his reign. It was also in the fourteenth year that the events of the last lesson took place. Isa. 36: 1. Hence "in those days" has reference to the time of Rabshakeh's challenge and Jerusalem's extremity, as recorded in the last lesson.

It would seem from Isaiah 38: 6 that the king's sickness took place at the time when Rabshakeh had come up with his army to Jerusalem to demand its surrender.

Verse 3. "Hezekiah wept sore." One cause for his weeping might have been the fact that he was childless. Manasseh was only twelve years old when Hezekiah died, fifteen years later, hence he was not born at this time. Was it possible that David's line through whom the Messiah should come would become extinct? Also, it was considered a great calamity in Israel to be childless.

Verse 8. "The sundial of Ahaz." Sundials were invented by the Babylonians. It is possible that Ahaz had obtained this dial at the time of his visit to Damascus. 2 Kings 16: 10. The dial

84 *Isaiah, the Gospel Prophet*

would naturally record the motion of the sun, and hence would move forward. To cause it to go backward would be a distinct and definite miracle. We are not told just how the Lord accomplished this, but apparently the Babylonians noticed it, for they sent word to inquire about "the wonder that was done in the land." 2 Chron. 32:31.

Verse 16. "By these things men live." Matt. 4:4.

Verse 18. Note Hezekiah's belief concerning the grave and death.

Verse 21. "The boil." The same word is used here as of the sixth plague. Ex. 9:8-11. It is used also in Leviticus 13:18-20 and Job 2:7. In Deuteronomy 28:35, where the word is used, the statement is made that "the botch," or boil, "cannot be healed." There was therefore no human help for Hezekiah. The lump of figs could not cure; only God could do that.

Isaiah 39:1. "Merodach-baladan" was a Babylonian prince who had taken advantage of the troublous times and made himself independent of Assyria.

Verse 7. "Thy sons." This could not refer to Manasseh or Amariah, great-grandfather to Zephaniah. Zeph. 1:1. Hence there must have been other sons, but of these we have no record. In Daniel's time children "of the king's seed" were taken captive, and became eunuchs in Babylon. Dan. 1:3.

Lessons for To-day

Isaiah 38:1. "Set thine house in order." This is a duty devolving upon all. It includes a spiritual and also a temporal preparation. We are to see to it that our "house" is in order, that the spiritual welfare of our children and relatives is not neglected, and that our own souls are ready for any eventuality.

Setting the house in order also includes the disposition of any property we may have, so that God's cause will not be forgotten. It is best to give to God's cause while we are living and can apportion it as we think best. Altogether too often property intended for God's cause is diverted into other channels by unbelieving children or relatives. Hence it is always best for a person to be his own executor. Where this is not done, there should be no hesitancy in making out a will that will assure to God's cause its proper share. And this should not be left until sickness comes. *Now* is the time.

Verse 5. "I have heard thy prayer." Hezekiah did not have long to wait for the answer. Before Isaiah had reached the middle

Hezekiah's Prayer Answered

court he was told to go back. 2 Kings 20:4. "I have seen thy tears." Every little thing comes under God's notice. Hezekiah turned to the wall so no one should see him weep, but God saw it. It is not only wicked things that God notices, nothing escapes Him.

Verse 8. It would be hard to conceive of a greater sign than that Hezekiah asked. It was a turning back of the clock of time. But God willingly complied with the request. He saw in that sign an opportunity to call the attention of nations afar off to the God of Israel. This was successfully effected, for the Babylonian astrologers immediately noticed the phenomenon, and an embassy was soon on its way to inquire about the wonder.

Thus God will sometimes answer our prayers, faulty though they may be, because there are larger interests at stake which we perhaps do not see.

Verse 16. "By these things men live." Men do not live by bread alone, but by "these things" which God speaks and does.
Verse 15.
Verse 17. "All my sins."

"My sin — O the bliss of the glorious thought! —
My sin, not in part, but the whole,
Is nailed to His cross and I bear it no more;
Praise the Lord, praise the Lord, O my soul!"

Verse 19. "The father to the children shall make known Thy truth." This is the ideal. The father should be the teacher, and he should lead his children into the truth. Mal. 4:6.

Verse 21. "A lump of figs." There is no healing but in God and of God. Isaiah was a man of faith, but that did not hinder him from using such remedies as were at hand. We are to have faith in God. We are also to use such means as God has given us.

Isaiah 39:2. "Showed them the house." "Hezekiah rendered not again according to the benefit done unto him; for his heart was lifted up." 2 Chron. 32:25. Without doubt Hezekiah had a beautiful house, and was proud of it and liked to show it. But God had other things in mind for the Babylonian ambassadors than to be shown a house.

We, too, sometimes like to show what we have or can do. If this is for the glory of God, well and good. God sometimes sends us visitors, not that we may show them our possessions in houses and lands, or how well we can entertain, or how good a feast we can prepare, but to bring them in contact with the truth. We need help and wisdom from God in visiting or in entertaining visitors, as well as in everything else. Hezekiah lost a golden opportunity of proclaiming the power of God. We should not repeat his mistake.

Verse 8. "Good is the word of the Lord." Submission to God's will is good. Obedience is better. God had done great things for the king. He had been cured of a fatal malady. God had defended Jerusalem, and Hezekiah had seen the Assyrian army melt away under the curse of God; yet that did not prevent Hezekiah from failing in the crisis. This must have been a grievous disappointment to Isaiah as well as to God. It would seem only natural to expect that the fifteen years granted to the king would be spent in deep heart searching and complete dedication to God's service. Yet who of us are sure of fifteen more years of life? And how do we spend our days? Hezekiah was sure of fifteen years. We are not sure of fifteen days. How much more, then, should we be sure to spend well each minute!

CHAPTER XIII
Warnings and Reproofs; An Unheeded Call to Repentance

Review

ISAIAH 1:18. The wonderful invitation of the Lord to come and reason with Him should ever excite our admiration. The Lord knows the advantage of close personal contact. He is sure that if men will but sit down and reason, they will see matters His way.

It is so in any estrangement among brethren. If they will but sit down together, not to quarrel, but to reason, and to reason *together*, they cannot long be at variance.

The proposition which the Lord presents is so good that it would seem that none could afford to neglect it. No sinner is too wicked, no sin too dark.

Isaiah 6: 1-10. Having studied many of Isaiah's experiences, it is well to go back to the original vision and call. It was this vision that gave Isaiah his idea of both sin and holiness. He saw the Lord, and he saw himself. Thrice holy was God, undone was man. Not until men have had such a vision of God and of themselves, can they rightly represent Him who is "holy, holy, holy."

Isaiah 8: 9-12. Men are associating together for mutual protection. Of this kind is the League of Nations. It is an effort to effect some union that shall mean greater security. We see the same tendency in other matters. Most of these confederacies are grounded in fear. God deplores the fact that men will seek one another for protection, and forget Him. There can be no combination formed that will protect any one when the judgments of God are in the land. God is our only security, both then and now.

One confederacy that God is specially anxious that we should avoid, is a union of believers with unbelievers, whether in family or business relations. A word of caution to both old and young may be needed.

Another mingling of the holy and the profane is commercializing religion and religious activity. To eliminate commercial work from our institutions, and yet retain the commercial spirit, is of doubtful value. We are to be diligent in our work, but we must ever remember that it is the Lord's work.

Verses 13-15. We are not to fear the fear of the world. The Lord is to be for a sanctuary. He is to be our refuge. We are to sanctify the Lord of hosts Himself.

While God will thus be a sanctuary to some, to others He will be a rock of offense, a gin, and a snare. When Christ was here on earth, His lowly birth, His unpretentiousness, His simplicity, was a stone of stumbling to many. "Have any of the rulers or of the Pharisees believed on Him?" was the question asked. John 7:48. As a result, many did " stumble, and fall," and lie " broken."

Verses 16, 17. " Bind up the testimony, seal the law." Of this Kay says in his commentary: " The testimony which the prophet was to bind up, related to the great central event of human history, and had to be recorded for the use of many generations of the faithful yet to come."

What could this be but the testimony concerning Immanuel? — that " testimony of Jesus " which from the time of the first preaching of the gospel had been " the spirit of prophecy." Rev. 19: 10.

" Seal the law "— that law which men are thinking to abrogate, but which is now ready to judge them; those " living oracles " which are full of the seeds of eternal life.

Verse 19. Spiritism is an old cult. It will have a revival in the last days. It will be one of the three great deceptions. Rev. 16: 13. The next war or plague will bring it more prominently to the front, as then there will be a greater demand for pretended communication with the dead. Strange that men will seek to the dead rather than to the living God!

Verse 20. " To the law and to the testimony." This is the watchword of God's people. When men bring any false doctrine for examination, we should go " to the law and to the testimony." If the doctrines do not harmonize with these, it is because there is no light in them.

Isaiah 17: 4, 6. God's people will pass through trying times. Isa. 24: 13. " The glory of Jacob shall be made thin." There will not be occasion for much boasting. The shaking that is coming will leave but " two or three berries in the top of the uppermost bough, four or five in the outmost fruitful branches." While we need not be discouraged, such statements as these should cause us to be very sober. Not all that say, " Lord, Lord," will be saved. A shaking is coming. And the shaking will " be caused by the straight testimony called forth by the counsel of the True Witness to the Laodiceans. This will have its effect upon the heart of the receiver, and will lead him to exalt the standard and pour forth the straight truth. Some will not bear this straight testimony. They will rise up against it, and this is what will cause a shaking among God's people.

"I saw that the testimony of the True Witness has not been half heeded. The solemn testimony upon which the destiny of the church hangs has been lightly esteemed, if not entirely disregarded. This testimony must work deep repentance; all who truly receive it will obey it, and be purified.

"Said the angel, 'List ye!' Soon I heard a voice like many musical instruments all sounding in perfect strains, sweet and harmonious. It surpassed any music I had ever heard, seeming to be full of mercy, compassion, and elevating, holy joy. It thrilled through my whole being.

"Said the angel, 'Look ye!' My attention was then turned to the company I had seen, who were mightily shaken. I was shown those whom I had before seen weeping and praying in agony of spirit. The company of guardian angels around them had been doubled, and they were clothed with an armor from their head to their feet. They moved in exact order, like a company of soldiers. Their countenances expressed the severe conflict which they had endured, the agonizing struggle they had passed through. Yet their features, marked with severe internal anguish, now shone with the light and glory of heaven. They had obtained the victory, and it called forth from them the deepest gratitude, and holy, sacred joy."—"*Early Writings,*" *pp. 270, 271.*

Isaiah 19: 18-22. We have come to the time when the message is to be preached in the whole earth. Men from all over the world shall learn "the language of Canaan." Even from "the city of destruction" shall men come. When they cry unto the Lord, "He shall send them a Saviour, and a great one, and He shall deliver them." What a blessed day it will be when "the Lord shall be known to Egypt"— Egypt that has always stood as symbolic of the oppressor of God's people! "The Egyptians shall know the Lord in that day." "They shall return even to the Lord, and He shall be intreated of them, and shall heal them."

We are sometimes afraid to ask great things of God. We hardly dare believe that God will hear us. Yet God counsels us: "Ask of Me, and I shall give thee the heathen for thine inheritance, and the uttermost parts of the earth for thy possession." Ps. 2:8.

According to the word of the Lord, the time will come when it may be said: "Blessed be Egypt My people, and Assyria the work of My hands, and Israel Mine inheritance." Isa. 19:25. Even as Saul, who had persecuted God's people, turned to the Lord, so some of God's enemies shall turn to Him. What a wonderful and strange time it will be when we may say, "Blessed be Egypt"!

Isaiah 21:11, 12. "Watchman, what of the night?" "The morning cometh."

What a cheerful message! "The morning cometh." The pilgrims are getting weary. Many years have passed since the first pioneers began the work. We should have been in the kingdom long ere this. But weary not. The morning is coming. The streaks of light show that the sun is about to rise. There are still a few more souls to be garnered in, and then the work will be done. Cheer up, faithful pilgrim. We are almost there.

"Also the night." The morning shall dawn for God's children, but the long night of sorrow and gloom shall come for the wicked. It is sad that any should be lost. God does not so intend it. Let us speed the work, for the night cometh when no man can work.

Isaiah 22:12-14. There has never been such a pleasure-mad age as the present. Nor has there ever been such a reckless, irreverent, God-defying age. "Let us eat and drink; for to-morrow we shall die," is the watchword of the world. While God is calling for weeping and mourning, men are eating and drinking and amusing themselves. No wonder that God is saying that "this iniquity shall not be purged from you till ye die."

Isaiah 26:4. "Trust ye in the Lord forever: for in the Lord Jehovah is everlasting strength." He is the "Rock of Ages," margin.

> "Rock of Ages, cleft for me!
> Let me hide myself in Thee;
> Let the water and the blood
> From Thy riven side that flowed,
> Be of sin the double cure,
> Save me from its guilt and power."

The Book of Isaiah

From "Mosaics of Bible History"

The Style and General Character of This Prophet's Writings

THE prophetic writings of Isaiah are among the noblest specimens of Hebrew poetry, and their style has been universally admired as a model of elegance and sublimity. The following tribute to the prophet's richness of imagery and his spiritual gifts, is from the pen of a distinguished Biblical scholar and critic:

"Isaiah stands pre-eminent above all other prophets, as well in the contents and spirit of his predictions, as in their form and style. Simplicity, clearness, sublimity, and freshness are the never-failing characteristics of his prophecies. Even Eichhorn mentions, among the merits of Isaiah, the harmony of his expressions, the beautiful outline of his images, and the fine execution of his speeches. In reference to richness of imagery, he stands between Jeremiah and Ezekiel. Symbolic actions, which frequently occur in Jeremiah and Ezekiel, are seldom found in Isaiah. The same is the case with visions, strictly so called, of which there is only one, namely, that in chapter 6, and even it is distinguished by its simplicity and clearness above that of the later prophets.

"[Yet the book of Isaiah is introduced as "The vision of Isaiah the son of Amoz;" so all his prophecies may be called visions, although only *one* of them is specially mentioned as such.]

"But one characteristic of Isaiah is, that he likes to give signs — that is, a fact then present, or near at hand — as a pledge for the more distant futurity. The instances in chapters 7 and 38 show how much he was convinced of his vocation, and in what intimacy he lived with the Lord. His spiritual riches are seen in the variety of his style, which always befits the subject. When he rebukes and threatens, it is like a storm; and when he comforts, his language is as tender and mild (to use his own words) as that of a mother comforting her son."— *Kitto*.

Another writer, well known as a critic and rhetorician, says: "Isaiah is, without exception, the most sublime of all poets. This is abundantly visible even in our translation; and, what is a material circumstance, none of the books of Scripture appear to have been more happily translated than the writings of this prophet. Majesty is his reigning character, a majesty more commanding, and more uniformly supported, than is to be found among the rest of the Old Testament poets. He possesses, indeed, a dignity of grandeur, both in his conceptions and expressions, which is altogether unparalleled, and peculiar to himself. There is more clearness and order, too, and a more visible distribution of parts, in his book, than in any other of the prophetical writings."— *Dr. Hugh Blair.*

The following is a general characterization of the style of this greatest of prophets and poets:

"Isaiah is at once elegant and sublime, forcible and ornamental; he unites energy and copiousness and dignity with variety. In his sentiments we find extraordinary elevation and majesty; in his imagery, the utmost propriety, elegance, dignity, and diversity; in his language, uncommon beauty and energy, and notwithstanding the obscurity of his subjects, a surprising degree of clearness and simplicity."— *Bishop Lowth.*

Dr. Blair cites the fourteenth chapter of Isaiah — from the 4th to the 23d verse inclusive — as containing "a greater assemblage of sublime ideas, of bold and daring figures, than is perhaps anywhere else to be met with."

Bishop Lowth also has the following remarks upon the style and composition of this wonderful poem:

"How forcible is its imagery, how diversified, how sublime! How elevated the diction, the figures, the sentiments! . . . One continued action is kept up, or rather a series of interesting actions are connected together in an incomparable whole. This, indeed, is the principal and distinguished excellence of the sublime ode,— and is displayed in its utmost perfection in this poem of Isaiah, which may be considered as one of the most ancient, and certainly the most finished specimen of that species of composition which has been transmitted to us.

"The personifications here are frequent, yet not confused; bold, yet not improbable: a free, elevated, and truly divine spirit pervades the whole; nor is there anything in this ode to defeat its claim to the character of perfect beauty and sublimity. If, indeed, I may be indulged in the free declaration of my own sentiments, I do not know a single instance in the whole compass of Greek and Roman poetry, which, in every excellence of composition, can be said to equal, or even to approach it."

We find in the following lines similar sentiments regarding Hebrew poetry in general:

> "Let those, who will, hang rapturously o'er
> The flowing eloquence of Plato's page,—
> Repeat, with flashing eye, the sounds that pour
> From Homer's verse as with a torrent's rage;
> Let those, who list, ask Tully to assuage
> Wild hearts with high-wrought periods, and restore
> The reign of rhetoric; or maxims sage
> Winnow from Seneca's sententious lore.
> Not these, but Judah's hallowed bards, to me
> Are dear; Isaiah's noble energy;
> The temperate grief of Job; the artless strain
> Of Ruth and pastoral Amos; the high songs
> Of David; and the tale of Joseph's wrongs,
> Simply pathetic, eloquently plain."
>
> — *Aubrey de Vere.*

Sabbath School Lesson
QUARTERLY

SENIOR DIVISION
Third Quarter, 1928

Lessons from
The BOOK of ISAIAH

Thirteenth Sabbath Offering, September 29, 1928
Work for INDIANS IN SOUTH AMERICA

Entered as second-class matter October 13, 1904, at the Post Office in Mountain View, Cal., under the Act of Congress of March 3, 1879. Acceptance for mailing at special rate of postage provided for in section 1103, Act of October 3, 1917, and authorized September 18, 1918.
PACIFIC PRESS PUB. ASSN. (A Corporation of S. D. A.)
No. 133   MOUNTAIN VIEW, CAL., JULY, 1928   20c A YEAR

Isaiah, The Gospel Prophet

Part I

By M. L. Andreasen

A Sabbath School Lesson Help for This Quarter

The historical setting. The times of Isaiah. The lessons for to-day. No other prophet had a clearer vision of the results of sin and of righteousness. But as Isaiah denounced sin, so he lifted up Him who only can save from sin.

The writer of this book, and the two parts which are to follow, has had a long experience in teaching the Bible in our colleges, and also as an evangelist. He therefore brings to this presentation the education and the study of many years.

Parts II and III of this book will be ready to use as Lesson Helps the last quarter of 1928 and the first quarter of 1929.

Bound in paper covers. Price, 25 cents; in Canada, 30 cents. Order of your Book and Bible House, or of the

REVIEW AND HERALD PUBLISHING ASSOCIATION
Takoma Park - - - Washington, D. C.

ANNOUNCEMENT

For a number of years the General Conference Sabbath School Department has printed in the Lesson Quarterly, in connection with each lesson, "Suggestions for Daily Family Study." Our purpose in this was to encourage daily study of the lesson by all members of the family.

We feel that we have come to the time when the "Suggestions for Daily Family Study" may be safely discontinued. The principal reason for this is our need of the space taken by the "Suggestions," for the full notes that must accompany these lessons on the book of Isaiah. Further, we hope our Sabbath school members are so established in the practice of daily lesson study that they no longer need the help of "Suggestions."

We sincerely trust that all will continue the Heaven-inspired plan of spending some time each day with the word of God as presented in the Sabbath school lessons. The usual recognition to all those maintaining a perfect record for a quarter or a year will still be given.

LESSON 1
THE TIMES OF ISAIAH; SPIRITUAL CONDITIONS; THE CALL OF ISAIAH

July 7, 1928

LESSON SCRIPTURE: Isaiah 6.
MEMORY VERSE: Isa. 6: 8.
LESSON HELP: "Prophets and Kings," pp. 303-310.

INTRODUCTION

Isaiah has been called the greatest of the Old Testament prophets, "the king of all prophets." His name signifies "Jehovah is salvation." Nothing is known of his father beyond the mere fact of his name, Amoz. Isaiah lived in Jerusalem, and it is concluded that he sprang from a family of some rank, as he seems to have had easy access to the king (Isaiah 7), and was on terms of intimacy with the priest (1sa. 8:2). He had two sons. Isa. 7:3; 8:3.

Various authorities state that Isaiah began to prophecy between the years 759-740 B. C. As his active labors continued more than sixty years, he must have died some time after 680 B. C., during the reign of Manasseh. (See "Prophets and Kings," pp. 310, 382.) Tradition records that he was sawn asunder, to which there may be a reference in Hebrews 11: 36-38.

THE LESSON

1. During the reign of what four kings did Isaiah prophecy? With whom do the visions especially deal? Isa. 1:1.

NOTE.—The chronology of the time of Isaiah is indicated by the reign of these kings. Uzziah, also called Azariah (2 Kings 14:21), who reigned fifty-two years (2 Chron. 26:3), died about the year 740 B. C. His son, Jotham, was associated with him on the throne after Uzziah was stricken with leprosy (2 Chron. 26:21), and reigned sixteen years. Jotham was followed by Ahaz, who is also said to have reigned sixteen years. 2 Chron. 28:1. He again was followed by Hezekiah, who reigned twenty-nine years. 2 Chron. 29:1. Manasseh, who followed Hezekiah, began to reign early in the seventh century, about 699 B. C., and reigned fifty-five years. 2 Chron. 33:1.

2. What is said of Uzziah's relation to God in the beginning of his reign? How long was he prospered? 2 Chron. 26:3-5, 15.

NOTE.—"The long reign of Uzziah in the land of Judah and Benjamin was characterized by a prosperity greater than that of any other ruler since the death of Solomon, nearly two centuries before. For many years the king ruled with discretion. Under the blessing of Heaven, his armies regained some of the territory that had been lost in former years. Cities were rebuilt and fortified, and the position of the nation among the surrounding peoples was greatly strengthened. . . . This outward prosperity, however, was not accompanied by a corresponding revival of spiritual power. The temple services were continued as in former years, and multitudes assembled to worship the living God; but pride and formality gradually took the place of humility and sincerity."—"Prophets and Kings," pp. 303, 304.

[3]

3. What caused Uzziah's downfall? Relate the story of his transgression, and the result. Verses 16-21.

NOTE.—"His heart was lifted up." (Compare Eze. 28:17.) The sin that resulted so disastrously to Uzziah was one of presumption. Neither his exalted position nor his long life of service could be pleaded as an excuse for the presumptuous sin by which he marred the closing years of his reign, and brought upon himself the judgment of Heaven.

4. What is said of the son of Uzziah? What did he fail to remove? What did the people continue to do? 2 Kings 15:32-35.

NOTE.—"The judgment that befell Uzziah seemed to have a restraining influence on his son. Jotham bore heavy responsibilities during the later years of his father's reign, and succeeded to the throne after Uzziah's death." The "high places" here mentioned in which the people continued to worship were altars for idolatrous worship. (See 2 Kings 17-32, 33.)

In trying to serve Jehovah and other gods at the same time, the Israelites were not unlike many professed Christians to-day. But God calls this doing "corruptly." 2 Chron. 27:2.

5. When God called to repentance and weeping, how did the people respond? Isa. 22:12-14.

6. In the year that King Uzziah died, what vision came to Isaiah? Where was the Lord? Isa. 6:1.

7. What description is given of the seraphim? Where did they stand? Verse 2.

NOTE.—The seraphim are an exalted order of angels that stand above or around the throne. The cherubim are another order, mentioned in Ezekiel, chapters 1 and 10. "Suddenly the gate and the inner veil of the temple seemed to be uplifted or withdrawn, and he [Isaiah] was permitted to gaze within, upon the holy of holies, where even the prophet's feet might not enter. There rose up before him a vision of Jehovah sitting upon a throne high and lifted up, while the train of His glory filled the temple. On each side of the throne hovered the seraphim, their faces veiled in adoration, as they ministered before their Maker, and united in the solemn invocation, 'Holy, holy, holy, is the Lord of hosts: the whole earth is full of His glory,' until post and pillar and cedar gate seemed shaken with the sound, and the house was filled with their tribute of praise."—"Prophets and Kings," p. 307.

8. What was their constant refrain? Verse 3. (Compare with Rev. 4: 8.)

9. How did the tribute of praise affect the very building? With what was the house filled? Isa. 6: 4. Compare with the experience on the day of Pentecost. Acts 2:1-4.

10. How did this view of God's holiness and glory affect the prophet? Isa. 6:5.

11. When the prophet realized and cried out that he was undone, how was help provided? Verse 6.

12. Where was the coal applied? What was said? Verse 7.

[4]

NOTE.—What was the significance of having a live coal touch the lips? James 3:2. It is "out of the abundance of the heart" that "the mouth speaketh." Matt. 12:34. It might be well to ask the Lord each day, "Lord, consecrate these, my lips, this day to Thee."

13. To what call was Isaiah now ready to respond? Verse 8.

14. To whom was Isaiah sent? Would the people understand his message? Why not? Verses 9, 10.

NOTE.—"It is not God that blinds the eyes of men or hardens their hearts. He sends them light to correct their errors, and to lead them in safe paths; it is by the rejection of this light that the eyes are blinded and the heart hardened."—"The Desire of Ages," p. 322.

15. As the prophet asks, "How long?" what answer is given? Verses 11, 12.

NOTE.—"The evils that had been multiplying for many generations could not be removed in his day. Throughout his lifetime he must be a patient, courageous teacher,—a prophet of hope as well as of doom. The divine purpose finally accomplished, the full fruitage of his efforts, and of the labors of all God's faithful messengers, would appear. A remnant should be saved."—"Prophets and Kings," p. 309.

16. What hope is given the prophet? Verse 13.

NOTE.—"The Promised Land was not to remain wholly forsaken forever. . . . This assurance [verse 13] of the final fulfillment of God's purpose brought courage to the heart of Isaiah."—Id., pp. 309, 310.

The last of the ten tribes were taken captive in 721 B. C., not many years after this vision. Jerusalem was taken more than a hundred years later.

LESSON 2

THE REBELLION OF ISRAEL AND ITS RESULTS; GOD'S CALL TO REPENTANCE

July 14, 1928

LESSON SCRIPTURE: Isaiah 1.
MEMORY VERSE: Isa. 1: 18.
LESSON HELPS: "Patriarchs and Prophets," pp. 634, 635 (new ed., pp. 661, 662); "Steps to Christ," pp. 26-33, 40, 41; "Prophets and Kings," pp. 599, 600, 605, 606.

INTRODUCTION

The first chapter of Isaiah is characteristic of the book. It is really a summary of all Isaiah's teachings. God has a controversy with His people. He calls heaven and earth to witness the awful fact that rebellion has sprung up in His family. God Himself is the plaintiff. His people are the defendants. The charge is rebellion. The court scene presented is most solemn. What can the people say in defense? They have kept up the form of worship, they have brought their sacrifices, they have made "many prayers;" but all this has been done only as a matter of form. The Lord is provoked. He is weary of all these empty forms, and hates them. But instead of pronouncing sentence

[5]

upon the people, He says: "Come now, and let us reason together, ... though your sins be as scarlet, they shall be as white as snow." How anxious God's people should be to accept the proffered pardon!

THE LESSON

1. What is God's complaint against His people? Isa. 1:2.

NOTE.—This scene has been called, "the great arraignment." Surely it must be a serious situation when God Himself makes the charge of rebellion against His people. "Rebellion originated with Satan, and all rebellion against God is directly due to satanic influence."—"Patriarchs and Prophets," p. 635. (See 1 Sam. 15:23.)

2. What impressive illustration does God use to show how low Israel has fallen? Verse 3.

3. How does God speak of His people? What is said of the Holy One of Israel? Verse 4.

NOTE.—What a fearful condition is here portrayed! In contrast with this, God is spoken of as "the Holy One of Israel." In vision, Isaiah had seen "the Holy One," and had heard the seraphim sing, "Holy, holy, holy." That impression never left him. God was to him, "holy, holy, holy." Twenty-five times this expression is used by Isaiah, and in the Old Testament elsewhere only six times.

4. How does God express the uselessness of further punishment? How completely had the body been afflicted because of their transgression? Verses 5, 6.

5. What had befallen their country? What would have taken place had there not been "a very small remnant"? Verses 7-9.

NOTE.—"Hearts that respond to the influence of the Holy Spirit are the channels through which God's blessing flows. Were those who serve God removed from the earth, and His Spirit withdrawn from among men, this world would be left to desolation and destruction, the fruit of Satan's dominion. Though the wicked know it not, they owe even the blessings of this life to the presence, in the world, of God's people whom they despise and oppress."—"The Desire of Ages," p. 306.

6. How does God now address the rulers? The people? To what should they give ear? Verse 10.

7. By what questions does God try to cause them to consider the real purpose of sacrifices? How does He speak of their offerings? Verses 11, 12.

8. What definite command does God give with reference to vain oblations? How is incense mentioned? New moons and sabbaths? Solemn meetings and appointed feasts? Verses 13, 14.

NOTE.—No form or ceremonies can ever take the place of heart service. Without Christ, without true repentance, no act is of any value in God's sight. Even prayer may become an abomination. Prov. 28:9.

9. When the people spread forth their hands in prayer, what would God do? Why would not God hear their "many prayers"? Verse 15.

10. What does God exhort them to do? What were they to cease to do? Verse 16.

11. What should they learn? What should be their attitude toward the oppressed? the fatherless? the widow? Verse 17. (See James 1:27.)

12. What invitation does God extend? What happy condition follows the acceptance of this invitation? Verse 18.

NOTE.—For comment on this verse see "Steps to Christ," pp. 48, 55.

13. On what conditions does God promise His people the good of the land? Verse 19.

14. What attitude on the part of the people will lead to their destruction? How sure is this? Verse 20.

NOTE.—"Here are the promises, plain and definite, rich and full; but they are all upon conditions. If you comply with the conditions, can you not trust the Lord to fulfill His word? Let these blessed promises, set in the framework of faith, be placed in memory's halls. Not one of them will fail. All that God hath spoken, He will do. 'He is faithful that promised.'"—"Testimonies," Vol. 5, p. 630.

15. What change had taken place in the city? How are the princes, or chief men, spoken of? Verses 21-23.

NOTE.—The city here spoken of is Jerusalem. It had been full of judgment, and righteousness had lodged in it. But now all was changed. The chief men had become companions of thieves, and justice was not to be had. How like conditions in the world to-day!

16. What will God do to His adversaries? What will He do for His own people? Verses 24-26.

17. How shall Zion be redeemed? Verse 27.

NOTE.—A "very little remnant" will be redeemed. "Her converts" literally means "those in her who turn." Some will turn, and they will be redeemed with judgment and with righteousness.

18. What will happen to transgressors and sinners? Verses 28-31.

LESSON 3

THE CALL OF THE PEOPLE TO THE HOUSE OF JACOB; A CONTROVERSY WITH ZION; A REFUGE IN ZION

July 21, 1928

LESSON SCRIPTURE: Isaiah 2 to 4.
MEMORY VERSE: Isa. 4: 5, 6.
LESSON HELPS: "Prophets and Kings," pp. 323, 324; "Patriarchs and Prophets," pp. 101, 102 (new ed., pp. 98, 99).

THE LESSON

1. For what time was this vision given? Where shall the mountain of the Lord's house be established? Who shall be drawn to it? Isa. 1, 2.

NOTE.—We make a distinction between "the Lord's house" and "the mountain of the Lord's house." "The Lord's house" is His people. (See Heb. 3:6.) "The mountain of the Lord's house" here mentioned is apparently a religious power of the latter days which exalts itself to rulership over other powers and to whom the nations of the earth will give honor. It is a power in which many, even of God's professed people, are led to put their trust, instead of trusting the Lord.

These verses can not refer to the time of the setting up of the true kingdom of God; for when the true kingdom is set up, all others are broken to pieces together. (See Dan. 2:35.) Here they are not broken to pieces, but this religious power merely exalts itself over the other mountains (or "hills"). Hence this power here spoken of does not refer to God's true people, but to the counterfeit power that will usurp God's place.

2. **What will many people say? Verse 3.**

NOTE.—"Many people shall go and say." This is not God's saying. It is not, "Thus saith the Lord," but the people "go and say." Compare "all nations shall flow unto it," verse 2, and "many people," verse 3, with Revelation 13:3, "all the world," and verse 8, "all that dwell upon the earth." When the power here mentioned shall be exalted over the kings of the earth,—the other mountains,—we may expect the whole world to wonder after the beast.

3. **What further will the people say? What will they propose to do with their swords and spears? What peace plans will they endeavor to establish? Verses 4, 5.**

NOTE.—Verse 4 has found a remarkable fulfillment in the peace talk and peace conferences of late years. Many nations, indeed, have said that they would not lift up the sword against other nations, and that they would not learn war any more. In contrast with what the people say, note what God says. Joel 3:9-13. Note also Isa. 8:9, 12.

4. **How does the prophet express God's displeasure with the house of Jacob? As the result of their idol worship, what will God refuse to do? Verses 6-9.**

NOTE.—Verse 5 mentions the house of Jacob as the ones addressed by the "people." Now God expresses His displeasure against those who say, "Let us go up to the mountain of the Lord" (verse 3), and yet have their land "full of idols" (verse 8). These people have all that man's natural heart could desire, yet God has forsaken them (verse 6), because of their idolatrous bowing and humbling themselves (verse 9), and He says, "Therefore forgive them not."

5. **How does God rebuke haughtiness and self-exaltation? Verses 10-17.**

NOTE.—When the last great deception shall come, the climax is shown in him who opposes and exalts himself above all that is called God, or that is worshiped. That power having been brought to view in Isaiah 2:1-4, God now tells how He regards it.

6. **In the day of the Lord, what will men do? Why do they seek to hide themselves? Verses 19-21.**

7. **What are we counseled to do? Verse 22.**

NOTE.—God's children had rebelled against Him, had so completely yielded themselves to the enemy, so debased themselves, that they were no longer to be accounted more than the breath they breathed. Instead of relying upon man's leadership, God would have men turn to Him.

8. **What did God say He would remove from Judah and Jerusalem? Who should rule over them? Isa. 3:1-5.**

NOTE.—Before Israel and Judah were taken captive, they suffered intensely for lack of bread during the straitness of the siege of both Samaria and Jerusalem. The countryside was also denuded. When the cities were captured, the leaders were disposed of by their conquerors. Of the house of Judah under Zedekiah it is written in "Prophets and Kings," pp. 459, 460, "Zedekiah was taken prisoner, and his sons were slain before his eyes. The king was led away from Jerusalem a captive, his eyes were put out, and after arriving in Babylon he perished miserably. . . .

"Many had escaped the horrors of the long siege, only to perish by the sword. Of those who still remained, some, notably the chief of the priests and officers and the princes of the realm, were taken to Babylon and there executed as traitors. Others were carried captive, to live in servitude." Without leadership, they preyed upon one another; seeking for leaders, but finding none, they have continued to this day a living testimony to the certainty of God's judgments.

9. **What was the condition of Jerusalem and Judah? What witnessed against them? Verses 8, 9.**

NOTE.—This chapter deals with conditions as they were in the time of Isaiah. "Only a-few short years, and the ten tribes of the kingdom of Israel were to be scattered among the nations of heathendom. And in the kingdom of Judah also the outlook was dark. The forces for good were rapidly diminishing, the forces for evil multiplying."—"Prophets and Kings," p. 324. As conditions were then, so they are now. Hence we may confidently apply the principles of this chapter to this time also. Of them it was said: "The child shall behave himself proudly against the ancient." Verse 5. Of this time it is written that the children shall be "disobedient to parents." 2 Tim. 3:2. Their countenance at that time showed their sin; the marks of dissipation were upon them. Isa. 3:9. The sins of Sodom are still prevalent. The poor were oppressed then. Isa. 3:14, 15. So they are now. James 5:1-6.

10. **What controversy does God have with the daughters of Zion? Verses 16-24.**

NOTE.—"The prophecy of Isaiah 3, was presented before me, as applying to these last days; and the reproofs are given to the daughters of Zion who have thought only of appearance and display."—"Testimonies," Vol. 1, p. 270.

11. **What is said of the men? Verse 25.**

NOTE.—"I was shown that this scripture will be strictly fulfilled."—Ibid.

12. **What is said of the women of Isaiah 4:1?**

NOTE.—This text is connected immediately in thought with the last verses of the preceding chapter. In its broader prophetic and spiritual application, we would note that "woman" designates a church. Rev. 12:1, 2; 17:3; 19:7-9; 21:9. Apparently these seven women are not above reproach. Isa. 4:1, last part. They are desirous of having a name, but they will eat their own bread and wear their own apparel.

We would therefore conclude that these seven women represent the fallen churches. They do not accept the wedding garment. They will wear their own apparel. They will not sit down at the feast and feed on the word of God. That they have rejected. They will eat their own bread. They want the name, not the person, of Christ. They are Christians in name only. They want the name of being Christians, but they will eat and dress as they please. In contrast with these, the true people of God are spoken of in the following verses.

13. How does the prophet speak of the Branch of the Lord? Verse 2. (See also Isa. 11:1; Jer. 23:5; Zech. 3:8; 6:12, 13.)

14. What shall they be called who are left in Zion and who remain in Jerusalem? Verse 3.

NOTE.—These verses speak of the remnant, they that are left, that remain, that "are escaped of Israel." Verse 2. The women spoken of in verse one are not above reproach, but these are holy. They are written among the living in Jerusalem. Moffatt translates it, "entered in the book of life." In the shaking time, many will be shaken out. Those that "remain," that are "left," will be holy, every one of them.

15. How will God accomplish His cleansing work? Verse 4. (See also John 16:7-11.)

NOTE.—"The word of the Lord to Israel was, 'I will turn My hand upon thee, and purely purge away thy dross, and take away all thy tin.' To sin, wherever found, 'our God is a consuming fire.' In all who submit to His power, the Spirit of God will consume sin. But if men cling to sin, they become identified with it. Then the glory of God, which destroys sin, must destroy them."—"The Desire of Ages," p. 107.

16. What precious promises has God given His people? Verses 5, 6.

NOTE.—These verses will find their fulfillment in the last great crisis. "In one of the most beautiful and comforting passages of Isaiah's prophecy [Isa. 4:5, 6], reference is made to the pillar of cloud and of fire to represent God's care for His people in the great final struggle with the powers of evil."—"Patriarchs and Prophets," p. 283.

LESSON 4

THE VINEYARD; THE SIX WOES; MESSIANIC PROPHECIES; THE REMNANT

July 28, 1928

LESSON SCRIPTURE: Isaiah 5; 7; 10; 11.
MEMORY VERSE: Isa. 9: 6.
LESSON HELPS: "Prophets and Kings," Introductory chapter, pp. 15-22; "Christ's Object Lessons," pp. 284-306 (new ed., pp. 287-311).

INTRODUCTION

The first part of the lesson deals with the Lord's vineyard. The Lord expected His people to bring forth good fruit, but, behold, they brought forth "wild grapes." Some of these wild grapes are mentioned and condemned under the six woes in the latter part of chapter five.

The other part of the lesson deals with prophecies concerning the Messiah. He shall be born of a virgin, His name shall be Immanuel, and Jesse of the house of David shall be His father. The Spirit of God shall rest upon Him in full measure, and of the increase of His government and peace there shall be no end.

THE LESSON

1. **What did God do for His vineyard? For what did He look? What was its fruitage? Isa. 5:1, 2.**

NOTE.—"As the Lord's vineyard they were to produce fruit altogether different from that of the heathen nations. These idolatrous peoples had given themselves up to work wickedness. . . . In marked contrast was to be the fruit borne on the vine of God's planting.

"It was the privilege of the Jewish nation to represent the character of God as it had been revealed to Moses. In answer to the prayer of Moses, 'Show me Thy glory,' the Lord promised, 'I will make all My goodness pass before thee,' 'And the Lord passed by before him, and proclaimed, The Lord, the Lord God, merciful and gracious, longsuffering, and abundant in goodness and truth, keeping mercy for thousands, forgiving iniquity and transgression and sin.' This was the fruit that God desired from His people. In the purity of their characters, in the holiness of their lives, in their mercy and loving-kindness and compassion, they were to show that 'the law of the Lord is perfect, converting the soul.' "—"Christ's Object Lessons," pp. 285, 286. (Compare Christ's parable, Matt. 21:33-44. See also Isa. 27:2, 3.)

2. **How does God appeal to the people? Verses 3, 4.**

3. **What does God say He will do? Who is the vineyard? What was the response to God's care? Verses 5-7.**

NOTE.—"God in His Son had been seeking fruit, and had found none. Israel was a cumberer of the ground. Its very existence was a curse; for it filled the place in the vineyard that a fruitful tree might fill. It robbed the world of the blessings that God designed to give. The Israelites had misrepresented God among the nations. They were not merely useless, but a decided hindrance. To a great degree their religion was misleading, and wrought ruin instead of salvation."—Id., p. 215.

4. **What does God condemn in the first of the six woes? Verses 8-10.**

NOTE.—"The outlook was particularly discouraging as regards the social conditions of the people. In their desire for gain, men were adding house to house and field to field."—"Prophets and Kings," p. 306.

"Dwell alone in the midst of the land." Verse 8, A. R. V. Having bought up all the land about them, they would have no near neighbors. Many houses would be desolate (empty). Verse 9.

This first woe deals with greediness. God's punishment is to reduce the yield. Ordinarily ten acres in those days would yield five hundred baths, or four thousand gallons. The "ephah" was one-tenth part of an homer.

5. **What is condemned in the second woe? Verses 11-17.**

NOTE.—Drinking and feasting are here condemned. Men drink until they "regard not the work of the Lord." The Lord is working, but drink has stupefied the people. Strong drink has always been a curse, and is condemned by God.

6. Against what form of sin is the third woe directed? Verses 18, 19.

NOTE.—The sin here mentioned is that of open defiance against God. Isaiah has been warning the people that judgments will come upon them for their sins. They scoff at him. "Let Him make speed," they say, "and hasten His work, that we may see it." This defiant unbelief seems to have been common in Isaiah's day. (See Isa. 28:14, 15.)

7. To whom does the fourth woe apply? Verse 20.

NOTE.—This verse brings to view a complete confusion of moral distinctions. Good is evil and evil is good. This lack of understanding or appreciating moral standards is a sign of deep moral corruption. The situation to-day is no better than in Isaiah's time.

8. On whom does the fifth woe descend? Verse 21.

NOTE.—True wisdom and prudence are gifts from God; but to be wise in one's own eyes is an abomination to Him.

9. Against whom is the last woe directed? Verses 22-30.

NOTE.—This woe is especially directed against the leaders of the people, the judges "which justify the wicked for reward." In verses 11-17 drunkenness is spoken of as a hindrance to spiritual progress. Here it is mentioned as a curse and a hindrance to justice. Drunken judges will "let off guilty men for a bribe, and deprive the innocent of his rights." Verse 23, Moffatt's translation. (See also Isa. 10:1-4.)

Note the judgments of God in verse 24. The reason for all this is that "they have cast away the law of the Lord," and that also they have "despised the word of the Holy One of Israel." "The law" and "the word" need to be emphasized at this time. Verses 25-30 deal with the sure destruction that shall come because of sin.

10. What sign was given to the house of David when the faithless King Ahaz had refused to seek a sign? Isa. 7:10-16.

11. How is the coming Messiah spoken of? Isa. 9:6, 7.

12. What is said of Christ and His ancestry? Isa. 11:1, 2.

NOTE.—Jesse was the name of David's father. 1 Sam. 17:12. Christ, then, should be of the house of David. Luke 1:32. Note the sevenfold spirit mentioned in Isaiah 11:2.

13. In what words does the prophet describe the Lord's dealings with man? How is the coming kingdom described? Verses 3-9.

14. What will the remnant do in "that day"? Isa. 10:20, 21.

NOTE.—"In that day" "the remnant of Israel, and such as are escaped of the house of Jacob, . . . shall stay upon the Lord, the Holy One of Israel, in truth." From "every nation, and kindred, and tongue, and people" there will be some who will gladly respond to the message, "Fear God, and give glory to Him; for the hour of His judgment is come." They will turn from every idol that binds them to earth, and will "worship Him that made heaven, and earth, and the sea, and the fountains of waters." They will free themselves from every entanglement, and will stand before the world as monuments of God's mercy. Obedient to the divine requirements, they will be recognized by angels and by men as those that have kept "the commandments of God, and the faith of Jesus."

15. Though many shall profess to belong to Israel, how many from among them will be saved? Verses 22, 23; Rom. 9:27, 28.

16. What shall the root of Jesse be in "that day"? What is said of His rest? Isa. 11:10.

17. Whom will the Lord set His hand to recover? From where will they be gathered? Verses 11, 12.

NOTE.—This will be the "second time" God recovers His people, and this prophecy has its fulfillment at the second coming of Christ. The first gathering was into the Promised Land in the time of Moses and Joshua.

18. What will become of envy and jealousy? Against whom will Israel use their united strength? Verses 13-16.

NOTE.—This has its application to God's people in all ages. Only as all envy and jealousy are banished from our hearts, can we ever successfully do the work given us. We must be a united people, or we shall fail.

LESSON 5

A SONG OF PRAISE; THE EARTH DESTROYED; THE FALL OF SATAN
August 4, 1928

LESSON SCRIPTURES: Isaiah 12; 13; 24; 14.
MEMORY VERSE: Isa. 12: 2, 3.
LESSON HELP: "The Great Controversy," pp. 653-661 (new ed., pp. 735-743).

INTRODUCTION

The twelfth chapter of Isaiah is a song of praise which God's people will sing "in that day." The twenty-fourth chapter deals with the destruction of the earth and the gathering of God's people from its four corners. Chapter fourteen deals with Satan, and the causes of his fall and final destruction. These three chapters are "present truth" for this time. Although we may not be able to understand every detail of each verse, the main lessons are clear.

THE LESSON

1. "In that day," what will God's people say? Isa. 12:1-3.

NOTE.—"That day" evidently has reference to the time just preceding the coming of the Lord, as brought to view in the latter part of the eleventh chapter of Isaiah.

The twelfth chapter is a song of the experience of the people of God. For a little while God has been angry with them, but now they are comforted.

2. **In what words will God's people further express their joy? Verses 4-6.**

NOTE.—"Declare His doings." Tell the people that God is the Creator. Tell what He has done for your soul. Exalt His name. God has not left His people. He is still "the Holy One" in the midst of His own.

3. **In the day of the Lord, who will be gathered to battle? How does that day come upon men? What will the effect be upon mankind? Isa. 13:4, 6, 7.**

4. **How is the day of the Lord spoken of? Verse 9.**

NOTE.—The day of the Lord will come as a day of deliverance to the saints, but to the wicked it will be a day of wrath and fierce anger. (See Zeph. 1:14-18.)

5. **What is said of the stars, the sun, and the moon? Verse 10. (See Matt. 24:29.)**

NOTE.—The signs in the sun, moon, and stars are here mentioned. The sun was darkened in accord with the words of this prophecy, May 19, 1780; the moon, the following night; and the great sign of the falling stars took place November 13, 1833. One additional item of note is here mentioned: "The sun shall be darkened in his going forth," that is, before noon. This was literally fulfilled, the darkening of the sun beginning about 10 A. M.

6. **What terrible destruction will God bring upon the world? What punishment will come to the wicked? Isa. 13:11, 13; 24:1, 3, 4.**

NOTE.—Of the condition of the earth at that time the following is written: "The whole earth appears like a desolate wilderness. The ruins of cities and villages destroyed by the earthquake, uprooted trees, ragged rocks thrown out by the sea or torn out of the earth itself, are scattered over its surface, while vast caverns mark the spot where the mountains have been rent from their foundations."—"The Great Controversy," p. 657.

7. **Why will this destruction come? Isa. 24:5, 6.**

NOTE.—God's charge against the people is that they have "transgressed the laws, changed the ordinance, broken the everlasting covenant." This is true in our day. The laws of both God and man are lightly regarded, crime and transgression are rapidly increasing, and the everlasting covenant is broken.

8. **What is the result of this destruction? Verses 7-12.**

NOTE.—God will speak in ways that can not be misunderstood. When the earth shall be given over to desolation, the merry-hearted will sigh, the harp shall cease as well as the song, all joy is darkened and mirth is gone. Men now seem to be pleasure mad, but when the cities are broken down and destruction reigns, there will be sorrow and anguish. How significant is the expression, "city of confusion,"— Babylon!

9. **What will be the experience of the remnant at this time? Verses 13, 14.**

NOTE.—This is the shaking time. As when an olive tree is shaken, or as when grapes are gathered, there are a few left still, so a remnant shall remain firm. Psalm 91.

10. **Whence will come this song of praise? Verses 15, 16.**

11. **How does the Lord state the hopeless condition of the wicked? Verses 17, 18.**

NOTE.—Fear, panic, shall seize the inhabitants. As they flee, some will be caught in the snare, some in the pit. And should they escape from the one, they will fall into the other. "For the windows from on high are open." This is a similar expression to the clause, "the windows of heaven" in Malachi 3:10. There God pours out a blessing, here He pours out the vials of His wrath.

12. **How complete will be the destruction of the earth? Verses 19, 20.**

13. **Who will be punished? Where will they be gathered? For how long a time are they shut up? What is said of the sun and moon? Verses 21-23.**

NOTE.—"The high ones that are on high," as contrasted with the kings of earth, are the fallen angels, including Satan. The pit and prison in which they will be shut up is the devastated earth. Rev. 20:1. "Many days" has reference to the one thousand years. "At the close of the thousand years the second resurrection will take place. Then the wicked will be raised from the dead, and appear before God for the execution of 'the judgment written.' . . . And Isaiah declares, concerning the wicked, 'They shall be gathered together, as prisoners are gathered in the pit, and shall be shut up in the prison, and after many days shall they be visited.' "—"The Great Controversy," p. 661. When the new kingdom is established, the glory will be so great that sun and moon will be pale in comparison, or, as the text expresses it, "be confounded" and "ashamed." (See Rev. 22:5.)

14. **By what name was Satan known before his fall? Isa. 14:12.**

15. **What caused the fall of Lucifer? What was the thought of his heart? Verses 13, 14.**

NOTE.—"Lucifer had said, 'I will be like the Most High;' and the desire for self-exaltation had brought strife into the heavenly courts, and had banished a multitude of the hosts of God. Had Lucifer really desired to be like the Most High, he would never have deserted his appointed place in heaven; for the spirit of the Most High is manifested in unselfish ministry. Lucifer desired God's power, but not His character. He sought for himself the highest place, and every being who is actuated by his spirit will do the same. Thus alienation, discord, and strife will be inevitable. Dominion becomes the prize of the strongest. The kingdom of Satan is a kingdom of force; every individual regards every other as an obstacle in the way of his own advancement, or a stepping-stone on which he himself may climb to a higher place."—"The Desire of Ages," pp. 435, 436.

16. How is Satan described by Ezekiel? Eze. 28:12, 13.

NOTE.—The king of Tyrus mentioned in verse 12 is evidently here used as a symbol of Lucifer, or Satan. The statement in verse 13, "Thou hast been in Eden the garden of God," coupled with the statements in verses 14-17, makes it plain that no other could have been intended.

17. What high position did Lucifer hold? What is said of his "ways"? Verses 14, 15.

NOTE.—Moffatt translates it thus: "From the day you were created, you lived a perfect life, till you were discovered doing wrong."

18. What did God say He would do to this covering cherub? Why was he "lifted up"? Verses 16, 17.

LESSON 6

THE TRIALS AND TRIUMPHS OF GOD'S PEOPLE

August 11, 1928

LESSON SCRIPTURE: Isaiah 25; 26.
MEMORY VERSE: Isa. 26: 3.
LESSON HELPS: "The Acts of the Apostles," pp. 593-602; "The Great Controversy," pp. 635-642 (new ed., pp. 717-724).

INTRODUCTION

The twenty-fifth chapter of Isaiah is a hymn of praise to Jehovah by the remnant church, which has just escaped the events mentioned in chapter 24. The twenty-sixth chapter is a song of the experience of God's people in connection with the events just preceding the coming of the Lord. This makes these chapters "present truth" in a very real sense. As this lesson is studied, these experiences will become more real to us, especially as we know that the events portrayed are just before us.

THE LESSON

1. What reason does Isaiah give for praising God? Isa. 25:1, 2.

2. What has God been to the poor and needy? When will protection especially be needed against the storm and the heat? Verse 4. (See Rev. 16; Ps. 91.)

NOTE.—"The darkest hour of the church's struggle with the powers of evil, is that which immediately precedes the day of her final deliverance. But none who trust in God need fear; for 'when the blast of the terrible ones is as a storm against the wall,' God will be to His church 'a refuge from the storm.'"—"Prophets and Kings," p. 725.

3. When will the events spoken of in verse 8 take place? 1 Cor. 15:54; Rev. 21:4.

NOTE.—"From garrets, from hovels, from dungeons, from scaffolds, from mountains and deserts, from the caves of the earth and the caverns of the sea, Christ will gather His children to Himself. On earth

[16]

they have been destitute, afflicted, and tormented. Millions have gone down to the grave loaded with infamy because they refused to yield to the deceptive claims of Satan. By human tribunals the children of God have been adjudged the vilest of criminals. But the day is near when 'God is judge Himself.' Then the decisions of earth shall be reversed. 'The rebuke of His people shall He take away.' White robes will be given to every one of them. And 'they shall call them the holy people, the redeemed of the Lord.'"—"Christ's Object Lessons," pp. 179, 180.

4. What will the redeemed say in that day? Isa. 25: 9.

NOTE.—"Those who would have destroyed Christ and His faithful people, now witness the glory which rests upon them. In the midst of their terror they hear the voices of the saints in joyful strains exclaiming, 'Lo, this is our God; we have waited for Him, and He will save us.' "—"The Great Controversy," p. 644.

5. What song will be sung? Isa. 26: 1.

6. To whom will the gates be opened? Verse 2. (See Rev. 22:14.)

NOTE.—The gates of the New Jerusalem will be opened wide for the righteous people that keep the truth. There will not enter into it anything that defiles.

7. Through all the struggles and turmoil of the last days, what may he have whose mind is stayed on God? Why? Verse 3.

NOTE.—"Those who take Christ at His word, and surrender their souls to His keeping, their lives to His ordering, will find peace and quietude. Nothing of the world can make them sad when Jesus makes them glad by His presence. In perfect acquiescence there is perfect rest. . . . Our lives may seem a tangle; but as we commit ourselves to the wise Master Worker, He will bring out the pattern of life and character that will be to His own glory. And that character which expresses the glory—character—of Christ, will be received into the Paradise of God. A renovated race shall walk with Him in white, for they are worthy."—"The Desire of Ages," p. 331.

8. What admonition does the Lord give? What reasons are given why we should trust in the Lord? Verses 4-6.

NOTE.—At this time when cities shall go down to destruction (verse 5), God counsels His people to put their trust in Him.

9. How is the way of the just defined? What name is here given to the One who will weigh men's actions? Verse 7.

NOTE.—The way of the just may be narrow, it may be steep, even stony, but it will not be crooked. It will be a "straight" path. Verse 7, Lesser's translation.

10. Where have the just waited for the Lord? What was their desire? Verses 8, 9, first part.

NOTE.—The people here spoken of have been waiting for the Lord. When His judgments were in the earth, they waited. Their desire was to the name of God and to His remembrance, or memorial. The American Revised Version of verse 8 reads: "Yea, in the way of Thy judgments, O Jehovah, have we waited for Thee; to Thy name, even to Thy memorial name is the desire of our soul." God's name and His memorial have a familiar sound. The name of God is His character. And the remnant people will have the name of God in their foreheads. Rev. 14: 1. The Sabbath is the outstanding memorial of creation. "It is to be remembered and observed as the memorial of the Creator's work. Pointing to God as the Maker of the heavens and the earth, it distinguishes the true God from all false gods. All who keep the seventh day, signify by this act that they are worshipers of Jehovah. Thus the Sabbath is the sign of man's allegiance to God as long as there are any upon the earth to serve Him. The fourth commandment is the only one of all the ten in which are found both the name and the title of the Lawgiver. It is the only one that shows by whose authority the law is given. Thus it contains the seal of God, affixed to His law as evidence of its authenticity and binding force."—"Patriarchs and Prophets," p. 307.

11. What is the effect of God's judgments upon mankind? Verses 9, last part, 10, 11.

NOTE.—Thus it has ever been. When God's judgments are in the land, men humble themselves. They promise to do right. Verse 9. Let the judgments be taken away, let the danger pass, and many forget all their good intentions. Verse 10.

12. What does God ordain for His own? What has He done for them? Verse 12; Eph. 2:10.

NOTE.—The American Revised Version reads, "Thou hast also wrought all our works for us." God works in us both to will and to do. We can do "no good thing" of ourselves. But, says the apostle Paul, "I have strength to do everything through Him who gives me power."

13. What confession do God's people here make? What has happened to all the wicked? Isa. 26:13, 14.

14. How has God blessed His people? What did God's chastisement lead them to do? Verses 15, 16.

15. What joyful news is proclaimed concerning those who have died in the Lord? Verse 19.

16. What invitation is given to God's people during the time of the "indignation"? Verse 20.

NOTE.—"If the blood of Christ's faithful witnesses were shed at this time, it would not, like the blood of the martyrs, be as seed sown to yield a harvest for God. Their fidelity would not be a testimony to convince others of the truth; for the obdurate heart has beaten back the waves of mercy until they return no more. If the righteous were now left to fall a prey to their enemies, it would be a triumph for the prince of darkness. Says the psalmist, 'In the time of trouble He shall hide me in His pavilion: in the secret of His tabernacle shall He hide me.' Christ has spoken: 'Come, My people, enter thou into thy chambers, and shut thy doors about thee: hide thyself as it were for a little moment, until the indignation be overpast. For, behold, the Lord cometh out of His place to punish the inhabitants of the earth for their iniquity.' Glorious will be the deliverance of those who have patiently waited for His coming, and whose names are written in the book of life."—"The Great Controversy," p. 634.

17. To what time does this refer? While God's people are safely hidden, what will come upon the wicked? Verse 21.

LESSON 7
THE VINEYARD; FALSE SECURITY
August 18, 1928

LESSON SCRIPTURE: Isaiah 27; 28.
MEMORY VERSE: Isa. 28: 16.
LESSON HELPS: "Patriarchs and Prophets," p. 726 (new ed., p. 761); "Prophets and Kings," pp. 587-592; "The Desire of Ages," pp. 597-600.

INTRODUCTION

We are considering events happening in "that day," that is, in close connection with the day of the Lord. Note how many times "that day" occurs in Isaiah 27, 28. At the beginning of this lesson, God assures His people that He will keep His vineyard, that He will water it every moment, and that He thinks of it tenderly. He will stay the "rough wind in the day of the east wind." Isa. 27:8. The same tender care is evidenced in the parable of the plowman in chapter 28. God's people will be tried and tested, but they will not be crushed. Not so with the wicked. God will there do His "strange act." Verse 21. And there is no escape, no hiding; the bed is too short, the covering too narrow.

THE LESSON

1. Whom does God say He will punish in "that day"? Isa. 27:1.

NOTE.—The symbols, serpent and dragon, here used, refer to Satan. Rev. 20:2.

2. To what does the Lord compare His people? In what impressive way does He express His care for them? Verses 2, 3. (See also Isa. 5:1-7; John 15:1-8.)

3. What will be done to the briers and thorns? Isa. 27:4; Mal. 4:1.

4. What gracious promise is given to the repentant sinner? Isa. 27:5.

NOTE.—"Whoever under the reproof of God will humble the soul with confession and repentance, as did David, may be sure that there is hope for him. Whoever will in faith accept God's promises, will find pardon. The Lord will never cast away one truly repentant soul. He has given this promise: 'Let him take hold of My strength, that he may make peace with Me; and he shall make peace with Me.' "—'Patriarchs and Prophets," p. 726.

5. Who will take root? Who will blossom? With what result? Verse 6.

NOTE.—How significant are the words "Jacob," "Israel"! They come "of Jacob," but they become "Israel." Jacob means a supplanter, a dishonest man. Israel meant a victor, an overcomer.

"Fill the face of the world with fruit." Of the early church it was said that they filled Jerusalem with their doctrine. Acts 5:28. Of the last church it is said that they will fill the whole earth with fruit.

6. **What else will come to pass in that day? How will they be gathered? Verse 12.**

NOTE.—"The Lord shall beat off," that is, gather in the harvest. The metaphor is taken either from the beating of olive trees to obtain the berries (see Isa. 17:6), or from the beating out of the grain on the threshing floor (Ruth 2:17; Isa. 28:27) "one by one." It is personal work that brings people to the Lord one by one. Even where multitudes come into the truth, personal work must be done to establish them.

7. **When will the great trumpet be blown? Whence will the redeemed come? What had been their condition? Verse 13.**

NOTE.—God's people will have gone through great trials before their final deliverance. It will seem to them that they must perish; but when the trumpet of the Lord shall sound, those of God's people who have been scattered in all the earth (Assyria and Egypt being here used as symbols of the nations of the earth), will come and worship with the redeemed of all ages in the Holy City, in the "holy mount," the dwelling place of God. Read "The Great Controversy," page 622, last paragraph.

8. **What will God be in that day to the residue of His people? Isa. 28:5, 6.**

NOTE.—The Lord in that day shall be a crown of glory to the remnant, a diadem of beauty. When men glory in this or that achievement, the remnant glories in the Lord. Jer. 9:23, 24. God will give His people good judgment as well as strength in the battle.

9. **What has strong drink caused both prophet and priest to do? Verse 7.**

NOTE.—Strong drink has ever been a curse. Here the results of its use is shown on religious leaders. They have wrong visions, they stumble in judgment. While God's people are promised the gift of good judgment, these stumble in judgment and are "out of the way through strong drink."

10. **Whom will God teach knowledge and doctrine? How will it be done? Verses 9, 10.**

NOTE.—Commenting on these verses, the servant of the Lord says: "Thus the word of the Lord is patiently to be brought before the children, and kept before them, by parents who believe the word of God." —"Testimonies to Ministers," p. 418.

11. **How did the word of the Lord come? For what purpose? Verse 13.**

NOTE.—"The most valuable teaching of the Bible is not to be gained by occasional or disconnected study. Its great system of truth is not so presented as to be discerned by the hasty or careless reader. Many of its treasures lie far beneath the surface, and can be obtained only by diligent research and continuous effort. The truths that go to make up the great whole must be searched out and gathered up, 'here a little, and there a little.'

"When thus searched out and brought together, they will be found to be perfectly fitted to one another. Each Gospel is a supplement to the others, every prophecy an explanation of another, every truth a development of some other truth."—"Education," pp. 123, 124. Why will they "fall backward, and be broken, and snared, and taken?"—"Because they did not heed the word of the Lord that came unto them."—"Testimonies to Ministers," p. 419.

12. What will scornful men say? Verses 14, 15.

NOTE.—"In the class here described are included those who in their stubborn impenitence comfort themselves with the assurance that there is to be no punishment for the sinner; that all mankind, it matters not how corrupt, are to be exalted to heaven, to become as the angels of God. But still more emphatically are those making a covenant with death and an agreement with hell, who renounce the truths which Heaven has provided as a defense for the righteous in the day of trouble, and accept the refuge of lies offered by Satan in its stead,— the delusive pretensions of Spiritualism. . . .

"They affect great pity for minds so narrow, weak, and superstitious as to acknowledge the claims of God and obey the requirements of His law. They manifest as much assurance as if, indeed, they had made a covenant with death and an agreement with hell,—as if they had erected an impassible, impenetrable barrier between themselves and the vengeance of God."—"The Great Controversy," pp. 560, 561.

13. What has God laid in Zion for a foundation? Verse 16; 1 Peter 2:6, 7.

NOTE.—"In infinite wisdom, God chose the foundation stone, and laid it Himself. . . . Christ is a 'tried stone.' Those who trust in Him, He never disappoints. He has borne every test. He has endured the pressure of Adam's guilt, and the guilt of his posterity, and has come off more than conqueror of the powers of evil. He has borne the burdens cast upon Him by every repenting sinner. In Christ the guilty heart has found relief. He is the sure foundation. All who make Him their dependence, rest in perfect security."—"The Desire of Ages," pp. 598, 599.

14. What will God measure by line and by plummet? Isa. 28:17.

NOTE.—Builders use the line and plummet in their work, the line for horizontal work, the plummet for adjusting walls to the vertical,— hence these terms are used figuratively for the standard of truth and righteousness. When God builds, it will be true to the line and the plummet, it will measure up to the standard of judgment,—the law. Eccl. 12:13, 14. But men's buildings will be swept away. Matt. 7: 24-27.

15. What will become of the covenant with death? By what will they be trodden down? Isa. 28:18, 19.

NOTE.—Men have thought to avoid God's judgments. But no one

can do this. The scourge, culminating in the seven last plagues will come. These plagues will take some time, for "morning by morning" and "by day and by night" they will harass.

16. What apt illustration does God use to show man's inability to save himself from the scourge? Verse 20.

17. Why is the act of punishing mentioned in verse 21 called "a strange act"?

NOTE.—"To our merciful God the act of punishment is a strange act. 'As I live, saith the Lord God, I have no pleasure in the death of the wicked.' . . . Yet He will 'by no means clear the guilty.' 'The Lord is slow to anger, and great in power, and will not at all acquit the wicked.' By terrible things in righteousness He will vindicate the authority of His downtrodden law. The severity of the retribution awaiting the transgressor may be judged by the Lord's reluctance to execute justice."—"The Great Controversy," p. 627.

18. What illustration from the field does God now use? With what intent? Verses 23-29.

NOTE.—The picture here used is one all can understand. After the plowing and sowing comes the harvest, when the different grains are threshed, each according to its nature. Fitch, black cummin (A. R. V., margin), is too tender to be threshed with the ordinary "threshing sledge," a heavy instrument that would crush it entirely. Nor "is a cart wheel turned about upon the cummin." This is another method of threshing that would be destructive to the seed. Another translation of verse 28 is: "Is bread grain crushed? Nay, he will not ever be threshing it, and driving his cart wheels and his horses over it: he doth not crush it." A. R. V., margin.

The lesson is plain. God will judge. God will punish. God will do His "strange act." His own people will not entirely escape. He will purify them in the fire, but the wicked will be destroyed. So take courage. God watches over His own. (See 1 Cor. 10: 13.)

LESSON 8

EVENTS CONNECTED WITH THE COMING OF THE LORD

August 25, 1928

LESSON SCRIPTURE: Isaiah 29; 30.
MEMORY VERSE: Isa. 30: 21.
LESSON HELPS: "Testimonies," Vol. 1, pp. 186-188; Vol. 8, pp. 41-44; "Thoughts from the Mount of Blessing," pp. 213-216.

INTRODUCTION

The first part of the twenty-ninth chapter of Isaiah evidently refers to the judgments that were to come on Jerusalem. The enemy would lay siege against it and also raise forts. Verse 3. God had forewarned of these calamities, but the people did not heed. Their eyes were closed. To them the vision was as the words of a sealed book.

Even the leaders were blind. Verses 11, 12. The lesson begins with verse 13 speaking to the people who confess God with the mouth, but their hearts are far away.

The lesson deals mostly with the events of "that day." Even as Christ in the twenty-fourth chapter of Matthew mingles the description of the fall of Jerusalem and of the end of the world, so also does Isaiah. But there need be no confusion. The two accounts can easily be distinguished.

THE LESSON

1. What does the Lord say of a certain class of people? How is their fear of God regulated? Isa. 29:13. (See Matt. 15:7-9.)

Note.—"It would be more pleasing to the Lord if lukewarm professors of religion had never named His name. They are a continual weight to those who would be faithful followers of Jesus. They are a stumbling-block to unbelievers, and evil angels exult over them, and taunt the angels of God with their crooked course. Such are a curse to the cause at home or abroad. They draw nigh to God with their lips, while their heart is far from Him."—"Testimonies," Vol. 1, p. 188.

2. What will God do among this people? What will become of the wisdom of their wise and prudent men? Isa. 29:14.

3. On whom does God pronounce His woe? What is said of their works? What do they say? Verse 15. (See John 3:19.)

4. How do they turn things? How will their work be esteemed? What two statements are mentioned as being made by the creature to the Creator? Verse 16.

Note.—This verse throws light on the two preceding verses. The wise men spoken of in verse 14, while they are said to "seek deep," verse 15, nevertheless turn "things upside down." They come to the conclusion that God is not the Creator,—"He made me not." They do not believe there is an intelligent Being back of the universe,—"He had no understanding." They have accepted evolution, or some other theory of "science falsely so called" (1 Tim. 6:20), instead of creation, and have thus rejected the Creator.

5. What will happen to the deaf and the blind in that day? Verse 18.

Note.—It is well for God's people to hold true to the words of the Book." It is thereby that the wise men shall be confounded. This is the "marvelous work" and "wonder" which God will perform. Verse 4. A small people who believe in their Creator and in "the Book" shall cause the wisdom of the wise men to perish.

6. In whom will the meek increase their joy? What is said of the poor? Verse 19.

7. What will happen to the scorner and to those that watch for iniquity? How is a man made an offender? Verses 20, 21.

Note.—There are those that "watch for iniquity," that will catch a phrase or word and enlarge upon it, and thus make a man an offender for a word."

8. What was the prophet commanded to do? For what time was is? Isa. 30:8, margin.

[23]

9. What should the prophet write? What will the people not hear? Verse 9.

NOTE.—God's charges against His people are for serious offenses, —rebellion, lying (Jer. 28:15-17), and disregard of law (Prov. 28:9).

10. What do the people say to the seers and the prophets? Verses 10, 11.

NOTE.—"The spirit of this generation is, 'Speak unto us smooth things.' But the spirit of prophecy speaks only the truth. Iniquity abounds, and the love of many who profess to follow Christ waxes cold. They are blind to the wickedness of their own hearts, and do not feel their weak and helpless condition. God in mercy lifts the veil, and shows them that there is an eye behind the scenes that discerns their hidden guilt and the motives of their actions.

"The sins of the popular churches are whitewashed over. . . . Many proclaim the law of God abolished, and surely their lives are in keeping with their faith. If there is no law, then there is no transgression, and therefore no sin; for sin is the transgression of the law."—"Testimonies," Vol. 4, p. 13.

Moffatt translates verse 11 as follows: " 'Out of our way,' they cry, 'clear out from us, and trouble us no more with talk of Israel's Majesty.' " This was the attitude of the Jewish nation toward the prophets, and it found its culmination in their rejection of the Son of God.

"By their actions they had long been saying, 'Cause the Holy One of Israel to cease from before us.' Now their desire was granted. The fear of God no longer disturbed them. Satan was at the head of the nation, and the highest civil and religious authorities were under his sway."—"The Great Controversy," p. 29.

11. What do they despise? In what do they trust? To what is their iniquity likened? Verses 12, 13.

NOTE.—The wicked rest in false security behind this "high wall," while at the same time they are despising "this word." But "suddenly" the break will come "at an instant." This harmonizes with 1 Thessalonians 5:3.

12. How complete will be the destruction? Verses 14.

NOTE.—The wall shall be broken in pieces. ⁄There shall not be left a piece large enough to take up a piece of burning coal on, or to dip water with.

13. Why does the Lord wait? What are they called who wait for Him? Verse 18; 2 Peter 3:9.

14. What will the people no longer do? What will God do when He hears? Isa. 30:19. (See also Rev. 21:4; Matt. 7:7, 8.)

15. Through what experience will God's people pass? Verse 20.

NOTE.—"Often the church militant is called upon to suffer trial and affliction; for not without severe conflict is the church to triumph. 'The bread of adversity,' 'The water of affliction,' these are the common lot of all; but none who put their trust in the One mighty to deliver will be utterly overwhelmed."—"Prophets and Kings," p. 723.

"Thine eyes shall see thy teachers." Isa. 54:13; John 3:2; 14:26. This whole experience is in contrast with Amos 8:11, where the "mul-

[24]

titudes will desire the shelter of God's mercy which they have so long despised." Instead, they will find a famine for the hearing of the words of the Lord, and although they seek they will not find.

16. What word will God's people hear? When will they hear it? Verse 21.

17. What is said of the light of the moon and of the sun at that time? Verse 26.

NOTE.—"Now the church is militant. Now we are confronted with a world in midnight darkness, almost wholly given over to idolatry. But the day is coming in which the battle will have been fought, the victory won. The will of God is to be done on earth, as it is done in heaven. Then the nations will own no other law than the law of heaven. All will be a happy united family, clothed with the garments of praise and thanksgiving,—the robe of Christ's righteousness. All nature, in its surpassing loveliness, will offer to God a constant tribute of praise and adoration. The world will be bathed in the light of heaven. The years will move on in gladness. The light of the moon will be as the light of the sun, and the light of the sun will be sevenfold greater than it is now. Over the scene the morning stars will sing together, and the sons of God will shout for joy, while God and Christ will unite in proclaiming, 'There shall be no more sin, neither shall there be any more death.' "—"Testimonies," Vol. 8, p. 42.

18. How is the coming of the Lord here portrayed? Verses 27, 28.

19. In contrast with this picture, how are God's people spoken of? Verses 29, 30.

NOTE. "It is now, in the hour of utmost extremity, that the God of Israel will interpose for the deliverance of His chosen. Saith the Lord: 'Ye shall have a song, as in the night when a holy solemnity is kept.' . . .

"With shouts of triumph, jeering, and imprecation, throngs of evil men are about to rush upon their prey, when, lo, a dense blackness, deeper than the darkness of the night, falls upon the earth. Then a rainbow, shining with the glory from the throne of God, spans the heavens, and seems to encircle each praying company. . . .

"By the people of God a voice, clear and melodious, is heard, saying, 'Look up,' and, lifting their eyes to the heavens, they behold the bow of promise. The black, angry clouds that covered the firmament are parted, and like Stephen they look up steadfastly into heaven, and see the glory of God, and the Son of man seated upon His throne."—The Great Controversy," pp. 635, 636.

20. What is ordained of old? For whom? How is it described as to size and inflammability? How is it kindled? Verse 33.

NOTE.—Tophet means a place of burning, that is, hell. The king is Satan.

THIRTEENTH SABBATH OFFERING—SEPT. 29, 1928

Work for the Indians in South America

LESSON 9

THE JUDGMENT AND THE TIME OF TROUBLE

September 1, 1928

LESSON SCRIPTURE: Isaiah 32; 33.
MEMORY VERSE: Isa. 33: 22.
LESSON HELPS: "The Desire of Ages," pp. 333-337; "Christ's Object Lessons," pp. 85-87 (new ed., pp. 87-89); "Thoughts from the Mount of Blessing," pp. 162-165.

INTRODUCTION

Isaiah is a prophet of the future. In chapter 32 the Man Christ Jesus is introduced as a king ruling in righteousness, and the princes in judgment. A special message is sent to rich women (churches), warning them of the calamities to come, and that troublous times may be expected until the Spirit is poured out from on high.

The thirty-third chapter is a most interesting chapter to the remnant church. Hypocrites will be in the church, but they will be "surprised." God will yet have a pure people. And they "shall see the King in His beauty," which is His holiness, His glory. For that saints and seers have longed. Then it will be a glorious reality.

THE LESSON

1. Who shall reign in righteousness? Who shall rule in judgment? Isa. 32:1.

NOTE.—The king is even the King of righteousness, Christ Jesus. The saints shall reign with Him in judgment. Matt. 19:28; Rev. 5: 10; 1 Cor. 6: 2, 3.

2. Under what different symbols is Christ mentioned? How will God estimate mankind in that day of judgment? Isa. 32:2-8.

NOTE.—Christ is here spoken of as a hiding place, a covert, rivers of water in a dry place, the shadow of a great rock in a weary land. Verse 2. Meditate on each of these descriptions. Christ is this, and much more.

The following verses apparently speak of the time of the judgment. God has given Christ "authority to execute judgment also, because He is the Son of man." John 5:27. God will "judge the world in righteousness by that Man whom He hath ordained." Acts 17:31. Hence it is as man that Christ is mentioned in connection with the judgment. Isa. 32:2. It is at that time that "the eyes of them that see shall not be dim." Verse 3. "Now we see through a glass, darkly." 1 Cor. 13: 12. Then we shall see face to face.

3. What will be the effect when the Spirit is poured out? Verses 15-17.

NOTE.—Verses 9-14 are addressed to the rich "women [churches] that are at ease," that are "careless," telling them that trouble is coming, that the harvest shall fail, that, as a result of this, the houses of joy in the city shall be forsaken as well as the palaces. They have been living in ease, a care-free existence,—now the time of trouble is at hand. These troublous times shall continue until the Spirit be

[26]

poured out from on high. Then the wilderness shall be a fruitful field. Then shall come the time when the latter rain shall fall, far exceeding the former. Then all bands shall be broken. "The work will be similar to that of the day of Pentecost. As the 'former rain' was given, in the outpouring of the Holy Spirit at the opening of the gospel, to cause the upspringing of the precious seed, so the 'latter rain' will be given at its close, for the ripening of the harvest. . . . The great work of the gospel is not to close with less manifestation of the power of God than marked its opening. The prophecies which were fulfilled in the outpouring of the former rain at the opening of the gospel, are again to be fulfilled in the latter rain at its close. . . .

"The message will be carried not so much by argument as by the deep conviction of the Spirit of God. The arguments have been presented. The seed has been sown, and now it will spring up and bear fruit. . . . Notwithstanding the agencies combined against the truth, a large number take their stand upon the Lord's side."—"The Great Controversy," pp. 611, 612.

4. Where will God's people be in the time of hail when the city shall be low? Verses 18, 19.

NOTE.—During the plagues when the hail descends and the cities fall (Rev. 16:19-21), there will be a tabernacle to shield God's people. Isa. 4:6.

5. In view of what is to come, who is called blessed? Verse 20.

NOTE.—Knowing that the judgments of God are in the earth, that soon we must give an account of our work, how well we ought to improve the opportunity of sowing the seed. "You are to sow the seeds of truth in every place. Wherever you can gain access, hold forth the word of God. Sow beside all waters. You may not at once see the result of your labors, but be not discouraged. Speak the words that Christ gives you. Work in His lines. Go forth everywhere as He did during His ministry on the earth."—"Testimonies," Vol. 7, p. 36.

6. What prayer ascends to God from His people in the time of trouble? Isa. 33:2.

7. How are conditions described when God begins to show His power? Verses 3-9.

NOTE.—These verses show the confusion at the beginning of the time of trouble. The people flee, the nations are scattered. Verse 3. There shall be complete destruction as when the caterpillar and the locust destroy. Verse 4. The valiant men shall cry, all travel ceases, cities go down. Verses 7, 8. Destruction shall even extend to nature. Verse 9. In the midst of this destruction, God's people will be safe. "The fear of the Lord" is their treasure. Verse 6.

8. What does God say He will do? What are the people likened to? Verses 10-13.

9. How will the sinners and hypocrites in Zion fare? What questions are asked? Verse 14.

NOTE.—"There are hypocrites now who will tremble when they obtain a view of themselves. . . . The people of God are unready for the fearful, trying scenes before us, unready to stand pure from evil and lust amid the perils and corruptions of this degenerate age. They have not on the armor of righteousness, and are unprepared to war against the prevailing iniquity. Many are not obeying the commandments of God; yet they profess so to do. If they would be faithful to obey all the statutes of God, they would have a power which would carry conviction to the hearts of the unbelieving."—"Testimonies," Vol. 2, p. 446.

God is Himself a devouring fire. Heb. 12:29. Hence the question really is, Who can dwell with God?

10. What six traits of character are mentioned as possessed by those who shall dwell with God? Verse 15.

11. What will be the reward? Verse 16.

NOTE.—"In the last great conflict of the controversy with Satan, those who are loyal to God will see every earthly support cut off. Because they refuse to break His law in obedience to earthly powers, they will be forbidden to buy or sell. It will finally be decreed that they shall be put to death. But to the obedient is given the promise, 'He shall dwell on high: his place of defense shall be the munitions of rocks: bread shall be given him; his waters shall be sure.' By this promise the children of God will live. When the earth shall be wasted with famine, they shall be fed."—"The Desire of Ages," p. 122.

12. What two things will His people be permitted to see? Verse 17.

NOTE.—To see the Lord was the deep desire of Moses. Yet the Lord could not grant it. "There shall no man see Me, and live." Ex. 33:20. But the time shall come when there shall be no veil before our vision. We shall see the Lord. Rev. 22:4. This is the climax of all experience throughout eternity. There is no higher. But only those who have experienced the power of Isaiah 33:15 will ever see the King in His beauty.

"The land that is very far off," rather "the land of far distances." Not Palestine, where on a mountain on a clear day one can see almost from one end of the land to the other. This refers to the new earth in all its glory.

13. What questions will be asked? What shall they not see? Verses 18, 19.

NOTE.—As the people of God see this "goodly land," for a moment the thought will come to them, Is all this true? Am I really saved? Or is it a dream? Ps. 126:1. Will there be no one to oppress or destroy any more? "Musing on the terror that has vanished, you ask, Where are the tyrant's officers who taxed us, charged us, took our tribute?" Isa. 33:18, Moffatt's translation. (See Isa. 60:18; 54:14.)

14. What are God's people to look on? What shall they see? What shall not be taken down, or removed, or broken? Verse 20.

NOTE.—The tabernacle in the wilderness was taken down and removed as Israel moved from place to place. Here the promise is given that it shall be so no more. How blessed it will be when God's people at last shall have "a place of their own, and move no more"! 2 Sam. 7:10.

15. What shall the Lord be unto His people? Verse 21.

NOTE.—Here the Lord is likened to a place of broad rivers and streams. "A river never raided by a galley, sailed by no ships of war," is Moffatt's translation.

16. What three things is the Lord said to be? What will He do? Verse 22.

NOTE.—It may be well to stress the word "our" in this verse. The Lord is our judge, our lawgiver, our King.

17. What picture is here introduced? Verse 23.

NOTE.—The picture of the Lord as a place of broad rivers suggests the picture in this verse of a boat with sails slack, ropes loose, and the mast dangling so it can not hold the sails. Such a boat could neither pursue nor escape the enemy. It would become a prey and be spoiled. Its utter helplessness is suggested by the fact that even "the lame take the prey." The spiritual lesson is obvious. We must always keep "in trim," always be prepared, not slack nor unready.

18. What shall the inhabitants not say? What is their condition? Verse 24.

LESSON 10

THE DESTRUCTION OF THE EARTH; THE NEW EARTH

September 8, 1928

LESSON SCRIPTURE: Isaiah 34; 35.
MEMORY VERSE: Isa. 35: 10.
LESSON HELP: "Great Controversy," pp. 672-678 (new ed., pp. 755-762).

INTRODUCTION

Two pictures are presented to us in this lesson. The thirty-fourth chapter of Isaiah should cause us to do all we can to help others who are now in sin to escape the terrible destruction that is coming. The study of chapter thirty-five should cause us to examine closely our own hearts to see if we are really and earnestly preparing for such a home. 'The unclean shall not pass over it" (Isa. 35:8); only "the redeemed shall walk there" (verse 9). Are we ready?

THE LESSON

1. Whom does the Lord call to hear what He has to say? What is coming upon the nations and their armies? What fearful picture of the slain is presented? Isa. 34:1-3.

2. What will be done to the host of heaven? What to the heavens? Verse 4.

3. What will come to pass in the day of the Lord's vengeance at the close of the millennium? Verses 5-8.

4. Into what are the streams as well as the land turned? Verse 9.

NOTE.—"Fire comes down from God out of heaven. The earth is broken up. The weapons concealed in its depths are drawn forth. De-pouring flames burst from every yawning chasm. The very rocks are on fire. The day has come that shall burn as an oven. The elements melt with fervent heat, the earth also, and the works that are therein are burned up. The earth's surface seems one molten mass,—a vast, seething lake of fire. It is the time of the judgment and perdition of ungodly men,—'the day of the Lord's vengeance, and the year of recompenses for the controversy of Zion.' "—"The Great Controversy," pp. 672, 673.

5. What book are we counseled to seek out and read? How sure are these predictions? Who commanded, and who gathered them? Verse 16.

6. What is said of the wilderness and solitary place? Isa. 35:1.

Note.—This text has an application to the gospel work now being done as well as to conditions as they will be in the new earth. "God's people have a mighty work before them, a work that must continually rise to greater prominence. Our efforts in missionary lines must become far more extensive. . . .

"The vineyard includes the whole world, and every part of it is to be worked. There are places which are now a moral wilderness, and these are to become as the garden of the Lord. The waste places of the earth are to be cultivated, that they may bud and blossom as the rose. New territories are to be worked by men inspired by the Holy Spirit. . . . The light is to shine to all lands and all peoples. And it is from those who have received the light that it is to shine forth. The day-star has risen upon us, and we are to flash its light upon the pathway of those in darkness."—"Testimonies," Vol. 6, pp. 23, 24.

"In the transformation of character, the casting out of evil passions, the development of the sweet graces of God's Holy Spirit, we see the fulfillment of the promise, 'Instead of the thorn shall come up the fir tree, and instead of the brier shall come up the myrtle tree.' We behold life's desert 'rejoice, and blossom as the rose.' "—Id., p. 308.

7. How shall the desert rejoice? What shall be given to it? What shall they see? Verse 2.

Note.—The desert "shall blossom abundantly." "Christ delights to take apparently hopeless material, those whom Satan has debased and through whom he has worked, and make them the subjects of His grace. He rejoices to deliver them from suffering, and from the wrath that is to fall upon the disobedient. He makes His children His agents in the accomplishment of this work, and in its success, even in this life, they find a precious reward."—Id., pp. 308, 309.

By "the glory of Lebanon" and "the excellency of Carmel and Sharon" are without doubt meant their fruitfulness. In the desert are no trees or grainfields. But this shall be changed. Those barren lives that have produced no fruit shall blossom abundantly. This seems to be a distinct prophecy of the times when those lands that have been unresponsive to the gospel shall be wide open.

"It was concerning the future fulfillment of this prophecy that Isaiah had heard the shining seraphim singing before the throne, 'The whole earth is full of His glory.' The prophet, confident of the certainty of these words, himself afterwards boldly declared of those who

[30]

were bowing down to images of wood and stone, 'They shall see the glory of the Lord, and the excellency of our God.'

"To-day this prophecy is meeting rapid fulfillment. The missionary activities of the church of God on earth are bearing rich fruitage, and soon the gospel message will have been proclaimed to all nations. 'To the praise of the glory of His grace,' men and women from every kindred, tongue, and people are being made 'accepted in the Beloved,' 'that in the ages to come He might show the exceeding riches of His grace in His kindness toward us through Christ Jesus.' "—"Prophets and Kings," pp. 313, 314.

8. What does God say should be done for the weak and feeble? Verse 3.

NOTE.—"Angels from a pure and holy heaven come to this polluted world to sympathize with the weakest, the most helpless and needy, while Christ Himself descended from His throne to help just such as these. You have no right to hold yourself aloof from these faltering ones, nor to assert your marked superiority over them. Come more in unison with Christ, pity the erring, lift up the hands that hang down, strengthen the feeble knees, and bid the fearful hearts be strong. Pity and help them, even as Christ has pitied you."—"Testimonies," Vol. 4, p. 131.

9. What encouraging word should be spoken to the fearful of heart? In view of what event is this counsel to be given? Verse 4.

NOTE.—The fearful, the faint-hearted, are not to be despised but rather encouraged. And this in view of the fact that Christ is soon coming. This is to be the keynote of every message, Christ is coming. He will come with vengeance, to punish. He will come with the recompense, to reward. He will come to serve, so be courageous. The Master is at the door.

10. What wonderful changes will take place when Christ comes? Verse 5.

11. What transformation will be wrought in the lame and dumb? Verse 6.

12. What will be done to parched ground and thirsty land? Verse 7.

NOTE.—This is another promise that the desert shall become fruitful. Nothing is much more uninviting or hopeless than a desert. Yet God has hope for it, and promises that it shall blossom. So let us not be discouraged, but rather work on in hope.

13. What name will be given to the highway of the Lord? Who shall not pass over the highway? For whom is the way? How clearly will it be marked? Verse 8.

NOTE.—The "way of holiness." What a highway that is! It begins down here and ends at the throne. "We believe without a doubt that Christ is soon coming. This is not a fable to us; it is a reality. We have no doubt, neither have we had a doubt for years, that the doctrines we hold to-day are present truth, and that we are nearing the judgment. We are preparing to meet Him, who, escorted by a retinue of holy angels, is to appear in the clouds of heaven to give the faithful and the just the finishing touch of immortality. When He comes, He is not to cleanse us of our sins, to remove from us the defects in our characters, or to cure us of the infirmities of our tempers and dispositions. If wrought for us at all, this work will be accomplished before that time. When the Lord comes, those who are holy will be holy still. Those who have preserved their bodies and spirits in holiness, in sanctification and honor, will then receive the finishing touch of immortality. But those who are unjust, unsanctified, and filthy, will remain so forever. No work will then be done for them to remove their defects, and give them holy characters. The Refiner does not then sit to pursue His refining process, and remove their sins and their corruption. This is all to be done in these hours of probation. It is now that this work is to be accomplished for us."—"Testimonies," Vol. 2, p. 355.

The American Revised Version of verse 8 reads: "It shall be for the redeemed," rather than, "It shall be for those."

14. What will not be found on God's highway? Who only will travel upon it? Verse 9.

15. What will the ransomed do? What will be their crown? What experience will come to them? Verse 10.

NOTE.—The picture presented in verse 10 was familiar to all Jews. At the annual feasts, the Israelites would come in groups from all parts of the land. They would bedeck themselves as well as their animals in festive adornment, and sing as they journeyed along.

It is with joy that God's redeemed people shall return to the heavenly Zion. No sorrow, no sighing, but everlasting joy shall be theirs. Lord, speed that day!

LESSON 11

INVASION OF JUDAH BY ASSYRIA; GOD DELIVERS HIS PEOPLE

September 15, 1928

LESSON SCRIPTURE: Isaiah 36; 37.
MEMORY VERSE: Isa. 37: 20.
LESSON HELP: "Prophets and Kings," pp. 349-366.

INTRODUCTION

For a long time Israel had been paying tribute to Assyria. Hezekiah continued this custom when he became king, while at the same time he did all he could to prepare himself for a possible war with Assyria. A few years after the beginning of his reign, Samaria was taken, and the ten tribes were carried into captivity, 721 B. C. As Samaria was only fifty miles from Jerusalem, Hezekiah might well expect that it would not be long before the Assyrians would be before the gates. Yet a few years intervened, and then came Sennacherib. It is at this point our lesson opens.

THE LESSON

1. Who came up to war against Judah in the days of King Hezekiah? What cities were taken? Isa. 36: 1.

2. **Whom did the king of Assyria send to Jerusalem? What was the substance of his proposals? Verses 2, 16-20.**

NOTE.—Rabshakeh counseled the Jews to surrender and give a present to the king of Assyria, else he would besiege Jerusalem. He warned them not to be persuaded by Hezekiah, who had told them that the Lord would deliver them. The king of Assyria had already taken several cities, and, according to the belief of the time, the gods of Assyria were therefore stronger than the gods of the cities that had been conquered. And could Jerusalem escape? Rabshakeh was sure that his gods were stronger than the God of Israel.

3. **What did Hezekiah, the king, do when Rabshakeh's message came to him? Isa. 37:1.**

4. **What message did Hezekiah send to Isaiah? What request did he make of the prophet? What did both do? Verses 2-4; 2 Chron. 32:20.**

5. **What encouraging answer did Isaiah send to the king? What did he say that God would send upon the king of Assyria? What would he hear and do? What would happen to him in his own land? Isa. 37:5-7.**

6. **What further message did Rabshakeh send to Hezekiah? Verses 8-13.**

7. **What did Hezekiah do when he received the letter? Verse 14.**

8. **What was the substance of Hezekiah's prayer? Verses 15-20.**

NOTE.—Hezekiah addresses Jehovah as the One dwelling between the cherubim, the Creator that made heaven and earth. He did not deny the power of Assyria, but says that the gods of the cities overthrown were only gods of wood and stone. He asks God to show Himself mighty,—"that all the kingdoms of the earth may know that Thou art the Lord, even Thou only."

"Hezekiah's pleadings in behalf of Judah and of the honor of their Supreme Ruler, were in harmony with the mind of God. Solomon, in his benediction at the dedication of the temple, had prayed the Lord to maintain 'the cause of His people Israel at all times, as the matter shall require: that all the people of the earth may know that the Lord is God, and that there is none else.' Especially was the Lord to show favor when, in times of war or of oppression by an army, the chief men of Israel should enter the house of prayer and plead for deliverance."—"Prophets and Kings," p. 359.

9. **What assurance did Isaiah give to Hezekiah concerning his prayer? Verse 21; 2 Kings 19:20.**

10. **Against whom had the king of Assyria really exalted himself? Isa. 37:23.**

11. **Through whom had he reproached the Lord? What boastful words did he speak? Verses 24, 25.**

12. **How does the Lord answer this boast? Verses 26, 27.**

NOTE.—These verses contain important principles. God will use one nation to punish another. That nation then becomes "the rod of" His "anger" (Isa. 10:5), to "take the spoil, and to take the prey" (verse 6), really an executor of the vengeance of God. Assyria had been so used, but had now lifted up itself and thought that all these things had been done through its own mighty power. "Hast thou not heard long ago," says God, "that thou shouldest be to lay waste defensed cities?" God had been using Assyria according to plans formed long ago. Now Assyria's time had come to be humbled.

13. What would God do to Assyria? Verses 28, 29.

14. Addressing Hezekiah, what sign did Isaiah say should be given? Verse 30.

NOTE.—In the third year conditions would again be normal so they could sow and reap as usual. In the meantime they would be enabled to live of that which "groweth of itself" or "springeth of the same." This would border on the miraculous, and would constitute a sign.

15. What is said of the remnant? Verses 31, 32.

NOTE.—God's own, the remnant, should again take root, become established, and bear fruit. This is not because of any inherent goodness. "The zeal of the Lord of hosts shall do this."

16. How would God defend Jerusalem? Verses 33, 34.

17. For whose sake would God defend the city? Verse 35.

NOTE.—God's honor was at stake. After the boasts made by the king of Assyria, had not God defended His city, the nations would draw the conclusion that after all Assyria was stronger than the God of Israel. For "David's sake." God had made promises to David. 2 Sam. 7:16; Ps. 89:29-37. These must be kept.

18. How did God's judgment come upon the Assyrian host? Verse 36.

19. What was the further history of the Assyrian king? How was Isaiah's word in verse 7 fulfilled? Verses 37, 38.

20. What lesson is there for the nations of to-day in the history of Assyria?

NOTE.—"The rise and fall of the Assyrian Empire is rich in lessons for the nations of earth to-day. Inspiration has likened the glory of Assyria at the height of her prosperity to a noble tree in the garden of God, towering above the surrounding trees."—"Prophets and Kings," pp. 362, 363. This description is given in detail in Ezekiel 31:3-9.

"But the rulers of Assyria, instead of using their unusual blessings for the benefit of mankind, became the scourge of many lands. Merciless, with no thought of God or their fellow men, they pursued the fixed policy of causing all nations to acknowledge the supremacy of the gods of Nineveh, whom they exalted above the Most High. God had sent Jonah to them with a message of warning, and for a season they humbled themselves before the Lord of hosts, and sought forgiveness. But soon they turned again to idol worship, and to the conquest of the world."—Id., p. 363.

"With unerring accuracy the Infinite One still keeps account with the nations. While His mercy is tendered, with calls to repentance, this account remains open; but when the figures reach a certain amount which God has fixed, the ministry of His wrath begins. The account is closed. Divine patience ceases. Mercy no longer pleads in their behalf."—Id., p. 364.

"The pride of Assyria and its fall are to serve as an object lesson to the end of time. Of the nations of earth to-day who in arrogance and pride array themselves against Him, God inquires: 'To whom art thou thus like in glory and in greatness among the trees of Eden? yet shalt thou be brought down with the trees of Eden unto the nether parts of the earth.' "—Id., p. 366.

LESSON 12
HEZEKIAH'S PRAYER ANSWERED; HIS PRIDE REBUKED
September 22, 1928

LESSON SCRIPTURE: Isaiah 38; 39.
MEMORY VERSE: Isa. 38: 19.
LESSON HELP: "Prophets and Kings," pp. 340-348.

INTRODUCTION

Hezekiah came to the throne at the time when the ten tribes were about to be carried into captivity. He determined to do all he could to save Judah from the fate about to overtake Israel. He cleansed the temple, which had long been neglected and was in a state of ruin, and reëstablished the sanctuary service. "Once more the temple courts resounded with words of praise and adoration. The songs of David and of Asaph were sung with joy, as the worshipers realized that they were being delivered from the bondage of sin and apostasy. 'Hezekiah rejoiced, and all the people, that God had prepared the people: for the thing was done suddenly.' "—"Prophets and Kings," p. 333.

Hezekiah invited all Israel to the feast of the Passover. 2 Chron. 30:1, 6, 10. "But they laughed them to scorn, and mocked them." This was the last invitation the ten tribes had. They refused it, and were carried into captivity. But God still spared Jerusalem.

THE LESSON

1. After the defeat of the Assyrian foes, what befell Hezekiah, king of Judah? What message did Isaiah bring to him? Isa. 38:1.

2. In what spirit did Hezekiah receive the message? What was the substance of his prayer? Verses 2, 3.

3. What message was Isaiah commissioned to bring? Verses 4-6.

4. What did Isaiah request should be placed on the boil? Verse 21.

NOTE.—"Those who seek healing by prayer should not neglect to make use of the remedial agencies within their reach. It is not a denial of faith to use such remedies as God has provided to alleviate pain and to aid nature in her work of restoration. . . . We have the sanction of the word of God for the use of remedial agencies. Hezekiah, king of Israel, was sick, and a prophet of God brought him the message that he should die. He cried unto the Lord, and the Lord heard His servant, and sent him a message that fifteen years should be added to his life. Now one word from God would have healed Hezekiah instantly; but special directions were given, 'Let them take a lump of figs, and lay it for a plaster upon the boil, and he shall recover.'

"On one occasion Christ anointed the eyes of a blind man with clay and bade him, 'Go, wash in the pool of Siloam. . . . He went his way therefore, and washed, and came seeing.' The cure could be wrought only by the power of the Great Healer, yet Christ made use of the simple agencies of nature. While He did not give countenance to drug medication, He sanctioned the use of simple and natural remedies."—"Ministry of Healing," pp. 231-233.

5. In agreeing to Hezekiah's request for a sign, what question did Isaiah ask? How did Hezekiah answer? What change came in the sundial of Ahaz? 2 Kings 20:8-11; Isa. 38:7, 8.

6. How does Hezekiah relate his experience? Verses 9-16.

NOTE.—It is evident from Hezekiah's own record of his feelings that he was not reconciled to God's message that he should die. "I am deprived of the residue of my years," he said, as though he had a contract with God for a certain number of years, and that God was about to cut him short. He would, of course, accept God's plan for him, but it would be in bitterness of soul.

7. What experience came to Hezekiah at the time of his healing? Verse 17; James 5:15.

8. What observation is made by Hezekiah regarding the grave and death? Isa. 38:18.

9. What will the living do? What will the father teach his children? Verses 19, 20.

10. What embassage came to Hezekiah after his recovery? Isa. 39:1.

NOTE.—"In the fertile valleys of the Tigris and the Euphrates there dwelt an ancient race which, though at that time subject to Assyria, was destined to rule the world. Among its people were wise men who gave much attention to the study of astronomy; and when they noticed that the shadow on the sundial had been turned back ten degrees, they marveled greatly. Their king, Merodach-baladan, upon learning that this miracle had been wrought as a sign to the king of Judah that the God of heaven had granted him a new lease of life, sent ambassadors to Hezekiah to congratulate him on his recovery, and to learn, if possible, more of the God who was able to perform so great a wonder."—"Prophets and Kings," p. 344.

11. What was God's purpose in allowing these messengers to be sent? 2 Chron. 32:31.

NOTE.—"The visit of the ambassadors to Hezekiah was a test of his gratitude and devotion. . . . Had Hezekiah improved the opportunity given him to bear witness to the power, the goodness, the compassion, of the God of Israel, the report of the ambassadors would have been as light piercing darkness. But he magnified himself above the Lord of hosts. He 'rendered not again according to the benefit done unto him; for his heart was lifted up.' "—Id., p. 346.

12. How did Hezekiah receive the ambassadors? What did he show them? Isa. 39:2.

NOTE.—"The visit of these messengers from the ruler of a faraway land gave Hezekiah an opportunity to extol the living God. How easy it would have been for him to tell them of God, the upholder of all created things, through whose favor his own life had been spared when all other hope had fled! What momentous transformations might have taken place had these seekers after truth from the plains of Chaldea been led to acknowledge the supreme sovereignty of the living God!

"But pride and vanity took possession of Hezekiah's heart, and in self-exaltation he laid open to covetous eyes the treasures with which God had enriched His people. . . . Not to glorify God did he do this, but to exalt himself in the eyes of the foreign princes. He did not stop to consider that these men were representatives of a powerful nation that had not the fear nor the love of God in their hearts, and that it was imprudent to make them his confidants concerning the temporal riches of the nation."—Id., pp. 344-346.

13. What conversation between Isaiah and Hezekiah followed their visit? Verses 3, 4.

14. What message did Hezekiah receive from the Lord? Verses 5-7.

NOTE.—"How disastrous the results which were to follow! To Isaiah it was revealed that the returning ambassadors were carrying with them a report of the riches they had seen, and that the king of Babylon and his counselors would plan to enrich their own country with the treasures of Jerusalem. Hezekiah had grievously sinned; 'therefore there was wrath upon him, and upon Judah and Jerusalem.'"—Id., p. 346.

"The story of Hezekiah's failure to prove true to his trust at the time of the visit of the ambassadors, is fraught with an important lesson for all. Far more than we do, we need to speak of the precious chapters in our experience, of the mercy and loving kindness of God, of the matchless depths of the Saviour's love. When mind and heart are filled with the love of God, it will not be difficult to impart that which enters into the spiritual life. Great thoughts, noble aspirations, clear perceptions of truth, unselfish purposes, yearnings for piety and holiness, will find expression in words that reveal the character of the heart treasure.

"Those with whom we associate day by day need our help, our guidance. They may be in such a condition of mind that a word spoken in season will be as a nail in a sure place. To-morrow some of these souls many be where we can never reach them again. What is our influence over these fellow travelers?"—Id., pp. 347, 348.

15. How did Hezekiah reccive the message? What relief was granted to him because he humbled himself? Verse 8; 2 Chron. 32:26.

NOTE.—"Filled with remorse, 'Hezekiah humbled himself for the pride of his heart, both he and the inhabitants of Jerusalem, so that the wrath of the Lord came not upon them in the days of Hezekiah.' But the evil seed had been sown, and in time was to spring up and yield a harvest of desolation and woe. During his remaining years, the king of Judah was to have much prosperity because of his steadfast purpose to redeem the past and to bring honor to the name of the God whom he served; yet his faith was to be severely tried, and he was to learn that only by putting his trust fully in Jehovah could he hope to triumph over the powers of darkness that were plotting his ruin and the utter destruction of his people."—Id., p. 347.

LESSON 13

WARNINGS AND REPROOFS; AN UNHEEDED CALL TO REPENTANCE

September 29, 1928

MEMORY VERSE: Isa. 21: 11, 12.
LESSON HELPS: "The Great Controversy," pp. 4l3-436, 451, 452, 631-633; "Patriarchs and Prophets," pp. 684-687 (new ed., pp. 714-718).

INTRODUCTION

In a brief survey of Isaiah such as is given in these Sabbath school lessons, it is impossible to emphasize all the texts that really demand notice. This lesson will take up scattered texts which either have not been used before, or which might justly be repeated for emphasis. While it is well that every scripture be considered in the setting in which it is found in the Bible, some texts are of such a general nature and application that no violence is done by considering them by themselves. Most of the texts in this lesson are of this character.

THE LESSON

1. What beautiful promise gives hope to all? Isa. 1:18.

2. What experience came to Isaiah when he was called to a prophet's work? Relate the circumstances. Isa. 6:1-10.

3. What is the word of the Lord in regard to associations and confederacies? Isa. 8:9-12.

NOTE.—Men may enter into confederacies and leagues, but they will not accomplish that for which they are intended. They will be broken in pieces. This phrase is thrice repeated in verse 9. (See 1 Thess. 5:3.) There is a lesson in this for the people of God.

"No confederacy should be formed with unbelievers, neither should you call together a certain chosen number who think as you do, and who will say Amen to all that you propose, while others are excluded, who you think will not be in harmony. I was shown that there was great danger of doing this."—"Testimonies to Ministers," pp. 462, 463.

"Those employed in any department of the work whereby the world may be transformed, must not enter into alliance with those who know not the truth. The world know not the Father or the Son, and they have no spiritual discernment as to the character of our work, as to what we shall do, or shall not do. We must obey the orders that come from above. We are not to hear the counsel or follow the plans suggested by unbelievers. Suggestions made by those who know not the work that God is doing for this time, will be such as to weaken the power of the instrumentalities of God. By accepting such suggestions, the counsel of Christ is set at naught."—Id., p. 463.

4. Whom are we to sanctify? What will He be to His people? What will be the experience of many? Verses 13-15.

5. What are we commanded concerning the testimony? What concerning the law? For whom will we look? Verses 16, 17.

NOTE.—"The Lord commands by the same prophet, 'Bind up the testimony, seal the law among My disciples.' The seal of God's law is found in the fourth commandment. This only, of all the ten, brings to view both the name and the title of the Lawgiver. It declares Him to be the Creator of the heavens and the earth, and thus shows His claim to reverence and worship above all others. Aside from this precept, there is nothing in the Decalogue to show by whose authority the law is given. When the Sabbath was changed by the papal power, the seal was taken from the law. The disciples of Jesus are called upon to restore it, by exalting the Sabbath of the fourth commandment to its rightful position as the Creator's memorial and the sign of His authority."—"The Great Controversy," pp. 451, 452.

6. What should be our answer to them that invite us to explore forbidden paths? Verse 19.

NOTE.—"The belief in communion with the dead is still held, even in professedly Christian lands. Under the name of Spiritualism, the practice of communicating with beings claiming to be the spirits of the departed, has become widespread. It is calculated to take hold of the sympathies of those who have laid their loved ones in the grave. Spiritual beings sometimes appear to persons in the form of their deceased friends, and relate incidents connected with their lives, and perform acts which they performed while living. In this way they lead men to believe that their dead friends are angels, hovering over them, and communicating with them. Those who thus assume to be the spirits of the departed, are regarded with a certain idolatry, and with many their word has greater weight than the word of God.

"There are many, however, who regard Spiritualism as a mere imposture. The manifestations by which it supports its claims to a supernatural character are attributed to fraud on the part of the medium. But while it is true that the results of trickery have often been palmed off as genuine manifestations, there have also been marked evidences of supernatural power. And many who reject Spiritualism as the result of human skill or cunning, will, when confronted with manifestations which they can not account for upon this ground, be led to acknowledge its claims.

"Modern Spiritualism, and the forms of ancient witchcraft and idol worship,—all having communion with the dead as their vital principle,—are founded upon that first lie by which Satan beguiled Eve in Eden."—"Patriarchs and Prophets," pp. 684, 685. (See Gen. 3:4, 5.)

7. What standard are we to uphold? Verse 20.

NOTE.—"While conflicting doctrines and theories abound, the law of God is the one unerring rule by which all opinions, doctrines, and theories are to be tested."—"The Great Controversy," p. 452.

"But however much one may advance in spiritual life, he will never come to a point where he will not need diligently to search the Scriptures; for therein are found the evidences of our faith. All points of doctrine, even though they have been accepted as truth, should be brought to the law and to the testimony; if they can not stand this test, 'there is no light in them.'"—"Testimonies," Vol. 5, p. 575.

8. To what is the remnant likened? Isa. 17:6; 24:13.

NOTE.—These texts bring to view the shaking time. Not very many will remain after the shaking is done. But those that remain will be a Gideon's band, and for them the Lord will work. Isa. 10:26; Judges 7:19-25.

9. What statements are made with regard to Egypt? Where will the altar of the Lord be placed? Whom will God send to the Egyptians? To whom will the Lord be known? Isa. 19:18-22.

NOTE.—While this prophecy may not be clear in all details, the main outline is sufficiently clear to be understood. According to this prophecy, the time shall come when some of the Egyptians shall learn the language of Canaan, some even that are living in the city of destruction, or the city of the sun. God's worship shall be exalted, and in their distress they shall call on the Lord, "and He shall send them a Saviour, and a great one, and He shall deliver them." These Egyptians shall know the Lord, and be known of Him. They shall not only vow to the Lord, but shall keep their vow. The Lord has smitten, but He will also heal.

While all this found a literal fulfillment, and a real temple and altar of the Lord was erected at Heliopolis, the city of the sun, by Onias in the time of Ptolemy Philometer, of which the ruins have been found, may we not believe this also to have a larger and a very definite spiritual fulfillment? From the darkness and superstition of heathenism, from the spiritual Egypts of this world, souls will be rescued, setting up the altar of God in the very midst of the spiritual darkness in all parts of the earth, in the strongholds of oppression and evil. Egypt has always stood for spiritual darkness and superstition. "Among all nations, kindreds, and tongues, He sees men and women who are praying for light and knowledge. Their souls are unsatisfied: long have they fed on ashes. The enemy of all righteousness has turned them aside, and they grope as blind men. But they are honest in heart, and desire to learn a better way. Although in the depths of heathenism, with no knowledge of the written law of God nor of His Son Jesus, they have revealed in manifold ways the working of a divine power on mind and character. . . .

"In various ways God will reveal Himself to them, and will place them in touch with providences that will establish their confidence in the One who has given Himself a ransom for all."—"Prophets and Kings," pp. 376, 378.

10. What cry is heard in the night? Isa. 21:11.

11. What answer is given? Verse 12.

NOTE.—"I saw that watch after watch was in the past. Because of this, should there be a lack of vigilance? Oh, no! There is the greater necessity of unceasing watchfulness, for now the moments are fewer than before the passing of the first watch."—"Testimonies," Vol. 2, p. 193.

12. For what does the Lord call? Isa. 22:12.

13. What is the response of the people? Verse 13.

NOTE.—God calls for repentance and weeping. Men turn from Him and continue their feasting. "Let us eat and drink; for to-morrow we shall die," never had more definite fulfillment than to-day.

14. What results will follow this transgression? Verse 14.

15. What precious promise has God given to His people in this time of trouble and turmoil? Isa. 26:4.

Isaiah, the Gospel Prophet
A Preacher of Righteousness

Lesson Notes and Helps, Volume 2

By M. L. ANDREASEN

"Wash you, make you clean; put away the evil of your doings from before Mine eyes; cease to do evil; learn to do well; seek judgment, relieve the oppressed, judge the fatherless, plead for the widow.

"Come now, and let us reason together, saith the Lord: though your sins be as scarlet, they shall be as white as snow; though they be red like crimson, they shall be as wool." Isa. 1: 16-18.

JOHN THE BAPTIST

"The voice of him that crieth in the wilderness, Prepare ye the way of the Lord, make straight in the desert a highway for our God." Isa. 40:3.

Contents

	INTRODUCTION	7
I.	BEHOLD YOUR GOD!	9
II.	JEHOVAH'S CHALLENGE TO FALSE GODS	15
III.	THE ELECT OF GOD; A LIGHT TO THE GENTILES	22
IV.	THE GATHERING OF ISRAEL — WITNESSES FOR GOD	29
V.	THE TRUE GOD; VANITY OF IDOLS; CYRUS THE SHEPHERD	37
VI.	THE VANITY OF FALSE GODS; ONE ONLY SAVIOUR	43
VII.	THE FALL OF BABYLON; GOD'S FINAL APPEAL TO HIS PEOPLE	49
VIII.	THE SERVANT; HOPE FOR THE DISCOURAGED	56
IX.	THY SAVIOUR AND THY REDEEMER	62
X.	THE RIGHTEOUSNESS AND POWER OF GOD; HIS CARE FOR HIS PEOPLE	69
XI.	ZION LED FROM UTTER DEFEAT TO TRIUMPHANT VICTORY	74
XII.	THE LAMB OF GOD	80
XIII.	STRICKEN BECAUSE OF ISRAEL'S TRANSGRESSION	86

F. ROBERT, ARTIST

"THE HOLY ONE OF ISRAEL"

"Behold the Lamb of God, which taketh away the sin of the world." John 1 : 29.

> What equal honors shall we bring
>   To Thee, O Lord our God, the Lamb,
> When all the notes that angels sing
>   Are far inferior to Thy name?
>
> Worthy is He that once was slain,
>   The Prince of Peace that groaned and died,
> Worthy to rise, and live, and reign,
>   At His almighty Father's side.
>
> Blessings forever on the Lamb,
>   Who bore the curse for wretched men;
> Let angels sound His sacred name,
>   Let every creature say, Amen!
>
>   — *Isaac Watts.*

Isaiah, the Gospel Prophet

Introduction

IN the introduction to Volume I the unity of Isaiah was discussed, so but little more on that subject need be said here.

Until modern times only one person — a Jewish scholar, Eben-Ezra, in the twelfth century — ever doubted the genuineness of chapters 40-66 of Isaiah. The whole book was conceded to be the work of one man, and that the man whose name it bears. The chief reason advanced for believing the latter part of Isaiah to be written centuries later than the first part, was that Isaiah *could not possibly* have foretold the name of Cyrus 150 years before he was born, nor that he would liberate the Jews. Hence it was claimed that the latter part of Isaiah was written by some unknown Jew toward the end of the captivity, about 450 or 500 B. C.

Having taken this position, it was soon found that to be consistent other chapters containing predictions must be discarded. Thus Isaiah was dismembered, and but little remained the undisputed work of the prophet.

The work of the critics has been carried forward under two suppositions, both of which we deem to be false: (1) Prophecy is impossible, for no prophet could possibly know events beforehand; (2) The style and language of chapters 40-66 are so different from chapters 1-39 that they could not possibly have been written by the same person.

The first proposition has no weight with a believer in the Bible. Prophecy is an essential element of Scripture. Thus to limit God is to reduce Him to the level of mere man. Indeed, the proposition is absurd. It takes for granted the very thing to be proved. It reminds one of another famous saying: " Miracles are an impossibility; therefore, no amount of evidence can establish one." By such reasoning anything can be proved or disproved.

The second proposition will not stand the test, either. Must Paul write in the same vein when he chastises the Galatians as when he writes his love letter to the Philippians or pleads with Philemon for the run-away slave Onesimus? There is as much difference between Romans and Ephesians as between the first and second parts of Isaiah. Must it be supposed that an author is bound to retain the same style when his subject matter changes? On that ground the "Hallelujah Chorus" could be rejected as not of the same authorship as the rest of the oratorio by Handel. Such reasoning leaves serious doubt in the mind concerning the right of the critics to be considered capable of judging even in the smallest matters.

Were it necessary, abundant proof could be submitted to establish the unity of the book. Kay, in his "Introduction to the Book of Isaiah," exposes some of the inconsistencies of the critics, and by their own line of reasoning and using their own proof, shows the falsity of their claims. Summing up, he says:

"The voice of criticism, then, is distinctly in favor of the unity of the work: and nothing, therefore, remains to derogate from the authority of the external evidence, which on its own ground is absolutely uncontested."

Under twenty-four heads he then proceeds to show how interrelated the two parts are, proving conclusively that the first part requires the second part for its explanation, and that only in the two parts have we a complete picture. With such evidence before us " we cannot think the remark of Sir E. Strachey unjustly severe, — that when he thought of the attempted disintegration, he was 'irresistibly reminded of the tradition that Isaiah was sawn asunder by those who misunderstood and denied his real office and powers.' "—" *Introduction to the Book of Isaiah,*" *W. Kay, p. 18.*

CHAPTER I

Behold Your God!

Lesson Scripture: Isaiah 40

GOD is presented to us in this chapter in the sevenfold capacity of Comforter, King, Judge, Shepherd, the All-wise One, Creator, and Upholder.

Verses 1, 2. God is a Comforter, and His message is one of comfort. How often the comforting words, "Fear not," or, "Be of good cheer," fell from the lips of the Saviour while on earth! He Himself was the Comforter; and when He left the earth, it was with the definite promise: "I will not leave you comfortless." He said, I will "pray the Father, and He shall give you another Comforter," even the Holy Spirit. John 14: 18, 16. How natural, therefore, that God's message should be, "Comfort ye, comfort ye My people, saith your God."

Verses 3-8. God is king. As in ancient days the road which the king expected to take was made ready for him, so now the way must be prepared for the King to come. Before His glory can be revealed, the crooked must be made straight and the rough places plain. He will rule over a people whose trust is not in themselves or in their "goodliness," but in the word of God, which "shall stand forever."

Verses 9, 10. God is Judge. He will come "with strong hand;" "His reward is with Him, and His work before Him."

Verse 11. God also is Shepherd. The prophet hastens to tell us that God is not only judge, but shepherd. The word "judge" savors of severity. And God indeed is severe, for He "will by no means clear the guilty." Ex. 34: 7. But His severity is just. When the final fearful judgments have been carried out, the witnesses will all cry out, "True and righteous are His judgments." Rev. 19: 2.

The picture of God as judge is not a complete picture, however. To that must be added another, that of shepherd, who gathers "the lambs with His arm," who carries "them in His bosom;" and most beautiful of all, who gently leads "those that are with young."

Verses 12-17. God is the "All-wise One," the Self-existent, the Underived One. No one directed Him or taught Him; He took counsel with no one; none instructed Him or taught Him knowledge or showed Him the way. God alone is God, and beside Him there is none else. Words could not express clearer the thought that God is not dependent on any one, that He is the First Cause, that He receives and requires no aid in planning or in executing. Father, Son, and Holy Spirit, the triune God, is the complete and perfect Godhead.

Verses 18-27. God is the Creator. Idols must needs be made by some one, but God is the Maker of all things. He "stretcheth out the heavens;" He marshals "their host by number: He calleth them all by names." "He is strong in power; not one faileth." In view of this mighty God, why should we be afraid?

Verses 28-31. God is the Upholder. Creation did not exhaust His strength or wisdom. He is never weary, and there is no searching of His understanding. Men may dig deep into the secrets of nature and bring forth wonderful things, as they indeed have done. Have they now learned all that God knows? No, God's wisdom is inexhaustible. "There is no searching of His understanding." "The Lord, the Creator of the ends of the earth, fainteth not, neither is weary." He has not retired to let matters take care of themselves. He is still working. He is a present God. "He giveth power to the faint; and to them that have no might He increaseth strength." He is the Creator, and He is looking after His creatures. He yet upholds "all things by the word of His power" (Heb. 1:3), and this upholding does not exempt the creatures He has made.

"Have you seen the Pacific Ocean?" one friend asked of another. "Yes," the friend replied, "a good many times." Yet, upon further reflection he wondered if the answer had been a strictly true one. He had indeed seen the ocean, he had stood upon the shore and viewed the mighty expanse of water. Yet how much had he seen? But a very little part of it. But had he not crossed it? Yes, but even that had given him a view of only a few miles at most on each side of the boat. But even though it were possible to cross and recross until every mile of the ocean had been covered, would he then have seen all? No, all he had seen would be a few inches of the surface of the ocean, a very thin top layer, and there would be ocean depths that he never had and never could fathom.

So with God. Man by searching tries to find out God and measure wisdom with Him. How futile! The wisest is but as a child on the shore, trying with a spoon to empty the ocean into his little bucket. Our God is infinite. Tender and strong, mighty in power, creating worlds by a word, and also gently leading those that are with young. There is indeed no searching of His understanding.

Notes

Isaiah 40: 2. " Speak ye comfortably; " " to the heart," margin. The words are those of a lover speaking to his beloved. The same words are used in Hosea 2: 14, and are those of a young man urging his suit.

" Warfare is accomplished; " " appointed time," margin. The word " pardoned " is really " accepted " as in Leviticus 26: 41, 43, where Israel is said to " accept of the punishment of their iniquity." The thought seems to be this, that Israel, by accepting their guilt and consequent punishment, receive pardon from the Lord.

Verses 3, 4. " In the wilderness " belongs to " prepare ye." Hence the reading should be as in the American Revised Version: " The voice of one that crieth, Prepare ye in the wilderness the way of Jehovah; make level in the desert a highway for our God." (See Matt. 3: 1-3.)

" Prepare," strictly " clear of obstacles." This was the usual preparation in getting the highway ready for the coming of the king.

Verses 6-8. In answer to the question, " What shall I cry? " the reply is twofold: The people are grass, and will soon pass away; the word of the Lord endures forever.

Verses 9-11. " Good tidings," the gospel.

" Behold your God! " The message deals with God, and calls upon the people to consider Him. His might and His gentleness are alike worthy of admiration.

Verses 12-14. These verses are a meditation on the greatness and wisdom of God. His greatness (verse 12) is shown by His wonderful works in creation; His wisdom, by the perfection of His knowledge.

Verse 12. These questions require no answer, but are rather intended to bring the mind to some such conclusion as this: How wonderful is the God who arranged the world in such perfection by measure, number, and weight! The thought is not merely that of creation, but of order, adjustment, and proportion. God " measured," " meted out," " weighed " oceans, heavenly bodies, and mountains, and did it with as much ease as and far greater precision than man is able to do in his small sphere. The accurate determination of mass, weight, distance, the balancing of the earth, the right proportioning of matter, all these are suggested in the verse.

Verse 13. "Directed the Spirit." "Directed" is from the same word as "meted out" in the previous verse. In creation the Spirit of God brooded over the face of the waters. Gen. 1:2. The question now is: Who limited or set any measure for what God was able to do when He set the Spirit "to brood over the formless waste with life-giving energy"? This seems to be a direct challenge to the evolutionist, who limits God. The form of the question suggests the answer: No one.

Verse 14. "Path of judgment." The "path" here suggests orderly procedure, such as we see in the six days of creation. The steps of creation followed in order and reveal intelligence.

Verses 15-17. "Drop of a bucket;" "small dust;" "very little thing;" "not sufficient;" "nothing;" "less than nothing;" "vanity."

Verse 22. "The circle of the earth;" the same word as in Job 22:14 and Proverbs 8:27.

Verse 24. The idea of the instability of things earthly is here presented. Scarcely have they been planted, etc., until they are rooted up again.

Verse 26. "Who hath created these?" A. R. V. "These" has specific reference to the heavenly bodies. The word "create" occurs twenty times in this part of Isaiah, and about ten times in all the earlier literature combined. Its frequent use in these chapters suggests the importance of creation as a determining factor in finding and worshiping the true God. This becomes so much the more significant in view of the widespread prevalence of the God-destroying theory of evolution.

Verse 28. "The everlasting God." God is not merely the God of creation, that is, the God that was and is not. God is a present God. He is the everlasting God. And He will "last" a good deal longer than men's theories.

Verse 31. "Mount up with wings as eagles." The promise to God's people is: "Thy youth is renewed like the eagle's." We understand this promise to be both physical and spiritual.

Lessons for To-day

Isaiah 40:1. "Comfort ye, comfort ye," twice repeated to give double assurance. There is a time to rebuke and chasten. There is also a time to comfort. Law and love combined constitute the gospel.

Verse 2. "Her warfare is accomplished." Forgiveness does not necessarily involve remission of punishment. God forgives, but the punishment may continue. (See David's experience in 2 Samuel 24.) So here. God forgives, but the "warfare," the "appointed time," must be accomplished.

"Is pardoned," not "will be" or "shall be."

Verse 3. "The voice." It is always well to take a humble attitude. We are but servants, voices, making audible to men God's message. No special glory is ours. We are not the authors of the message, but its proclaimers. This prophecy should be of special interest to us, as it speaks of the message that will prepare a people for the Lord's coming. Its first fulfillment was in John the Baptist (Luke 1:17); its second and final, in this people. Mal. 4:5, 6.

"Prepare ye the way." This preparation has a double aspect,— the preparation of our own hearts and lives, and the giving of the message to others. Both are neglected at the peril of our souls.

Verses 6-8. "What shall I cry?" The answer is: The insecurity and frailty of things human as contrasted with the surety of the word of God. The timeliness of this message will become more apparent to us as the years go by. All things earthly will vanish and pass away, God's word alone will stand. We must ever stress the abiding value of the word.

"The word of our God." Note the word "our." That makes it personal. The people proclaiming the message of preparation have a personal religious experience. "Lo, this is *our* God."

Verse 9. "Behold your God!" The same God whom they have found they now present to others. "Our" God should also be "your" God.

"With strength;" "be not afraid." There are those who would intimidate us. "Be not afraid," God says, "lift up thy voice with strength."

Verses 10, 11. "Behold the Lord God." Lest some should think that "our" God or "your" God is some other than the true God, He is now mentioned as "the Lord God." "Our" God is not a god, but "*the* Lord God."

Do not miss the contrast between these two verses. God comes with a "strong hand." "His arm shall rule for Him." He also comes to "gather the lambs," to "carry them in His bosom," to "gently lead" them. "Behold therefore the goodness and severity of God." Rom. 11:22.

Verse 12. Do not from this verse try to get an idea of the size of God. It is not God's size that is here in question, but His power. And this mighty God is our God. The storm may roar and the waves beat high, but the ocean, being " in the hollow of His hand," we need not fear.

Verse 15. "Nations are as a drop of a bucket." We speak of this or that nation as being strong or mighty. In this verse we get God's viewpoint. They are but as a drop of a bucket, or as the "small dust of the balance," which a man blows away. This is written for our encouragement when nation shall rise against nation and the trials of the last days come.

Verse 23. Nations are nothing; princes are nothing; judges are vanity. Even as God is superior to, and Lord of, nature, so God also is superior to nations and kings, and Lord of them.

Verse 26. "Who hath created these things?" An embarrassing question for an evolutionist to answer.

"Calleth them all by names." Stars have individual characteristics by which they are known. (See Job 38:31.) God knows them all, even as He knows His sheep and calls them by name. John 10:3.

Verse 27. If God thus knows all things, does He not know our difficulties? And do we need to think that God has forgotten us?

Verse 29. We might sometimes be tempted to read this: He giveth power to the strong. That might be true, but the promise is to the faint, to those who "have no might."

"Increaseth strength." At times sudden strength may be given, but ordinarily strength comes by a gradual increase. The promise here is of increasing strength.

Verses 30, 31. Physical strength may fail, even the young men (literally, selected men) may faint; but those that wait upon the Lord, the remnant, shall renew their strength. As the eagle is thought to molt and renew his feathers, so the waiting people of God shall gather new courage, they shall mount up on eagles' wings above all discouragements and disappointments.

CHAPTER II

Jehovah's Challenge to False Gods

Lesson Scripture: Isaiah 41

THE power of prediction is not the greatest of God's characteristics. Love, mercy, justice, righteousness, holiness,— these are what constitute God's character and make Him what He is. Prediction is important, but is not to be classed with the others. Yet this chapter and the following chapters stress the predictive power of God, and for very good reasons, which we shall now consider.

Most false religions have prophets as well as priests. Thus we read of the prophets of Baal and of the groves. 1 Kings 18: 19. These prophets professed to be able to foretell the future, as illustrated in the case of Nebuchadnezzar's dream in Daniel 2. The prognostication was sometimes made by observing the position of the stars, at other times by examining the entrails of beasts. Often it was done through pretended revelations or communications from the gods. These last-named methods were very popular, and the messages thus procured were called oracles. From this the place where the messages originated came to be called oracles also. Of these oracles there were many, specially among the Greeks.

Whenever a king made war or peace, enacted laws, changed the constitution, or did any other public act, the oracle was consulted. In private life also, marriage, business, a journey, building a house — all called for an expression by the oracle. The future has always held a deep interest for mankind, and as the gods were supposed to know the future, men would naturally seek to those who pretended to have intercourse with the gods. Hence the oracles became very popular.

In chapter forty God does not appeal to His power of prediction as proof that He is God. He refers to His creative power, His omnipotence, His tenderness, His faithfulness. In this present chapter, however, He condescends to the heathen's own idea of what a god should be able to do. First and foremost would be the idea of prediction. And God now challenges the heathen on their own ground. Let them tell the future, He says.

Cyrus, who is introduced in this chapter under the title of the "righteous man," is also called God's shepherd, the Lord's anointed.

16   *Isaiah, the Gospel Prophet*

Isa. 44:28; 45:1. These are strange titles to give to a king of whom there is uncertainty as to his even being a monotheist. However, in view of the work he accomplished and the part he had in restoring Israel to Palestine, God might well use these titles of him. Cyrus was God's instrument, His chosen, His anointed, to do a certain work.

Isaiah 41: 1-7. God's challenge to the nations.

God calls the people together to ask them concerning the one whom He will raise up, to whom He will give authority over the nations, who always is victorious, and who marches so swiftly that he does not tread the path with his feet. It is God who has done this. Verses 1-4.

When the people see this conqueror coming, they are afraid. They decide to appeal to their idols, and immediately set about to make some new gods to help them. Verses 5-7.

Verses 8-20. God's care for His people.

Israel is God's servant. They have been taken from the ends of the earth and are a chosen people. They need not fear, for God will uphold them. Their enemies shall be confounded and be as nothing. Verses 8-12.

God will help them, and though it may seem that they will be crushed as a worm when the mighty nations clash, they need not fear. God will not only protect them, but will use them to punish other nations. Verses 13-16.

God will not forsake His own. When they are thirsty, He will open fountains for them even in the wilderness, and make dry lands springs of water. This will be done in such a way that the hand of the Lord will be clearly seen. Verses 17-20.

Verses 21-29. God's challenge to the idols.

God calls upon the idols to produce evidence that they can predict future events. Have they anything to show that in the past they have foretold the future, and that the events really came to pass? Have they, in fact, done anything at all, good or evil? The idols in reality are nothing. Verses 21-24.

God will now do what He asks the idols to do. He will foretell the future. One, even Cyrus, shall come from the north and from the east. He shall call upon the Lord, and be successful in his career. Has any one predicted this? No, no idol has predicted it, nor announced it. The Lord is the first to proclaim it to Zion.

Jehovah's Challenge to False Gods

Among the idols there was no one to answer when the Lord challenged. They are all vanity. Verses 25-29.

Notes

Isaiah 41:1. "Keep silence." "Let them speak." God is speaking; let men keep silence; afterward they may speak.

Verse 2. "The righteous man," Cyrus. On the "Cyrus cylinder" he is called "the righteous prince," an interesting parallel. (See Goodspeed's "History of the Babylonians and Assyrians," page 375.)

Cyrus is one of the greatest men of history, "not only because of high personal character, but because of extraordinary powers of heart and intellect and will. Magnanimous, tolerant, wise, daring, he swayed men and nations with equal ease. He had a genius for evoking loyalty."—*Bailey and Kent's "Hebrew Commonwealth," page 268.*

"In his own land his name is still a household word. . . . No man outside the Greek and Roman world has been so much the theme of classical writers, historians, poets, and philosophers. No one outside of Israel has such a place in the Hebrew literature. . . . We may take for granted what may be called his Napoleonic qualities, force of will, energy, enterprise, versatility. But these are not the substance of his traditional reputation, which was that of a good rather than of a great man."

"Cyrus, Alexander, Cæsar, these three changed the face of the ancient world. Men of the after time, even more than men of their own day, have been awe-struck by the almost superhuman genius and force of these rulers of the race. . . . Such men can have no successors; and when they pass away, the world after them has to be made over again."—*McCurdy's "History, Prophecy, and the Monuments," Book II, pars. 1412, 1417.*

These words seem almost extravagant, yet history is a unit in imputing to Cyrus unusual virtues as well as extraordinary abilities. For the Bible student the chief interest lies in him as an instrument of God and as a subject of prophecy. More than a hundred years before his appearance God speaks of him. Later chapters bring out more fully the work he is to do in furthering Israel's return to Palestine, but already in this chapter the prediction of his appearance is used as a challenge to the false gods.

"From the east," "from the north," "from the rising of the sun," east.

Verse 25. Cyrus came from the east, went north of the Arabian desert to get to Palestine, hence came from both the north and the east.

Verses 2, 3. A paraphrase of these verses reads: "Who hath raised up one from the east who is always victorious? Who hath given him authority over the nations and made him rule over kings? His sword drives them like dust, his bow like chaff before the wind. He pursues them and marches forward safely, and that so swiftly that he does not tread the path with his feet."

The rapidity of Cyrus' movements and the vast extent of his conquests "admit of no doubt." "The space which he overran covered no less than fifty degrees of longitude, from the coast of Asia Minor to the Oxus and the Indus."—*Grote's "History of Greece," Vol. III, pp. 244, 248.*

Verses 5-7. "The ends of the earth were afraid." The nations became alarmed at the rapid conquests of Cyrus. Crœsus, the rich king of Lydia, consulted the oracle of Delphi, and received the answer that should he attack Cyrus he would destroy a great empire, which in this case proved to be his own. An alliance between Egypt, Babylon, and Lydia was formed, but Cyrus overcame them. In their perplexity the nations turned to the idols and oracles for help, and decided to make a "particularly good and strong set of gods." Having finished the making of the idols, all that remained was to fasten them with a nail, lest perhaps they should fall. The irony of this passage is patent.

Verse 9. "Chief men;" "corners," American Revised Version.

Verse 14. "Worm Jacob, and ye men of Israel;" "few men," margin.

"Thy Redeemer." Here used for the first time in Isaiah. The Hebrew word "Goel" is that used for the "nearest of kin" charged with the duty of buying back the forfeited property of a kinsman and of avenging his death. Lev. 25: 48, 49; Num. 35: 19 ff.; Ruth 3: 12. Thus our Redeemer must be one "near of kin." Christ, to save the "worm Jacob," became as "a worm, and no man." Ps. 22: 6.

Verses 15, 16. "Threshing instrument." This is a "heavy sledge studded on its under surface with sharp stones or knives, and drawn by oxen over the floor." Note the contrast: Jacob, meaning the people of Israel, has just been spoken of as a worm. Now that nation shall thresh mountains. These verses may have reference to the judgment. (See Dan. 2: 35; Matt. 3: 12.)

Verse 22. "Show the former things." Produce "past predictions which have already been verified by the event."

Verse 23. "Do good, or do evil." Do anything, whatever it may be, to show any sign of life or intelligence.

Verse 26. "He is righteous;" rather, "He is in the right."

Verse 27. Cheyne translates: "I, the first one, announced it to Zion." That is, the idols do not have power of prediction.

Verse 28. "No man," "no counselor." There was none among the idols who could advise or help in the present crisis.

Verse 29. "All of them," A. R. V. Both worshipers and idols, all of them, are nothing.

ORACLES.— The oracles became very influential institutions among the ancients. This was true of many, but especially of the oracle of Delphi, above referred to. A woman selected first among the young virgins, but later from the married class, known as the Pythoness, was the organ of inspiration. At certain stated seasons, after having first prepared herself by chewing some leaves of the sacred laurel and drinking water from an underground stream, she would seat herself on a tripod over a fissure in the earth from which ascended mystic vapors. These vapors would cause a kind of epileptic seizure, and under this influence she would utter unintelligible sounds which were taken down and interpreted by the priests who were seated about her and who already had in hand the questions to be answered. These answers were worded in ambiguous language, so that whichever way events turned out, the oracle would seem to have predicted it. The classical example of this is the instance mentioned above concerning Crœsus. When he asked the oracle if he would be victorious should he attack Cyrus, the answer came back that in doing so he would destroy a great empire. Thinking this meant Cyrus' empire, he attacked — and destroyed his own.

In the beginning of his reign, Crœsus had cast about to find which gods he should serve. The test he proposed was to ask all the oracles to tell him what he would be doing on a certain day. If they were able to disclose that, his confidence in them would be established. All the oracles were consulted, and the one at Delphi came nearest being correct.

This was a common method of procedure. The power of prediction was counted among the heathen as the supreme test of communication with the gods. God now condescends to be tested by their own standards. He predicts the coming of Cyrus, as yet nearly 150 years in the future. What can the oracles do to meet the challenge? Will they also predict something? The challenge in verse 23 is most impressive. At the close of the verse there is a pause, while God is waiting for the answer. But there is no answer. The idols are silent, and the silence is almost oppressive. It is eloquent with defeat. The idols are vanquished on their own ground and with their own weapons.

Lessons for To-day

Isaiah 41:1. "Keep silence," "then speak." It is always well to listen before speaking. Prov. 18:13.

Verse 4. "Calling the generations from the beginning," that is, guiding the destinies of men through all ages. God is still at the helm. Things do not run at loose ends. God was present at "the beginning." He is still "with the last." "I am with you alway, even unto the end of the world." Matt. 28:20.

Verses 6, 7. "Helped every one his neighbor." In this case they were making idols, but the spirit of helpfulness was present. "Be of good courage," said one to the other. This might be contrasted with the spirit of criticism manifested at times by those who should know better.

"So the carpenter encouraged the goldsmith," might be paraphrased: "So the elder encouraged the Sabbath school superintendent," or "the pastor encouraged the colporteur," or "the parents supported the church school teacher."

Note, they helped "every one." All are needed. Every little bit helps. No one must be a slacker.

We may think it strange that these people should resort to making idols to help them in their distress. They should have known that there is no help in an idol. But so should we know that there is no help in subterfuge, no strength in stimulants, no refuge in lies, no real pleasure in worldly amusements, no safety in human alliances.

Verses 8, 9. "My servant." We are called not merely to enjoy ourselves, or to special privileges, but to service. "I have chosen thee." God has picked us out for service. He has a place for us. It is honorable, useful service.

"My friend." The servants are also friends. (See John 15:14, 15.) They are really friends that serve. Christ was Master and Lord, yet He served. (See John 13:13, 14.) So we are not servants, but friends who serve, friends of God. What a wonderful privilege!

Verse 10. As the small boy feels safe when his big brother is with him, so we are safe in the promise: "I am with thee." Note, "I am with thee," "I am thy God," "I will strengthen thee," "I will help thee," "I will uphold thee."

Verses 14-16. "Worm;" "few men," margin. God's people may never be many. They may not seem strong. It may look as if they could be trodden underfoot easily. But God is their helper. He will make them a new threshing instrument, and "thresh the mountains" (nations) with them.

That has been true of nations in the past. Egypt went through a severe "threshing" before Israel was let go. So have the other great nations that were unduly severe with God's people.

Within a smaller sphere how often have not the enemies of God's truth determined to crush all opposition! And how often has not God turned their hatred into victory for His people! The little hated sect, how easy to crush them and their arguments as you crush a worm! But it is not so easily done. One valiant man to-day, alone against all the prophets of Baal and Astarte, as was Elijah of old, has "threshed" many a Goliath who defied the armies of the living God. We shall see more of this in the future. Evolution and science falsely so called will give God and His people unparalleled opportunities to proclaim the truth and "beat them small."

Verse 17. This power, however, can only be entrusted to a people who themselves feel their need and poverty. When "the poor and needy seek water, . . . the God of Israel will not forsake them." The self-sufficient, the boastful, the proud, have no such promise. Let every one beware of putting his trust in arguments rather than in the living God.

Verses 18-20. These verses present the results that will come when God's people seek Him. The wilderness and the desert — places that appear most unpromising — shall bring forth of the choicest. Seven kinds of trees, here symbolical of the people that will be attracted by the message, shall spring up from unexpected sources.

CHAPTER III

The Elect of God; A Light to the Gentiles

Lesson Scripture: Isaiah 42

THE word "servant" in this chapter is held by the critics not to refer to Christ. This would not need to disturb us, were it not for the fact that many well-meaning Christians accept statements made by such men as the latest result of ripe scholarship which cannot be refuted, and hence must be believed. A few words may therefore be in order.

We do not contend that every time the phrase "servant of God" or "servant of the Lord" is used it refers to Christ. On the contrary, we find that Jeremiah speaks of Nebuchadnezzar as God's servant. Jer. 25:9; 27:6. Jacob also is so named. Isa. 45:4; 44:1. So are Israel and David. Isa. 41:8; 37:35. In fact, any one who, wittingly or unwittingly, is part of God's plan and does His bidding, may rightly be named God's servant.

In these verses, however, we do not have an ordinary servant to deal with. While some of the expressions might indeed refer to a faithful human servant, others can be predicated only of the Divine One. Of whom, other than Christ, has it ever been, or can ever be, true that He did "not fail"? Verse 4. Of whom, other than Christ, can it be said that the isles "wait for His law"? Verse 4. Of whom, other than Christ, can it be said so truly that He was "a covenant of the people"? Verse 6. Are not the expressions, "He shall bring forth judgment unto truth" (verse 3), called "in righteousness" (verse 6), "set judgment in the earth" (verse 4), applicable to Christ and none else? The Servant here mentioned is God's "Elect;" God's Spirit is upon Him; and He "delights" in Him. Verse 1. God keeps Him and holds His hand. Verse 6. He opens the eyes of the blind, and frees the prisoners that sit in darkness. Verse 7. As *all* these statements fit the character and work of Christ, and as many of them could not possibly fit any one else, we conclude that the Servant spoken of in these verses is the Lord Christ Jesus.

Letting the context and the plain reading of the word decide the question, we conclude that of the twenty times the word "servant" is mentioned in Isaiah, in chapters 41-53, nine times in chapter 41:8, 9; 44:1, 2, 21; 45:4; 48:20; 49:3, it refers to Israel or Jacob; six times in chapter 42:1; 49:5, 7; 50:10; 52:13; 53:11, it refers to Christ; and five times in 42:19; 43:10; 44:26; 49:6, it may refer to both Christ and the people.

It is interesting to note that the title, "Servant of the Lord," though it occurs twenty times in these chapters, disappears entirely after chapter 53:11. Instead another title appears, which has not occurred before, "Servants of the Lord." The "Servant" disappears, and the "servants" take the place. This title is used ten times in chapters 54-66. We can hardly believe it to be merely a happening that this should be so. In chapter 53 we have Christ's suffering and death portrayed. He sees there "the travail of His soul," He sees "His seed." Verses 11, 10. How fitting, then, that as the "Servant" dies, the "servants" should take His place and carry on His work.

Isaiah 42: 1-9. The calling, equipment, and mission of the Servant.

Christ is here spoken of as the "Elect, in whom My soul delighteth." This calls to mind the voice from heaven which at Christ's baptism proclaimed, "This is My beloved Son, in whom I am well pleased." Matt. 3:17.

God's Spirit will be upon Christ, and His message will be sounded, not merely to the Jews, but also to the Gentiles. Verse 1.

This mighty work is not to be with outward pomp and ceremony. The Servant will quietly go about His work, and will neither cry nor lift up His voice to draw attention to Himself. Verse 2.

He will show great consideration and sympathy for the weak and discouraged, and will work for them as long as there is the least hope. Though the outlook is not always bright, He will not give up. He will accomplish His task of bringing the true religion to the whole earth, and far-off places will wait for His instruction. Verses 3, 4.

The true God has called the Servant in righteousness to do His work, and will sustain and keep Him. He will give Him "for a covenant of the people, and for a light of the Gentiles." The blind shall receive their sight, and prisoners shall be given their freedom. The Lord will not yield His glory and praise to any graven idol. He has declared beforehand what shall come to pass. Verses 5-9.

24 *Isaiah, the Gospel Prophet*

Verses 10-17. A new song unto the Lord.

Let the whole earth unite in a song of praise unto the Lord. Let the seafaring men and those that dwell in far-off lands repeat the chorus. Let the wilderness and the cities join in. Let those that dwell in solitary places and in the mountains make their voices heard. Verses 10-12.

The reason they are thus to sing praises is that the Lord is about to vindicate Himself against His enemies. For a long time He has remained quiet and said nothing when they exulted, but now the time has come when He will refrain Himself no longer. Verses 13, 14.

He will make waste the mountains, and dry up the rivers and pools; that is, He will destroy His enemies. Those, however, who are blind He will tenderly lead to the light. That which seemed to them crooked, He will make straight. On the other hand, they that trust in graven images will be turned back and be ashamed. Verses 15-17.

Verses 18-25. A call to the deaf and blind.

This call invites the people to consider two great facts: first, the Servant of God through whom the law is to be magnified; and second, their own condition and the reason for it.

God's Servant has seen and heard "many things," but not laid them to heart. And "the Lord is well pleased." "He will magnify the law, and make it honorable." Verses 18-21.

The people are in a pitiable condition. They are "hid in prison houses," and have none to deliver them. The Lord has permitted this because the people "would not walk in His ways" nor keep His law. God's anger has been poured out upon them, but they "laid it not to heart." Verses 22-25.

Notes

Isaiah 42:1. "My servant," Christ. Matt. 12:18.

"Whom I uphold." Christ, who upholds all things, is Himself upheld by the Father. Heb. 1:3.

"Put My Spirit upon Him." Luke 2:40; 3:22; 4:18-21.

"Bring forth judgment to the Gentiles." The word "judgment," while meaning literally "judicial decisions," is here used in a special and larger sense. "It means the religion of Jehovah regarded as a system of practical ordinances."—*Cambridge Bible.* Hence Moffatt translates: "Carry true religion to the nations."

Verse 2. For a commentary on this verse, see Matt. 12: 15-19.

Verse 3. "Bruised reed," such as are weak, broken, dejected. "Smoking flax;" rather, "dimly burning wick." A. R. V.

Verse 4. "He shall not fail." The word for "fail" here is "dimly burning," the same word as in verse 3.

"Discouraged," bruised, the same word as in verse 3.

The meaning therefore is that Christ's light will not burn dimly, nor will He show any of that weakness which He compassionates in others.

"Judgment." See verse 1.

"Wait for," rather "long for."

Verse 5. "God the Lord." Hebrew, the God; that is, the God who alone is truly God.

"That which cometh out of it," vegetation and minerals.

God has created, according to this verse, first the inanimate, the earth; second, vegetation, "that which cometh out of it;" and third, life itself, breath and spirit.

Verse 6. "A covenant." Christ is the mediator of the new covenant, also the surety of it. Heb. 8:6; 7:22. Here He is called the covenant itself. The old covenant was between God and Israel. Christ, being both God and man, combines in Himself the two contracting parties, hence He is not only the mediator of the new covenant, He *is* the covenant.

Verse 9. "The former things are come to pass." That which had been prophesied before had all been fulfilled. This should cause them to have faith in future predictions.

Verse 11. "Kedar," probably the Arabs.

"Inhabitants of the rock" (A. R. V.), "the inhabitants of Sela," or Petra, the capital city of Edom. Isa. 16:1.

Verse 13. "Mighty man," "a man of war."

"Stir up jealousy," His own. God is a jealous God. Ex. 20:5. His name is "Jealous." Ex. 34:14. He will no longer permit His glory and praise to be given to graven images. Verses 8, 12.

Verse 14. "Long time;" literally, "for an eternity." Same word as "evermore" in 1 Chronicles 17:14; Psalms 18:50, etc.

"I will destroy and devour at once." "I will gasp and pant," A. R. V. A strong expression, showing God's deep emotion at the "strange work" He is about to do.

Verse 15. "Make waste mountains," destroy the mighty ones of earth. The result of God's stirring up His "jealousy" will be the destruction of worldly kings and kingdoms.

Verse 16. " The blind," the spiritually blind, but honest in heart, God will cause to see the light.

Verse 17. Verses 16 and 17 should be contrasted. The honest, though blind, God will lead. Those that trust in graven images " shall be turned back," literally " driven back " in confusion and defeat.

Verse 19. " My messenger." (Cf. Mal. 3: 1.) " He that is perfect." " He that is at peace with Me," A. R. V. It may also mean " the surrendered One." These expressions would seem to have definite reference to Christ, though it should not be forgotten that they may also apply to " any one that the Lord may select and appoint to do a certain work."—" *Testimonies," Vol. IX, page 138.*

Verse 21. " Magnify the law." (See Matt. 5: 17-48.) " Make it honorable; " margin, " make Him honorable."

Verses 22-25. If Israel had kept the law and permitted God to magnify it in their lives, God would indeed have made a great nation of them. Now they are " a people robbed and spoiled " because " they would not walk in His ways, neither were they obedient unto His law." The Lord permitted this to come to them because they had sinned against Him.

Lessons for To-day

Isaiah 42: 1. God delights in His Son, He is well pleased with Him. May the same be said of us.

Verse 2. Mighty powers are often silent. The tremendous energy of the sun, the all-pervading law of gravitation, the abounding life forces of vegetable and animal growth, the mysterious electricity, the powerful tides,— all these are silent forces. So in the spiritual and intellectual realms. Thought, conscience, will — what mighty forces and what silent ones! Christ's work was not spectacular. Neither should ours be.

Verse 3. " A bruised reed," how valueless! A bruised life, a challenge to the power of God! Even as a skillful surgeon covets a difficult case that his skill may be apparent to all, so God covets the opportunity of showing what He can do with a poor, bruised soul. In this He asks our co-operation. We all need to take Matthew 9: 13 to heart.

Verse 4. If any one ever had an apparently hopeless task, it was Christ. He came to this world to reveal the Father, but His own received Him not. Being most temperate in all things, He was accused of being a glutton and a winebibber. Matt. 11: 19.

Being most upright, He was accused of deceiving the people. John 7:12. Being most reverent, he was accused of blasphemy. John 10:33. His neighbors attempted to throw Him over a precipice to kill Him. Luke 4:28-30. One of the twelve sold Him to His enemies for thirty pieces of silver. Matt. 26:15. His own kinsmen believed Him insane. Mark 3:21. The twelve upon whom He depended to carry on His work after Him, so far failed to comprehend His mission that at the close of His ministry there was strife among them as to who should be the greatest. Mark 9:33-37. Of a truth, if any one ever had reason to be discouraged, Christ had. In view of this, how marvelous are the words: "He shall not fail nor be discouraged." Can there be any conceivable circumstances under which we should be discouraged or talk of failure if Christ was not downcast?

Verse 6. The same promises given to Christ, hold for us. Note, "I have called," "and will hold," "and will keep," "and give." Blessed promises! Note also that God will hold our hand, not that we hold His. There is a difference.

Verse 7. In a minor way the work given to Christ is given to us.

Verse 8. This verse harmonizes with Revelation 14:7. We are to give glory to God, not to man or science.

Verse 16. This verse should be an encouragement to all. We sometimes wonder why certain people do not see and accept the truth. To us it seems so plain that we are almost tempted to doubt their honesty. This verse tells us that the time will come when God "will lead them in paths that they have not known." That which has been obscure to them will be made light, and that which has seemed crooked will be made straight. Is there a gentle suggestion in the latter part of the verse that if God does not forsake them, neither should we? Have we been too quick in thinking that people have rejected the truth because they have not moved as fast as we think they should? If God has not forsaken them, neither should we.

Verses 19, 20. It is well at times not to notice all we see. The teacher in school must sometimes be both blind and deaf. The parents at home will find occasions when they must overlook or appear not to notice certain things. In the world we are constantly confronted with sounds and sights to which we must be deaf and blind.

So in our Christian experience. We will be spoken against; let us not notice it. Temptation may be whispered to us; let us turn a deaf ear. Evil reports will clamor for attention; let us not listen. Impure thoughts and words will intrude; let us banish them.

There are many things in the world which we cannot avoid hearing and seeing. We can, however, refrain from having them make an impression on us. Even as we need to pray God to help us remember that which ought to be remembered, so also we need to pray God to help us forget some of the things which we see and hear. It is as important to learn to forget as to learn to remember.

Verse 21. The law is not magnified by argument, but by life. The beauty and virtue of a law is seen in its workings. The law of God condemns sin, and demands purity of life. Hence the life is the revealing and magnifying of the law.

CHAPTER IV

The Gathering of Israel -- Witnesses for God
Lesson Scripture: Isaiah 43

Isaiah 43: 1-7. Israel ransomed and restored.

THIS section is closely connected with the last part of the previous chapter. The connection, however, is both a strange and an interesting one.

The Lord has plainly told Israel that He is the author of their calamities. Isa. 42:24. They have not been obedient nor kept His law, and this is the reason of the Lord's anger. It would be natural to expect God to say that because of this they had been cut off, and that there was no salvation for them. On the contrary, the Lord now assures them of His continued good will, that He will protect them, that He loves them, that they are so precious in His sight that He will give both men and nations to redeem them, and that He will gather them from the ends of the earth.

In the next section, verses 8-28, the prophet brings clearly to view one of his fundamental teachings, namely, that God's people are His witnesses. The significance of this should not escape us. Witnesses are used or summoned in a trial. The question at issue here is: "Who is the true God?" The nations are challenged to bring their witnesses, and God will bring His. On the testimony of these witnesses hangs the case.

A witness may tell only that which he knows. He may not relate hearsay. He may not preach a sermon. He may strictly adhere to the one thing only: his own experience. If *you* were put on the witness stand and restricted to these rules, how would you prove God to be the true God?

The rest of the chapter deals with the prediction of Babylon's fall and God's provision for leading His people out of Babylon, as in former times He brought Israel out of Egypt, and ends with a reproof of and promise to Israel.

God is addressing Jacob and Israel. He has punished them (Isa. 42: 24, 25), now He comforts them. God has redeemed them, they bear His name, they belong to Him. Whether they pass through water or through fire, God will be with them. He is their Saviour, and considers them worth more than great nations. He loves them. Verses 1-4.

He will gather them from the east and from the west, every one. None shall be missing. They were created for God's glory. Verses 5-7.

Verses 8-13. Witnesses for God.

God calls upon all nations to assemble, and challenges them to produce proof of their power of prediction. Let them bring forth their witnesses, He says, and prove their contention; or if they cannot do this, let them accept the testimony of His witnesses.

God's people are His witnesses that He is God. He is the self-existent One. There was none before Him, nor shall there be any after. He is the Lord, and besides Him there is no Saviour.

Verses 14-21. A declaration against Babylon and the promise of a " new thing."

God now proceeds to explain two things that He is about to do. He will humble Babylon and bring down all their nobles to be fugitives. Verse 14. As God formerly destroyed Pharaoh and his host, so now Babylon shall be destroyed. "The army and the power; they shall lie down together, they shall not rise: they are extinct, they are quenched as tow." Verse 17.

The second thing, the "new thing," God will do, is to make a way in the wilderness for His people. This deliverance shall be so much greater than the deliverance from Egypt that they shall not remember the former experience. Verse 18.

Verses 22-28. Remonstrances and Promises.

In spite of all that God has done for Israel, they have not appreciated His goodness. They have wearied of God, and have not brought Him their offerings as they should. He has not exacted much of them, but even the little that would have satisfied Him they have refused. Even as they are weary of God, so He is weary with their sins. Verses 22-24.

Instead of scolding them, however, God now gives them one of the most glorious promises in the whole Bible. He not only forgives all their transgressions, but blots out their sins, and remembers them no more. He counsels them to put Him in mind of His promise. Verses 25, 26.

The people have nothing to plead why they should be so well treated. Their fathers and leaders have sinned from the very beginning. Because of this, God has punished both the priest and the people. Verses 27, 28.

Notes

Isaiah 43: 1. "But now," introducing the contrast to the verse before, Isaiah 42: 25.

Note, "created thee," "formed thee," "redeemed thee," "called thee,"— an ascending scale. First creation of matter; then forming man of the dust of the ground; then the fall and consequent redemption; and last the calling by name, even the new name that is ours by reason of redemption. Rev. 3: 12. We belong to God by reason of each of these four steps. Hence God says, "Thou art Mine."

Verse 2. "Walkest through the fire." (See Daniel 3.)

Verse 3. "I gave Egypt for thy ransom;" rather, "I give." Commentators agree the meaning to be that Egypt, Ethiopia, and Seba would be given to the Persians as a reward for letting Israel return to their own land. These lands were actually annexed by Cambyses, the son and successor of Cyrus. It seems more reasonable, however, to think that it is an expression of God to show that He thinks more of His people than of all Egypt, Ethiopia, and Seba together; that is, that their worth cannot be computed in money.

Verse 4. This verse might be rendered: "So precious art thou to Me, so honorable, so beloved, that I will give men for thee, and nations for thy life." God so loved the world that He spared nothing, but freely gave the best He had, even His Son. John 3: 16.

Note, "I have created him," "I have formed him," "I have made him." "The three verbs describe the process of formation from the first rough cutting to the perfecting of the work."— *Cheyne.* The third verb would, perhaps, best be translated, "I have perfected." All three acts — creation, formation, completion — are done by God for His own glory.

Verses 8, 9. "Bring forth the blind," "let all the nations be gathered together." The picture here presented is that of a tribunal before which the whole world is called. Who can "show us former things"? that is, can the nations or any one show by well-attested documents where they have made predictions that have been fulfilled? If so, let them bring forth their witnesses. If they cannot, let them hear the record of what God has done, and they will be compelled to admit their truth.

32   *Isaiah, the Gospel Prophet*

Verse 10. "Ye are My Witnesses." This was spoken to the Jews. Their whole history is a testimony to the truthfulness of God's predictions. From the very first they were subjects of prophecy, and step by step they have proved God's prophecies true.

It was prophesied that Israel should go down into Egypt, that they should be afflicted, but that they also should be brought out again. Gen. 15: 13-16. This was exactly fulfilled, even to the "selfsame day." Ex. 12: 41.

Samuel gave the people an exact description of what would happen if they rejected the Lord and chose a king. 1 Sam. 8: 10-18. This was abundantly fulfilled in their later history.

God told Solomon that He would "rend the kingdom" from him in the time of his son, which came to pass. 1 Kings 11: 11-13, 31.

Jeroboam did evil in the sight of God, and he was told what would happen because of it. 1 Kings 14:7-16. This was fulfilled even to the detail of the dogs eating the flesh. 1 Kings 14: 11; 21: 23, 24; 2 Kings 9: 36, 37.

God foretold of Israel's going in captivity. That was fulfilled in 721 B. C. 2 Kings 17: 23.

In fact, all the history of Israel was a witness to the truthfulness of God's predictions. "The Jews, therefore, are a kind of standing miracle, being a monument of the wonderful fulfillment of the most extraordinary prophecies ever delivered, which prophecies they themselves preserve and bear witness to, though they shut their eyes to the fulfillment of them."—*Archbishop Whately's "Evidences," pp. 89, 90.*

Verse 12. "I have declared" (beforehand what I would do) "and have saved" (in accordance with that declaration), "and I have showed" (announced or proclaimed or proved it). God has done what the idols could not do. He told beforehand just what He would do, and did it.

"Therefore ye are My witnesses." That is, your own history and testimony prove the truth of what I have said.

Verse 13. "Before the day was," that is, "since time began." "Who shall let it?" or, "Who shall turn it back," or reverse it, or undo it?

Verse 14. "I have sent," or "I will send," Septuagint.

"Have brought," or "will bring," A. R. V.

The American Revised Version translates the latter part of the verse: "I will bring down all of them as fugitives, even the Chaldeans, in the ships of their rejoicing." The sense seems to be that Babylon shall be taken, as it was by Cyrus, and that the nobles shall be carried as fugitives in the very boats they have used for their pleasure excursions. "Whose cry is in the ships," "ships of their rejoicing" (A. R. V.), pleasure boats.

Verse 16. "A way in the sea." The reference is to the deliverance from Egypt, when Israel marched through the Red Sea.

Verse 18. "Remember ye not the former things." This does not, of course, mean that they are to forget what the Lord has done for them, but rather that their minds must not be on the past to the extent that they forget that God is still able to do and will do great things for them.

Verses 19-21. We are not told what the "new thing" is, beyond the statement that it is "a way in the wilderness" and that God will provide water and "give drink to My people, My chosen," and that as a result the people "shall show forth My praise." As the preceding verses have mentioned the fall of Babylon and referred to the going out of Egypt, and as this is a "new thing" of such great importance that the "former things" should not be remembered, we conclude that it stands for a greater deliverance than either of these two events, and that therefore it has reference to the spiritual deliverance through Christ.

Verses 22-24. Note the three statements: "Thou hast been weary of Me;" "I have not . . . wearied thee;" "thou hast wearied Me." God is not reproaching His people for not having brought their offerings, but is merely stating the true situation. The thing that made this serious, however, was the fact that even as they had not brought any offerings, neither had they called on the Lord. This was a serious condition.

"Made Me to serve with thy sins." There is no power but of God. When we sin, we prostitute the powers God has given us.

Verses 27, 28. "Thy first father," Adam.

"Thy teachers," the same as the "princes of the sanctuary." All these have sinned and been punished. Israel deserves the same punishment and more, yet God will be merciful to them.

Lessons for To-day

Isaiah 43:1. "Fear not: for I have redeemed thee." If we have paid a great price for an article, we value it highly, and are anxious that it shall not be lost and that no harm shall come to it. Christ has paid a great price for us, we belong to Him, He has bought us,

34   *Isaiah, the Gospel Prophet*

and He will see to it that no harm shall come to us. Hence we need not fear.

Verse 2. God sometimes saves from trouble, but often He permits the waters of affliction to come even to the soul. Daniel was not saved from the lions' den, but in it. So when we pass "through the waters," God will be with us. The promise here is not that God will save us from the waters, but that He will be with us. And so when financial losses come; when sore disappointments in ourselves and others threaten to overwhelm us; when sickness and sorrow knock at the door; when old age, dependency, and death stare us in the face,— at such times the promise, "I will be with thee," becomes very precious.

Verses 3, 4. "I gave Egypt. . . . I give men for thee." God's people are very precious in His sight, for He has paid a great ransom for them. These terms are here used to give Israel an idea of how much He valued them. In Christ we have an even higher valuation.

Verses 5-7. God's people will be gathered from all parts of the earth, east, west, north, south. Matt. 8:11. That is the great meeting to which we are looking forward.

"Every one that is called by My name." Only those will be called who belong to the family, who bear the name. The question is not one of being red or brown, white or black, male or female, but of having the Father's name. (See Rev. 14:1.)

Verse 10. "Ye are My witnesses." Israel were God's witnesses. So are we. "Ye shall receive power, . . . and ye shall be witnesses unto Me." Acts 1:8. A preacher or a layman must first of all be a witness himself to the mighty power of God before he can recommend it to others.

A witness is one who has had a personal experience. When he testifies, he does not tell what he has heard or read, or what he thinks or surmises. He tells only that which he knows, that which he has seen with his own eyes. John 3:11; 1 John 1:1-3. If a minister therefore speaks on conversion, or on the power of God or His love, he must in his own life have experienced conversion and the power and love of God, or he cannot be a witness to the things he preaches.

But this applies not to the ministers only. "Ye" are My witnesses. That means *you*, every one. And before any one condemns any one else, let him look to his own case.

The Gathering of Israel — Witnesses for God

A witness is under oath to tell the truth, the whole truth, and nothing but the truth. Does your life bear witness to the truth you profess? When you speak of creation, not evolution, have you the witness of creative power in your own life, or is your argument a theory of creation rather than a witness to creation? What is your testimony as to Bible study, tithe paying, Sabbath keeping, prayer, sanctification, in the light of witnessing rather than of argument? God desires "truth in the inward parts," the heart, rather than in the mouth. Ps. 51:6. Only such truths as have been translated into life, are ours.

Verse 13. "Who shall let it?" Who shall hinder it? Balaam tried to curse Israel, but could not. Numbers 22 to 24. Pharaoh tried to keep Israel in Egypt, but could not. Exodus 5 to 12. Satan tried to keep Moses in the tomb, but could not. Jude 9. Whatever God sets out to do, that He does. God will finish His work in the earth on time. Rom. 9:28. None can hinder Him. God will build His church, and the gates of hell shall not prevail against it. Matt. 16:18. God, who is both the author and finisher of our faith and who has begun in us the good work, will also finish it. Heb. 12:2; Phil. 1:6, margin.

Verse 16. "A way in the sea, and a path." A path might be made almost anywhere else on earth easier than in the sea. God chooses that which we think hard, to encourage our faith. If God can make a path in the sea, if He can dry it up if need be so His people can walk over dry shod, "is anything too hard for the Lord?" The God who did this is our God.

Verses 22-24. "Not called upon Me." This is a justifiable complaint of God's. We do not call upon Him, we do not pray, as we ought. We may have good excuse for not being able to give as we should like to. We may not be able to work as we should like to. But it will be harder to find any excuse for not praying as we should. And if we do not do that which we can do, are we sure we would do that which we say we would like to do if we had the opportunity?

"Weary of Me." Are we getting weary of God's service,— weary of the prayer meeting, of the missionary service, perhaps even of the preaching? weary of the many calls and campaigns and offerings? weary of asking others to do what they ought to do without urging? Weary of Christ's long-delayed coming? Weary of the long journey which we had hoped would end long before this? Remember, dear one, God has borne a long while with you. Remember also that we are nearing the journey's end. You your-

36   *Isaiah, the Gospel Prophet*

self have made God weary many times. Verse 24. Now bear with patience that which comes to you. God loves you and cares for you. Hold out a little longer.

Verse 25. "Will not remember." We suppose God *could* remember if He wanted to, but He *will* not. Sometimes the question is asked if God knows all things. To that the answer is, There is nothing hid from God. He knows all things, *if He wants to know them.* But there are some things He does not want to know. And there are some things He does not want to remember.

CHAPTER V

The True God; Vanity of Idols; Cyrus the Shepherd

Lesson Scripture: Isaiah 44; 45: 1-4

Isaiah 44: 1-5. The outpouring of God's Spirit.

God, addressing Jacob and Israel, announces the outpouring of the Spirit upon their seed and upon their offspring. Verses 1-3. This refreshing will be so abundant that others not of Israel will be affected and join the people of God. Verses 4, 5.

Verses 6-8. The true God.

The King of Israel is also the Lord of hosts, the only God. He is the first and the last; there is no other. Verse 6. He is the only one that can declare the future long before it comes to pass. Therefore the people need not be afraid. God has foretold what is coming, and they are His witnesses. Verses 7, 8.

Verses 9-20. The vanity of idols.

Those that make graven images are wanting in understanding. Their images cannot profit them. How can any one be so foolish as to make an idol? Verses 9, 10.

How can men think that they can produce a god? If they all come together, they are still but men, and shall be ashamed. The smith does his work with tongs and hammer. He is strong, but he is only a man, and soon gets hungry and thirsty. Verses 11, 12. The carpenter uses his rule and plane and compass, and marks out the figure of a man. He cuts down the trees necessary for his idol. A part of the trees he will use for warmth, another part for baking his bread and roasting meat, and another part he will worship as a god, praying to it, " Deliver me." Verses 13-17.

Such men have no knowledge or understanding. Their eyes are bedaubed so they cannot see, and their minds are closed to knowledge. If they but considered, they would see the folly of using part of the wood to burn in roasting flesh, and worshiping the other part. Such are feeding on ashes. It is only a deceived heart that cannot see the folly of this. Verses 18-20.

Verses 21-23. An admonition, a promise, a song of praise.

Israel must remember this, for he is the Lord's servant, and shall not be forgotten of God, who has blotted out his transgressions and sins and redeemed him. Verses 21, 22. Let the heavens and the earth rejoice over this, let the mountains and the forest break forth into singing. Verse 23.

Verses 24-28; 45: 1-4. Cyrus the shepherd.

The Lord again calls attention to the fact that He is the Creator of heaven and earth. He confounds the signs of the boasters, and makes sport of the diviners; He turns the wisdom of the wise men into folly. On the other hand, He confirms the word of His servant and of His messengers. He says that Jerusalem shall be built and the waste places restored. Verses 24-26.

Cyrus is the Lord's shepherd, and he shall perform the Lord's will. He shall command that both Jerusalem and the temple be built. Verse 28. Cyrus is also the Lord's anointed. God holds his hand, and will open the way. Isa. 45: 1. The gates of brass and the bars of iron shall God cut in sunder for him, and shall reveal to him treasures and hidden riches so that he may know that the God of Israel is doing it. Verses 2, 3. God is doing this for His people's sake. He has even called Cyrus by name, though Cyrus has not known the Lord. Verse 4.

Notes

Isaiah 44: 1. The last verse of the previous chapter states that God has "given Jacob to the curse, and Israel to reproaches." "Yet now," do not be discouraged. All is not lost. Not all of Jacob or of Israel is to be condemned.

Verse 2. "The Lord . . . will help thee; fear not." Blessed promise!

"Jeshurun," the "upright one," an endearing term, used only here and in Deuteronomy 32: 15; 33: 5, 26.

Verse 3. "Water," "floods," "Spirit," "blessing." These four words denote the outpouring of the Spirit "in rich measure." Note that it comes only upon "the thirsty," the "dry ground." Matt. 5: 6.

Verse 4. "As among the grass, as willows." Grass in chapter 40: 6-8 denotes frail mankind. The idea here seems to be that the outpouring of the Spirit shall cause those to take their stand who previously have been held back by fear of man. "A compelling power moved the honest, while the manifestation of the power of God brought a fear and restraint upon their unbelieving relatives

Verse 5. This speaks of the work of God among the Gentiles, that many shall say, "I am the Lord's." "Subscribe," literally, "inscribe his hand 'To Jehovah;'" that is, dedicate his service to the Lord.

"Surname himself;" "give for a title the name of Israel," A. R. V., margin; that is, be proud that he may belong to God's people, counting it as a title.

Verse 6. The first and the last, Alpha and Omega. Rev. 1:8, 17.

Verse 7. A paraphrase might read: " Who can do what I do,— call events into being, declare them and set them in order beforehand — who can do this for Me or in My stead? No one. I have done it from the very beginning. Now let some one declare what is in the future, events that will really come to pass."

Verse 8. "From that time," "from of old," from the beginning. "No God;" "no Rock," margin.

Verse 9. "Vanity," literally "chaos," confusion, lacking in understanding.

"Delectable things," objects in which they delight, idols.

"Their own witnesses," they testify against themselves.

Verse 10. "Who is there?" that is, "Can there be any so foolish as to do this?"

Verse 11. "His fellows," all those engaged in the worship of an idol.

"They are of men," they are but human.

Verse 12. The smith, though he be strong, yet will he soon faint from thirst and hunger.

Verse 16. The carpenter also becomes cold and exhausted, and needs warmth and refreshment. Can these who are human produce a god?

Verse 18. Any one who thinks so, certainly has no understanding; his eyes are "daubed" (margin), so he cannot see.

Verse 20. "He feedeth on ashes." Surely not a very nourishing diet. Yet on such do they live who do not worship the living God.

"A deceived heart." Fearful words!

"He cannot deliver his soul." There is no salvation apart from God.

Verse 21. "Remember these." Remember the instruction just given concerning the futility of trusting to a deceived heart, or to anything or any one but God.

Verse 24. "Stretcheth forth the heavens alone; that spreadeth abroad the earth by Myself." God uses angels to do many things. Some things He does Himself, personally. Among these is the making of the heavens and the earth.

Verse 25. "The tokens of the liars." God brings to naught the prognostication of astrologers and soothsayers. "Maketh diviners mad," that is, shows them to be fools and madmen. (See Job 12:17.)

"Turneth wise-men backward," shows their pretended wisdom to be folly.

Verse 28. "Saith of Cyrus, He is My shepherd." The only other instance of a person's being prophesied of by name long before his birth, is that of Josiah. 1 Kings 13:2.

"My shepherd." The ten tribes had already been carried into captivity previous to this writing. The other two would soon follow. God would cause Cyrus to gather His people together and send them back to their own land. "Even saying to Jerusalem, Thou shalt be built; and to the temple, Thy foundation shall be laid."

There can be no reasonable doubt that Cyrus issued his edict for the building of the temple at Jerusalem after having read these verses in Isaiah. Note the reading in Ezra 1:2: "Thus saith Cyrus king of Persia, The Lord God of heaven hath given me all the kingdoms of the earth; and He hath charged me to build Him a house at Jerusalem, which is in Judah. Who is there among you of all His people? his God be with him, and let him go up to Jerusalem, which is in Judah, and build the house of the Lord God of Israel, (He is the God,) which is in Jerusalem."

Where did Cyrus get the wording of the edict or the idea, if not from Isaiah 44:24-28? This is the only way his language can be accounted for. "The Persians were systematically opposed to the practice of worshiping in temples; so that very strong inducement would be needed to make Cyrus issue such a decree."— *Kay's "Introduction," p. 8.* When Cyrus in the decree says: "The Lord God of heaven hath . . . charged me to build Him a house at Jerusalem," and the only authority for such a statement is found in Isaiah 44, the burden of proof must rest upon those who deny the authenticity of the record. Josephus, in his "Antiquities," book XI, par. 1, mentions this very thing as being the common belief among the Jews at his time.

Isaiah 45:1. "His anointed." It must be admitted that some extraordinary titles are used of Cyrus, specially as he was not an Israelite. We have mentioned before the unusual character of the

The True God; Vanity of Idols; Cyrus the Shepherd

man, that he was both kindly and gracious, with many enviable traits, and that his ability was unquestioned. All these, however, would not weigh heavily with God were it not for the fact that the Lord had a work for him to do. Cyrus overthrew Babylon in 538 B. C., and two years later became its king. After Cyrus had read the record of himself in Isaiah, "his heart was profoundly moved, and he determined to fulfill his divinely appointed mission." —"*Prophets and Kings," p. 557.*

As Cyrus thus overthrew Babylon, and as he also liberated God's people from their bondage, he becomes in some sense a type of Him who overthrew mystical Babylon, the kingdom of darkness, and told His people to go out thereof.

"Whose right hand I have holden," rather, "strengthened."

"Loose the loins of kings," that is, render them weak and incapable of resistance. (See Dan. 5:6.)

"The two-leaved gates." Herodotus tells us that the gates of Babylon were of brass. The night of the attack they were left unbarred.

Verse 3. "Treasures of darkness," "hidden riches." Probably the references here are to the treasures of Babylon, the golden city (Jer. 51:7, 13), and those of Crœsus, the latter of which were estimated at $630,000,000 — an enormous sum in those days.

Verse 4. "I have surnamed thee," that is, given Cyrus such honorable titles as "Shepherd," "My anointed."

"Though thou," or "while thou." We have no record that Cyrus ever accepted Jehovah as his God.

Lessons for To-day

Isaiah 44: 1, 2. Note the three names: Jacob, My servant; Israel, My chosen; Jeshurun, the upright one, that is, the righteous one. We are, first Jacob, then Israel, then Jeshurun.

Verses 3, 4. The outpouring of the Spirit. Water is the symbol used. Note some of the qualities of water:

It is common and abundant.
It is absolutely necessary to life.
It is cleansing, purifying.
It is refreshing and satisfying.

All these qualities can be transferred spiritually to God's grace, and applied to the outpouring of the Spirit.

Thirst is one of the strongest cravings in the body. A man who is thirsty simply *must* have water or he will die. God wants us to be just that much in earnest in our desire for His Spirit.

Isaiah, the Gospel Prophet

Verse 4. The outpouring of the Spirit is not for our own individual enjoyment. It is that we may bear more fruit. God will bless both the seed and the offspring, and results will " spring up as among the grass, as willows by the water courses." Let first the " water courses " come, and results will not tarry. We all need to pray for the latter rain.

Verse 5. " One," " another," " another." One by one they shall come.

Verse 8. " Fear ye not." How often these words occur! God knows what is before us; and knowing that, He says, " Fear ye not."

Verse 9. " Vanity," really " confusion." Those that reject God as the Saviour and Creator, and accept instead the teachings of men, surely are wallowing in confusion. As compared to the simple story of creation, how confused and confusing are men's theories!

Verse 10. " Profitable for nothing." Recount some of the many things which men — and women — do that are " profitable for nothing."

Verse 19. " None considereth." We are to serve God with the mind as well as with the heart. Mark 12: 30. We are to consider, to reason. Isaiah 1: 18. If men would but use the mind God has given them, they would soon discover the inconsistency of some of the things they do and believe.

Verse 20. No one can live on ashes, nor can the soul live on the theories and opinions of men. It is sad to go to church expecting to hear the message of God, and then be treated to a lecture on psychology, or a review of some book, or plain fables. Ashes instead of manna from heaven!

Verses 21-23. " Remember these." This is written to God's people. It is an admonition to us, that while we see the emptiness of the things of the world, we may take warning and abstain from even the appearance of evil.

" God's forgiveness is not a future event but an accomplished fact. " The Lord hath done it." No wonder heaven and earth are called on to rejoice.

Verse 25. God in His own time will do all that this verse indicates. We can afford to be patient and wait. Men's so-called science, pretended wisdom, and profound theories will some day be made to look " foolish." Anything or any one that is not in harmony with the word, that pretends to be wise above that which is written, is riding toward a fall.

CHAPTER VI

The Vanity of False Gods; One Only Saviour

Lesson Scripture: Isaiah 45: 5-25; 46

Isaiah 45: 5-8. The Lord is the only God.

THE Lord again announces that He is the only God. He has strengthened Cyrus, though Cyrus did not know Him. Verse 5. The purpose of God's helping Cyrus was to cause men to know the true God. Verse 6. God is the Creator of both light and darkness; He also makes peace and causes calamities to come. Verse 7. Let the heavens and the earth rejoice together, and pour forth righteousness and salvation. Verse 8.

Verses 9-13. The clay and the potter.

Woe to him that tries to take God to task. Man is but a potsherd among other potsherds. And shall the clay question its maker? As well might the child murmur against its parents. Verses 9, 10. God is the Holy One of Israel, He does all things well. We may not criticize God, nor presume to dictate to Him concerning His work. Verse 11. God that made the earth and man upon it, that made the heavens and commanded their host, has also raised up Cyrus in righteousness and directed his ways. He shall cause Jerusalem to be rebuilt, and shall let the people go back to their own land, not for price or reward. Verse 13.

Verses 14-17. Heathen nations turn to God.

Heathen nations, such as Egypt, Ethiopia, and Seba, shall turn to the Lord. They shall come humbly as slaves do, ready to serve, ready to take any position. They shall recognize that God is with His people, and that there is no other God than Jehovah. At last they have found Him who seemed to hide Himself from them, the God of Israel. Verses 14, 15. They that trust in idols shall be confounded and confused, but Israel " shall not be ashamed nor confounded world without end;" they " shall be saved with an everlasting salvation." Verses 16, 17.

Verses 18-25. God as Creator and Saviour.

The God who has made the heavens and also the earth did not create the earth in vain; He formed it to be inhabited. He does not speak in secret nor misguide His people. Verses 18, 19. Let the people that have escaped assemble themselves. Let them consider the unwisdom of praying to gods that cannot save. God is the only one who can reveal the future. There is none besides Him, "a just God and a Saviour." Let "the ends of the earth" look to Him and be saved. Verses 20-22. God has sworn that the time shall come when every knee shall bow and every tongue shall swear. In the Lord shall Israel be justified. Verses 23-25.

Isaiah 46: 1-7. Contrast between the true God and false gods.

The Babylonian gods cannot save themselves. They cannot even walk, but must be carried upon beasts of burden. They are unable to save themselves, much less others, but are carried into captivity. Verses 1, 2. The true God, on the other hand, does not need to be carried, but carries His people and saves them. Verses 3, 4. Can there be any comparison between Him and the god that a goldsmith has carved, a god that must be carried and set in his place and cannot move, a god that cannot answer nor save? Verses 5-7.

Verses 8-13. An admonition to the people.

Once more remember that the Lord is the only God. He declares the end from the beginning, and His counsel shall stand. Verses 8-10. He calls Cyrus from the east, and through him executes His purpose. Let all note this, for God's salvation will not tarry. Verses 11-13.

Notes

Isaiah 45:5. "I girded thee," as God girded David with strength. Ps. 18:32.

Verse 6. "That they may know." God intended that the nations of the world should learn of the true God through Cyrus and his dealings with the Jews.

Verse 7. "I . . . create evil." "Evil" here is rather calamity than sin; that is, the result of sin rather than sin itself. It is the same thought as in Amos 3:6: "Shall there be evil in a city, and the Lord hath not done it?" God punishes sin, hence He creates calamities that come as a result of sin.

The Vanity of False Gods; One Only Saviour

The Persians believed in the two eternal principles, light and darkness. This verse may have reference to that belief.

Verse 8. Righteousness is here represented as coming down from heaven as the gentle rain falls; and the earth is represented as opening its bosom to receive it, causing salvation and righteousness to spring up together, a most beautiful picture.

Verse 9. "Potsherd," a broken fragment or piece of earthenware. Job 2:8. The thought of the verse is that if puny man wishes to strive, he better not strive with God, but with one of his equals — another potsherd.

Verse 11. The language of the verse demands that the comma be placed after "come," and not after "sons." (See the A. R. V.)

Moffatt renders this part of the verse: "Would you question Me about the future? Would you dictate to Me about My work?"

Verse 13. This verse refers to Cyrus.

"In righteousness," to carry out My righteous purposes.

"My city," Jerusalem.

"He shall let go My captives." Ezra 1:3.

Verse 14. "Men of stature," tall men.

"In chains," not literally, but symbolic of their willingness to serve.

Verse 17. "An everlasting salvation." The deliverance from Egypt culminated in the wilderness, and was only temporary. This shall be everlasting.

"World without end;" literally, to all eternity.

Verse 18. "God Himself," no one else.

"Not in vain;" literally, not a chaos. There were order, beauty, and arrangement in creation.

"To be inhabited." God will not finally abandon the earth, but will make it "the home of the saved."

Verse 19. "Not spoken in secret." God's word is found everywhere and in almost all languages. God is certainly not trying to hide His messages from mankind. Openly God challenges all to read and compare prophecy with fulfillment. God has no secrets that He is not willing to reveal to His servants. Amos 3:7.

Verse 21. "A just God and a Saviour." God unites in Himself those two apparently incompatible virtues, justice and mercy. (See Rom. 3:26; Ps. 85:10.)

Verse 23. "Sworn by Myself." Gen. 22:16; Heb. 6:13. The form of the oath is given in Isaiah 49:18: "As I live, saith the Lord." "Every knee shall bow to Me. and every tongue shall confess." or swear. Rom. 14:11; Phil. 2:10, 11.

God could crush all opposition, did He so desire. A much greater victory, however, would be His if all at last should confess that God is right and that their punishment is just. And that very thing God will bring about.

"With all the facts of the great controversy in view, the whole universe, both loyal and rebellious, with one accord declare, 'Just and true are Thy ways, Thou King of saints.'" "And now Satan bows down, and confesses the justice of his sentence."—"*The Great Controversy,*" *pp. 671, 670.*

How much better such an ending of the controversy, than if the wicked should go to their doom unconvinced of God's justice! If God can so conduct His work that those who go to their final destruction will exclaim, "Just and true are Thy ways," and Satan "confesses the justice of his sentence," *that is victory.*

Isaiah 46: 1. Bel and Nebo are the Babylonian counterparts of the Roman Jupiter and Mercury. Bel is the Babylonian form of the Hebrew Baal. Nebo, the same as Mercury, was the "speaker" of the gods. (See Acts 14: 12.) Not a few of the Babylonian kings were named after him,— Nebu-chadnezzar, Nabo-polassar, Nabo-nidus.

Verse 11. "A ravenous bird;" "as the eagle or vulture: to cleanse the earth from this rank and foul mass of idolatry. Cyrus was singularly rapid in his movements. It is remarked that he took for his ensign a golden eagle standing with outstretched wings on the top of a spear."—*Kay.*

Verse 13. "I will place salvation in Zion." God always works in harmony with His church. He places salvation in Zion.

Lessons for To-day

Isaiah 45: 5. God "girded" Cyrus, though he did not know Him. Many are the blessings we receive from God not only unasked, but undeserved. Of many God may say, "I have blessed him abundantly, but he has not even thanked Me."

Verse 6. "That they may know." God always has a saving purpose in what He does. He wants us to reason not only from cause to effect, but from effect to cause. God helped Cyrus, and He wanted men to see in that help the intervening hand of God. Is there anything in the world to-day in which we can see the hand of God?

Verse 8. "Let the skies pour down, . . . let the earth open." The work of salvation is twofold: God must give, we must receive. God does not, indeed God cannot, save a single individual without his co-operation. It is when we open our mouth wide that God will fill it. Ps. 81: 10.

Verse 9. A critical attitude toward God's work is not the best. God is more interested in His work than we can possibly be. And if God tolerates some people, cannot we do the same? We sometimes forget that what we do to one of the least, we do unto God. We therefore at times criticize God in the person of some brother or sister. And that is always dangerous.

God knows more than we do, as the commanding general of an army knows more than the private soldier. A company of soldiers in a battle may be commanded to make a certain charge which to them may seem futile. A minor officer may view the charge and predict failure, and failure may indeed result. And the lower officer may feel justified in his criticism, especially as the result confirmed his prediction.

Was the general wrong? Not necessarily so. What the minor officer saw was only his own small sector. He did not understand the plan of battle, and that it was necessary to make the charge in question, which was intended, not to result in success, but to draw a sufficient number of the enemy away from other parts of the field where the real attack was to be made. And so the charge which seemed to be a failure was a success from the larger point of view.

To criticize or murmur is to assume that we know and that others do not. It is therefore based on self-confidence and pride. There is no point in accusing the papacy of changing God's law, thus putting itself above God, if we ourselves have the idea that some of God's other plans should be changed.

Verse 15. Sometimes —

"God moves in a mysterious way
His wonders to perform."

Yet we may believe that God never hides Himself just for the sake of hiding. When the two angels came to Lot, they had to be "pressed greatly" to induce them to stay overnight, though it was evidently their intention to stay. Gen. 19: 3. When the three men came to Abraham to talk with him, he had to urge them not to "pass on," though they came for the very purpose of visiting him. Gen. 18: 3-5. When Christ walked with the two disciples to Emmaus, "He made as though He would have gone further." Luke 24: 28.

God wants to make very sure that He is welcome. If He hides Himself, it is that we may seek Him. And "he that seeketh shall find."

Verse 19. It must be a dreadful experience to seek God in vain. We know that the time will come when men will run "to seek the word of the Lord, and shall not find it." Amos 8:12. After probation closes, the world will seek God in vain. But also now there are some who worship the Lord in vain, "teaching for doctrines the commandments of men." Mark 7:7. The Lord does not so ask us to seek Him.

Verse 22. "Be ye saved, all the ends of the earth." Salvation is for all, even for "the ends" of the earth. Out-of-the-way places, backward nations, all shall hear the gospel.

Verse 23. "Every knee shall bow." All shall at last confess the justice of their sentence, but it will be too late for them to be saved. To admit and to receive justice is one thing; to accept Christ and receive mercy is another. Knowing that there are but two classes in the world, how interested we should be in presenting to all the wonderful advantage of humbling themselves now, rather than later.

Verse 24. "In the Lord." Some may claim holiness and superior goodness for themselves. Let all such beware. It is only "in the Lord" that we have any goodness at all. And if it is "in the Lord," we will not do any boasting.

Verse 25. Some have wondered if the people in the Old Testament knew anything of real salvation. Most certainly. "In the Lord shall all the seed of Israel be justified, and shall glory." That is the Old Testament, and that is the New. "All Israel." Whoever is saved before or after Christ must be "justified."

Isaiah 46:4. "Even to your old age." Let not the old be discouraged. "I am He." God still lives.

Verse 8. "Show yourselves men." God is not pleased with weakness. He wants men to be men. Paul was small of stature, but he was every inch a man. So was John the Baptist, and Elijah, and Moses, and most of all, Christ. Men, faithful, noble, courageous, kind, capable, true to duty as the needle to the pole — such God is seeking.

Verse 11. "The man that executeth." Not the man that talks, or intends to do, or promises, or makes excuses, but the man that executes, is the man God wants.

CHAPTER VII

The Fall of Babylon; God's Final Appeal to His People

Lesson Scripture: Isaiah 47 and 48

IN chapter 47 God announces and describes the fall of Babylon. It was Babylon's boast, according to Herodotus (1:191), that the city had never been taken. This, however, is not true, for history records several such captures. After the time of Cyrus, Babylon was never the capital of a kingdom, the Persians making Susa the seat of empire. Afterward Babylon gradually dwindled until it became a ruin.

Isaiah 47: 1-10. God's judgment upon Babylon for its unmercifulness and pride.

Babylon is told to sit in the dust, for there is no throne. Henceforth she will have to work and grind meal, instead of being waited upon. She shall become a fugitive, crossing rivers, and God will take vengeance upon her and will not relent; to His people, however, God will be a redeemer. Verses 1-4.

Babylon shall sit in silence and hide herself in darkness. God had sent Israel into captivity because of their sins, but Babylon was too cruel to them, even compelling the aged to perform heavy labor. Verses 5, 6. Babylon did not consider what such action would lead to, but thought that her care-free existence would last forever. She never considered becoming a widow or losing her children, yet those two things were to come in one day. Verses 7-9. Her wisdom and knowledge perverted her, and she came to believe herself supreme. Verse 10.

Verses 11-15. The surety of the coming destruction.

Because of Babylon's pride, evil shall come upon her, and there is no way in which it can be averted. It shall come suddenly, and though she practice her enchantments and sorceries, they shall not help her. Even her astrologers and stargazers are helpless. Verses 11-13. Babylon shall be as stubble which the fire devours, and shall not be able to save herself. The destruction shall be complete; there shall not be anything left. Verses 14, 15.

50   *Isaiah, the Gospel Prophet*

Isaiah 48 is largely a repetition and summary of prophecies given before. Cyrus is here mentioned for the last time in Isaiah, as is also God's appeal to prophecy and creation as proof of the true God. Henceforth the predictions of Babylon's fall cease, and there is no more reference to " former things " and " new things " or the vanity of idols. This chapter closes one section of Isaiah's later prophecies.

Verses 1-8. God's complaint against His people.

Jacob and Israel have not called on God in truth and righteousness, though they claim to belong to the holy city and to stay on God. Verses 1, 2. God predicted coming events because He knew that Israel was obstinate and hard to handle. By thus predicting events beforehand, they would be unable to give the credit to their idols. Verses 3-5.

Israel had heard God's prophecies proclaimed, and now see them fulfilled. To that they should bear witness. God is about to show them new things, which they did not know and had never heard of, lest they should say, " We knew them." God must deal thus with His people because He knows them to be treacherous transgressors.

Verses 9-11. God proclaims mercy to His people.

For His name's sake, God will defer His anger. He will not cut them off now. The refining process has not been completed. God's name and glory demand that mercy be shown.

Verses 12-16. The last prophecy concerning Cyrus.

He that is the first and the last is speaking. He has created the heavens and the earth, and when He calls they stand before Him. Let all now hear: Which of your idols have predicted this, that He whom the Lord loves shall execute God's pleasure on Babylon and on the Chaldeans? I now foretell it. I have called him and will cause him to prosper. Let all hear this. I have never spoken in secret. From the beginning I have declared it.

Verses 17-22. God's call to consecration.

God is the one that teaches men the way they should go. If they would but hearken to His commandments, their peace would be secure and their posterity assured. Verses 17-19.

Let God's people flee out of Babylon, and declare to the ends of the earth the Lord's salvation. He who formerly brought His people out of Egypt and led them safely through the wilderness, is still leading. But to the wicked there is no peace. Verses 20-22.

The Fall of Babylon; God's Final Appeal to His People 51

Notes

Isaiah 47:1. Babylon is here likened to a virgin, "tender and delicate." In chapter 23:12 Tyre is also called a virgin. "Virgin" may here have reference to the boast of Babylon that the city had never been taken. "Sit on the ground," in deep humiliation. "No throne," the kingdom had departed.

Verse 2. "Take the millstones, and grind meal." Women slaves ordinarily did this work, turning the heavy upper stone all day long. (See Ex. 11:5.)

Verse 3. "I will not meet thee as a man." The reading is somewhat obscure. The probable meaning is, leaving out the italicized words, that there will be none to oppose God's plan.

Verse 5. "Get thee into darkness," a symbol of imprisonment. (See Isa. 42:7.)

Verse 6. "I have polluted." (See Isa. 43:28.)

"No mercy." We have no record how the captives were treated while in Babylon, aside from Daniel, his three brethren, and the king Jehoiachin. (See Daniel 1 to 3 and 2 Kings 25:27-30.)

"The ancient," the aged people. It is not improbable that even of the aged many were put to forced labor.

Verse 7. "A lady forever." It is strange that Babylon could engage in such cruelty and yet think herself "a lady." There was apparently no thought that there would ever come a day of reckoning, and this thought of security made Babylon cruel.

"Didst not lay these things to heart." She was light-hearted, thoughtless.

"The latter end." She did not think or believe that we reap what we sow.

Verse 8. "Carelessly." Herodotus tells us that when the Babylonians heard of Cyrus' intention of taking the city, they made light of it. No special preparations were made, for they thought none were needed. In careless confidence Babylon awaited the coming of Cyrus, and danced the very night the city was taken. Daniel 5.

Verse 9. "In a moment, in one day." Babylon's fall came suddenly. One day men were dancing and carousing, the next day they had been killed or taken captive. Rev. 18:8.

"Widowhood," the figure of desolation. Rev. 18:7.

"Loss of children," loss of population or loss of provinces.

"In their perfection;" "in their full measure," A. R. V. Rev. 18:6.

"For the multitude of thy sorceries;" rather, "in spite of thy sorceries." The Babylonians were noted for their enchantments, incantations, and "spells." Note the array of wise men and astrologers in Daniel 2. In spite of all that the wise men and sorcerers could do, however, Babylon should go down.

Verse 10. "None seeth me;" God does not keep account or remember.

"It hath perverted thee." This verse reminds of Ezekiel 28: 17, where the cause of Lucifer's fall is laid to his wisdom and brightness, as well as to his pride.

Verse 11. "Not be able to put it off;" rather, "not be able to charm it away."

Verse 12. "Stand now." A challenge similar to that of Elijah on Mt. Carmel. 1 Kings 18:27. It contains a bit of irony. "Do your very best," the prophet says, "perhaps you can charm away the evil the Lord will send upon you."

Verse 13. "Thou art wearied." The Babylonians had consulted so many oracles and wise men and had received so much confusing counsel, that they themselves tired of it.

"The astrologers, the stargazers, the monthly prognosticators." Really only one class of persons, all consulting the heavens to determine the future from the position of the stars. The latter specialized in making almanacs in which coming disasters were foretold, also lucky and unlucky days.

Verse 14. "They shall not deliver themselves," much less others.

Isaiah 48: 1. "Not in truth, nor in righteousness." God is now speaking to that portion of His people who are Christians only in name. The rebukes in this chapter are among the severest in the whole book.

Verse 2. "They call themselves of the holy city." They belong to God's people and are members of the church. They put emphasis on the outward, as in Christ's day: "We be Abraham's seed." John 8: 33.

Verse 4. "Obstinate," hard; "iron sinew," cruel; "brass." This seems to be the origin of our expressions "brazen," "brazenfaced."

Verse 6. "Thou hast heard, see all this." That is, you have known the prophecies, and now you see the fulfillment. "Will not ye declare it?" Will you not bear your testimony to the truthfulness of the predictions of which you are witnesses?

Verses 7, 8. The "new things" of verse 6 are here referred to. God is about to do something, to make a new prediction — concerning Cyrus. Of all old prophecies the people might affirm that they "knew them," or as they do now, say they were written after the

The Fall of Babylon; God's Final Appeal to His People

events transpired. That could not be the case in this new prediction.

Verses 9-11. God will defer His anger, and give the people another chance. This He does for His own sake. For "not with silver" read "not as silver."

Verse 13. "When I call unto them, they stand up" in reverence to their Maker, a mark of respect.

Verse 14. Cyrus is here introduced. God loved him. This calls to mind the rich young ruler whom, when Jesus saw, He "loved him." Mark 10:21. We cannot but believe God had a special interest in seeing Cyrus saved.

Verse 15. God has called Cyrus, brought him, and made him to prosper.

Verse 16. God has not spoken in secret. This He repeats again and again. The Lord is open and above board.

"From the time that it was, there am I;" rather, "from the beginning I have been in it."

Verses 17-19. Some have taken the position that these verses are addressed to Cyrus, and that they reveal God's solicitude for his salvation. The statements made are of general application, but we see no objection to the view that God has Cyrus specially in mind.

Verses 20, 21. This is the call to come out of Babylon. As God of olden times led the children of Israel through the wilderness, so God will lead His children now.

Lessons for To-day

Isaiah 47:1. "Sit in the dust: . . . there is no throne." Life holds many strange experiences. Kings and princes, brought up in luxury, suddenly find themselves destitute, as was the case in the World War. It is well for all of us to learn what Paul had learned when he wrote: "I know both how to be abased, and I know how to abound." Phil. 4:12.

Verse 6. "No mercy." We never know what the future may bring. The person in authority may soon be under the jurisdiction of the one he now treats disdainfully. To be kind and merciful to all is good Christianity, and therefore good sense.

"The ancient." God loves and cares for the aged. To be old and to be made to feel in the way is one of life's saddest experiences. All should be specially solicitous for the old and infirm.

Verse 7. "A lady forever." A woman to be worthy the name must be refined and well-bred, a gentlewoman. Character, not position, makes a lady. To show no mercy, to illtreat the aged, to be proud and haughty, and yet think herself a lady — what a lack of appreciation of the meaning of the name!

"Didst not lay these things to thy heart." God wants no one to carry unnecessary burdens, but there are some things He wants us to lay to heart. There are times when it is sin to be light-hearted and gay. May God give us the right balance.

Verse 8. "Given to pleasures." This is one of the sins of Babylon.

"Carelessly." Some are careless of both temporal and eternal interests. This also is a sin.

Verse 10. "None seeth me." What a man does in leisure hours, what he does when he is alone and thinks no one sees, that is what he is and that is where his interests lie.

"Thy wisdom and thy knowledge, it hath perverted thee." How strange that wisdom and knowledge should pervert! And yet that is what they often do,— not indeed true wisdom and knowledge, but worldly. "Knowledge puffeth up." 1 Cor. 8:1. Unless heart education follows step with head education, the result will be disaster. The religious and moral powers must be developed equally with the mental, or there will be power without control; and that is always dangerous.

Isaiah 48 1. "Swear by the name of the Lord, and make mention of the God of Israël, but." That "but" is significant. These people worshiped God, *but*. Many people nowadays go to church, *but*. Some belong to the church, *but*.

There must be no "but" in our Christian experience. God calls for whole-hearted and undivided service.

Verse 2. "They call themselves of the holy city." Outward forms and ceremonies will not satisfy God. We may call ourselves of the holy city, we may belong to God's people, but that is not sufficient.

Verse 4. "Obstinate." The difference between firmness and obstinacy is not clear to some people. We should all be firm, none should be obstinate. Obstinacy is defined as persistent and unreasonable adherence to one's own opinion; stubbornness. One serious result of obstinacy is heart-hardening.

"Brass." To be brazen-faced is to be impudent and shameless, not a very desirable trait.

Verse 10. The refining process. God's reason for causing us to pass through the furnace of affliction is our refining. Every spot and wrinkle must be removed from our character. Spots can be

The Fall of Babylon; God's Final Appeal to His People

washed out, but wrinkles cannot. They can be removed only by a hot iron. God will refine His people, but not as silver. Silver is tried "in a furnace of earth, purified seven times." Ps. 12:6.

Verse 13. "When I call unto them, they stand up." Reverence is one of the virtues we all need to cultivate. Here heaven and earth are represented as standing up when God speaks. Why should there not be profound reverence wherever and whenever God's word is spoken or read?

Verse 14. "The Lord hath loved him." If God loved Cyrus, may it not be possible that there are rulers and great men to-day of whom the same may be said? And is there no way of reaching them? Will not God co-operate with us when we seek out those in the highways as well as in the byways? We sometimes neglect those whom we consider great, not thinking that there are longing hearts among them also. Who will prepare himself to work among the great, the learned, the rich? How will we give an account to God for the neglected souls of millions of high school and university trained men and women as well as the submerged classes, unless we include them in our plans?

Verse 17. "I am the Lord thy God which teacheth thee to profit." Every ability is of God, and should be dedicated to Him. Profit here may not have reference to money, but rather to anything which is for our good, but whatever the special application may be, the lesson is clear: all talents are of God, and should be sanctified to His service.

Verse 18. Some may think that the keeping of the commandments brings strife rather than peace. We are not, however, promised peace in this world as regards outward conditions, but rather tribulation. But "in Me," He says, we shall have peace. That peace Christ left with us. John 16:33; 14:27.

Verse 22. "There is no peace . . . unto the wicked." There is no true peace in compromise. Peace bought at the cost of giving up the keeping of the commandments is but temporary and delusive. It does not pay.

CHAPTER VIII

The Servant; Hope for the Discouraged

Lesson Scripture: Isaiah 49: 1-23

THIS chapter contains the second of the four so-called "servant passages" in Isaiah, the first one of which we studied in chapter 42. The "servant" in this chapter is undoubtedly Christ, though some of the statements also have an application to Israel.

"The Desire of Ages," pp. 678, 679, quoting verses 4, 5, 7-10, refers them to Christ. "Testimonies," Vol. VII, pp. 191, 192, quoting verses 2, 3, 6, speaks of them as applying to the people. We therefore take it for granted that some apply to Christ, some to the people, and some to both. In verse 6, for example, the Servant is to "raise up" Jacob and Israel. The Servant therefore is differentiated from both. As He is to "raise up" and "to restore" Israel, He is not Israel, but the Restorer of Israel. But in verse 3 Israel is definitely called the servant. Verses 1 and 2 find a better and more complete fulfillment in Christ than in Israel, and so does verse 7. We therefore take the statements in this lesson to refer to Christ primarily, and in a secondary sense to His people.

Verses 1-6. The Servant's call and work.

Countries and peoples afar off are invited to hear the story of the Servant. The Lord has called Him from the womb and named Him. From His mouth proceeds a sharp sword, and He is like a polished arrow. He is the Lord's Servant, in whom God will be glorified. Verses 1-3.

The Servant is almost cast down, as it seems to Him He is not accomplishing very much. But He determines not to be discouraged, and leaves His case with God. And the Lord sends Him the comforting word, that even though Israel be not gathered, the Servant's work is yet glorious; that in fact He has a larger work in mind for the Servant to do than merely ministering to Israel: He expects to give Him for a light to the Gentiles, and to be God's salvation to the ends of the earth. Verses 4-6.

The Servant; Hope for the Discouraged

Verses 7-13. Despised of men, yet their Saviour.

The Servant has been despised of men and as a slave of despots, but the time is coming when kings shall arise before Him and princes worship Him. God has heard and helped Him, and will give Him for a covenant to the people, to raise up the earth and cause it to be inhabited. Verses 7, 8. The Servant shall also cause the prisoners to go forth and shall feed them. They shall not hunger or thirst any more, nor shall the sun smite them. The mountains shall not detain them, but shall be as a road, and the highways shall be exalted. They shall come from afar, even from the land of Sinim. Let the heavens and the earth rejoice, for the Lord has comforted His people. Verses 9-13.

Verses 14-23. Zion comforted.

Zion is despondent and believes the Lord has forsaken her. But can a woman forget her little one? She may, but the Lord will not forget His own. They are graven upon His hands. They are continually on His mind. Verses 14-16. No, God has not forgotten Zion. They that destroyed her shall be separated from her, and instead she shall be given a multitude of children. Her place of habitation shall be too small by reason of her increase, and those that swallowed her up shall be far away. Verses 17-19. The children that shall come to her after she has lost those that tormented her, shall be many, so that her place must be enlarged and she will wonder where they have all come from. The answer which the Lord gives is that they shall come from the Gentiles; that even kings and queens shall come and worship. They that wait for the Lord shall not be ashamed. Verses 20-23.

Notes

Isaiah 49: 1. "Isles;" rather, "countries."

"People;" or "peoples," A. R. V.

"The Lord hath called Me from the womb. . . . He made mention of My name." Christ was called and named "from the womb." "Behold, thou shalt conceive in thy womb, and bring forth a son, and shalt call His name Jesus." Luke 1: 31.

Verse 2. "My mouth like a sharp sword." "Out of His mouth goeth a sharp sword." Rev. 19: 15. (See also Heb. 4: 12.)

"In the shadow of His hand." God kept and protected Him until the fullness of time came.

"A polished shaft" or arrow. An arrow will go even deeper than a sword. Christ is an arrow that will go straight to the hearts of men, convincing and converting, or else killing.

Verse 3. "Thou art My servant, O Israel." This states that the servant is Israel. Kay, however, believing that Christ here is meant, speaks of "God's Servant [who] would stand as a new federal Head, a true 'Israel' or 'Prince with God,' and in Him God would be glorified." Another writer, believing it to mean the nation, says: "It is possible that 'Israel' may be a gloss, and for that reason no great stress can be laid on the word as an argument for the national interpretation of the passage."— *Cambridge.*

Verse 4. "I have labored in vain." When Christ viewed His work, it must have seemed to Him that very little had been accomplished. The leaders of the nation had rejected Him. The Pharisees sought His life. His neighbors had once taken Him to the brow of the hill to kill Him. The twelve whom He had selected were not perfect. One sold Him, one denied Him, all fled and left Him alone.

"I have labored in vain." In these words we get a little view of the inmost heart of Christ. What soul-anguish these words reveal! And what courage it must have taken to continue the work in spite of personal feelings!

"My judgment is with the Lord." I leave the matter with God. I will do My duty, and leave the results with Him.

Verse 5. "Though Israel be not gathered." All that Christ did could not save any man against his will. "He came unto His own, and His own received Him not." John 1:11. Yet Christ's work was not a failure even if all literal Israel was "not gathered." He was still "glorious in the eyes of the Lord."

Verse 6. "It is a light thing," "too light a thing," A. R. V. The plan of salvation is "too light" if it only includes the Jews. It must take in the whole world. "Whosoever will, let him come." (See Rev. 22:17; Acts 13:47.)

Verse 7. "Him whom man despiseth." Christ was despised. Isa. 53:3.

"Servant of rulers." He was treated as a slave by such rulers as Herod and Pontius Pilate. Luke 23:11; John 19:1, 16.

"Kings shall see and arise." Christ was despised and rejected of men; but the time will come when kings shall arise and stand in reverence, when they "shall worship" Him whom they abhorred.

Verse 8. "I helped Thee," and "will preserve Thee," and "give Thee." These promises are for all who will appropriate them.

The Servant; Hope for the Discouraged

"To establish the earth;" rather, "to raise up the land" out of its long degradation.

Verse 9. "They shall feed." Those who have been prisoners, when they accept the light, "shall feed" "in all high places." Christ is their shepherd. John 10: 11-16.

Verse 10. This verse reminds of the twenty-third psalm.

Verse 11. Even the mountains shall not be a hindrance, but rather constitute "a way."

Verse 12. "Land of Sinim," now generally conceded to refer to China. Though the Tsin dynasty dates only from 255 B. C., the name Tsin, from which Sinim is derived, was known as early as 1122 B. C.

Verse 13. In view of this large ingathering from the ends of the earth, sing and rejoice.

Verse 16. "I have graven thee upon the palms of My hands." Christ bears the marks of the crucifixion in the nail prints, emblems of His sacrifice for us. He will never forget.

Verse 17. "Thy children shall make haste." God "will finish the work, and cut it short." Rom. 9: 28.

Verses 18-20. The great increase in the church here signified shall be as "an ornament," and there shall be so many that there is hardly room.

Lessons for To-day

Isaiah 49: 2. God's word can pierce to the heart, and must do so if it is to do its work. A pointless sermon is no sermon. "In His quiver." God takes care of His tools even as a good workman does. "I am immortal till my work is done."

Verse 4. We may not always count success as men count it. Christ's work seemed a failure. Yet it was a most glorious success, even though it ended in death. It is enough that we do our duty and leave results with the Lord.

Verse 5. "Though Israel be not gathered." Verses 1-5 must have been a wonderful consolation to Christ while on earth. With all His love and entreaty, men turned from Him. Christ loved the young ruler, but could not hold him. So we may not always be successful. But we have the blessed assurance, as He had it, that God knows and loves.

Verse 6. Applying this text to the people of God, which we have a right to do, according to the "Testimonies," Vol. VII, p. 192, we would say that it is "too light" a thing to minister only to those who are well grounded in the truth. Some must stay at home "by the stuff," but even these must "look on the fields," and by their prayers and means help those who can go. When a church or denomination lose their world view, when they cease to pray for and give to world missions, when they consume their tithes and offerings on themselves, demanding preachers to serve them "like the nations about them," then that church or that denomination is headed for a spiritual graveyard.

Verse 7. Some of the treatment accorded Christ may be ours also. Why should we escape when Christ did not, nor His disciples? Read what Paul says in 1 Corinthians 4: 10-13: "We are despised. Even unto this present hour we both hunger, and thirst, and are naked, and are buffeted, and have no certain dwelling place; and labor, working with our own hands: being reviled, we bless; being persecuted, we suffer it: being defamed, we entreat: we are made as the filth of the world, and are the offscouring of all things unto this day."

One of the serious situations in the more favored lands is that our people are apt to forget that another day is coming when persecution will rage, when war and turmoil will be the order of the day. For that time we all need to prepare.

Verse 8. "An acceptable time." There is no more acceptable time than now. Neither yesterday nor to-morrow equals now. Of all recorded time, this year, this day, is the most important. "Teach us to number our days," the psalmist prayed. Ps. 90: 12. That is easily done. We have but one day that is ours. That day is to-day. This being the only day we have of which we are sure, it is a most important day.

To-day is the day to make matters right with God and man. To-day is the day to decide for the Lord. To-day is the day to begin being faithful in tithe paying and to make up arrears. To-day is the day to make the confession contemplated a long while. To-day is the day to start family worship. To-day is the day to decide to make a real sacrifice for God. Above all, to-day is a day of dedication of all that we are, and all that we have, to the Lord.

Verses 10-12. These verses doubtless find their special fulfillment in connection with the coming of the Lord, when the great gathering will take place. What a blessed time when all the saints of God shall meet from all parts of the earth!

Verse 16. "Graven thee upon the palms of My hands." Those nail prints will ever remain there. There is "the hiding of His power." Hab. 3: 4.

Verse 17. The day shall come when the "destroyers" in the church — the criticizers, the backbiters, the ruiners of reputations, and those that "made the waste," that started factions, that by their lives brought ill repute upon the cause — "shall go forth of thee." What a blessed day when the church shall consist only of such as have the cause at heart, and live it!

Verse 18. "An ornament." Those that come into the church are here spoken of as ornaments. That is what all of God's people should be. Some are a reproach instead. We should show forth the virtues of Him who has called us out of darkness into His marvelous light. (See 1 Peter 2:9.)

Verses 19-21. There shall come a time of shaking, when the "destroyers" and the wasters shall "go forth" out of the church. That will create vacancies, but these will be more than filled by the influx of new believers. The children which thou shalt have, after thou hast lost the other," will be far more than those that went out. That "the shaking" will be a great one, is clear from the expression: "I have lost my children, and am desolate." Verse 21.

Verse 23. "They shall not be ashamed that wait for Me." This is a blessed promise. We need to cling to it in these days of waning faith.

CHAPTER IX

Thy Saviour and Thy Redeemer

Lesson Scripture: Isaiah 49: 24-26; 50

Isaiah 49:24-26. The captives delivered.

Can a strong man's prey be taken from him when he has a lawful captive? The answer is, Yes. The prisoners may be taken away even from a strong man. The Lord will contend with the mighty, and save thy children. Those that oppressed them shall be made to eat their own flesh and drink their own blood. Thus shall all the world know that the Lord is both a Saviour and a Redeemer.

Isaiah 50. This chapter consists of three separate sections not very closely connected. The teaching, however, is as beautiful as in any portion of the book.

Verses 1-3. A rebuke to Israel.

The Lord here defends Himself against the unfounded charge that He has put away His people. He has not put them away, He has not sold them. What has happened, however, is that they have sold themselves, but for that the Lord is not to blame. The Lord is not only willing to take them back, but He is calling them to come. He is perplexed to find that no one responds to His call. Is it because they believe He is unable to save, that His hand is shortened? They should know better than that. The Lord is the one who dried up the Red Sea for Israel to pass over. He clothes the heavens with blackness, and makes sackcloth their covering.

Verses 4-9. Perfect through suffering.

This section deals with the work and sufferings of Christ. Though "the Servant" is not mentioned by name, the references are so clear that no one need misunderstand. The subject is presented in the form of a soliloquy, as though Christ were thinking aloud for our benefit.

The Lord has taught me how to speak and when to speak so that I might be of help to the despondent. Morning by morning He wakens Me to teach Me. He opened My ears, and I did not rebel or turn back. Verses 4, 5. I willingly took the scourgings they gave Me, and when they plucked off the hair of My beard and spit in My face, I did not retaliate; for the Lord helped Me, therefore I did not fail. I have set my face like flint, and I know I shall not be ashamed. Verses 6, 7.

God who justifies Me is near. Who, then, can contend with Me? Let us stand together. Let My adversary come near. The Lord will help Me, who then can condemn Me? Behold, they are as an old garment which the moth will eat up.

Verses 10, 11. A message of encouragement and warning to the people.

There may be some that fear the Lord and do all He commands, and yet do not have the experience they long for, but rather seem to walk in darkness and have trying experiences. What shall they do? Let them continue to trust in the Lord and keep near Him. Light will come.

There are some that kindle a fire of their own, thinking they are thus walking in the light. They are but walking in the sparks of their own kindling. Such are doomed to disappointment.

Notes

Isaiah 49:24. Applying this text spiritually, the "mighty" is Satan. His captives are such as have deserted the banner of Christ and gone over to the enemy. While some are unwilling captives, many have gone over to him of their own free will. The question now is whether they can be delivered, or must they ever remain captive?

Verse 25. The answer is definite. The captive can be delivered. God will enter the battle, and contend with the "mighty," and "will save thy children."

Christ must have had something like this in mind when He said: "How can one enter into a strong man's house, and spoil his goods, except he first bind the strong man? and then he will spoil his house." Matt. 12:29. Christ is the Man that enters into the "strong man's house" and binds him. "When He ascended up on high, He led captivity captive." Eph. 4:8. Satan will at last be bound. Rev. 20:1, 2.

Verse 26. The punishment meted out to those who at last are lost is not a pleasant one to contemplate. (Compare Rev. 19:17, 18.)

Isaiah 50:1. "Where is the bill of your mother's divorcement?" Moses, because of the hardness of Israel's heart, suffered them to put away their wives; though from the beginning it was not so. Matt. 19:8. A man was permitted to put away his wife, giving her a bill of divorcement. After that was done, he might never take her back. The divorce was final and irrevocable. Deut. 24:1-4. God in this verse is telling His people that He has not put them away finally. There is yet hope for them.

"To whom have I sold you?" The law permitted, without approving, the selling of persons into bondage. Ex. 21:7. (See also 2 Kings 4:1; Neh. 5:5.) Had the Lord sold His people? By no means. They had sold themselves by reason of their iniquities, and on that ground also the mother had been put away.

The point of the verse is this: Israel had separated themselves from God. God had not done it. If He had divorced them, there was no hope, for a divorce was final. Hence, as God had not divorced them, it was their own doing; and if they wished to come back, they might.

Verse 2. "None to answer." God expresses His astonishment that no one answers when He calls. It certainly cannot be because they believe Him unable to save. He has in the past shown His great power in drying up the sea.

Verse 4. "Tongue of the learned;" "the tongue of them that are taught," A. R. V. Christ was taught of the Father. "The Son can do nothing of Himself, but what He seeth the Father do." John 5:19. "As My Father hath taught Me, I speak these things." John 8:28.

"He wakeneth morning by morning." The communication between Father and Son was uninterrupted. At no time did the Father leave Jesus alone. John 8:29. "Whatsoever I speak therefore, even as the Father said unto Me, so I speak." John 12:50. From this we learn that Jesus received communications constantly from heaven, and that when He spoke, it was the Father's word He uttered.

Verse 5. "The Lord God hath opened Mine ear." A contrast to Israel, whose "ear was not opened." Isa. 48:8. The meaning here is that Christ had an open ear, a willing mind, and gladly did the biddings of the Lord.

Verse 6. "I gave My back to the smiters." A reference to the scourging of Jesus. John 19:1; Mark 15:15.

"Plucked off the hair." We have no record in the New Testa-

ment of this. Plucking off the hair of the beard is an extreme insult to an Oriental, to whom the beard is a symbol of dignity.
" Shame and spitting." Matt. 26 : 67 ; 27 : 30.

On " scourging," note what Dr. C. Geikie says : " Jesus was now seized by some of the soldiers standing near, and after being stripped to the waist, was bound in a stooping posture, his hands behind his back to a post, or low pillar, near the tribunal. He was then beaten till the soldiers chose to stop, with knots of rope or plaited leather thongs, armed at the ends with acorn-shaped drops of lead, or small sharp-pointed bones. In many cases, not only was the back of the person scourged cut open in all directions; even the eyes, the face, and the breast were torn and cut, and the teeth not seldom knocked out. The judge stood by, to stimulate the sinewy executioners by cries of 'Give it him!' but we may trust that Pilate, though his office required his presence, spared himself this crime. Under the fury of the countless stripes, the victims sometimes sank, amidst screams, convulsive leaps, and distortions, into a senseless heap; sometimes died on the spot. Sometimes they were taken away, an unrecognizable mass of bleeding flesh, to find deliverance in death, from the inflammation and fever, sickness and shame."

Verse 7. " I set My face like a flint," a figure of determination. (See Eze. 3 : 9.) It is worthy of note that Christ again and again speaks of His dependence upon the Father. " The Lord God will help Me," Christ says cheerfully and trustingly, " and I know that I shall not be ashamed."

Verse 8. " He is near that justifieth Me." Christ on the cross was dying condemned as a criminal, crucified between two criminals. But the Lord was near. Even in the thick darkness that enveloped the cross the Father's presence was hidden. And He would justify Him. Christ had been condemned on the charge that in claiming to be the Son of God He had committed blasphemy. Matt. 26 : 63-66. God did justify Christ in raising Him from the dead. Rom. 1 : 4. (See also 1 Tim. 3 : 16.) By that He was " declared " by the Father to be " the Son of God."

" Who will contend?" (Compare Rom. 8 : 33, 34.)

Verse 9. " The moth shall eat them up." A figure of corruption. Ps. 39 : 11.

Verse 10. The question is addressed to those who live up to all the light they have, and yet do not experience the happiness and joy that should be theirs. The answer is to wait and trust.

Verse 11. Instead of accepting God's light, these start a fire of their own, and walk in that light and in the sparks they have kindled. This shall be to their own sorrow.

Lessons for To-day

Isaiah 49:24. The question raised in this verse is a most important one. Can a man be saved who has transgressed all the laws of God and man? Is there really hope for a woman who is down in the mire? What about the slave to drink? or drugs? or tobacco, or sensual pleasures? or the debased? or the demon-possessed? or the insane? or the criminal? All of these are Satan's captives. Some of them are willingly so, others are not as yet reconciled to their fate. Is there any hope?

Verse 25. The answer comes back loud and strong: *There is deliverance for all.* The question is not as to the strength of the captive, but as to the strength of the Deliverer. The captive may have no might at all. That makes no difference. If the Deliverer has the power, that is all that counts. And our Saviour is a strong God. Christ entered the grave, "the strong man's house," "that through death He might destroy him that had the power of death, that is, the devil; and deliver them who through fear of death were all their lifetime subject to bondage." Heb. 2:14, 15. Through the death of Christ there is deliverance for all. To God be the glory.

Isaiah 50:1. "Ye sold yourselves." The separation from God was not His fault, but theirs. They had sold themselves.

Men and women still sell themselves. The woman who barters her virtue for gold is justly abhorred. The man who sells his soul for unjust gain is in no better position. Truth, integrity, honesty, virtue, loyalty — what wealth can be compared to these? Yet men sell these every day, and for a pittance. "What shall it profit a man, if he shall gain the whole world, and lose his own soul?" Mark 8:36.

Many a young woman has sold eternal life for a few hours of fleeting pleasure followed by years of bitter regret. Many a young man has given up his title to heaven for promotion here on earth and an accusing conscience. For note this, there is no mere worldly enjoyment but has a corresponding sorrow added to it. It is only in God that we can have true joy, and "He addeth no sorrow with it." Prov. 10:22.

Verse 4. "A word in season." "A word fitly spoken is like apples of gold in pictures of silver." Prov. 25:11. What a blessing "a word in season" is! And what a curse a word may be if it is not "fitly spoken"! "When you get into deep waters, keep your mouth shut," is good advice, not only for swimmers, but for all.

What opportunities for good we miss because we do not know how to speak the right word! And yet, in the words of the text, " I should know how to speak a word in season to him that is weary."

> "Lost for the want of a word —
> A word that you might have spoken!
> Who knows what eyes may be dim,
> Or what hearts may be aching and broken?"

Verses 5, 6. Christ did not turn back. He knew the future, and what He must suffer physically. He knew the greater soul-anguish through which He must pass. He knew the lack of understanding and appreciation on the part of those who were closest to Him. But He did not turn back. Courageously He went forward, facing misunderstanding, suffering, death.

The servant is not greater than his Master. "All that will live godly in Christ Jesus shall suffer persecution." 2 Tim. 3:12. Do we have the courage, the fortitude, and the faith we need? Can we go quietly on our way facing scorn, neglect, injustice? "If any man draw back, My soul shall have no pleasure in him." Heb. 10:38.

Verse 7. "Face like a flint." Flint is unyielding. Christ was unmovably determined to go on. He had set His face like a flint. With Him there was no compromise, no halfway measure. No more than John the Baptist was He " a reed shaken with the wind."

One of the greatest dangers before us to-day is the spirit of compromise. John the Baptist could probably have saved his life had he not rebuked sin in high places. Matt. 14:3-12. Yet " among them that are born of women there hath not risen a greater than John the Baptist." Mark 11:11. He was "Elias. which was for to come." Verse 14. And before the Lord comes He will again send Elijah the prophet; that is, a people that will go forth " in the spirit and power of Elijah." Mal. 4:5; Luke 1:17.

Verse 9. "The Lord God will help me." We can never face the future, we can never get through even one day, without God's help.

Verses 10, 11. Experiences come to all of us that we do not fully understand. This verse propounds a question and presents a solution which should interest all.

Every one that is bound for the kingdom will sooner or later go through Gethsemane. The road to heaven leads to Galilee, but it goes by way of Golgotha. Dark hours will come to every soul, as came to Jesus in the garden. Has God forsaken us? Did God forsake Christ? Yet He prayed three times, and the cup did not pass. "Trust in the name of the Lord," is God's advice when the dark days come. Stay upon God. Your prayers may not be answered immediately, but do not give up. To learn to walk with God in the dark is one of life's lessons, and a most precious one. It develops faith, courage, hope, and trust, as no experience walking with Him in the light ever can. So when the dark days come, do not try to make a light of your own and to walk in the sparks of your own kindling. Put your hand in God's, walk a little closer, trust a little more, and a richer, nobler, larger faith shall be yours.

CHAPTER X

The Righteousness and Power of God; His Care for His People

Lesson Scripture: Isaiah 51: 1-16

Isaiah 51: 1-8. Encouragement to the people of God.

This section consists of three parts, each one of which begins with "Hearken." Verses 1, 4, 7. It is an earnest appeal to the true Israel to put away all fear and grasp God's promises in their full import.

Verses 1-3. A retrospect.

Let those that seek the Lord and earnestly desire righteousness hear what the Lord says: Look at your past history; consider your origin. Look at Abraham and Sarah. I called him when he was alone, and blessed and multiplied him. So the Lord shall comfort Zion and make her waste places fruitful, even as the garden of Eden. And there shall be joy and gladness.

Verses 4-6. God's righteousness and salvation are near.

Let My people give ear to Me. A law shall proceed from Me, and true doctrines shall be a light to the people. My righteousness is ready to be revealed, and My salvation has already gone forth. Mine arms shall judge the people, and far-off lands are waiting for Me. The heavens shall vanish away, and the earth grow old as a garment; but My salvation and My righteousness shall always endure.

Verses 7, 8. Do not be afraid of men.

Let My people that know righteousness, that keep My law, hearken to Me. Do not be afraid of the reproaches of men or of their revilings, for they shall soon be destroyed. But My righteousness and My salvation shall always endure.

Verses 9-11. An appeal to Jehovah to put on His strength.

Awake, O arm of the Lord, and put on strength as in the days of old, when Thou didst hew Rahab in pieces and wounded the dragon. Thou didst dry up the Red Sea, and made a way for Thy people to pass over. The redeemed shall return and come to Zion with song and gladness, and sorrow and mourning shall be no more.

Verses 12-16. Jehovah again comforts His people.

I am the Lord that comforts you. Why, then, should you be afraid of man that shall die and forget that your God made heaven and earth? Those that are captive shall speedily be loosed, and shall not die in the pit, neither shall their bread fail. I am the Lord of hosts; I divided the sea when the waves roared, and I will put words in your mouth and protect you, that I may plant the heavens and lay the foundation of the earth, and say to Zion, "Thou art My people."

Notes

Isaiah 51:1. "Justice, justice, shalt thou follow." Deut. 16:20, margin. The word rendered "justice" there is the same as "righteousness" here. "Righteousness, righteousness," was therefore the call to Israel of old, "shalt thou follow, that thou mayest live and inherit the land which the Lord thy God giveth thee." The call here is to them that follow after righteousness, earnestly desiring it, and that seek the Lord.

"Look unto the rock." The figure here used is that of a rock quarry whence the rock for a building is hewn. The original stone, rough as it comes from the pit, does not much resemble the finished product as it appears later in the building. Much work and labor must be expended on it before it is fit and ready. And when at last it is polished and given a place of honor, it seems so much unlike the uncouth original rock that hardly any resemblance remains.

"And to the hole of the pit." The hole left after the rock is removed would give an idea both of the shape and size of the original piece, as well as of the general surroundings whence it came.

Verse 2. "Look unto Abraham . . . and unto Sarah." Abraham was called when he was "alone," that is, childless. The original call is recorded in Genesis 12:1-3. There God promises to make of him "a great nation;" but Sarah, "Abraham's wife, bare him no children." Gen. 16:1.

Now look upon Abraham and Sarah. Abraham was old and "as good as dead;" Sarah the same and "past age." Heb. 11:11, 12; Rom. 4:19. Yet from these two sprang a great nation as they in faith grasped the promises of God.

Verse 3. "The Lord shall comfort Zion." The same God who could make a great nation of Abraham when he was as good as dead, can bless Zion and make all her waste places blossom like the garden of Eden. Hence, let not God's people lose courage because they are few in number.

Verse 4. "A law;" rather, "law" in general. "Judgment," doctrines, "the true religion."

Verse 5. "My righteousness is near." By "righteousness" here we must understand all that is included in God's plan of salvation, both as to the salvation of His people and the punishment of the wicked. The salvation and judgment spoken of in the text are the two parts of the "righteousness."

Verse 6. "The heavens shall vanish away, . . . and the earth shall wax old." The contrast here is between that which shall vanish away, and that which is eternal. Look at the heavens, look at the earth. Can anything appear more solid and substantial or more likely to endure forever? Yet the heavens shall vanish away as smoke, and the earth and its inhabitants perish; but God's salvation and righteousness, His eternal law of right, shall not cease nor be abolished.

"In like manner;" "perhaps, like gnats," A. R. V., margin.

Verse 7. "Ye that know righteousness." We have here a definition of who those are that know righteousness. They are "the people in whose heart is My law." In verse 1 we have those mentioned that "follow after" and "seek" righteousness. Here we have those who have found it, who "know righteousness," and, lo, in their heart is the law! The same is said of Christ, that He had the law within His heart. And the next statement is: "I have preached righteousness." Ps. 40:8, 9. Law and righteousness go together.

It would seem from the next statements in the verse that those who keep the law would be reproached and reviled. At that we need not be surprised. The previous chapters brought to view Christ's sufferings. And we shall not escape. But we need not fear or be afraid.

Verse 8. The moth and the worm will do their work, but God's righteousness and salvation shall be forever.

Verses 9, 10. Rahab and the dragon are both symbolic names for Egypt. (See Ps. 89:10, margin; Eze. 29:3.) The American Revised Version of Isaiah 30:7 says: "Egypt . . . I called her Rahab." The word means "the proud one." The dragon, of course, is also another name for Satan. Rev. 12:7-9.

Rahab and the dragon are therefore symbolic of Egypt, which formerly held God's people in bondage. The Lord with a mighty hand delivered His people, and Pharaoh and his army were destroyed in the Red Sea.

This whole incident is called to the mind of the prophet as he has a view of the events of the last days. Again God's people are oppressed. The governments of earth unite themselves against the elect. They are reproached — blamed for the calamities that are coming on the earth — and reviled. To the view of the prophet it appears as if they will be overwhelmed, and that God does not interfere. In his anxiety Isaiah calls upon God to awake, as if He were asleep. But God is not asleep. He knows what is going on. And He will speedily answer the cry that goes up to Him. He is merely waiting until the right time comes. They must drink the cup.

Verse 11. "Therefore." The Lord has interfered. In the "zero hour" deliverance came. "Therefore the redeemed of the Lord shall return, and come with singing unto Zion; and everlasting joy shall be upon their heads."

Verse 12. "Afraid of a man that shall die." Verses 9-11 are put in the midst of the description of what shall happen in the last days. They represent the prophet's appeal to God as he sees what God's people are passing through. He now continues the description that was interrupted by these verses.

Verse 13. "Feared continually every day." The trials of the last days are severe ones. It will seem to God's people that "the fury of the oppressor" can be restrained no longer. They fear "every day" that he is "ready to destroy."

Verse 14. But it will not be long. "The captive exile shall speedily be loosed; and he shall not die and go down into the pit, neither shall his bread fail," A. R. V.

Verse 16. God has shielded His people in the shadow of His hand, that He "may plant the heavens, and lay the foundations of the earth." The word "plant" is the same as is used in Genesis 2:8. God's people are a "holy seed," and He will use them when the new heavens and the new earth are called into being.

Lessons for To-day

Isaiah 51:1. It is well for all of us to look back once in a while, and consider where we would have been if the truth had not found us. It is also well to consider what the truth has done for us. And those that are inclined to think themselves important may look at the hole of the pit whence they were digged. Not a very large hole, likely. In a large quarry, acres, perhaps miles in extent, one little stone makes not much difference. Hence it is well for our own good to look back, to find our right place.

Verse 2. To look at Abraham and Sarah should establish our faith. Here were two old people who apparently had outlived their usefulness. But God takes hold of matters, these two take hold of Him, and things happen. We often speak of the work of the young people and their opportunities. Let not the old forget that God can do as much for them.

Verse 3. God "will comfort all her waste places." All of us have some unfruitful traits, some waste and uncultivated places in our lives. God can make them blossom "like Eden."

Verse 6. "Lift up your eyes," that is, consider, think. Look upon things as God looks upon them. Value that which He values. Some things will vanish, others will remain. The true value of anything is that which God places upon it.

Verse 7. Make no mistake in this matter. The statement is not that the law is in their heads or upon their lips, but in their hearts. And if the law is where it belongs, in the heart, it will not reveal itself in a cold, formal, legal religion, but in a warm, helpful, happy life. The lips indeed will speak, and they will speak out of the abundance of the heart. The law will find expression in words as well as deeds, but the expressions will come from a heart filled with the love of God.

"The reproach of men." God's people will be charged with bringing calamities and disasters. Do the best we can, yet the charges will be brought. But is it not worth while now to live in such a manner that men will be convinced of our integrity and honesty, so that when the charges are brought, *they* will be condemned, not *us?*

Verses 9, 10. Man's extremity is God"s opportunity. God, after all, is our strength, not our own wisdom or cunning. We should have that faith in God that will cause us not to fear, but to rest our case with Him. God may seem to be asleep and not to care. At such times all we can do is to watch and pray. We may have to wait,-- and waiting is said to be man's hardest task,— but we shall not need to wait long.

CHAPTER XI

Zion Led From Utter Defeat to Triumphant Victory

Lesson Scripture: Isaiah 51: 17-23; 52: 1-12

Isaiah 51:17-23. God's judgment on Jerusalem.

JERUSALEM is told to rouse herself and stand up. She has drunk the cup of the Lord's fury to the dregs. Among her sons there are none to help her, nor any among the many she has brought up. Desolation and destruction are everywhere, and there is none to comfort. The sons have fainted, and are lying in the streets like an antelope caught in a net. They also have drunk the cup of the Lord's fury. Verses 17-20.

"Hear now this, thou afflicted, and drunken, though not with wine!" The Lord has taken away the cup of trembling; thou shalt drink it no more again. I will now give it to them that afflict thee, that have humbled thee in the dust and walked over thee. Verses 21-23.

Isaiah 52: 1-6. God redeems and saves His people.

Zion is told to awake and put on her "beautiful garments" and her strength. Henceforth no uncircumcised or unclean shall come into her. Let her shake off the dust, and loose the bands that bind her. She has sold herself for nothing, and shall be redeemed without money. Verses 1-3.

God's people at one time went down into Egypt. The Assyrians also oppressed them without cause. And now the Babylonians have taken them and rule over them, and God's name is blasphemed. The Lord will reveal Himself that He is Jehovah, and that He is all that the name signifies. Verses 4-6.

Verses 7-12. The gospel to the whole world.

How beautiful are the feet of them that bring good tidings of peace and salvation, that proclaim: "Thy God reigneth!" The watchmen shall sing together, and see eye to eye when the Lord shall bring again Zion. Verses 7, 8.

Zion Led From Utter Defeat to Triumphant Victory

Let the waste places rejoice and sing together, for the Lord has comforted and redeemed His people. He has made bare His holy arm, and the whole world shall see His salvation. Let all that are unclean depart; those that bear the vessels of the Lord must be clean. They shall not go out hastily, for the Lord shall go before them, and He also shall be their rereward. Verses 9-12.

Notes

Isaiah 51:17. "Awake;" rather, "rouse thee." Not the same word as in verse 9.

"The cup of His fury, ... the dregs." Jerusalem did drink the dregs of God's wrath in the destruction of the city by Nebuchadnezzar. Not only were the houses burned and the wall broken down, but famine prevailed in the city, the king was captured, his sons were killed before his eyes, and then his own eyes were put out; the palace was burned, and last of all the temple was destroyed, and the people were carried into captivity. 2 Kings 25:3-11. Jerusalem did indeed drink the dregs of the Lord's wrath.

Verse 18. "None to guide her." Jerusalem had rejected the prophets sent to her. The last one, Jeremiah, she mistreated, and then took him to Egypt. Jer. 43:5-7. Now there was none left, and God had no mouthpiece through which to communicate His will to them.

Verse 19. "Two things." These two things are desolation caused by the famine, and destruction caused by the sword.

"By whom shall I comfort thee?" God would have comforted and helped His people, as evidenced in the forty-second chapter of Jeremiah, but they would not hear. When God sent a message to them through the prophet, they answered, "Thou speakest falsely." Jer. 43:2. God could then do no more.

Verse 20. "Thy sons have fainted." The people were all exhausted.

"A wild bull in a net;" rather, "an antelope," "swift, strong, and handsome, but hunted down into the net, and now exhausted with fruitless attempts to escape."

Verse 22. "Thy Lord the Lord, and thy God that pleadeth the cause of His people," the Lord Jesus.

Isaiah 52:1. "Awake, awake;" the same words as in 51:9. The words there addressed to Jehovah are here addressed to the church. The strength is there, the garments are there. Put them on. The beautiful garments are Christ's righteousness.

The words in this verse evidently go beyond any local or restricted meaning. When the statement is made that no uncircumcised or unclean shall henceforth come into the city, it cannot have reference to Jerusalem. It must have an application to the time when God will have a pure church that shall henceforth never know defilement.

Verse 2. "Shake thyself," "loose thyself." Zion has not only wallowed in the dust, but has also been bound about the neck. Captives in ancient times were often fastened together by chains passed around the neck. To this custom reference is here made.

Verse 3. "Redeemed without money." This does not mean that the redemption costs nothing. On the contrary, the price paid was so enormous that no comparison with money can be made.

Verse 4. There were three captivities:
The first in Egypt. Ex. 1:13, 14.

The second to Assyria under Tiglath-pileser (2 Kings 15:29); Sargon (2 Kings 17:6); Sennacherib (2 Kings 18:13).

The third is the Babylonian captivity referred to in the next verse, Isaiah 52:5.

Verse 5. "What have I here?" paraphrasing freely: "What had I better do?" now that My people are taken to Babylon.

God still has a care for His people. The Babylonians are oppressing them, making "them to howl," and God's name "is blasphemed."

Verse 6. "Therefore," because of the "howling" and "blaspheming."

"My people shall know My name." God will reveal Himself as the great "I AM," the powerful God.

Verse 7. "Good tidings," the gospel.

"Thy God reigneth!" rather, "Thy God has become King." This has reference to the time when the seventh angel shall proclaim that "the kingdoms of this world are become the kingdoms of our Lord, and of His Christ." Rev. 11:15. Then it will be true that "the Lord God omnipotent reigneth." Rev. 19:6.

Verse 8. "Watchman," God's ministers.

"With the voice together," in unison.

"For they shall see eye to eye." While the original Hebrew phrase may not have the same meaning of harmony and unity which it bears in English, it can hardly have any other sense here than that of harmony, agreement.

Verse 10. "Made bare His holy arm." All nations shall see this. And when the Lord has finished His work, there will be no

Zion Led From Utter Defeat to Triumphant Victory

doubt in the mind of any as to who has done it. The Lord has bared His arm in the sight of the nations. The work will not be finished in a corner.

Verse 11. "Depart ye." This is the call out of Babylon, and to touch no unclean thing.

"Be ye clean." It was the work of the priests to bear the vessels. Num. 4: 15; Ezra 8: 24-28. Hence this is a call for a clean ministry to minister to a clean people.

Verse 12. "Not go out with haste;" that is, unprepared. If we follow on to know the Lord, we shall be taught from time to time just what to do. The lesson is: Be ready.

"Before you," "be your rereward." God being both before and after His people, they are safe.

Lessons for To-day

Isaiah 51: 17. The picture is one of horrible degradation. It is a true picture, however, of one who has been left of the Lord and given over to reap the fruit of his own doing. In that picture every one — man or woman — may see himself as he will be when God finally lets him have his own way. It should cause all to pause, lest taking the first step may lead to taking the last.

Verse 18. "None to guide her;" none "that taketh her by the hand." In prosperity friends are many. When we are reduced to low levels, pretended friends depart.

Verse 19. "Who shall be sorry for thee?" The punishment was well deserved. It is thus in most if not in all cases. We are generally treated better than we deserve, though we do not always think so.

Verse 20. "Wild bull in a net." No animal would run into a net if it saw and realized the danger. But the net is ingeniously hidden, and the animal is caught before it is fully aware of its situation.

Men are caught the same way. They think they are in no danger. They can "take care of themselves." They have "their eyes open." But before they know it, they are caught.

A net is not made of heavy steel bars. Men look at it, thinking they can easily break those feeble threads if they should get caught. But when they are in the meshes, they find their vitality sapped. How many a young man has said that he was "able to quit any time," only to find himself unable to do so when he came to realize his need.

Verse 22. "God that pleadeth the cause of His people." No man can help. "Cures" cannot be depended on. Only One can help; He is the Lord.

Verse 23. "Bow down, that we may go over." Whatever it is that afflicts us, whatever sin or habit has caused us to be slaves to it, there is victory. We need not let it keep us in the gutter and walk over us. Deliverance is coming.

Isaiah 52:1. "Put on thy strength," "put on thy beautiful garments." God wants us to do what we can. We cannot provide the strength, we do not have it. But we can put it on. We cannot provide the beautiful garments. God will do that. But we can put them on. God will provide strength for any need, if we will but put it on. That is our part.

"The unclean." God does not want any unclean among His people, nor any that are uncircumcised in heart.

Verse 2. "Shake thyself," "loose thyself." Get rid of every sin, gain the victory over every besetment, break every chain that binds. Do that now, to-day.

Verse 3. "Sold yourselves for naught." It is strange what some will choose instead of heaven. Filthy, unclean habits and debasing passion; a greedy disposition, an ungovernable temper, and a backbiting tongue. And for such, men will sell eternal life!

Verse 5. "My name continually every day is blasphemed." Taking the Lord's name in vain is a useless and disgusting habit. Let all learn to avoid doubtful expressions of all kinds. Nor is blaspheming the name of God confined to spoken words. He who professes to be a child of God, but knowingly continues in sin, wrongly representing God's love and righteousness to the world, is guilty of the worst form of blasphemy.

Verse 7. Whatever the means of spreading the good news, the gospel, it is a "beautiful" work. Let the minister, the Bible worker, the editor, the doctor, the nurse, the teacher, the colporteur, the institutional workers — let all who have any part in "publishing" the good tidings rejoice in their work and take courage. And let all who help support this army of workers, who pray for them and stand by them, rejoice in the work being done.

Verse 8. What a glorious time when all shall be as one in love and harmony! No discordant note shall be heard. It is almost too good to be true. And if it is to be true and we are to be among that company, we may have to step rapidly.

Verse 10. "Made bare His holy arm." Symbolic of taking hold of the task whole-heartedly. To "roll up the sleeves" means going to work. That is what some need to do, in both a literal and a spiritual sense. When God is making bare His holy arm, He would be pleased if we would take hold with a will also.

Verse 11. "Touch no unclean thing." God wants His people to leave unclean things alone, whether it be in eating, in reading, in thoughts, in conversation, or in life.

Verse 12. "Not go out with haste." It is hard to conceive of Christ's being in haste. He had much to do, but He so planned His work that there was time for every needful task.

So might we. God never requires any one to do that for which there is no time. It may be that we have not planned our work so as to make first things first. There never should be any reason for saying, "I have no time to do that," if it is a task worthy of being done, and that you should do.

CHAPTER XII

The Lamb of God

Lesson Scripture: Isaiah 52: 13-15; 53: 1-5

WITH this lesson begins the last of the four great "Servant" sections. Even critics admit that the picture presented in these chapters is a remarkable anticipation of the sufferings of Christ and the glory that should follow. To the believer no proof is needed of the genuineness of the prophecy. Remove the fifty-third chapter of Isaiah from the Bible, and an irreparable loss would be sustained.

Isaiah 52: 13-15. The Servant exalted and marred.

The Servant shall deal wisely and prosper. He shall be highly exalted, very highly indeed. When men shall see Him, they shall be astonished and amazed. His countenance is so cruelly marred, and His form so unlike that of the sons of men. He shall startle many nations, and kings shall reverently keep silent; they shall see that which they had not been told, and they shall consider that which they had not heard.

Isaiah 53: 1-5. For our sakes.

Who could have believed that which we have heard? Whoever has had such a revelation of the Lord's power? He grew up as a tender plant and as a shoot from dry soil. He had no beauty of countenance or form, so that we should be attracted to Him. Men despised and rejected Him; He knew the meaning of pain and sickness. We shunned Him; He was despised, and held of no account.

Yet it was our sicknesses that He bore, our pains that He carried; but we thought Him suffering from a stroke at God's own hand. But He was wounded because of our transgressions, and crushed because of our iniquities. He was chastised that we might have peace, and the blows that fell on Him brought us healing.

Notes

When we last considered the "Servant" in the third of the four "Servant" sections, He was presented to us as suffering, giving

His back to the smiters, while men spit upon Him and illtreated Him. Isa. 50:6. His faith was steadfast; but we were not told of the outcome of the struggle. Would God interfere? would the "Servant" die? would men change their minds? or what would happen? We left the "Servant" in the midst of His sufferings, not knowing what the end would be.

The story is now continued in the fifty-second chapter, and carried to its conclusion in the fifty-third. These fifteen verses contain more suffering, more love, more hope, deeper insight into the mysteries of the plan of salvation, clearer vistas of the whole plan of God, and more profound revelations of God's character, than almost any other part of the Bible. He who, unmoved, can read these verses need pray God mightily for a clearer vision and deeper appreciation as well as an insight into his own spiritual condition.

Isaiah 52:13-15. "My Servant shall deal prudently;" rather, "shall prosper," as in Jeremiah 23:5. The primary idea means to deal wisely or prudently, but includes more than that. It means having insight, being able to see events in their bearing on the future, and so to conduct oneself that in the end success will come. It is expressed in the words we use when we see a person noted for his farsighted wisdom doing something the full meaning of which we do not comprehend: "He knows what he is about."

Consider now the use of this word in connection with Christ. In chapter 50 we find Christ suffering. We are not told why. He has not sinned. Yet He patiently and willingly suffers. He says God will help Him. But we are left in suspense whether God does actually help Him. The chapter leaves us in deep mystery both as to the reason for the suffering and the outcome.

In this section the mystery is solved. It is not for Himself that He is suffering. There is another purpose. There are larger interests at stake. When men understand the real situation, they will be astonished. Nations will be startled; kings will do Him reverence; He will be exalted and extolled; it will seem such an unheard-of thing that One willingly suffers and dies for another that men can hardly believe the report.

It is God speaking: "My Servant shall deal prudently." He knows what He is about. The suffering you see is part of the plan to save man. He is not suffering for Himself, but for others. I am standing right by Him. We know what we are doing.

"He shall be exalted," when the purpose of the suffering is known, and when the work is accomplished. It was when Christ became obedient unto death that God "highly exalted Him." Phil. 2:8, 9.

Verse 14. "Many were astonied." "The word 'astonied' expresses the blank amazement, mingled with horror, excited in the minds of beholders by the spectacle of the Servant's unparalleled sufferings." This astonishment was not merely because a man suffered. Many men had suffered before, and thousands had been crucified. But the astonishment was caused by the knowledge of the stupendous fact that this suffering was part of a world plan to save man; that an innocent One was suffering for the guilty; that God was suffering, and that through this suffering healing and salvation would come to mankind.

"His visage was so marred." The physical pain was so intense that Christ's countenance became almost unrecognizable. And yet the bodily suffering was as nothing compared to the spiritual agony.

Verse 15. "Sprinkle;" rather, "startle." This verse also registers the astonishment of nations and kings when they shall learn the truth of the sacrifice of Christ, when "they shall see what they were never told, a sight unheard of." (Moffatt's translation.)

Isaiah 53:1. "Who hath believed?" The implication of the question is that few have believed. It is still true to-day that few believe.

"To whom is the arm of the Lord revealed?" The statement might be paraphrased: Who can see the plan and purpose of God in the suffering of the "Servant"? In this case it is a metaphor for the Lord's operation in history.

Verse 2. "A tender plant." (See Luke 2:40, 52.) If God had not shielded Christ, the tender plant, Herod would have killed Him. Matt. 2:12-18.

"A root out of a dry ground." First a tender plant, now a root. So Christ grew as in Luke 2:52.

"Dry ground," the Jewish nation.

"No form nor comeliness." Probably a reference, not to the physical appearance of Christ, but to the fact that He came with no outward display or kingly splendor. "Comeliness" should be translated "majesty."

"No beauty." There must be nothing in Christ to attract men because of His physical beauty. While we cannot conceive of Christ with anything but a winning personality, it must be the spiritual qualities rather than the physical that are the attraction. We know indeed that the law required the sacrifice to be "without blemish," so we may draw the conclusion that Christ likewise was physically perfect. Lev. 1:3; 6:6. We are told that even under the most trying circumstances, Christ was "dignified and composed." His form was "perfect," He "appeared more like a king than any of the rulers." "His eye was mild, clear, and undaunted, His forehead broad and high. Every feature was strongly marked with benevolence and noble principle. His patience and forbearance were so unlike man that many trembled. Even Herod and Pilate were greatly troubled at His noble, Godlike bearing."— "Early Writings," p. 172.

Verse 3. "A man of sorrows, and acquainted with grief." "Sorrow" may also be translated "pain," and is used specially of pains which accompany a wound or disease. But the rendering of our version may well stand, since there are many places where the word used certainly means "sorrow" and nothing else. The same word is used in the beautiful wording in Lamentations 1:12: "Is it nothing to you, all ye that pass by? behold, and see if there be any sorrow like unto My sorrow."

"Grief;" Hebrew, "sickness," A. R. V., margin.

"We hid as it were our faces from Him;" literally, "There was as it were a hiding of face from Him." This may have reference to the hiding of God's face at the cross. It may also refer to the altogether too common occurrence of men being ashamed of Christ.

Verse 4. The vicarious suffering of Christ is here plainly brought to view. It was not *His* sorrows or griefs that He carried, but *ours*. The Jews believed, as many do now, that every affliction is the result of some wrong-doing. Hence a great sufferer must be a great sinner. It was to prevent the Jews from rejecting Christ because of His sufferings that this part of Isaiah was written. Had the Jews read their own book and believed it, they would have known that One must come who would suffer, not for Himself, but for others, and that the very reason they considered Him "accursed" was part of God's plan for their salvation. Gal. 3:13. (See also "The Desire of Ages," pp. 470, 471.)

Verse 5. "Wounded," by the thorns, the nails, the spear; but wounded more by His people's lack of understanding, their unsympathetic attitude, their failure to appropriate the blessings He came to bestow.

"Bruised," or "crushed." A stronger expression can hardly be found to denote the crushing weight He carried and the extremity of the Sufferer's affliction.

"The chastisement of our peace;" paraphrasing: "the chastisement which brought us peace."

"With His stripes we are healed." "Stripes," or "stripe wounds," really the wales that are raised because of the flogging. Besides the smiting with rods (Matt. 26:67, margin) and with the reed (Matt. 27:30), Jesus was scourged (Matt. 27:26). It is this scourging that would leave the "stripe wounds."

Lessons for To-day

Isaiah 52:13. "Deal prudently." To be prudent is to be "habitually careful to avoid errors; to exercise sound judgment and foresight; judicious; to be characterized by practical wisdom or discretion; not extravagant."

Christ dealt prudently. We should do the same. Avoid speculation, shun debt, beware of installment buying. In association with others, speak wisely or not at all, shun evil companions, avoid "going security." In religious matters be neither too forward nor too backward in expressing an opinion; shun extreme positions, keep pace with God and man.

Verse 14. "His visage was so marred." Do not judge by outward appearance. Do not judge men great sinners because they may be great sufferers.

Isaiah 53:2. "No beauty." Cathedrals do not make churches, nor houses homes, nor outward beauty inward worth. The temple Solomon built was the most beautiful structure on earth. That did not make Solomon a better man nor help the Jews in their relation to Jehovah. Rather, they came to worship the temple instead of the God of the temple. So God destroyed the temple.

God could have sent His Son to this world, and dazzled men by the splendor of His kingdom. Had He done so, doubtless many would have accepted Him who now rejected Him. But the basis of their acceptance would be wrong. God wants men to accept Him, not because of what He *has,* but because of what He *is.* Outward splendor would have vitiated God's plan.

This principle is worth remembering in building houses of worship or any institution. And it applies to many other phases of life.

Verses 3, 4. "Sorrows," "griefs," or sicknesses. While sickness is often a result of sin, not all sickness is directly caused by sin. The disciples once asked Jesus: "Master, who did sin, this man or his parents, that he was born blind? Jesus answered, Neither hath this man sinned, nor his parents: but that the works of God should be made manifest in him." John 9:1-3. When Lazarus was sick, and Jesus heard of it, He said, "This sickness is not unto death, but for the glory of God, that the Son of God might be glorified thereby." John 11:4.

We do not suppose that Christ meant to say that the blind man or his parents had never sinned, but that this affliction had not come to them because of any specific evil they had done. Christ was trying to counteract the idea of the Jews who believed that when people are afflicted, they must necessarily have sinned.

According to these texts, some are sick that "the works of God should be made manifest;" others are sick "for the glory of God." Paul's "thorn in the flesh" may be an illustration of the latter kind.

If, when we are sick, we have searched our hearts for any hidden and unconfessed sin, and have found none, we need not continually distress ourselves over the outcome. God knows best. It may be "that the works of God should be made manifest" in healing; for God will do great things for us if He is asked.

Some are afflicted for the "consolation and salvation" of others. 2 Cor. 1:6. This should be a great comfort to many who wonder why God sends certain afflictions to them. Remember, dear one, there may be some poor struggling soul going through deep waters whom God is preparing you to help by causing you to go through afflictions that will make you more understanding and sympathetic. So do not despair. God is giving you certain experiences that will make you a better worker, a better Christian.

"We hid our faces," in shame. Ashamed of Christ! Blasphemous conduct! Even the world will honor the one who is not ashamed of his faith. As the man is blessed who honors his father and mother, so the man is cursed who dishonors them or is ashamed of them. We despise one who is ashamed of his mother, though she may be plainly dressed. Is that any worse than to be ashamed of Christ?

> "Jesus, and shall it ever be,
> A mortal man ashamed of Thee?
> Ashamed of Thee, whom angels praise,
> Whose glories shine through endless days?
>
> "Ashamed of Jesus! sooner far
> Let evening blush to own a star;
> He sheds the beams of light divine
> O'er this benighted soul of mine.
>
> "Ashamed of Jesus! just as soon
> Let midnight be ashamed of noon;
> 'Twas midnight with my soul till He,
> Bright Morning Star, bade darkness flee."

CHAPTER XIII

Stricken Because of Israel's Transgression

Lesson Scripture: Isaiah 53: 6-12

THE fifty-third chapter of Isaiah "is the most central, the deepest, and the loftiest thing that the Old Testament prophecy, outstripping itself, has ever achieved."—*Delitzsch, on Isaiah, Vol. II, p. 303.* These words are not exaggerated. Words fail in describing the beauty, the sweep, the profundity and stateliness of the passage.

Eleven times expressions occur in this chapter emphasizing the vicarious character of the sufferings of Christ: 1. "He hath borne our griefs." 2. "Carried our sorrows." 3. "He was wounded for our transgressions." 4. "He was bruised for our iniquities." 5. "The chastisement of our peace was upon Him." 6. "With His stripes we are healed." 7. "The Lord has laid on Him the iniquity of us all." 8. "For the transgression of My people was He stricken." 9. "When thou shalt make His soul an offering for sin." 10. "He shall bear their iniquities." 11. "He bare the sin of many."

In these expressions the whole gospel is contained. Christ here is the Lamb of God that bears our sins and sorrows, our transgressions and iniquities. But the suffering is not merely vicarious; it is redemptive: "By His stripes we are healed." The scourging was His, the healing is ours. Ours is the peace, His the chastisement.

Isaiah 53: 6-9. The sinless Lamb of God.

We have all gone astray like sheep; every one has turned to his own way. The guilt of the whole world was placed on Him. When He was oppressed, He submitted Himself and opened not His mouth. As a lamb that is led to the slaughter and as a sheep that before her shearers is dumb, He opened not His mouth. Verses 6, 7.

Through oppression and judgment was He taken away; and who among His generation cared that He was cut off out of the land of the living for the transgression of My people, to whom the stroke was due? His grave was made with the wicked and with the rich at His death, although He had done no violence, neither was deceit found in His mouth. Verses 8, 9.

Verses 10-12. Christ the sin offering.

It was the Lord's will that Christ should die as well as suffer. "When Thou shalt make His soul a [trespass] offering, . . . He shall see His seed, He shall prolong His days, and the pleasure [purpose] of the Lord shall prosper in His hand." He shall see the result of His agony of soul, and " be satisfied." Through the knowledge which He has of the deep things of God, shall He " justify many," and " He shall bear their iniquities." Therefore will I give Him His " portion with the great," and " with the strong; " because He " poured out His soul unto death," and was " numbered with the transgressors." " He bare the sin of many, and made intercession for the transgressors."

Notes

The Jews looked for a Messiah who as a conquering hero should lead Israel to victory and bring back the glorious days of David and Solomon. And in this they were not without Scriptural support, though they completely confused the events of the first and second comings of Christ. The very first reference in the Bible to a Deliverer (Gen. 3: 15) presents Him as a conqueror, bruising the serpent's head. They were well acquainted with the fact that He would be called " Wonderful, Counselor, The mighty God, The everlasting Father, The Prince of Peace." Isa. 9: 6. They knew that He would " smite the earth with the rod of His mouth," and with His breath " slay the wicked." Isa. 11: 4. The isles should " wait for His law," and He would " set judgment in the earth." Isa. 42: 4.

Up to the time of Isaiah, very little had been said in prophecy concerning the suffering of the Messiah, and to the Jews it seemed an impossibility that one could be " the mighty God," " the Prince of Peace," who should " slay the wicked," and yet Himself be slain by them. How could it be true that He should " smite the earth," and at the same time be smitten Himself? Their views of the future included a Messiah to sit on the throne of David, ruling the nations with a rod of iron, and a return of the golden age, but did not include a suffering " Servant " who at last should die.

And yet they were without excuse; for though up to the time of Isaiah not much had been said in *prophecy* of a Lamb of God to be slain for the sin of the world, the whole Jewish ceremonial worship had been built around the idea of sacrifice. No Jew who had come to years of accountability could fail to see the significance of the temple worship. As the morning and evening sacrifices were made, as he brought his own offering at the specified season, as the solemn services of the day of atonement were carried out while Israel lay on their faces on the ground, he could not escape the conviction that sins were forgiven and blotted out only as some one died in his place. What else could be the meaning of taking two birds, in the case of the leper, killing one and dipping the other living bird in the blood of the dead one, then sprinkling the blood on the leper, pronouncing him clean, and letting the living bird fly away? Lev. 14:1-7. Surely death had something to do with the forgiveness of sin, or the whole Jewish worship was meaningless. And when the great day of atonement came, every Jew knew that his life depended upon God's acceptance of the sacrifice provided. He knew that he escaped only because God had provided a Lamb Himself. Gen. 22:8, 13.

No Jew can read the fifty-third chapter of Isaiah, and not be reminded of the day of atonement. Nor can any one read it, and fail to see the resemblance between the Man of sorrows there spoken of and the Root and Offspring of David promised in prophecy. If the Jewish nation had never understood their ritual service before, this chapter would certainly bring the necessary light. On God's "righteous Servant" (verse 11) should be laid "the iniquity of us all" (verse 6); He should be "brought as a lamb to the slaughter" (verse 7); He should die (verses 8, 12), be buried (verse 9), and be raised again (verse 10). He should make "intercession for the transgressors" (verse 12), and be made "an offering for sin" (verse 10), and thus justify many (verse 11). And all this was according to the plan of the Lord, and pleasing to Him. Verse 10.

Verse 6. "Like sheep." Sheep follow the leader. Where one goes, all go.

"Laid on Him the iniquity of us all." (See 1 Peter 2:24.)

Verse 7. "Opened not His mouth." This means more than merely refraining from complaint. Christ was submissive, willing. It was His own desire to give His life, not something forced on Him.

Verse 8. The Hebrew of this verse is difficult. The meaning is probably that unjustly, "by violence which cloaked itself under the formalities of a legal process," He was condemned, and that none of His generation cared that He was cut off out of the land of the living for the transgression of the people who deserved to be stricken instead of Him.

Verse 9. "Grave with the wicked." Christ was counted a criminal, and was crucified as such.

"With the rich." (See Matt. 27: 57-60.)

"In His death," Hebrew, "deaths."

"Neither was there any deceit." (See Rev. 14: 5.)

Verse 10. "It pleased the Lord." The idea is not that God delights in suffering, but rather that all was a part of the plan of God, according to His own "predetermined counsel." (See Acts 2: 23; 3: 18.)

"An offering for sin;" Hebrew, a "trespass offering" (Leviticus 6), not a "sin offering" (Leviticus 4).

"See His seed." See souls saved because of His life and death.

"Prolong His days," seemingly a contradiction of verses 8, 9, where He is "cut off" and is buried. Note also that it is "when" His soul is made an offering for sin, that is, after His death, that He shall prolong His days. The resurrection is the only explanation of this statement. (See Rev. 1: 18; Rom. 6: 9.)

Verse 11. "Travail of His soul." Those for whom He has died.

"Shall be satisfied." Apparently Christ is not quite satisfied until "His own" are with Him. Is there really a yearning in God's heart for the companionship of "the whole family"? And is mankind destined to fill that deep longing?

"By His knowledge." Another difficult sentence in Hebrew. The meaning seems to be: "Through the intimate knowledge of the divine counsels and purposes, which He will impart to His disciples, shall My righteous Servant justify many."

Verse 12. "Divide Him a portion with the great." Christ, who had been "numbered with the transgressors" and classed with "wicked men" (verse 9), now shall receive His rightful place. He shall be accounted a conqueror, "surrounded by the mighty ones who share His triumph."

Lessons for To-day

Isaiah 53: 6. "Like sheep." Sometimes we are too much like sheep. Where one goes, all go. Sheep have a tendency to go in groups without knowing just where they may be led. This is good if all go the right way, otherwise not.

"His own way." Apparently a contradiction. How can we be like sheep, all blindly following the leader, and yet go our own way? The truth is that some are like sheep and some are not. Some go where the crowd goes, and others are just the opposite — do not follow leadership at all, but go their own way. Both are wrong. We are not blindly to follow where others lead, neither are we stubbornly to refuse leadership, and go our own way.

God has a church. That church has leaders. We are to follow the leaders in so far as they follow Christ. God has given His church certain rights and prerogatives which must not lightly be set aside for private opinion.

Verse 7. "He opened not His mouth." Christ was unjustly accused; He said nothing. He was contemptuously treated; He did not retaliate. He was cruelly scourged; He did not invite sympathy. The nails were driven through His hands; He flinched not. And this is not merely negative goodness, a stoical refusal to admit defeat. Rather, He prays for those that mistreat Him; He speaks words of courage to a fellow sufferer; He asks not pity for Himself, but for those that mistreat Him. Luke 23: 34, 42, 28; 1 Peter 2: 21-25.

The lesson is obvious. Instead of anxiously letting people know about our aches and pains, as we so often do, angling for sympathy and disappointed if it is not given, we should, with the Saviour, seek to comfort others, to help and uplift them. Instead of dwelling on our personal wrongs, let us pray and work for the souls of the wrong-doers.

Verse 8. "He was taken from prison and from judgment." Christ did not receive justice. He was to be judged according to law, but contrary to it He was condemned; yet He said nothing.

Sometimes we think that we do not get justice, do not, in the language of the day, " get a square deal." Perhaps not, and yet in the long run we are generally treated better than we deserve. But whether we are treated right or not, we can afford to wait. Nothing is ever settled until it is settled right, and if we can have patience, we shall see all things adjusted. Have faith in God.

"Who shall declare His generation?" really, "Who cares?" That is the thing that hurts at times. We are, or think we are, unjustly treated, and some of whom we thought better and who could have interfered, or at least have said a word, did nothing. We lose confidence in our brethren, and thus in humanity. We become grouchy and suspicious, and our whole Christian experience is affected. No one cares, we think.

Christ went through that experience, and it did not affect His equanimity. He rather prayed for those that abused Him.

Verse 9. No "deceit." He was absolute truthfulness in word and act. There are times when we need not speak; but when we do, it must be to tell the truth. And to tell the truth, one must live the truth. Truth is not merely a matter of words, but of life.

Verse 10. "It pleased the Lord to bruise Him." "God so loved the world, that He gave His only begotten Son, that whosoever believeth in Him should not perish, but have everlasting life." And the Son gave Himself. "As He is, so are we in this world." 1 John 4: 17. As He gave, so should we give ourselves for others.

There are times when we do not see or understand the purpose of the Lord. We are as perplexed as Job was when his calamities came. But it was because Christ suffered that He is able to help them that suffer. Heb. 2: 18. It is only one who has passed through an affliction that is able to appreciate the trial and sufferings of another passing through the same.

It is good for a physician to be sick once in a while, and to suffer. It helps him to be more understanding and sympathetic to others. It is well for the field missionary secretary to sell books himself once in a while. He will better understand the difficulties others labor under. It is well for the minister to put himself in the place of the lay member, and look at matters from their viewpoint; and it is just as helpful for the lay members to place themselves in the position of the ministry and conference officials, and see their difficulties.

"An offering for sin." We have as truly a sacrificial system as Israel of old. We may yet bring our sin offering, even Jesus; we may bring thank offerings and sacrifices of praise. Our prayers as sweet incense may ascend on high, and the table of the Lord takes the place of the showbread. We have an altar, and we have a mercy seat. (See Heb. 13: 10; Rom. 3: 25. "Propitiation" is the same word that is used for "mercy seat" in Heb. 9: 5.) We have a priesthood, and we have a High Priest. 1 Peter 2:9; Heb. 8: 1.

Verse 11. "Be satisfied." Christ will be satisfied only when He sees souls saved as the result of His labor. We should not be satisfied with our work until we see results. There is a divine satisfaction, and also a divine dissatisfaction. We are to be satisfied and thankful, whatever may be our lot. We are to be dissatisfied with present achievements, and ever strive for something better and higher. The man who does not try to improve, has come to the peak, and after that must necessarily go downhill.

Isaiah
53:3-5

SABBATH SCHOOL LESSON
QUARTERLY

SENIOR DIVISION
Fourth Quarter, 1928

Lessons from
The BOOK of ISAIAH

Thirteenth Sabbath Offering, December 29, 1928
INTER-AMERICAN DIVISION

Entered as second-class matter October 13, 1904, at the Post Office in Mountain View, Cal., under the Act of Congress of March 3, 1879. Acceptance for mailing at special rate of postage provided for in section 1103, Act of October 3, 1917, and authorized September 18, 1918.

PACIFIC PRESS PUB. ASSN. (A Corporation of S. D. A.)

No. 134   MOUNTAIN VIEW, CAL., OCTOBER, 1928   20c A YEAR

LESSON 1—OCTOBER 6, 1928

"BEHOLD YOUR GOD!"

LESSON SCRIPTURE: Isaiah 40.
MEMORY VERSE: Isa. 40: 9.

INTRODUCTION

Many of the chapters we shall study this quarter have a special application to the latter days. This is true of chapter forty. The keynote of the chapter is, Behold your God! Behold Him as Creator, Saviour, Judge, Shepherd, and coming King. Help on this chapter may be found in "The Desire of Ages," pp. 132-135.

THE LESSON

1. What message does God send to His people? Isa. 40:1, 2.

NOTE.—Sin, wherever found, is abhorrent to God, but doubly so in the case of those who know the truth. Light brings responsibility. Those who know the truth and still persist in sin are more guilty than those who do not have a knowledge of God's message for this time. For this reason God's people have received double punishment. But God does not hate His people any more than the gardener hates the vine which he prunes. God loves His people, and sends them a message of comfort and love.

2. What message is proclaimed by "the voice"? Who is spoken of as having fulfilled this scripture? Verses 3-5; Matt. 3:1-3.

NOTE.—"In this age, just prior to the second coming of Christ in the clouds of heaven, such a work as that of John is to be done. God calls for men who will prepare a people to stand in the great day of the Lord. The message preceding the public ministry of Christ was, 'Repent; publicans and sinners; repent, Pharisees and Sadducees; "repent ye; for the kingdom of heaven is at hand."' . . .

"In order to give such a message as John gave, we must have a spiritual experience like his. The same work must be wrought in us. We must behold God, and in beholding Him lose sight of self."—"Testimonies," Vol. 8, pp. 332, 333.

3. What further does "the voice" say? What is all flesh said to be? In contrast with this, what is said of the word of our God? Isa. 40:6-8.

NOTE.—Man and his wisdom shall perish, but "the word of our God" shall stand forever. Men's theories will go down. Their ideas of future peace and of a millennium will not bear the test of "the word." It is well to build on something that will "stand" when everything else is shaken.

4. Where are those who bring good tidings instructed to go? What is Jerusalem to do? What are the people of God to say to the cities? Verse 9.

NOTE.—The message is not to be given in a corner. The messenger is to get up into a high mountain where all can see and hear, and lift up the voice with strength. This is nothing but "the loud cry." And the first part of the message is, "Behold your God!"

"The children of God are to manifest His glory. In their own life and character they are to reveal what the grace of God has done for them. The light of the Sun of Righteousness is to shine forth in good works,—in words of truth and deeds of holiness."—"Christ's Object Lessons," pp. 415, 416.

5. What is a vital part of the message to be given? Verse 10.

NOTE.—"The Lord God will come." This is the advent proclamation, and should be the keynote of every message. The Lord will come "with strong hand." He will "rule." Ps. 2:8, 9. He will also bring the "reward" with Him. Rev. 22:12. The Lord will come to punish and to reward.

6. Under what symbol is Christ presented? How are His love and care revealed? Verse 11; see also John 10:1-16.

7. How does the prophet illustrate the mighty power of God? Isa. 40:12.

8. What further questions are asked? Verses 13, 14.

NOTE.—These questions are so put as to require the negative answer. "No one,"—the strongest way in which such statements can be placed. The positive would be, God has not been taught by anyone; no one has shown Him "the way of understanding." That is, God is the Original One, the Ultimate One, the Source of all things. There was none before Him. No one "instructed" or "taught" Him.

9. To what is the importance of the nations compared? Verses 15-17.

NOTE.—The dripping of a bucket or a little dust blown from the scales are not regarded as great or important. Yet if whole nations are so counted, how much smaller must the individual be? And yet puny man sets himself up against God, and attempts to teach Him! Such indeed must be counted by Heaven "less than nothing, and vanity."

10. What shows that it is impossible to make any comparison to the great God of heaven? How are idols made? Verses 18-20.

NOTE.—The inference is plain. God is the Creator. He has made all things. Idols can not create. They themselves must be made.

11. In what four ways is the question asked concerning our knowledge of God? Where is God represented as sitting? What is said of the inhabitants of earth? of princes and judges? Verses 21-23.

12. How is the shortness of human life spoken of? Verse 24.

NOTE.—The American Revised Version, margin, renders verse 24: "Scarce are they planted, scarce are they sown, scarce hath their stock taken root in the earth, when He bloweth upon them." That is, men hardly begin to live ere they are taken away.

13. In what words are the questions of verse 18 repeated? What are we counseled to do? How are God's wisdom and power shown? Verses 25, 26.

NOTE.—"God calls upon His creatures to turn their attention from the confusion and perplexity around them, and admire His handiwork.

As we study His works, angels from heaven will be by our side, to enlighten our minds, and guard them from Satan's deceptions. As you look at the wonderful things that God's hand has made, let your proud, foolish heart feel its dependence and inferiority. How terrible it is when the acknowledgment of God is not made when it should be made! How sad to humble one's self when it is too late!"—"Counsels to Teachers," p. 457.

14. What do Jacob and Israel say? Verse 27.

NOTE.—The complaint of Jacob and Israel seems to be that "my way," that is, their course and condition of life, is hidden from the Lord, and that "my judgment" or, rather, "my right," escapes His notice. It is really a complaint from the people that God does not pay enough attention to them, that He "passes them by."

15. How does God meet the complaint of the people, and assure them of His knowledge and of His care? Verses 28, 29.

NOTE.—"There is no searching of His understanding." That is, God knows. You may think He does not know your perplexities, or, even worse, that He does not care. Be assured, dear soul, God knows and He cares. Your God not only understands, but He will give you the needed power and increase your strength.

"God's workers will meet with turmoil, discomfort, and weariness. At times, uncertain and distracted, they are almost in despair. When this restless nervousness comes, let them remember Christ's invitation, Come apart, and rest awhile. The Saviour 'giveth power to the faint; and to them that have no might He increaseth strength.' "—"Testimonies," Vol. 7, p. 244.

16. What may be the experience of the youth? What is noted of them "that wait upon the Lord"? Verses 30, 31.

NOTE.—"Remember that prayer is the source of your strength. A worker can not gain success while he hurries through his prayers, and rushes away to look after something that he fears may be neglected or forgotten. He gives only a few hurried thoughts to God; he does not take time to think, to pray, to wait upon the Lord for a renewal of physical and spiritual strength. He soon becomes weary. He does not feel the uplifting, inspiring influence of God's Spirit. He is not quickened by fresh life. His jaded frame and tired brain are not soothed by personal contact with Christ."—Id., p. 243. Read Ps. 27:14.

LESSON 2—OCTOBER 13, 1928

JEHOVAH'S CHALLENGE TO FALSE GODS

LESSON SCRIPTURE: Isaiah 41.
MEMORY VERSE: Isa. 41: 10.

INTRODUCTION

"Study the forty-first chapter of Isaiah, and strive to understand in all its significance."—"Testimonies," Vol. 8, p. 39.

In Isaiah 40, God is presented as the Creator. In this chapter the nations are challenged to appear and witness to God's foreknowledge.

The Lord is about to tell them concerning the future, concerning one "who hath raised up one from the east, whom He calleth in righteousness to His foot." Isa. 41:2, English Revised Version. God will give this man "the nations." He will give him "rule over kings." Verse 2. Though this man is unnamed as yet, he is without doubt Cyrus mentioned by name first in Isaiah 44:28; 45:1, and many years before he was born.

God gives each man ample ground for faith. In this chapter He says in substance to Israel, "I will foretell the future. By that you may know that I am God. I challenge the idols to tell us what shall come to pass. They can not do this. When I now tell you concerning the man I will raise up and you see this come to pass just as I say, then you may know that I am indeed the true God, the Creator of heaven and earth."

Help on this chapter may be found in "Prophets and Kings," pages 143-154, the challenge of Elijah to the false gods.

THE LESSON

1. How does God address the islands and the people? Isa. 41:1.

NOTE.—God calls the nations before Him. He is about to speak to them, so He asks them to keep silence. After God has spoken, "then let them speak."

2. What questions does God ask? What would the "man from the east" do? Verses 2, 3.

NOTE.—The sense of these two verses may perhaps best be presented by this paraphrase: "Who hath raised up one from the east who is always victorious? Who hath given him authority over the nations, and made him rule over kings? His sword drives them like dust, his bow like chaff before the wind. He pursues them and marches forward safely and that so swiftly that he does not tread the path with his feet."

Cyrus is the "man from the east." See Introduction.

3. Who had used Cyrus to do these things? How is God spoken of? Verse 4.

NOTE.—This verse does not say that God is the first and the last. That indeed is true. Rev. 1:11. But here it states that God is with the last. Even as God was in the beginning, so He will be with His people to the end, with the last.

4. How is the coöperative spirit of the builders of idols described? Verses 5-7.

NOTE.—The prophet is here describing the condition which would accompany the conquests of Cyrus. The islands and the nations would be afraid; they would "draw near," but not to God. This drawing near probably has reference to the league between Lydia, Babylon, and Egypt against Cyrus. But instead of trusting God, they appeal to their idols, and decide to make a particularly good and strong set of gods.

"Well might the words written of the idol builders of old be, with worthier aim, adopted as a motto by character builders of to-day: 'They helped every one his neighbor; and every one said to his brother, Be of good courage.' "—"Education," p. 286.

5. How does God speak of His people? Whence have they come? Verses 8, 9.

NOTE.—"Abraham my friend"! What a wonderful designation! And we are the children of Abraham, God's friend. God's people will come from the ends of the earth. They may not be perfect, but God has not cast them away.

6. Why should we not fear? Why not be dismayed? What exceedingly precious promises are given? Verse 10.

7. What will be the experience of those who are incensed against God's people? Verses 11, 12.

8. How does God lead His people? Why need no one fear? What two names are given to God? Verses 13, 14.

9. What will God make of His people? What will God's people do to the mountains? In whom will God's people glory? Verses 15, 16.

NOTE.—The time was to come when Israel should again reign. As the instrument of the Almighty they would thresh the nations (mountains). A day also lies just ahead when the Israel of God will no longer be a savor of life to a rebellious world. No more will God spare a world in rebellion because of the righteous remnant. Instead, because of their rebellion and their oppression of His people, the vials of His wrath will be poured upon them. The land will be emptied and desolate (Rev. 5:14-17; Jer. 4:23-28) like Babylon of old (Jer. 51:2). But in that day God's people shall rejoice in Him and "glory in the Holy One of Israel." (See Isa. 25:8, 9.)

10. What precious promise does God give the poor and needy? What will God open for them? Verses 17, 18.

NOTE.—This text has a literal application as well as a spiritual one. Speaking of the time of trouble, we read in "The Great Controversy," page 629:

"The people of God will not be free from suffering; but while persecuted and distressed, while they endure privation, and suffer for want of food, they will not be left to perish. That God who cared for Elijah will not pass by one of His self-sacrificing children. He who numbers the hairs of their head will care for them; and in time of famine they shall be satisfied. While the wicked are dying from hunger and pestilence, angels will shield the righteous, and supply their wants. To him that 'walketh righteously' is the promise, 'Bread shall be given him; his waters shall be sure.' 'When the poor and needy seek water, and there is none, and their tongue faileth for thirst, I the Lord will hear them, I the God of Israel will not forsake them.'"

11. What will God plant in the wilderness and in the desert? Why does God do this? Verses 19, 20.

NOTE.—These trees are of the choicest. The desert itself shall be transformed into a grove of stately, beautiful trees. And the object is that men may see in this a demonstration of the creative power of God.

12. What does God call upon the idols of the nations to do? What does He challenge them to show? Verses 21, 22.

13. How does God further challenge the idols? What does God declare them to be? Verses 23, 24.

NOTE.—God's challenge is definite, "Show us the future. Prove your power to predict, or give any proof of life and activity." (See Jer. 10:5.) God's idea of these idols is well expressed in the margin, "worse than nothing," "worse than of a viper."

14. Whom does God say He has raised up? What shall he do to princes? Verse 25.

NOTE.—Cyrus is here again introduced. He is said to have come from the north, also from the east. In fact, he came from the east, though all armies from the east came around the Arabian desert, and hence attacked Palestine from the north. "Call upon My name." The Cambridge Bible, page 23, makes the following comment: "It is true that in Isaiah 45:4 it is said that Cyrus had not known Jehovah; but it is also said (verse 3) that the effect of his remarkable successes will be 'that thou mayest know that I am Jehovah that calleth thee by thy name, the God of Israel.' There is therefore no difficulty in the idea that Cyrus, who was at first the unconscious instrument of Jehovah's purpose, shall at length recognize that Jehovah was the true author of his success."

15. What questions does God again ask concerning the idols? Verse 26.

16. What will God give to Jerusalem? Verse 27.

NOTE.—The first part of verse 27 in the American Revised Version reads, "I am the first that said unto Zion, Behold, behold them."

17. What does God say He did not find among the idols? What are they again declared to be? Verses 28, 29.

LESSON 3—OCTOBER 20, 1928

THE ELECT OF GOD; A LIGHT OF THE GENTILES

LESSON SCRIPTURE: Isaiah 42.
MEMORY VERSE: Isa. 42: 3, 4.

INTRODUCTION

The work of Christ is definitely set forth in this chapter. He is the elect of God, a term which occurs six times in this portion of Isaiah. He is gentle, quiet, compassionate. He does not come to crush life, but to develop it; not to despise the weak, but to help them. If there is but a dimly burning wick, He does not give up hope. He will not stop until the work is accomplished. Many of the blind shall yet see the light, and the whole earth shall praise the Lord.

THE LESSON

1. What two names does the prophetic word give to Christ? What has God put upon Him? What will He bring to the Gentiles? Isa. 42:1.

NOTE.—Christ is the servant (John 6:38), sent to do the Father's will. He is the elect whom the Father has chosen, and whom He upholds.

"Bring forth judgment." The word "judgment" occurs three times in these first verses, and may be translated "law;" but commentators agree that the word is used here in a larger sense, some rendering the sentence thus: "He shall carry the true religion to the Gentiles."

2. What will be the manner of Christ's working? Verse 2.

NOTE.—Moffatt's translation is, "He shall not be loud and noisy, He shall not shout in public."

"In marked contrast to all this [the manner of the Pharisees] was the life of Jesus. In that life no noisy disputation, no ostentatious worship, no act to gain applause, was ever witnessed. Christ was hid in God, and God was revealed in the character of His Son. To this revelation Jesus desired the minds of the people to be directed, and their homage to be given."—"The Desire of Ages," p. 261.

3. What two examples show Christ's love and tenderness for the weak? Verse 3, margin.

NOTE.—There are few more beautiful passages in the Bible. The reed may be bruised, Christ will not break it. The candle may burn dimly, but He will not blow it out. There may not be much strength, the life may be bruised and broken; there may not be much light, rather smoke and darkness. But Christ does not give up hope. His own light does not burn dimly. By gentle measures the smoking flax may be fanned into a flame. His purpose shall not be broken, and the true religion shall be extended to all the earth.

4. What is Christ's attitude toward His work? What will He accomplish? For what do the isles wait? Verse 4.

NOTE.—The words "fail" and "be discouraged" correspond in the original to "dimly burning" and "broken" in verse 3. (See margin, American Revised Version.)

5. How is the true God revealed? Verse 5.

NOTE.—Again and again the true God is mentioned as the Creator. Here the reading really is, Thus saith the God who alone is truly God. "That which cometh out of it," probably refers to all that the earth produces,—gold, silver, and vegetation.

6. How does God speak of Christ's appointment to His work? How will God sustain Him? For what will He give Him to the people and to the Gentiles? Verse 6.

7. What is further prophesied concerning the work of Christ? Verse 7.

8. What does God say of His name? What is said concerning the Lord's glory and praise? Verse 8.

9. What has been true of "the former things"? What is said of the future? Verse 9.

NOTE.—The former things which God had foretold had all been fulfilled. He was now telling of new things. These would as surely come to pass.

10. What are we exhorted to do? Who are to sing this song? Verses 10-12.

11. What is the Lord about to do? Verses 13-15.

NOTE.—The reason for singing the new song is given in these verses. God is about to manifest Himself. The second coming of Christ is here brought to view. For a long time God has refrained Himself and kept still when iniquity raised its ugly head. But now God will restrain Himself no more. He will go forth. He will prevail against His enemies.

12. What is God's promise to the blind? How will He lead them? Verses 16-18.

NOTE.—The blind here must have reference to the spiritually blind. In "Prophets and Kings," page 378, this text is applied to "all the honest in heart in heathen lands." There are many who are blind, but honest. That which seems to them to be darkness will then be made light, and the crooked things will be made straight. This should give us hope for many who apparently are rejecting light.

13. Who is spoken of as being blind and deaf? Though many things may be seen and heard, what does the Lord's servant not do? Verses 19, 20.

NOTE.—"The terms 'My servant,' 'Israel,' 'the servant of the Lord,' mean anyone that the Lord may select and appoint to do a certain work. He makes them ministers of His will, though some who are selected may be as ignorant of His will as was Nebuchadnezzar."—"Testimonies," Vol. 9, p. 138.

"God does not wish us to hear all that is to be heard, or to see all that is to be seen. It is a great blessing to close the ears, that we hear not, and the eyes, that we see not. The greatest anxiety should be to have clear eyesight to discern our own shortcomings, and a quick ear to catch all needed reproof and instruction, lest by our inattention and carelessness we let them slip, and become forgetful hearers, and not doers of the work."—"Testimonies," Vol. 1, pp. 707, 708.

14. What is the Lord well pleased to do? Verse 21.

NOTE.—"The beloved disciple, who listened to the words of Jesus on the mount, writing long afterwards under the inspiration of the Holy Spirit, speaks of the law as of perpetual obligation. He says that 'sin is the transgression of the law,' and that 'whosoever committeth sin transgresseth also the law.' He makes it plain that the law to which he refers is 'an old commandment which ye had from the beginning.' He is speaking of the law that existed at the creation, and was reiterated upon Mount Sinai."—"Thoughts from the Mount of Blessing," p. 77.

"The third angel's message, embracing the messages of the first and second angels, is the message for this time. We are to raise aloft the banner on which is inscribed, 'The commandments of God, and the faith of Jesus.' The world is soon to meet the great Lawgiver over His broken law. This is not the time to put out of sight the great issues before us. God calls upon His people to magnify the law, and make it honorable."—"Testimonies," Vol. 8, p. 197.

15. What calamities had come upon God's people? What appeal did the Lord make? Verses 22, 23.

16. Who permitted the calamities to come? Why were they permitted? Yet what did the people not do? Verses 24, 25.

LESSON 4—OCTOBER 27, 1928

THE GATHERING OF ISRAEL; WITNESSES FOR GOD

LESSON SCRIPTURE: Isaiah 43.
MEMORY VERSE: Isa. 43: 25.

INTRODUCTION

The lesson of this chapter centers around two main topics. The first seven verses tell of God's great love for His people, His willingness to make any sacrifice to insure their salvation, even to the lives of men and of peoples, to make certain that no honest heart should be lost. He then makes the promise that every member of His family, those called by His name, should all be gathered to Himself.

The second topic deals with the weighing of men in the balances, a testing of their loyalty. God depends upon the witness of His children. We are to testify of what He has done for us, of what we know by personal experience. A witness is allowed to tell only of that which he personally knows to be true. Now what has God done for you? God is looking for witnesses to testify to what He has done for them.

THE LESSON

1. What comforting statement is made by the Lord to His people? Isa. 43:1.

NOTE.—"Fear not." This blessed assurance that we need not fear is especially comforting in view of the last verses of the preceding chapter, where it is stated that God will pour out His fury against them that walk not in His ways nor keep His law.

"Called thee by thy name." "Jesus knows us individually, and is touched with the feeling of our infirmities. He knows us all by name. He knows the very house in which we live, the name of each occupant. He has at times given directions to His servants to go to a certain street in a certain city, to such a house, to find one of His sheep. Every soul is as fully known to Jesus as if he were the only one for whom the Saviour died."—"The Desire of Ages," p. 479.

2. What promises are given to God's people when in trial? Verses 2, 3.

NOTE.—God's promise to help His people has been wonderfully fulfilled in the past. For example, see Daniel 3: 27 and Exodus 14: 21, 22. When the trials of the last days shall come, these promises will become very precious indeed.

"Often the church militant is called upon to suffer trial and affliction; for not without severe conflict is the church to triumph. 'The

[11]

bread of adversity,' 'the water of affliction,' these are the common lot of all; but none who put their trust in the One mighty to deliver will be utterly overwhelmed."—"Prophets and Kings," p. 723.

3. How much does God think of His people? Verse 4.

NOTE.—God loves His people. He loves them so much that their worth can not be expressed in terms of money. He would gladly give Egypt, Ethiopia, and Seba for them. "I will give men for thee." That which is of immeasurably greater value than silver or gold, than property of any kind—men, human lives—God would give for His people. He spared not His own Son, but freely gave Him. He has permitted some of His own to give their lives for those "other sheep" who have not known Him.

4. Why need we not fear? From what parts of the earth will God call His people? Verses 5, 6.

NOTE.—This scripture is now being fulfilled. The message is sounding in all parts of the earth, and God is calling men from every nation, kindred, tongue, and people.

5. What will those who come from the ends of the earth be called? Why was man created? Verse 7.

NOTE.—"Called by My name." Of a certain company it is written that they will have the Father's name written in their foreheads. Rev. 14: 1. God's name is what He is. Ex. 3: 14. Hence, to be called by the name of God means to have His character.

6. What call does God now issue to all nations? What challenge does He make? Verses 8, 9.

NOTE.—God is calling all nations together as to a judgment scene. "Let them bring forth their witnesses," He says. The question is, Who is the true God? He challenges them to "show us former things," that is, things that they have predicted and which have come to pass. If they profess to do this, let them bring forth their witnesses to support their contention. If they can not do this, let them hear God's side of the case and say, "It is truth."

7. What does God call His people? What may they know, believe, and understand? What does God say of Himself? Verse 10.

NOTE.—"Our confession of His faithfulness is Heaven's chosen agency for revealing Christ to the world. We are to acknowledge His grace as made known through the holy men of old; but that which will be most effectual is the testimony of our own experience. We are witnesses for God as we reveal in ourselves the working of a power that is divine. Every individual has a life distinct from all others, and an experience differing essentially from theirs. God desires that our praise shall ascend to Him, marked with our own individuality. These precious acknowledgments to the praise of the glory of His grace, when supported by a Christlike life, have an irresistible power, that works for the salvation of souls."—"Ministry of Healing," p. 100.

8. What does God say of Himself? What three things does God say He has done to which His people are called to witness? Verses 11, 12.

NOTE.—"The people of the world are worshiping false gods. They are to be turned from their false worship, not by hearing denunciation of their idols, but by beholding something better. God's goodness is to be made known. 'Ye are My witnesses, saith the Lord, that I am God.' "—"Christ's Object Lessons," p. 299.

As to being a witness, "This also we shall be in eternity."—"Education," p. 308.

"The redeemed only, of all created beings, have in their own experience known the actual conflict with sin; they have wrought with Christ, and, as even the angels could not do, have entered into the fellowship of His sufferings; will they have no testimony as to the science of redemption,—nothing that will be of worth to unfallen beings?"—Ibid.

9. How does God declare His omnipotence? Verse 13.

NOTE.—The first statement, "Before the day was I am He," is variously translated. The sense seems to be, "I am ever the same." Before the day was, that is, before time began, "I am He." "From this day forth I am He." American Revised Version, margin.

10. How is the fall of Babylon announced? Verses 14-17.

NOTE.—In these verses the fall of Babylon is announced, but in very general terms. We are told that the chariot and horse, the army and the power, shall lie down together and not rise again, that they shall become extinct. When this calamity should come, His people were to know that the Holy One, the Creator of Israel, is their King, and that He will make a way for them in the sea and a path in the mighty waters.

11. What does God say His people are not to remember? What will God do? Who shall show forth His praise? Verses 18-21.

NOTE.—These verses are evidently to be understood in a spiritual sense. God will do a new thing. He will make a way in the wilderness, and rivers in the desert, and there He will give drink to His people, His chosen.

12. What complaint does God bring against His people? What have they not brought? With what has God not wearied them? Verses 22, 23.

NOTE.—God's people have neglected prayers; they have become weary of Him. What an indictment! Against this charge God defends Himself. He has not required very much of His people. He has not wearied them either with offerings or with incense.

13. What further complaint does God make? What does He say they have done? Verse 24.

NOTE.—God now speaks of His weariness of His people. "I have not caused thee to serve," He says, "but thou hast made Me to serve with thy sins." I have not "wearied thee with incense," but "thou hast wearied Me with thine iniquities." All power is of God. When we sin, we use for a base purpose the power God has given us. We make Him to serve with our sins. What a fearful condition!

14. What does God say He is doing? Why? What will He not remember? Verse 25.

Note.—It would be natural to expect God to be so weary with our sins that He would turn us away. On the contrary, God blots out our sins, not for our sakes, not because we deserve it, but for His own sake.

15. Of what does God say we are to put Him in remembrance? What invitation is given? Verse 26.

Note.—The more probable interpretation is, "Put Me in remembrance of My promises; plead them before Me; declare them, that I may justify thee." What a gracious invitation!

16. Who has sinned? Who have transgressed? What was God therefore forced to do? Verses 27, 28.

Note.—"You have no good thing wherewith to come before Me. Your first father sinned; your teachers have sinned. I have punished them. If you escape, it is only because of My great mercy."

LESSON 5—NOVEMBER 3, 1928

THE TRUE GOD; VANITY OF IDOLS; CYRUS, THE SHEPHERD

LESSON SCRIPTURE: Isaiah 44; 45: 1-4.
MEMORY VERSE: Isa. 44: 22.

INTRODUCTION

God will pour out His Spirit, but only upon them that are thirsty. Many will be converted also among the Gentiles and heathen. These shall all acknowledge the true God and keep themselves from idols.

Two things distinguish the true God from false gods. God is the Creator. God is the God of prophecy. He can tell the future.

We may not worship idols of wood and stone. But if we do not acknowledge God as Creator, if we accept evolution as a substitute for creation, we have formed another god and rejected the true One.

God may use nations and kings to fulfill His word. So He did in the case of Cyrus. Our faith should be strengthened as we see fulfilled prophecy.

THE LESSON

1. Whom is God addressing in the first verse of this lesson? How does God again call attention to the fact that He is the Creator? Isa. 44:1, 2.

Note.—It is interesting to note how God uses every opportunity to emphasize the fact of creation. Here He announces Himself as the One who made and formed man.

Jeshurun means the "upright one." It may here be used to show the change from "Jacob, the supplanter."

2. Upon whom will God pour water, symbolic of the Spirit? What will be the result of this outpouring? Verses 3, 4.

Note.—"There are certain conditions upon which we may expect that God will hear and answer our prayers. One of the first of these

[14]

is that we feel our need of help from Him. He has promised, 'I will pour water upon him that is thirsty, and floods upon the dry ground.' Those who hunger and thirst after righteousness, who long after God, may be sure that they will be filled. The heart must be open to the Spirit's influence, or God's blessing can not be received."—"Steps to Christ," p. 99.

The result of the outpouring of the Spirit is the springing up here and there of life,—new believers.

3. **What will one say? What will others do? Verse 5.**

NOTE.—This verse tells of the ingathering of Gentiles as a result of the outpouring of the Spirit.

4. **How does God speak of Himself? What proof does He present to show that beside Him there is no god? Verses 6-8.**

NOTE.—God is here King, Redeemer, the First and the Last, the only One.

A paraphrase of verse 7 would read: "Who is like Me? For since the beginning, I have prophesied and declared and set in order. Now let them,—the false gods,—tell us the future."

God repeatedly calls attention to prophecy as incontestable proof of divinity. We may do the same. We need not fear. God stands by His predictions.

5. **What does God call the maker of graven images? Who makes these images? Verses 9-11.**

NOTE.—"Their delectable things." Another name for their idols which are "pets, favorites, treasures." They are their own witnesses. They witness against themselves, for they can neither see nor know. How, then, can they help others? Verse 10 is a rhetorical question, "Who is so foolish as to make an image?"

"His fellows," that is, worshipers.

The workmen are men. And how can men make a god?

6. **How is the fashioning of an idol described? Verses 12-17.**

7. **What have the makers of idols not known? What have they not considered? On what do they feed? What has turned them aside? Verses 18-20.**

NOTE.—"He hath shut their eyes." Rather, their eyes are plastered over.

"None considereth." They do not think, they do not reflect. If they did, they would see the folly of their action.

"Feedeth on ashes." (See Prov. 15: 14; Hosea 12: 1.)

"A deceived heart." We need to ask God to help us not to deceive ourselves.

"Can not deliver his soul." Help must come from some outside source. We can not save ourselves. An idol is a lie. Men believe an idol can help. But it is a vain hope.

8. **What are Jacob and Israel told to do? What has God blotted out? What invitation is given? Verses 21, 22.**

NOTE.—God tells His people to remember these things of which He has just been speaking. And if they do, God will remember them. They shall not be forgotten. God not merely promises to forgive, but in this text it is spoken of as already done. "I have blotted out." I is as though a father were speaking to a wayward son or daughter who had caused the parents much sorrow and grief, "I have forgiven the past. All is well. Come home. Return to me. I have redeemed you.'

9. Why are heaven and earth called upon to break forth into singing? Verse 23.

NOTE.—Rejoice, for the Lord hath done it! The Lord hath redeemed Jacob.

10. How does the Lord again note His creative power? What other references does He make to His power? Verses 24-27.

11. What is said of Cyrus? What should be done to Jerusalem? Verse 28.

NOTE.—The mention of Cyrus by name, one hundred fifty years before his appearance, has been one of the chief factors in the decision of the critics that Isaiah did not write this part of his prophecies. It seems impossible to them that God could give a man's name even before his birth. Such an attitude shows a great lack of faith, and, indeed, most of the work of the critics is founded in unbelief. Josiah's name was announced three centuries before his birth. 1 Kings 13:2. And why should it be thought a thing incredible that God should do this? These very chapters in Isaiah emphasize again and again that God is different from idols. He can foretell the future. They can not. For anyone to hold the view that God can not tell what is to come, is to put Him on a level with idols.

12. What is Cyrus here called? What had God done? What did He say He would do for him? Isa. 45:1.

NOTE.—"His anointed." The only place in the Scriptures where this is spoken of a Gentile.

"The advent of the army of Cyrus before the walls of Babylon was to the Jews a sign that their deliverance from captivity was drawing nigh. More than a century before the birth of Cyrus, Inspiration had mentioned him by name, and had caused a record to be made of the actual work he should do in taking the city of Babylon unawares, and in preparing the way for the release of the children of the captivity. Through Isaiah the word had been spoken. . . .

"In the unexpected entry of the army of the Persian conqueror into the heart of the Babylonian capital by way of the channel of the river whose waters had been turned aside, and through the inner gates that in careless security had been left open and unprotected, the Jews had abundant evidence of the literal fulfillment of Isaiah's prophecy concerning the sudden overthrow of their oppressors."—"Prophets and Kings," pp. 551, 552.

13. What would God do for Cyrus? Who would break in pieces the gates of brass? Why would this be done? Verses 2, 3.

NOTE.—God would go before and help Cyrus. He is the One who would cause the gates to open. God would so work that Cyrus could not fail to know that some supernatural power was helping him. Babylon, according to Herodotus, had one hundred gates, all of brass. The city could not be taken in any ordinary manner.

14. For whose sake was Cyrus called by name? Verse 4.

NOTE.—To establish the faith of His people, God called Cyrus by name. When we see prophecy fulfilled, our faith should become stronger. The fulfillment of prophecy in the signs of the times occurring all about us should have the same effect.

LESSON 6—NOVEMBER 10, 1928

THE VANITY OF FALSE GODS; ONE ONLY SAVIOUR

LESSON SCRIPTURE: Isaiah 45: 5-25; 46.
MEMORY VERSE: Isa. 45: 18.

INTRODUCTION

The warnings against idolatry do not have reference only to the time of Isaiah. Anything that comes between us and our God is a false god, an idol. Whether it be worldly pleasure, the lusts of the flesh or of the eye, worldly wisdom, the follies and fashions of the hour, or position or honor, or the plaudits of the crowd,—all these are condemned as idolatry.

But there are other dangers,—dangers threatening the church of God. Anything or anyone besides Christ which we trust to help us to obtain God's favor, becomes a vain hope, a false god. No works of our own can take the place of Christ. There is only one Saviour. Isa. 45:21. He saves to the uttermost. Remember the admonition, "Keep yourselves from idols." 1 John 5: 21.

THE LESSON

1. What does the Lord proclaim concerning Himself? What had He done for Cyrus? Isa. 45:5.

NOTE.—"I girded thee." As God loosed the loins of the adversaries (verse 1), to weaken them, so He "girded" those of Cyrus, to strengthen him.

2. For what purpose was this done? Verse 6.

3. What does God form? Create? Make? Verse 7.

NOTE.—"Create evil." The "evil" here mentioned is not moral evil but physical, and could well be translated calamity. God punishes for sin, and it is these calamities to which the prophet refers. (See Amos 3:6.)

4. What blessings are promised to God's people? Verse 8.

NOTE.—These words indicate in figurative language the blessed consequences of opening the heart to God's righteousness. Reference is here made to the creative power of God manifested in the new life.

5. What warning is given concerning murmuring against our Maker? Verses 9, 10.

6. How does God here make known His creative power and foreknowledge? Verses 11-14.

NOTE.—God had raised up Cyrus, and would direct his ways. He was to conquer Egypt and Ethiopia, and they were to acknowledge God's dealings.

7. What is God said to do? What will be the experience of idolaters? What contrast is shown in the experience of Israel? Verses 15-17.

NOTE.—God sometimes hides Himself. He "moves in a mysterious way, His wonders to perform." Rom. 11:33.

"An everlasting salvation." Not saved to-day and lost to-morrow. Not a wonderful mountain-top experience one year at some great meeting, and then an intermediate lapse into the valley.

"World without end." Literally, to all eternity.

8. For what purpose did God form the earth? Verse 18.

9. How has God spoken to mankind? Verse 19.

NOTE.—God may at times hide Himself, but He does not speak in secret. Deut. 30:11-14. He does not ask men to seek Him in vain, literally, in chaos, that is, without definite guidance and without hope of result.

10. Who are told to assemble themselves? What do those do who have no knowledge of God? What questions are asked? What answers are given? To whom are the ends of the earth to look? Verses 20-22.

NOTE.—"Ye that are escaped of the nations." This call is to all who "are escaped," that is, those whom God has called and who have responded.

"Tell ye." Announce, or, as in the American Revised Version, "declare," His message of mercy to the nations.

11. What has God sworn concerning the people of earth? Verse 23.

NOTE.—Referring to events to take place at the close of the millennium, the following description is given: "Now Christ again appears to the view of His enemies. Far above the city, upon a foundation of burnished gold, is a throne, high and lifted up. Upon this throne sits the Son of God, and around Him are the subjects of His kingdom. The power and majesty of Christ no language can describe, no pen portray."—"The Great Controversy," pp. 664, 665.

"As if entranced, the wicked have looked upon the coronation of the Son of God. They see in His hands the tables of the divine law, the statutes which they have despised and transgressed. They witness the outburst of wonder, rapture, and adoration from the saved; and as the wave of melody sweeps over the multitudes without the city, all with one voice exclaim, 'Great and marvelous are Thy works, Lord God Almighty; just and true are Thy ways, Thou King of saints;' and falling prostrate, they worship the Prince of life."—Id., pp. 668, 669.

12. In whom do we have righteousness and strength? In whom are we justified? Verses 24, 25.

13. What is said of the downfall of the Babylonian gods? What will happen to them? Isa. 46:1, 2.

NOTE.—Bel and Nebo were Babylonian gods, answering to Jupiter and Mercury. (See Acts 14:12.) Bel is the same as Baal, mentioned elsewhere in the Bible.

The picture here is of the Babylonians trying to save their gods. They put them on beasts, and they make a load. "They could not deliver." Their gods can not save them. They themselves, the gods, are "gone into captivity."

14. How does God, by contrast, speak of Himself? What beautiful promises are given to those who are growing old? Verses 3, 4.

Note.—The contrast here is striking. While the Babylonians must carry their idols to save them, God carries and delivers. God will not forsake. "Even to your old age I am He."

15. How is an idol made? Verses 5-7.

16. What does God counsel us to remember? Verses 8, 9.

Note.—Remember this, and show yourselves men! In a time of idolatry, when the whole current of life is downward, it takes courage to stand against popular superstitions and customs. God calls for men. "The greatest want of the world is the want of men,—men who will not be bought or sold; men who in their inmost souls are true and honest; men who do not fear to call sin by its right name; men whose conscience is as true to duty as the needle to the pole; men who will stand for the right though the heavens fall."—"Education," p. 57.

17. What does God declare from the beginning? What shall stand? Verse 10.

Note.—God again calls attention to the prophetic word, saying He has declared "the end from the beginning." Even in the first chapter of the Bible the heavenly bodies are mentioned as being signs.

"My counsel shall stand." Isa. 14:24.
"My pleasure," rather, My purpose.

18. How is Cyrus spoken of? To whom does God appeal? What will He bring near? What does He say of His salvation? Verses 11-13.

Note.—Cyrus is here likened to a ravenous bird, as Nebuchadnezzar was likened to an eagle. Eze. 17:3. The royal Persian ensign was an eagle.

LESSON 7—NOVEMBER 17, 1928

THE FATE OF BABYLON; GOD'S FINAL APPEAL TO HIS PEOPLE

LESSON SCRIPTURE: Isaiah 47; 48.
MEMORY VERSE: Isa. 48:18.

INTRODUCTION

Babylon was given to pleasure, was tender and delicate. Vice and folly sapped her strength. Gluttony, effeminacy, overrefinement, luxury, pride, self-exaltation, were among her besetting sins. Babylon said in her heart, "I am, and none else beside me." Pride was a dominant trait. And pride goes before destruction.

The sins that caused Babylon's fall are prevalent now, and will bring about the same results.

In Isaiah 48, God makes another appeal to His creative power and to prophecy as the proof of His being the true God. In Isaiah's day it was the Creator against false gods, idols. To-day it is the same. False, evolutionary teachings are among the many theories by which a scientific age would set aside the true God, the Creator of the heavens and the earth.

THE LESSON

1. **What message came to the ruler of Babylon? Dan. 4:31; Isa. 47:1-5.**

NOTE.—"To the ruler of Babylon came the sentence of the divine Watcher: O king, 'to thee it is spoken: The kingdom is departed from thee.'

" 'Come down, and sit in the dust, O virgin daughter of Babylon,
Sit on the ground; there is no throne. . . .
Sit thou silent,
And get thee into darkness, O daughter of the Chaldeans;
For thou shalt no more be called the lady of kingdoms.' "—"Education," p. 176. This was fulfilled in the time of Belshazzar.

"While still in the festal hall, surrounded by those whose doom had been sealed, the king is informed by a messenger that 'his city is taken' by the enemy against whose devices he had felt so secure; 'that the passages are stopped, . . . and the men of war are affrighted.' Even while he and his nobles were drinking from the sacred vessels of Jehovah, and praising their gods of silver and of gold, the Medes and the Persians, having turned the Euphrates out of its channel, were marching into the heart of the unguarded city. The army of Cyrus now stood under the walls of the palace; the city was filled with the soldiers of the enemy, 'as with caterpillars;' and their triumphant shouts could be heard above the despairing cries of the astonished revelers. 'In that night was Belshazzar the king of the Chaldeans slain,' and an alien monarch sat upon the throne."—"Prophets and Kings," p. 531.

2. **Because of the sins of His people, what had God done to His inheritance? How had Babylon treated the captives? Isa. 47:6.**

NOTE.—God's people had sinned, and He had been wroth. Isa. 64: 5, 9. The inheritance, the holy land, had been polluted, and Israel carried into captivity. Babylon had shown Israel but little mercy, and the ancient people, literally, aged people, had been compelled to work hard.

3. **What had Babylon said? To what was Babylon given? How did she not expect to sit? What should come in one day? Verses 7-9; Rev. 18:7, 8.**

NOTE.—"Given to pleasures." Babylon is not much different now. "Dwellest carelessly." Belshazzar was dancing and drinking while Death stalked without! Dancing the last night of probation! Dancing on the brink of the abyss! Dancing while the Hand was about to write Babylon's doom!

4. **What had Babylon further said? What had perverted her? What had she said in her heart? Isaiah 47:10.**

Note.—"None seeth me." So think they that are now of Babylon.

5. What would Babylon not be able to put off? How was desolation to come? What challenge was given? Verses 11, 12.

Note.—Punishment for sin is sure. It may be delayed, but it can not be put off indefinitely. Destruction will come, and come suddenly. Verse 12 is a challenge to the sorcerers and enchanters to come forth with their enchantments, to see if they can avert the evil. The prophet here taunts the sorcerers as Elijah did the prophets of Baal.

6. What further challenge does the prophet issue? What does he say of those who make false claims? What can they not do for themselves? Verses 13-15.

Note.—"The astrologers and stargazers were men who pretended to read the future from a study of the position of the stars. The monthly prognosticators were such as prepared monthly almanacs in which coming disasters were foretold, and lucky and unlucky days pointed out."—Cambridge Bible.

The destruction of Babylon by fire would not be a "fire to sit before," not one merely to warm one's self by, but an all-consuming destruction.

7. Whom does God here address? What is said of their sincerity? Of what city do they boast? In whom do they profess to take refuge? Isa. 48:1, 2.

8. What has God declared from the beginning? What does He say of the fulfillment of His word? How does He speak of His people? Why did God make known the events of the future? Verses 3-5.

Note.—If God had not prophesied beforehand what should come to pass, some would have given the credit to idols, saying that their idols had done it or commanded it.

9. What has God shown? Why had He not shown them before? Verses 6-8.

Note.—These verses might be paraphrased thus: "Thou hast heard all this, and now thou seest it fulfilled. I will show thee from this time new things, which thou hast not known before. They are entirely new, and before to-day thou hast not heard them, lest thou shouldest say, Behold, I knew them."

10. For His own sake, what did God do? What had He done to Israel? Whence did He choose them? For whose sake does He do this? Verses 9-11.

Note.—Instead of cutting off Israel, God purified them in the furnace of affliction. He might leave Israel, but it would mean destruction. The only alternative is the furnace. So it is with us. God has good reason for leaving us to our own way. But that would mean eternal loss. Our only hope is God's purifying fire,—trials.

11. In what terms does God again proclaim Himself the Creator? How do heaven and earth obey Him? Verses 12, 13.

12. What will God do to Babylon? Whom has He called? Verses 4-16.

NOTE.—God now again calls upon the nations to hear Him. Babylon shall fall. Verse 14. God has called him, that is Cyrus, and will prosper him. Verse 15. Now, let every one hear this, for God is not speaking in secret. One hundred fifty years before Cyrus appears, God is saying this: Cyrus shall destroy Babylon. My word has always been fulfilled; and when you see this come to pass, when you see Babylon fall by a man whom I have named years before his birth, you may know that I am God.

This is the last time Cyrus is mentioned in Isaiah. And with this chapter God closes the argument which He has so often used to prove His divinity, the facts of prophecy and creation.

13. By what names is God called? What does God teach His people? How does He lead? Verse 17.

14. What desire does God express? If the desire had been realized, what would result? Verses 18, 19.

NOTE.—"Those who take Christ at His word, and surrender their souls to His keeping, their lives to His ordering, will find peace and quietude. Nothing of the world can make them sad when Jesus makes them glad by His presence. In perfect acquiescence there is perfect rest."—"The Desire of Ages," p. 331.

15. What call is given to God's people in Babylon? In what spirit will this call be given? How far will the message be sent? What will they say? Verse 20.

NOTE.—This verse is prophetic of the last call to come out of Babylon. Rev. 18:4.

"With a voice of singing." Clear, definite, musical. Not gloomy, but happy, for a way of escape has been found.

This message will go to the end of the earth, and with it the blessed assurance that God has redeemed His people.

16. How did God preserve His people when they fled from Egypt? Verse 21.

NOTE.—This verse should be a source of comfort to God's people at this time. The way may be rough and thorny, but God will not leave His own. Psalm 91.

17. What do the wicked lack? Verse 22.

NOTE.—God "gives no one liberty to gloss over the sins of His people, nor to cry, 'Peace, peace!' when He has declared that there shall be no peace for the wicked. Those who stir up rebellion against the servants whom God sends to deliver His messages are rebelling against the word of the Lord."—"Testimonies," Vol. 4, p. 185.

THIRTEENTH SABBATH OFFERING

December 29, 1928

INTER-AMERICAN DIVISION

LESSON 8—NOVEMBER 24, 1928

THE SERVANT: HOPE FOR THE DISCOURAGED

LESSON SCRIPTURE: Isa. 49: 1-23.
MEMORY VERSE: Isa. 49: 15, 16.

INTRODUCTION

With this chapter begins a new section of the book of Isaiah. The term "the servant" is often mentioned. This refers to Christ, but in some cases it has a double application and refers also to God's people. However, there need be no confusion on this point, as the references are clear.

THE LESSON

1. In the beginning of this chapter, who are called upon to listen? To what has God compared the mouth? What does God say of His people? Isa. 49:1-3.

NOTE.—"Isles," literally, countries; "people," literally, peoples. The whole world is called upon to hear the announcement, for it concerns the whole world.

"The Lord hath called Me." Luke 1:31-33.
"Mention of My name." Matt. 1:21.
"Sharp sword." Heb. 4:12.
"A polished shaft," or arrow, even sharper than a sword.
The description of "the servant" is that of Christ.

"The Desire of Ages," pages 678, 679, quoting Isaiah 49:4, 5, 7-10, applies the scripture to Christ. "Testimonies," Vol. 7, pages 191, 192, quoting Isaiah 49:2-6, applies it to the people of God. Hence we accept these references as having a double application, first to Christ, then to Israel, old and new.

2. What brought discouragement to "the Servant"? In what words did He leave the matter with God? Verse 4.

NOTE.—"As the world's Redeemer, Christ was constantly confronted with apparent failure. He, the messenger of mercy to our world, seemed to do little of the work He longed to do in uplifting and saving. Satanic influences were constantly working to oppose His way. But He would not be discouraged. Through the prophecy of Isaiah He declares, 'I have labored in vain, I have spent My strength for naught, and in vain: yet surely My judgment is with the Lord, and My work with My God.' "—"The Desire of Ages," p. 678.

If Christ could feel a sense of discouragement, is it surprising that we sometimes feel the same way? Let us follow His example: leave ourselves with the Lord, and take courage.

The American Revised Version translates the latter part of the verse: "Yet surely the justice due to Me is with Jehovah, and My recompense with My God."

3. For what purpose was "the Servant" called? How was He regarded by the Lord? Verse 5.

NOTE.—This verse seems to have definite reference to Christ. He was called to bring "Jacob" back to God, and also, as the American Revised Version has it, "that Israel be gathered unto Him."

Christ was glorious, or honorable, in the sight of God. Yet He did not take glory to Himself. He said, "I can of Mine own self do nothing." John 5: 30.

4. What does God say is a light thing? To whom did God say He would also make the Servant a light? For what purpose? Verse 6.

NOTE.—"This prophecy was generally understood as spoken of the Messiah, and when Jesus said, 'I am the light of the world,' the people could not fail to recognize His claim to be the Promised One."—"The Desire of Ages," p. 465.

"Prophets and Kings," pages 688, 689, says that it was generally understood that the coming of the Messiah was referred to in the prophecy of Isaiah 49:6.

This prophecy, however, also has an application to the people of God. After quoting Isaiah 49:6, "Testimonies," Vol. 7, page 192, says:

"This is the word of the Lord to all who are in any way connected with His appointed institutions. They are favored of God, for they are brought into channels where the light shines. They are in His special service, and they should not esteem this a light thing."

A paraphrase of Isaiah 49:6 would read: "It is too small a work for you to labor only among those who already know the truth. I will send you for a light to the heathen, that you may bring salvation to the ends of the earth."

This is an excellent foreign-missionary text. God's ministers are not constantly to hover over the churches. The call is to send the message to the ends of the earth. Nor must the people demand that their tithes and offerings be spent in ministering to themselves, thus consuming their own gifts.

5. How is Christ spoken of? What prophecy is made concerning Him? Verse 7.

NOTE.—This verse refers definitely to Christ. "It is to Christ that the promise is given," says "The Desire of Ages," page 678, quoting Isaiah 49:7-10. He was despised of men. Isa. 53:3. It is not the Jews only who cry, "Away with Him." John 19:15. "A servant of rulers," taunted and scourged by such rulers as Herod and Pontius Pilate. Luke 23:11; John 19:1, 16. Nevertheless the time will come when kings and rulers shall "see and arise." Wonderful change!

6. When did God hear? When did He help? For what would God give Christ to the people? What should be done to the earth? Verse 8.

NOTE.—Christ is here again spoken of as the covenant. (Compare chapter 42:6.) He has become the mediator of a new covenant (Heb. 8:6), and hence may be spoken of in the terms of our text.

"Establish the earth," rather, raise up the earth, that is, lift it out of its present degraded, sin-cursed condition. Christ came to seek and to save that which is lost, and this includes the earth.

7. What shall be said to the prisoners? What to those in darkness? What shall these liberated prisoners do? Verse 9.

NOTE.—Compare Isaiah 61:1. Moffatt translates the latter part of the verse thus: "On the road home food shall never fail them, they shall find pasture even upon bare hills."

8. What experience shall they not have? How are they protected from these? Verse 10; Ps. 121:6.

9. How shall the way be prepared? Whence do these prisoners come? Isa. 49:11, 12.

NOTE.—By many commentators Sinim is thought to refer to China.

10. Why are the heavens and the earth to rejoice? But what does Zion, or God's people, say? Verses 13, 14.

11. What illustration is used to show forth God's remembrance of His people? What assurance is given? Where are we graven? Who shall be separated from God's people? Verses 15-17.

NOTE.—"Not a single soul who puts his trust in Him will be forgotten. God thinks of His children with the tenderest solicitude, and keeps a book of remembrance before Him, that He may never forget the children of His care."—"Testimonies," Vol. 4. pp. 329, 330.

Verse 17 contains an interesting statement. "Thy destroyers and they that made thee waste shall go forth of thee." While God's people are to go out of Babylon, when it comes to the church, it is not the church that leaves and goes out, but the destroyers, the wasters. It is not those that "go forth" that constitute the church. The church remains.

12. After the wasters and destroyers have gone forth from the church, who shall come to take their place? What solemn statement does the Lord make? Verse 18.

13. What shall be too narrow? What shall these new children say? Verses 19, 20.

14. What questions shall Zion ask? What answer does the Lord give? What is said of kings and queens? Who shall not be ashamed? Verses 21-23.

NOTE.—These latter verses without doubt found their first fulfillment in the coming in of the Gentiles in the Christian era. May we not believe they will find another and even more complete fulfillment, and that they that wait for the Lord shall not be ashamed?

LESSON 9—DECEMBER 1, 1928

"THY SAVIOUR AND THY REDEEMER"

LESSON SCRIPTURE: Isa. 49: 24-26; 50.
MEMORY VERSE: Isa. 50: 10.

INTRODUCTION

To Isaiah had been revealed a comprehensive view of the plan of salvation. He understood that man was Satan's captive, and also that there is One mightier than the mighty who could take away the prey, and that this One was the Lord, "thy Saviour and thy Redeemer."

To the Jew, the word Redeemer was most expressive and meaningful. Sometimes a poor man might sell himself. If so, he could be redeemed, but only by one near of kin. Lev. 25:47-49. The redemption was effected by the kinsman's paying the just demand in full. Lev. 25:27; 1 Peter 1:18, 19. The story of Ruth is a beautiful illustration of redemption.

This lesson also brings to view the suffering Saviour. What a wonderful picture is given of His passion! He feels the insults to the quick, but does not draw back. His face is set like a flint; that is, He is determined to go through to the end. The Lord will help Him. They will "stand together." Christ passed through darkness. Let others who may be doing God's will, yet are confronted with difficulties and perplexities, take courage. God is still living.

THE LESSON

1. What question is asked concerning the mighty, and the lawful captive? Isa. 49:24.

2. What answer does the Lord give? What does the Lord promise to do? Verse 25.

NOTE.—"The mighty" here spoken of, is Satan. He has some captives, some who have given themselves over to evil, and are justly his captives.

"All who willfully depart from God's commandments are placing themselves under the control of Satan. Many a man tampers with evil, thinking that he can break away at pleasure; but he is lured on and on, until he finds himself controlled by a will stronger than his own. . . .

"Yet his condition is not hopeless. God does not control our minds without our consent; but every man is free to choose what power he will have to rule over him."—"Ministry of Healing," pp. 92, 93.

3. What terrible punishment will be meted out to the oppressors? What shall all men know? Verse 26.

4. What two questions does the Lord ask? Who had sold them? Why were they put away? Isa. 50:1.

NOTE.—When Isaiah wrote this, God had not as yet put away His people, Israel. They deserved this treatment, but God was still merciful. Later on He did divorce Israel. Jer. 3:8.

In Isaiah 50:1 God asks for proof that He has put Israel away. The answer, of course, is that He has not put them away, nor sold them to the creditors as was sometimes the custom. Neh. 5:5; 2 Kings 4:1. They had, however, sold themselves. Isa. 52:3.

5. What questions does God now ask? Verses 2, 3.

NOTE.—If I have not put you away, but have called you, how is it that no one responds? Is it because you think My hand is shortened so I can not redeem, or that I have no power? God is astonished and perplexed that no one answers His call. He offers the riches of heaven, and men are not interested.

6. What has God given His servant? For what purpose? What does God do every morning? Verse 4.

NOTE.—" 'The Son of man came not to be ministered unto, but to minister.' Not for Himself, but for others, He lived and thought and prayed. From hours spent with God He came forth morning by morning, to bring the light of heaven to men. Daily He received a fresh baptism of the Holy Spirit. In the early hours of the new day the Lord awakened Him from His slumbers, and His soul and His lips were anointed with grace, that He might impart to others. His words were given Him fresh from the heavenly courts, words that He might speak in season to the weary and oppressed."—"Christ's Object Lessons," p. 139.

"Words of kindness are as welcome as the smile of angels."—"Ministry of Healing," p. 158.

7. How did Christ show His willing submission to God? Verse 5.

NOTE.—The ears of the true servant are always open, and those of the rebellious servant are closed. The true servant will hear the word and do it. The wicked servant will not hear. Matt. 7:24-29.

8. To whom did Christ submit His back? His cheeks? From what did He not hide His face? Verse 6.

9. When were these prophecies fulfilled? Matt. 27:26-31; Mark 15:19.

10. What confidence did Christ express in God? How did Christ set His face? What did He know? Isa. 50:7.

NOTE.—"Difficulties will arise that will try your faith and patience. Face them bravely. Look on the bright side. . . . Never let your courage fail. Never talk unbelief because appearances are against you. As you work for the Master, you will feel pressure for want of means, but the Lord will hear and answer your petitions for help. Let your language be, 'The Lord God will help me; therefore shall I not be confounded: therefore have I set my face like a flint, and I know that I shall not be ashamed.' Isa. 50:7.

"If you make a mistake, turn your defeat into victory. The lessons that God sends will always, if well learned, bring help in due time. Put your trust in God. Pray much, and believe. Trusting, hoping, believing, holding fast the hand of Infinite Power, you will be more than conquerors."—"Testimonies," Vol. 7, p. 244.

11. Who is said to be near? What other question is asked? What challenge is made? Verse 8.

NOTE.—Christ was mocked and condemned by the Jewish Sanhedrin and by Rome. But He knew that though He was condemned by man, God would justify Him.

"Let us stand together." With God on his side, who need be afraid? The challenge is issued: "Who is mine adversary? let him come near to me." God is on our side, and victory is sure.

12. Who will ever be our help? What shall happen to the opposers? Verse 9. (Compare with Rom. 8:33, 34.)

13. What questions are asked? In whom are we counseled to trust? Verse 10.

NOTE.—There are those that fear the Lord and obey the voice of His servant, and yet walk in darkness, literally in dark places, that is, in trouble. Many are doing the best they know, and live up to all the light they have, and still are not free from trouble. What shall they do? "Let him trust in the name of the Lord, and stay upon his God."

14. What is said to those that compass themselves about with sparks of their own kindling? What shall be their end? Verse 11.

NOTE.—The picture is that of a man in darkness, trying to get light by kindling a fire. All that results, however, is a few sparks. Refusing God's light, he tries to make one of his own. But he shall not succeed.

"Many look to their ministers to bring the light from God to them, seeming to think this a cheaper way than to be at the trouble of going to God for it themselves. Such lose much. If they would daily follow Christ, and make Him their guide and counselor, they might obtain a clear knowledge of His will, and thus be gaining a valuable experience. For want of this very experience, brethren professing the truth walk in the sparks of others' kindling; they are unacquainted with the Spirit of God and have not a knowledge of His will, and are therefore easily moved from their faith. They are unstable, because they trusted in others to obtain an experience for them. Ample provisions have been made for every son and daughter of Adam to obtain individually a knowledge of the divine will, to perfect Christian character, and to be purified through the truth. God is dishonored by that class who profess to be followers of Christ, and yet have no experimental knowledge of the divine will or of the mystery of godliness."—"Testimonies," Vol. 2, p. 644.

LESSON 10—DECEMBER 8, 1928

THE RIGHTEOUSNESS AND POWER OF GOD; HIS CARE FOR HIS PEOPLE

LESSON SCRIPTURE: Isa. 51: 1-16.
MEMORY VERSE: Isa. 51: 3.

INTRODUCTION

It is well sometimes to look back. It helps us not to despise the day of small things. We need to look back to the days of the beginnings of this message, when hardship, toil, and privation were the portion of minister and of people. We are living in an age of extravagance and luxury, and there is danger that we partake of the spirit of the times. What we are, we are by the grace of God. Let us keep to the simplicity of the gospel.

The contrast between mortal man and his Maker is clearly brought out in this lesson. Man is like a garment which the moths eat, like a gnat that dies, like wool which the worms eat, like grass which is burned. There is very little place in those terms for the doctrine of natural immortality. On the other hand, God's salvation is everlasting, and His righteousness, that is, His character, His law, shall not be abolished.

THE LESSON

1. Who are asked to hearken unto the Lord? Where are they asked to look? Isa. 51:1.

NOTE.—"Righteousness here means, not salvation, but righteousness in conduct, a way of life in accordance with the will of God."—Cambridge Bible.

It is well, sometimes, to look back on our own personal history and consider where we would be, and what we would be, had not God found us. Looking back on these things would probably make us more humble and more thankful.

2. To whom are we to look? How was Abraham called? Verse 2.

NOTE.—"Called him alone," literally "as one," before he had children.

"Blessed him." Gen. 24:1.

"Increased him," made him father of many nations. Gen. 17:5.

3. What will the Lord do to Zion and to the waste places? What will He make of the wilderness and of the desert? What shall be found there? Verse 3.

NOTE.—This refers definitely to the new earth state.

"Like Eden," like the garden of the Lord.

"There we shall know even as also we are known. There the loves and sympathies that God has planted in the soul will find truest and sweetest exercise." Read "Education," pp. 306, 307.

4. What will proceed from the Lord? What will God make to rest for a light? Verse 4.

NOTE.—"I will make My judgment to rest." A somewhat unusual construction. Judgment is the same word as in Isaiah 42:1, and might be rendered religion, as the Cambridge Bible has it. God, then, will send the true religion to all peoples, and it will be to them for a light.

5. What is near? What has gone forth? How will the people be judged? On whom do the isles wait? On what do they trust? Verse 5.

NOTE.—This verse may rightly, as does the preceding one, have reference to the last days. God's righteousness and salvation are near. He is about to judge the people. The same arm that brings destruction to sinners will bring salvation to the saints.

6. What change will take place in the heavens? What changes will come to the earth? To the inhabitants? What will remain forever? What will not be abolished? Verse 6.

NOTE.—This verse brings to view the contrast between the things that shall perish and the things that shall remain. The world has this reversed. That which God says shall vanish, men say will stand forever. That which God says shall not be abolished, men professedly believe to be abolished.

7. Who are now directly addressed? Of what are they not to fear or be afraid? Verse 7.

NOTE.—Apparently those who have God's law in their heart will be reviled and reproached.

"Through Satan's temptations the whole human race have become transgressors of God's law; but by the sacrifice of His Son a way is opened whereby they may return to God. Through the grace of Christ they may be enabled to render obedience to the Father's law. Thus in every age, from the midst of apostasy and rebellion, God gathers out a people that are true to Him—a people 'in whose heart is His law.' "—"Patriarchs and Prophets," p. 338.

8. What contrast is made between men and God's righteousness and salvation? Verse 8.

9. What is the Lord exhorted to do? What question is asked of God? Verse 9.

NOTE.—Rahab, literally, the proud one, is symbolically an expression for Egypt. Ps. 89:10, margin. The dragon is another symbol for Egypt. Eze. 29:3. The reference here is to the destruction of Pharaoh's army at the Red Sea. The dragon originally is Satan. Rev. 12:7-9. This term is therefore applied also to the adversaries of God generally.

10. What reference is made to Israel's experience at the Red Sea? Verse 10.

NOTE.—The reference here is clear to the drying up of the Red Sea, that the Israelites might pass over. Ex. 14:21, 22.

11. To what is the prophet's mind now turned? Verse 11.

NOTE.—This verse is nearly identical with Isaiah 35:10, and furnishes a good illustration of how an event of the past, as Israel's deliverance from Egypt, will suggest the greater deliverance that shall soon come to God's people.

12. Of whom should we not be afraid? Whom should we not forget? What question is asked? Verses 12, 13.

13. What will God do for the captive exile? Verse 14.

NOTE.—The American Revised Version is a little clearer: "The captive exile shall speedily be loosed; and he shall not die and go down into the pit, neither shall his bread fail."

14. How does God speak of His power? What is His name? Verse 15.

NOTE.—Reference is again made to the crossing of the Red Sea.

15. What has God done for His people? What does He say to Zion? Verse 16.

NOTE.—The Septuagint renders this verse: "I will put My words into thy mouth, and I will shelter thee under the shadow of Mine hand, with which I fixed the sky, and founded the earth; and the Lord shall say to Zion, Thou art My people."

"The knowledge of God that works transformation of character is our great need. If we fulfill His purpose, there must be in our lives a revelation of God that shall correspond to the teaching of His word."—"Testimonies," Vol. 8. p. 329.

253

LESSON 11—DECEMBER 15, 1928

ZION LED FROM UTTER DEFEAT TO TRIUMPHANT VICTORY

LESSON SCRIPTURE: Isa. 51: 17-23; 52: 1-12.
MEMORY VERSE: Isa. 52: 7.

INTRODUCTION

The first picture presented to us in the lesson is that of Jerusalem figured as a woman lying drunk and senseless, unable to help herself. She has drunk to the very dregs the cup of the Lord's indignation, and no one can help her.

The second picture is much more encouraging. Zion is asked to awake, put on her strength and her beautiful garments. God will cleanse and beautify His church, and henceforth no unclean thing shall enter.

The third picture is that of the gospel proclamation to the whole world. God's people are united. They sing together. They are one. And God is baring His holy arm for them. They have left Babylon; they are "clean." God goes before them, and victory is assured.

THE LESSON

1. Who is told to awake? What experience has Jerusalem gone through? Isa. 51:17.

NOTE.—The prophet here by anticipation speaks of the destruction of Jerusalem by Nebuchadnezzar, and the resulting calamities. 2 Kings 25:8-11; compare Jer. 42:18.

2. Who is there to help her? What two things have come upon her? What is said of her sons? Verses 18-20.

NOTE.—"None to guide." When Jerusalem was destroyed and most of the people taken into captivity, the leaders were also taken. Not a few people remained in the land, but there were no leaders. When Jeremiah and Baruch were taken to Egypt, there was none left. Jer. 43:5-7.

"These two things." "Desolation," or wasting produced by the "famine" within the city; and "destruction," produced by the "sword" without the city.

3. Whom does God now address? How does God speak of Himself? What will God do to the cup? What have the nations done to the people of God? Verses 21-23.

NOTE.—"Thy God that pleadeth the cause of His people." This can be none other than Christ.

"I have taken out of thine hand the cup." God will take the cup away from Jerusalem, and give it to the nations that afflicted her. These have trampled upon His people, and now retribution comes.

4. To whom does the call come to awake? Who shall henceforth no more come into the holy city? Isa. 52:1.

NOTE.—The church is here bidden to put on her strength and the beautiful garments of Christ's righteousness. "Souls are perishing out of Christ, and those who profess to be Christ's disciples are letting them die. Our brethren have talents intrusted to them for the very work of saving souls; but some have bound these up in a napkin, and buried them in the earth. How much do such idlers resemble the angel who is represented as flying in the midst of heaven, proclaiming the commandments of God and the faith of Jesus? What manner of entreaty can be brought to bear upon the idlers that will arouse them to go to work for the Master? What can we say to the slothful church member to make him realize the necessity of unearthing his talent and putting it out to the exchangers? There will be no idler, no slothful one, found inside the kingdom of heaven. O that God would set this matter in all its importance before the sleeping churches! O that Zion would arise and put on her beautiful garments. O that she would shine!"—"Testimonies," Vol. 6, p. 434.

5. **What are Jerusalem and the captive daughter of Zion told to do? Verse 2.**

NOTE.—"Shake thyself from the dust." Get rid of all sin.

"Loose thyself from the bands of thy neck," literally, the bands of thy neck are unloosened; that is, I have caused thy chains to fall from thee.

6. **For what had they sold themselves? How shall they be redeemed? Verse 3.**

NOTE.—"The enemy is buying souls to-day very cheap. 'Ye have sold yourselves for a thing of naught,' is the language of Scripture. One is selling his soul for the world's applause, another for money; one to gratify base passions, another for worldly amusements. Such bargains are made daily. Satan is bidding for the purchase of Christ's blood, and buying them cheap, notwithstanding the infinite price which has been paid to ransom them."—"Testimonies," Vol. 5, p. 133.

7. **Where did the people aforetime go? How did the Assyrians treat them. Verse 4.**

NOTE.—Israel experienced three captivities. The first when they "went down" into Egypt and were made to serve. Ex. 1:13, 14.

The second was the Assyrian captivity. 2 Kings 15: 29; 17:6; 18:13.

The third is the Babylonian captivity, referred to in Isaiah 52:5.

8. **What question does the Lord ask? How did Babylon treat the captives? What is said of the name of the Lord? What shall they know? Verses 5, 6.**

NOTE.—"To the prophet [Isaiah] was given a revelation of the beneficent design of God in scattering impenitent Judah among the nations of earth. 'My people shall know My name,' the Lord declared; 'they shall know in that day that I am He that doth speak.' And not only were they themselves to learn the lesson of obedience and trust; in their places of exile they were also to impart to others a knowledge of the living God. Many from among the sons of the strangers were to learn to love Him as their Creator and their Redeemer; they were to begin the observance of His holy Sabbath day as a memorial of His creative power; and when He should make 'bare His holy arm in the eyes of all the nations,' to deliver His people from captivity, 'all the ends of the earth' should see of the salvation of God. Many of these converts from heathenism would wish to unite themselves fully with the Israelites, and accompany them on the return journey to Judea."—"Prophets and Kings," pp. 371, 372.

9. **What is said of him that bringeth good tidings? What is said to Zion? Verse 7.**

NOTE.—The good tidings referred first to the news to Israel in Babylon that they were free to leave the land of their captivity and return to the land of Judea. It is also the gospel proclamation: good tidings, peace, good tidings of good, salvation.

"Thy God reigneth!" God is still ruling in the affairs of men. It may seem that things are going to pieces, that evil is triumphant and the right is perverted. But be of good cheer. "Thy God reigneth!"

10. **What do the watchmen do? How do they sing? How do they see? When? Verse 8.**

NOTE.—"Never was there so great a diversity of faith in Christendom as at the present day. If the gifts [Eph. 4:11-13] were necessary to preserve the unity of the primitive church, how much more so to restore unity now! And that it is the purpose of God to restore the unity of the church in the last days, is abundantly evident from the prophecies. We are assured that the watchmen shall see eye to eye, when the Lord shall bring again Zion. Also, that in the time of the end the wise shall understand. When this is fulfilled there will be unity of faith with all whom God accounts wise; for those that do in reality understand aright, must necessarily understand alike. What is to effect this unity but the gifts that are given for this very purpose?"—"Early Writings," p. 140.

11. **How may the joy of God's people be fitly expressed? What has the Lord done? Verse 9.**

12. **What has the Lord done in the sight of the nations? What shall the ends of the earth see? Verse 10.**

13. **What are His people told not to touch? Who must be clean? Verse 11.**

NOTE.—God's ministers must be holy, clean. So must His people. This scripture applies to ministers and people.

"The church will rarely take a higher stand than is taken by her ministers. We need a converted ministry and a converted people. Shepherds who watch for souls as they that must give account will lead the flock on in paths of peace and holiness. Their success in this work will be in proportion to their own growth in grace and knowledge of the truth. When the teachers are sanctified, soul, body, and spirit, they can impress upon the people the importance of such sanctification."—"Testimonies," Vol. 5, p. 227.

14. **How should God's people not go out? Why is haste and secrecy unnecessary? Verse 12.**

NOTE.—"Not go out with haste." This refers first to the departure from Babylonian captivity, as described in Ezra; but the scripture also has a wider application. God wants His people to be ready, and to do deliberately and with forethought that which needs to be done. God is not in a hurry, and He will go before us. He will also be our rearward. The final triumph of His people at Christ's coming shall likewise be a complete victory in full sight of the nations.

LESSON 12—DECEMBER 22, 1928

THE LAMB OF GOD

LESSON SCRIPTURE: Isa. 52: 13-15; 53: 1-5.
MEMORY VERSE: Isa. 53: 5.

INTRODUCTION

"It would be well to spend a thoughtful hour each day reviewing the life of Christ from the manger to Calvary. We should take it point by point, and let the imagination vividly **grasp each scene**, especially the closing ones of His earthly life. By thus contemplating His teachings and sufferings, and the infinite sacrifice made by Him for the redemption of the race, we may strengthen our faith, quicken our love, and become more deeply imbued with the spirit which sustained our Saviour."—"Testimonies," Vol. 4, p. 374.

The wrong views which the Jews held in regard to sin and suffering helped decidedly to cause them to reject Christ. If any man suffered, it was clear to them that he must be a great sinner. God knew this, and in the fifty-third chapter of Isaiah corrects the idea. Christ was indeed smitten of God, but it was for our sake; He was scourged, but it was that we might be healed.

Help on this lesson may be found in "Testimonies," Vol. 2, pages 200-215.

THE LESSON

1. What will God's Servant do? Because of this, what will be His position? Isa. 52:13.

NOTE.—"My Servant shall deal wisely."—American Revised Version. The word here used primarily means wisely, but it also includes the success which is normally the result of wise action; hence the margin has "prosper."

Christ did deal wisely in all acts of life. Wisely He chose His disciples not from the rich or learned, lest it be said that influence or learning was the cause of His remarkable success. Wisely He refused to be made king, lest ambition be laid to His charge. Wisely He hid His divinity and did most of His miracles unnoticed, so that the supernatural should not have undue influence in deciding men. Wisely He submitted Himself to civil authority. Wisely He answered subtle questions and avoided others. Wisely He dealt with the erring and downtrodden. No unwise word or action has ever been laid to His charge,—not even by His enemies.

"Shall be exalted." Christ was highly exalted. Phil. 2:9-11.

2. Why were many astonished? Verse 14.

NOTE.—The word "astonied" expresses the thought of blank amazement, mingled with horror, aroused in those who should behold the Saviour's extreme anguish and suffering.

"He bore insult, mockery, and shameful abuse, until His 'visage was so marred more than any man, and His form more than the sons of men.'

"Who can comprehend the love here displayed! The angelic host beheld with wonder and with grief Him who had been the Majesty of heaven, and who had worn the crown of glory, now wearing the crown of thorns, a bleeding victim to the rage of an infuriated mob, fired to insane madness by the wrath of Satan. Behold the patient Sufferer! Upon His head is the thorny crown. His lifeblood flows from every lacerated vein. All this in consequence of sin! Nothing could have induced Christ to leave His honor and majesty in heaven, and come to a sinful world, to be neglected, despised, and rejected, by those He came to save, and finally to suffer upon the cross, but eternal, redeeming love, which will ever remain a mystery."—"Testimonies," Vol. 2, p. 207.

3. What will He do to many nations? What will kings do? Why? Verse 15.

NOTE.—This verse speaks of the results of Christ's humiliation.

"So shall He sprinkle many nations," rather, "startle." The American Revised Version, putting verses 14 and 15 together, reads, "Like as many were astonished at Thee (His visage was so marred more than any man, and His form more than the sons of men), so shall He startle [astonish] many nations." (See margin.) It should be an astonishing thing that from such an act, the suffering and death of an innocent person, should come such wonderful results.

"Kings shall shut their mouths at Him," in reverence, as princes did in the case of Job before calamity came upon him. Job 29:8, 9.

4. What two questions are now asked? Isa. 53:1.

5. How should Christ grow up? What is said of His appearance? Verse 2.

NOTE.—In the Old Testament it was required that the sacrifice should be perfect, without blemish. Lev. 1:3; 6:6. Concerning Christ's personal appearance, read "Early Writings," page 172.

It was in the spiritual rather than in the physical sense that the Jews rejected Christ. If He had come as a prince and received honor of men; if He had used His miraculous power to free them from the Roman yoke; if He would even continue to feed them as He had done with the five thousand, they might have accepted Him.

"For more than a thousand years the Jewish people had waited the coming of the promised Saviour. Their brightest hopes had rested upon this event. For a thousand years, in song and prophecy, in temple rite and household prayer, His name had been enshrined; and yet when He came, they did not recognize Him as the Messiah for whom they had so long waited. 'He came unto His own, and His own received Him not.' To their world-loving hearts, the Beloved of heaven was 'as a root out of a dry ground.' In their eyes He had 'no form nor comeliness;' they discerned in Him no beauty that they should desire Him."—"Prophets and Kings," p. 710.

6. How did men treat Christ? What is He called? With what is He acquainted? How did they treat Him? What did they not do? Verse 3.

NOTE.—"Mark the humble life of the Son of God.... Behold His ignominy, His agony in Gethsemane, and learn what self-denial is. Are we suffering want? so was Christ, the Majesty of heaven. But His poverty was for our sakes. Are we ranked among the rich? so was He. But He consented for our sakes to become poor, that we through His poverty might be made rich. In Christ we have self-denial exemplified. His sacrifice consisted not merely in leaving the royal courts of heaven, in being tried by wicked men as a criminal and pronounced guilty, and in being delivered up to die as a malefactor, but in bearing the weight of the sins of the world. The life of Christ rebukes our indifference and coldness."—"Testimonies," Vol. 3, p. 407.

7. What has Christ borne and carried? Verse 4, first part; Matt. 8:16, 17.

NOTE.—"The Majesty of heaven pleased not Himself. Whatever He did was in reference to the salvation of man. Selfishness in all its forms stood rebuked in His presence. He assumed our nature that He might suffer in our stead, making His soul an offering for sin. He was stricken of God and afflicted to save man from the blow which he deserved because of the transgression of God's law. By the light shining from the cross, Christ proposed to draw all men unto Him. His human heart yearned over the race. His arms were opened to receive them, and He invited all to come to Him. His life on earth was one continued act of self-denial and condescension."—"Testimonies," Vol. 4, p. 418.

8. How did we esteem Him? Isa. 53:4, last part.

NOTE.—It was generally believed by the Jews that sin is punished in this life. Every affliction was regarded as the penalty of some wrongdoing, either of the sufferer himself or of his parents. It is true that all suffering results from the transgression of God's law, but this truth had become perverted. Satan, the author of sin and all its results, had led men to look upon disease and death as proceeding from God,—as punishment arbitrarily inflicted on account of sin. Hence, one upon whom some great affliction or calamity had fallen had the additional burden of being regarded as a great sinner.

"Thus the way was prepared for the Jews to reject Jesus. He who 'hath borne our griefs and carried our sorrows,' was looked upon by the Jews as 'stricken, smitten of God, and afflicted;' and they hid their faces from Him."—"The Desire of Ages," pp. 470, 471.

9. Why was Christ wounded? And bruised? What was upon Him? How are we healed? Verse 5.

NOTE.—"Christ was treated as we deserve, that we might be treated as He deserves. He was condemned for our sins, in which He had no share, that we might be justified by His righteousness, in which we had no share. He suffered the death which was ours, that we might receive the life which was His. 'With His stripes we are healed.' "—"The Desire of Ages," p. 25.

10. What is sometimes the cause of affliction? John 9:1-3; 11:4.

NOTE.—While sickness is often a result of sin, all sickness is not directly caused by sin. We do not suppose that Christ meant to say that the blind man or his parents had never sinned, but that this affliction had not come to them because of any specific evil they had done. Christ was trying to counteract the idea of the Jews who believed that when people are afflicted, they must be great sinners.

According to these texts, some are sick that "the works of God should be made manifest;" others are sick "for the glory of God." Paul's "thorn in the flesh" may be an illustration of the latter kind.

If, when we are sick, we have searched our hearts for any hidden and unconfessed sin, and have found none, we need not continually distress ourselves over the outcome. God knows best. It may be "that the works of God should be made manifest" in healing; for God will do great things for us if He is asked.

11. Why does affliction sometimes come to God's children? 2 Cor. 1:3-7.

NOTE.—God comforts us in our tribulation, with the intent "that we may be able to comfort" others. According to this, some are afflicted for the "consolation and salvation" of others. Verse 6. This should be a great comfort to many who wonder why God sends certain afflictions to them. Remember, dear one, there may be some poor struggling soul going through deep waters whom God is preparing you to help by causing you to go through afflictions that will make you more understanding and sympathetic. So do not despair. God is giving you certain experiences that will make you a better worker, a better Christian.

LESSON 13—DECEMBER 29, 1928

STRICKEN BECAUSE OF ISRAEL'S TRANSGRESSIONS

LESSON SCRIPTURE: Isa. 53: 6-12.
MEMORY VERSE: Isa. 53: 11.

INTRODUCTION

The suffering, death, and resurrection of Christ must ever be vital in the life and message of every Christian. The subject of the atonement can never grow old. Righteousness by faith rightly understood and practiced is needed more than ever.

"The proud heart strives to earn salvation; but both our title to heaven and our fitness for it are found in the righteousness of Christ. The Lord can do nothing toward the recovery of man until, convinced of his own weakness, and stripped of all self-sufficiency, he yields himself to the control of God. Then he can receive the gift that God is waiting to bestow. From the soul that feels his need, nothing is withheld. He has unrestricted access to Him in whom all fullness dwells. Isa. 57:15."—"The Desire of Ages," p. 300.

Contemplation of the last scenes in the life of Christ will draw the soul nearer to God. This lesson should serve that purpose.

THE LESSON

1. How has mankind gone astray? Which way have we gone? What has the Lord laid on Christ? Isa. 53:6.

NOTE.—When a whole flock goes astray, it is generally because the leaders have gone astray. Let the first sheep lead the way, and all the rest follow. While God does not excuse those who have thus gone after their own way, He understands that the chief responsibility is upon the leaders.

"The Lord hath laid on Him the iniquity of us all." "Whether they know it or not, all are weary and heavy-laden. All are weighed down with burdens that only Christ can remove. The heaviest burden that we bear is the burden of sin. If we were left to bear this burden, it would crush us. But the Sinless One has taken our place. . . . He has borne the burden of our guilt. He will take the load from our weary shoulders. He will give us rest. The burden of care and sorrow also He will bear. He invites us to cast all our care upon Him; for He carries us upon His heart."—"The Desire of Ages," pp. 328, 329.

2. How was Christ treated? What did He not do? By what word is His death here named? How was His attitude before His judges described in the prophecy? Verse 7.

NOTE.—"He was oppressed." The word denotes harsh, cruel, and arbitrary treatment, such as that of a slave driver. The same word is used in Exodus 3:7.

"As a lamb to the slaughter." Christ's trial was neither just nor legal. It was not an execution but a slaughter.

"He opened not His mouth." "Patiently Jesus listened to the conflicting testimonies. No word did He utter in self-defense. At last His accusers were entangled, confused, and maddened. The trial was making no headway; it seemed that their plottings were to fail. Caiaphas was desperate. One last resort remained; Christ must be forced to condemn Himself. The high priest started from the judgment seat, his face contorted with passion, his voice and demeanor plainly indicating that were it in his power he would strike down the prisoner before him. 'Answerest Thou nothing?' he exclaimed; 'what is it which these witness against Thee?' Jesus held His peace."—"The Desire of Ages," p. 706.

The power of silence! Many people understand the power of words, of oratory. Few understand the power of silence. And yet it is just as important to know when not to speak as to know when to speak.

3. How was the scripture that "He opened not His mouth" fulfilled? Matt. 27:12-14; Luke 23:8, 9.

NOTE.—"Herod was irritated by this silence. It seemed to indicate utter indifference to his authority. To the vain and pompous king, open rebuke would have been less offensive than to be thus ignored. Again he angrily threatened Jesus, who still remained unmoved and silent. . . . Christ's silence was the severest rebuke that He could have given."—Id., p. 730.

4. Where was Christ taken? What is said of the generations? Why was Christ stricken? Isa. 53:8.

NOTE.—A paraphrase of this verse might read: "They did away with Him unjustly, and who of His generation cared? 'He was cut off out of the land of the living for the transgression of my people to whom the stroke was due.'" See American Revised Version.

5. Where was His grave made? What had He not done? What was not found in His mouth? Verse 9.

NOTE.—The preceding verse states that Christ was unjustly condemned, and verse 7 calls the judicial murder a "slaughter." This verse emphasizes the fact that Christ was sinless, that He had done no violence, and that there was no deceit in Him. Had the leaders in Israel diligently studied the prophecies, they could not but have seen the parallel between Christ and Isaiah 53. They would have known that Isaiah spoke of One who should be condemned unjustly, who should patiently take the insults offered, who should not retaliate or open His mouth in His defense. And when at last the rich Joseph buried Him, had they read the prophecies they could but have seen the climax of what was foretold.

6. How was the prophecy as to Christ's burial fulfilled? Matt. 27:57-60.

7. What did it please the Lord to do? What will take place when His soul is made an offering for sin? Isa. 53:10.

NOTE.—"It pleased the Lord." It was by "the determinate counsel and foreknowledge of God" (Acts 2:23) that Christ suffered. It was according to the plan laid from eternity.

"His soul an offering for sin." Christ "made Himself an offering for sin, that we might be justified before God through Him."—"Testimonies," Vol. 4, p. 374.

Now when we shall present that offering before God, "He shall see His seed," that is, we shall then be reckoned among "the seed," we shall be "heirs according to the promise." Gal. 3:29; Ps. 22:30. Christ "shall see His seed" among His true followers. "He shall prolong His days." This is the resurrection. He shall live again.

8. What will Christ see? What effect will this have upon Him? Verse 11, first part.

NOTE.—Christ shall see "the travail of His soul," that is, those for whom He labored and suffered. "Then, in the results of His work, Christ will behold its recompense. In that great multitude which no man could number, presented 'faultless before the presence of His glory with exceeding joy,' He whose blood has redeemed and whose life has taught us, 'shall see of the travail of His soul, and shall be satisfied.'"—"Education," p. 309.

9. How will many be justified? Why? Verse 11, last part.

NOTE.—The American Revised Version reads, "By the knowledge of Himself shall My righteous Servant justify many." The knowledge spoken of here is the knowledge of experience. Christ was made a perfect Saviour by the things He suffered. Heb. 2:10. To really know Christ, that is, to know Him as we ought, is eternal life (John 17:3); but such knowledge is gained only by experience. (See Phil. 3:10, 11.)

10. **What has stood throughout the ages as a great beacon of truth?—Ans. Righteousness by faith.**

NOTE.—"Through all the ages the great truth of justification by faith has stood as a mighty beacon to guide repentant sinners into the way of life. It was this light that scattered the darkness which enveloped Luther's mind, and revealed to him the power of the blood of Christ to cleanse from sin. The same light has guided thousands of sin-burdened souls to the true Source of pardon and peace."— "Acts of the Apostles," pp. 373, 374. It should be noted that justification and righteousness by faith mean the same thing.

11. **Of what do our churches sadly stand in need?**

NOTE.—"Our churches are dying for the want of teaching on the subject of righteousness by faith in Christ, and on kindred truths."— "Gospel Workers," p. 301.

12. **What is righteousness, and how do we receive it? Rom. 4:3; Gen. 26:5.**

NOTE.—"Righteousness is holiness, likeness to God; and 'God is love.' It is conformity to the law of God; for 'all Thy commandments are righteousness;' and 'love is the fulfilling of the law.' Righteousness is love, and love is the light and the life of God. The righteousness of God is embodied in Christ. We receive righteousness by receiving Him.

"Not by painful struggles or wearisome toil, not by gift or sacrifice, is righteousness obtained; but it is freely given to every soul who hungers and thirsts to receive it."—"Thoughts from the Mount of Blessing," p. 34.

13. **What is the glory of God which closes the work of the third angel? Rev. 18:1.**

NOTE.—"The message of Christ's righteousness is to sound from one end of the earth to the other to prepare the way of the Lord. This is the glory of God, which closes the work of the third angel."—"Testimonies," Vol. 6, p. 19.

14. **What will God divide or give to Christ? Why is this given to Him? Isa. 53:12.**

NOTE.—The picture here is of a conqueror returning from battle and dividing the spoil. Men here make themselves a name by their heroism and valor, and so Christ also is to be given "a name which is above every name." Phil. 2:9. His "spoil" is the souls He has won in battle. And this victory is won and this reward given "because He hath poured out His soul unto death."

The last time we gave a Thirteenth Sabbath Offering to the Inter-American Division, there was an overflow of $4,352.66. The call this quarter is for $105,000. Make your offering generous, so there will be a liberal overflow.

Isaiah, the Gospel Prophet
A Preacher of Righteousness

Lesson Notes and Helps, Volume 3

By M. L. ANDREASEN

"Wash you, make you clean; put away the evil of your doings from before Mine eyes; cease to do evil; learn to do well; seek judgment, relieve the oppressed, judge the fatherless, plead for the widow.

"Come now, and let us reason together, saith the Lord: though your sins be as scarlet, they shall be as white as snow; though they be red like crimson, they shall be as wool." Isa. 1: 16-18.

THE GATHERING OF ISRAEL

"I will rejoice in Jerusalem, and joy in My people: and the voice of weeping shall be no more heard in her, nor the voice of crying." Isa. 65 : 19.

Contents

	INTRODUCTION	6
I.	THE GOD OF COMFORT	7
II.	GOD CALLS TO RETURN; THE WORD THAT TRANSFORMS	14
III.	BLESSINGS TO JEW AND GENTILE; BLIND WATCHMAN .	21
IV.	THE RIGHTEOUS AND THE WICKED IN THE DAY OF TROUBLE	28
V.	TRUE FASTING; THE SABBATH RESTORED . . .	36
VI.	A REDEEMER PROMISED TO A PENITENT PEOPLE . .	43
VII.	THE FINAL TRIUMPH OF THE RIGHTEOUS . . .	50
VIII.	BUILDERS OF THE OLD WASTE PLACES	58
IX.	THE HOLY PEOPLE; THE LORD'S REDEEMED . . .	64
X.	AFFLICTED FOR HIS PEOPLE'S SAKE	69
XI.	A PRAYER FOR THE REVEALING OF GOD'S POWER . .	76
XII.	A PEOPLE PREPARED FOR A NEW HEAVEN AND A NEW EARTH	83
XIII.	THE INGATHERING FROM THE GENTILES; WORSHIP IN THE NEW EARTH	90

Introduction

MANY authors tell all they have to say in the first few chapters of their book. Not so Isaiah. Until the very last his book is filled with most precious instruction. Even as the Bible ends in a blaze of glory with a description of the new earth and the life hereafter, so Isaiah keeps some of the best things till the last.

Those who will read the portion of Isaiah covered by this booklet will find many things of great interest. Among the prominent subjects discussed in Isaiah 44-66 are the coming of the Lord, the Sabbath, and the new earth. These have special value for this time. Of no less interest should be the sections dealing with the great ingathering of souls before the coming of Christ. God's work will not be finished in a corner. Before the end comes, the earth will be lightened with the glory of God. We are now living in the time when this is about to be fulfilled.

The reader will please take notice that very frequently the several scriptures under review in this book are not in the exact words of any one version, but are more in the nature of a paraphrase, following in each instance the translation that seems to make the meaning of the text most clear. The student will, of course, have at hand and use freely one or other of the several recognized versions.

It is our sincere prayer and hope that the following chapters may be of help in making clearer some of the greatest prophecies ever given to man.

CHAPTER I

The God of Comfort

Lesson Scripture: Isaiah 54

Isaiah 54: 1-10. The enlargement of Zion.

Verses 1-3. Zion, under the symbol of a childless woman, is told to sing aloud; for the time is coming when she shall have more children than the married wife. For that reason it will be necessary to enlarge her place of abode to accommodate the increased numbers. Hence the tent where she has dwelt must be made larger, for the increase shall come to her from all directions. In fact, her seed shall take possession of the nations, and even the desolate cities shall be inhabited.

Verses 4-8. As though this were almost too good to be true, Zion is assured that she need not fear its fulfillment. She will not be disappointed or put to shame. She shall forget the shame of her youth and widowhood in the joy that shall come to her. Her husband is her Maker, even the Lord of hosts; He is also her Redeemer, the Holy One of Israel, the God of the whole earth. As a wife forsaken and grieved in spirit, yes, as a young wife who has been cast off, the Lord has recalled her to His side again. It was only for a small moment that God forsook her, and now with great mercies He will restore her. In a little wrath God hid His face, but with everlasting loving-kindness will He have mercy.

Verses 9, 10. This experience is parallel to that in the time of Noah, when God swore that the waters should not again cover the earth. So now God swears that He will nevermore be wroth with His people, nor rebuke them. The mountains may depart and the hills be removed, but God's loving-kindness shall not depart nor His covenant of peace be removed.

Verses 11-17. God's care for His own.

Verses 11-14. God's people have been afflicted and tossed about as Noah was in the ark, but now He will establish them in a city with foundations of sapphires, windows of agates, and gates of carbuncles. All shall be taught of the Lord, and great shall be their peace. They shall be established in righteousness, and fear and terror shall not come nigh them.

7

Verses 15-17. Should the enemy gather against them, they need not fear, for such attack is not of "My doing," hence it shall fail. I have created all, even the smith who makes the weapon whereby he intends to harm them. No weapon, therefore, that is lifted against them shall prosper, and every tongue that tries to condemn them shall itself be condemned. This is the heritage of God's servants, whose righteousness is of Me, says the Lord.

Notes

Isaiah 54:1. In the fourth chapter of Galatians Paul quotes part of this section of Isaiah, making it apply to the story of Sarah and Hagar. Gal. 4:27. "Sarai was barren; she had no child." Gen. 11:30. Hagar, on the other hand, "bare Abram a son: and Abram called his son's name, which Hagar bare, Ishmael." Gen. 16:15. Abraham believed that Ishmael was the one through whom God's promises would be fulfilled. Gen. 17:18. When God told him to change Sarai's name to Sarah, because "I will bless her, and give thee a son also of her: yea, I will bless her, and she shall be a mother of nations; kings of people shall be of her," "Abram fell upon his face, and laughed." Gen. 17:16, 17. Yet the promise was fulfilled through Isaac, the child of promise. Gen. 22:18.

"Which things are an allegory." Hagar "answereth to Jerusalem which now is,"— the first covenant. Gal. 4:24, 25. Sarah answers to "Jerusalem which is above,"— the second covenant. Verse 26. Hagar stands for the flesh, for works. Sarah stands for the spirit, for faith. Looking at the world, we see multitudes adhering to Hagar's doctrine of salvation by works, while very few indeed walk by faith. The promise is sure, however. The children of the barren, of Sarah, shall be more than the children of Hagar. "Cast out the bondwoman and her son," is the divine command. Gal. 4:30. In eternity there will be no children of works, but there will be multitudes, even as the sands of the sea, of those saved by faith. And thus Isaiah 54:1 will be fulfilled.

This scripture has another application. The Jews were God's peculiar people, married to Him, and apparently enjoying the special favor of God. The Gentiles, on the other hand, "were without Christ, being aliens from the commonwealth of Israel, and strangers from the covenants of promise, having no hope, and without God in the world." Eph. 2:12. A Jew would hardly admit the possibility of salvation for one not of Israel. Yet God had far larger plans than the salvation of the Jews. That would be too small a thing. Isaiah 49:6. God is "God of the whole

The God of Comfort

earth" (Isaiah 54:5), not of the Jews only. His plan embraces the Gentiles and the desolate places. Verse 3. It did not seem possible when this was written that the time would ever come when the few Gentiles who were grudgingly admitted to the privileges of Israel should swell to such numbers as to eclipse Israel, that the children of the desolate should be more than the children of the married wife. Yet this scripture has been abundantly fulfilled. Hosea says: "I will call them My people, which were not My people; and her beloved, which was not beloved. And it shall come to pass, that in the place where it was said unto them, Ye are not My people; there shall they be called the children of the living God." Rom. 9:25, 26; quoted from Hosea 1:10; 2:23.

Verse 2. Compare Isa. 49:20, 21.

"Spare not." Let nothing hinder you or stand in the way. The work is so important that it must have the right-of-way.

Verse 3. "On the right hand and on the left"— in all directions.

"Inherit the Gentiles," rather "take possession of nations," a fulfillment of Genesis 22:17.

Verse 4. "The shame of thy youth." God united Himself in covenant relation with Israel at Sinai. That was in the days of Israel's youth. Eze. 16:60. God considered Himself married to them. Jer. 3:14. But Israel soon left the Lord. "As a wife treacherously departeth from her husband," so Israel left God. Jer. 3:20. She "played the harlot" "and she went after her lovers, and forgot Me, saith the Lord." Hosea 2:5, 13. This constituted the shame of her youth.

"The reproach of thy widowhood." When Israel had thus gone after her lovers, God said, "She is not My wife, neither am I her husband." Hosea 2:2. Israel became a widow. Lam. 1:1. The reproach of widowhood consisted in being untrue to the marriage vows, and therefore she was forsaken of her husband.

Verse 5. "Maker," "husband." Both these words are in the plural. The Hebrew language has three numbers,— the singular, meaning one; the dual, meaning two; and the plural, meaning three or more. When these words therefore are in the plural, at least three are meant. The Newberry Bible has in the margin of Isaiah 54:5: "Maker, plural, the Triune God." It is interesting to note that "God" in Genesis 1:1 is also in the plural.

Note the six names for God in this verse. "God of the whole earth." God is not limited to any nation or people. He is God of the whole earth, and also ruler of all the forces of the universe.

Verse 6. " The Lord hath called thee as a woman forsaken "—
" as a wife," A. R. V. Israel had left the Lord and gone after
other gods. Now God calls her back to resume her former status
as wife, as " a wife of youth."

Verse 7. " For a small moment have I forsaken thee "—" forsook I thee," Hebrew. Moffatt translates: " I did forsake you for
awhile, but I will take you back right tenderly."

It has been suggested that the " small moment " may have reference to the forty years in the wilderness; or as some think, to the
seventy years' captivity, the prophet projecting himself into the
future. Some, however, think it more reasonable that it should
have reference to a more immediate event, such as the Assyrian
captivity of 721 B. C.

[NOTE.— Should not the study of this scripture be approached
from the standpoint of the original promise as given (1) to the
Seed (Gen. 3:15); (2) to Abraham (Gen. 15:7), compare Rom.
4:13; (3) to Isaac (Gen. 26:2-4); (4) to Jacob (Gen. 28:13);
and finally (5) to David (2 Sam. 7:16)?

This, then, brings us to the question, Of what time was it or
could it be said, " For a small moment have I forsaken thee " ?
Surely not of the forty years in the wilderness, of which time it
is said in chapter 63:9: " He bare them, and carried them all
the days of old." During all those forty years they were fed
every day with manna, " the corn of heaven." Ps. 78:24.

But at the time of the Babylonian captivity, God's chosen
people were " refused " and " forsaken." Later, however, Judah
was called out of their captivity in ancient Babylon, and restored
to their earthly Canaan, as God's people are now being called out
of modern Babylon, presently to be put in possession of the
heavenly Canaan. In this the experience of Judah was different
from that of Israel; there was no general return of Israel from
the Assyrian captivity. To this day the northern kingdom is
spoken of as the ten lost tribes. It seems impossible, therefore,
that verse 7 could refer to the captivity of B. C. 721, from which
there was no return, and in the very nature of the case can be
none.—ED.]

Verse 8. " In a little wrath," rather " an outbreak of wrath."
(See 2 Kings 17:18.)

" Everlasting kindness." God's anger endures but a moment.
His kindness is everlasting. (See Ps. 30:5.)

Verse 9. " As the waters of Noah." The older versions, except
the Septuagint, read: " As the days of Noah." In the days of

Noah God said that He would not destroy the earth or its inhabitants any more with a flood. Gen. 9:11, 15. In this verse God says that He will not be wroth with His people any more. "This" has reference to a present calamity. As the ten tribes had recently been carried into captivity (721 B. C.), the reference is probably to that event.

Verse 10. "My kindness"—"loving-kindness," A. R. V. "Covenant of My peace." This covenant will not find its complete fulfillment until in the new-earth state. (See Num. 25:12, 13; Eze. 34:25; 37:26.)

Verse 11. God here comforts His people. As Noah was tossed about in the ark, so these have been exposed to the tempest. Now God will build them a firm city that has foundations.

"Sapphires," a transparent blue. (See Rev. 21:19.) This description draws the mind to the New Jerusalem.

Verse 12. "Windows of agates"—"rubies," R. V. Agate is a variegated quartz, in which the colors are usually in bands, as in some of the children's playing marbles. Rubies are transparent gem stones of a deep-red color.

"Gates of carbuncles." John tells us that the gates of the city are each of one pearl. Rev. 21:21. Here the gates are said to be of carbuncles. Anciently this meant any gem of brilliant fire and deep-red color.

"All Thy borders," probably the outer wall.

"Pleasant stones," precious gems.

Verse 13. This and the following verse may be partly fulfilled in this world, but not until Christ comes will it find complete fulfillment.

Verse 15. The prophet, after having been given a view of the blessing to come, turns back for a moment to the present. The sense of the verse is this: If any should attempt to stir up strife, I want you to know that it is none of My doing. Hence it shall not prosper.

Verse 17. "This is the heritage," inheritance, or lot.

Lessons for To-day

Verse 1. "Barren." To be barren was considered a great curse in Israel. Note Hannah's prayer in 1 Samuel 1:11. To be spiritually barren is an even greater curse. How many of the fruits mentioned in Galatians 5:22, 23, are you bearing? Check them off: Love, joy, peace, long-suffering, gentleness, goodness, faith, meekness, temperance. These are the virtues that should appear in your own life. Having checked these off, take another inventory of your active fruit bearing in missionary lines: Souls saved through your ministry or life; faithful attendance at services; tithes and offerings; prayer life; various activities of the church, such as Harvest Ingathering, Big Week; daily study of the lesson and the word of God; ministry to the sick, the poor, the needy; loyalty. Add to this list that which fits your case, and decide that this year, by the grace of God, shall see advance in all lines.

"Thou that didst not travail." Children are not born into this world without travail and agony. Neither are spiritual children. Yet travail of soul is almost unknown. It was when "Zion travailed, she brought forth her children." Isa. 66: 8. Paul knew what that meant. Gal. 4: 19. There must be more travail of soul among us if we are to see any large increase of souls.

Verse 2. "Enlarge," "stretch forth" "lengthen," "strengthen." There must be constant effort to enlarge our work at home and abroad. That enlargement must not, however, be at the cost of strength. Every lengthening, every stretching forth, must be so planned as to strengthen, and not to weaken, the work.

Verse 3. "Desolate cities." There are large cities with thousands and even millions of inhabitants, which God counts desolate. "Your house is left unto you desolate," said Christ. Matt. 23: 38. There were as many people in the temple as before, *but Christ was not there.* That is what makes a city desolate. God is interested in the cities. Jonah 1: 2; 3: 2; 4: 10, 11. We should be also.

Verse 4. "Fear not." "Thou shalt forget, . . . and shalt not remember." Both a command and a promise. Some seem unable to forget. They remember a reproach for years. Let such claim God's promise, and not sear their own minds by harboring a grudge. Forget the mournful past, and press forward to better things.

Verse 5. "God of the whole earth." We are inclined to limit God. Men in the late war would pray for victory for their respective nations, as though there were a German, a British, a French, and an American God. God is God of the whole earth. As we do not know the many interests that must be reckoned with in order to have our prayers answered, it is always well to add, as did Christ, "Not my will, but Thine, be done." Luke 22: 42.

Verse 6. "The Lord hath called thee." That is true of all, whatever their condition. In this case the call is to a woman, a wife gone wrong, than which there is no sadder condition. But

God calls, and the call is sincere. Whosoever will may come. Let the woman come, and let the man who led her into sin come. There is still mercy with God.

Verse 10. "My kindness shall not depart."

> "There's no place where earthly sorrows
> Are more felt than up in heaven;
> There's no place where earthly failings
> Have such kindly judgment given.
>
> "For the love of God is broader
> Than the measure of man's mind;
> And the heart of the Eternal
> Is most wonderfully kind."

Verse 11. What a blessing when earth's storm-tossed children at last shall find a haven of rest!

Verse 13. "All thy children shall be taught of the Lord." As a result of this, "great shall be the peace of thy children." If great peace results from being taught of God, may we not draw the conclusion that where there is strife and contention, men have not been taught of God? According to this rule, measure your own life. Do you easily become irritated? Are you impatient? Do you scold? Those that are taught of God have great peace. Do you have peace? What is the condition in your church? Are all taught of God so that there is peace?

Verse 15. "They shall surely gather together." There will be opposition; it will surely come. But we need not and should not fear. Lack of faith brings apprehension. Trust brings confidence. After Christ had promised His disciples peace, He said, "Let not your heart be troubled, *neither let it be afraid.*" John 14:27. That is, do not worry, but trust. Peace comes as a result of faith.

Verse 16. In this verse God really takes upon Himself the responsibility of all that happens to any of His children. He says in effect: "I have created both the smith and his instrument of torture. He cannot go beyond what I permit. So do not fear. Nothing shall happen to you but what I conceive to be for the best.

Verse 17. "No weapon," "every tongue." We are here promised that no weapon shall prosper against us. One of the weapons to be used is evidently the tongue, both in argument and in slander. We must so live that there can be no just accusation brought against us, and our faith must be buttressed with such sound reasoning that our adversaries will be confounded.

CHAPTER II

God Calls to Return; The Word That Transforms

Lesson Scripture: Isaiah 55

Isaiah 55:1-7. God's call to return.

Verses 1, 2. God issues a call to all those that are thirsty to come to Him, and without money or price buy milk and wine. With gentle reproach He asks why men will continue to spend both labor and money for that which does not satisfy, when with Him they may have their wants supplied freely. They should eat only that which is good, and delight themselves in it.

Verses 3-5. Let all listen to the message of the Lord, that their souls may live. He will make an everlasting covenant with them according to the sure promises He made to David concerning Him whom the Lord has made a Witness to the world as well as a Prince and Commander of nations. He shall call a nation whom He had not hitherto recognized as His own, and nations who had not known Him shall flock to Him because of the Lord, the Holy One of Israel, who has glorified Him.

Verses 6, 7. The Lord is not always to be found, hence the time to seek Him is now while He is near. To obtain the Lord's mercy and pardon, however, it is necessary for the wicked to give up their sinful habits and thoughts, and turn whole-heartedly to the Lord.

Verses 8-13. The word that transforms.

Verses 8-11. God's thoughts are not as our thoughts, and our ways are not like His. Even as the heavens are high above the earth, so are His ways and His thoughts high above ours. His word is like the rain and the snow that come down from heaven, and water the earth and cause the seed to grow so that the hungry may be fed. They accomplish the intent of the Lord, and do not return until their work is accomplished. So also is the word. It shall not return to God until it has done the Lord's pleasure, and prospered therein.

God Calls to Return; The Word That Transforms

Verses 12, 13. God's people shall be joyful as they go out, and all nature shall rejoice with them. Instead of thorns and briers, shall be trees of beauty; and all this shall redound to the Lord's glory; it shall be an everlasting monument to His praise.

Notes

Verse 1. In Oriental countries water even to this day is not abundant, but must often be bought. The water seller will carry skins filled with water on the back of his donkey while he is crying his wares. It was to people who were acquainted with such conditions that this verse was first written. To be invited to come and get water without money would be very unusual indeed. And not only water, but wine and milk!

"That thirsteth" after righteousness. Matt. 5:6; Rev. 21:6; 22:17.

"The waters" are symbolic of Christ, divine grace, the Word, spiritual life, baptism! (See "Patriarchs and Prophets," pp. 413, 412; "Steps to Christ," p. 93; "The Desire of Ages," pp. 190, 148.)

"He that hath no money," and realizes and confesses his poverty. (See Luke 1:53.)

"Wine." Symbolic of the blood of Christ. (See "The Desire of Ages," p. 148; 1 Cor. 11:25-27.) Also of gladness. (See Ps. 104:15.)

"Milk." "Desire the sincere milk of the word." 1 Peter 2:2.

Verse 2. "Spend money," literally "weigh silver." Silver was the usual medium of exchange, and was weighed.

"That which is not bread," that which has no real value; which cannot sustain you. (See John 6:27, 32.)

"Your labors," your earnings.

"That which satisfieth not." Most things perish with the using. Only that which is of eternal value satisfies.

"Hearken diligently," rather "hearken, oh, hearken." This is a strong plea, suggesting disinclination on the part of Israel to listen and an attempt of God to overcome it.

How strange it is that the Creator must beg lost men and women to hear the message of salvation! Said the Saviour in the days of His earthly ministry, "He that hath ears to hear, let him hear." Matt. 11:15. That is, let him hear who is willing to be instructed. The thought is made very clear by another figure, in Revelation 22:17, "Let him that is athirst come." "Blessed are they which do hunger and thirst after righteousness: for they shall be filled." Matt. 5:6.

It need hardly be stated that these verses are primarily to be spiritually understood. God has spread for the soul a table of spiritual dainties that are completely satisfying. (See Ps. 36:8; 63:5; Isa. 25:6; Ps. 23:5.)

Verse 3. "Incline your ear, and come," that is, hear and obey, listen and do.

"An everlasting covenant." This covenant David speaks of as "all my salvation, and all my desire." 2 Sam. 23:5. It was made concerning "the Seed" who should "endure forever, and His throne as the days of heaven," "as the sun" "to all generations." Ps. 89:3, 4, 28, 29, 36. This Seed is Christ. Gal. 3:16.

Verse 4. "Him," Christ.

"A witness." Rev. 1:5; Ps. 89:37.

"A leader," rather "prince," A. R. V., margin. Same word as in Daniel 9:25.

Verse 5. "A nation that Thou knowest not." Of Israel God says, "You only have I known of all the families of the earth." Amos 3:2. They were God's peculiar people, His own. Of the heathen He says that they are "a people whom I have not known." Ps. 18:43. We therefore take the people mentioned in this verse to be the Gentiles.

"Nations that knew not Thee shall run unto Thee." This has been true of the Gentile nations.

"He [the Father] hath glorified Thee [the Son]." (See John 17:1, 5; Acts 3:13.)

Verse 6. In this verse the people are again addressed. The statements are of general application, but in view of Israel's coming captivity, they must have had special emphasis at the time they were written. (See Deut. 4:29; Jer. 31:13, 14.) Israel is said to be "a people near unto Him." (See Ps. 148:14; Deut. 4:7.)

Verse 7. "His way," his mode of life, his habits.

"Let him return." This is spoken to those who have known God. One that has never known God may "turn" to Him; one that has known God but is fallen away "returns."

"Abundantly pardon," not grudgingly. What God does He does whole-heartedly.

Verse 8. "For." This has reference to the preceding. that God "abundantly pardons." Unregenerate man does not do that. He is apt to hold a grudge and seek revenge. With all the evil we have done against God, He says: "I alone know the thoughts that I entertain respecting you, saith the Lord, thoughts of peace and not of evil, to give you a (happy) future and hope." Jer. 29:11, Leeser's Jewish Translation.

God's thoughts concerning us include the plan of salvation, the heights and depths of which no human mind can fathom.

Verse 9. How high are the heavens above the earth? So high are God's thoughts and ways above ours.

Verse 10. The rain and the snow are God's ministers, " fulfilling His word." Ps. 148:8. They have their appointed work. They come down from heaven, and do not return with their mission unfulfilled. The Septuagint reads: " As rain shall come down or snow, from heaven, and shall not return until it have saturated the earth," etc. Isaiah evidently knew, as did the writer of Ecclesiastes (1:7) that the rain and the snow which fall to refresh the earth ascend again in the form of vapor.

"Maketh it bring forth and bud." Rain has a very definite mission in plant life. The seed would never swell and burst without moisture, nor could the plant afterward grow.

Verse 11. "So," in like manner.

"My word." "Every word that proceedeth out of the mouth of God " is " quick and powerful." Deut. 8:3; Heb. 4:12. No scientific explanation of life and growth which leaves God out of the reckoning is satisfying or complete. God upholds " all things by the word of His power." Heb. 1:3. The origin of life, the mystery of growth, the productive powers of the earth, the germination of seed, the nutritive properties of the corn — all find their explanation in Him who is the Word. "In Him was life." John 1:4. It was the Son of God who came down from heaven and gave life to the world. John 6:33. That is the scientific explanation of how life came to this planet, and explains the origin of life.

"It shall not return unto Me void." The figure is that of a messenger returning to report the outcome of his mission. In Zechariah 1:7-11 the angels are thus shown as God's messengers who go to and fro in the earth and return to report to " the Angel of the Lord," Christ.

Verse 12. Commentators generally explain this verse as the " going out " of Babylon. In view of the previous verses, however, where God's word is spoken of as the rain and snow which cause the seed to grow; and in view of the following verse which describes the result of this " going out,"— that vegetation shall flourish,— we prefer to see in these verses the picture of God's people going out to sow the seed of the word, with the result that the mountains and the hills break forth into singing and the trees clap their hands.

Verse 13. This verse explains the change which the word will accomplish in the hearts and lives of men. Thorns and briers — sarcasm, criticism, bitterness — shall give place to the graces of the Spirit. This change shall be "to the Lord for a name," that is, it shall be to His glory. The Jewish Targum paraphrases this verse: "Instead of the wicked shall rise up the righteous; and instead of transgressors men that fear sin."

Lessons for To-day

Verse 1. "Every one that thirsteth." The call is not confined to the rich or the learned, but issued to all that are thirsty. It is the felt need that is the qualification.

A hungry man will lie down quietly and die. A thirsty man will spend himself in mad strivings. Of the two, thirst is by far the more powerful craving.

As satisfying as is water to the thirsty traveler, so satisfying is Christ to the thirsty soul. And the verse presents the blessed fact that the deepest needs and longings of the human heart are understood by God, and that abundant provision is made for their satisfaction. Whatever may be the legitimate desire of the heart, Christ can satisfy it, and will do so.

There is perhaps no true child of God, however humble and obscure, whose eyes have been opened to eternal realities, but has secret longings for purity, love, power, and larger service, which he perhaps never has dared admit even to himself, much less speak of to others. Shall there always be such unfulfilled and unexpressed longings? Shall there in the earth made new be suppressed wishes and ambitions that shall vainly strive for expression? No, no! Even as the thirsty soul drinks and drinks and drinks until he is satisfied, so the time shall come when every one of God's children shall see his highest ambitions realized and his deepest soul-longing satisfied. "I shall be satisfied, when I awake, with Thy likeness." Ps. 17: 15.

Water refreshes, wine cheers, milk nourishes. All our wants will be supplied, and that without money and without price.

Verse 2. How much money is spent for that which is not bread! and how much labor for that in which there is no satisfaction!

Literally speaking, much of that which is on our tables is "not bread." Others may be suffering for the necessities of life, but our tables are loaded with dainties and delicacies, mostly useless and often harmful, the price of which would keep many starving children alive. God admonishes us to deal our bread to the hungry. Isa. 58:7. Might it not be well to have this in mind when we are smugly thanking God that *we* are well provided for?

Much of our reading is "not bread." Few are the books or magazines published to-day worth while. Some of them are trash, some are literary jazz, some plain filth, some rank poison. The world reads as it eats — unwholesome concoctions that stimulate but do not produce strength.

"Spend money." How many foolish plunges men have made! Unwise investment has claimed its thousands, and the desire to get rich quickly its ten thousands. The lure of speculation, the fascination of large returns, the inability to learn lessons from past experiences, all combine to rob God's cause of means. It is high time that all of God's people kept themselves from the world in this respect.

But it is not only in large matters but also in small ones that we should be careful in spending money. Why is it that we freely spend money for knick-knacks, but forget to put our Sabbath school offering by when it happens that we do not get to the service some Sabbath? Why should we not lay the money by, and bring it the following Sabbath? "Every little counts."

"Eat ye that which is good." That is sound advice, whether literally or spiritually applied. Not that which tastes good, or looks good, or smells good, but that which *is* good.

"Let your soul delight itself in its fatness;" that is, learn to like that which is good.

Verse 6. "While He may be found." God may be found to-day. To-morrow may be too late. "Thou shalt find Him, if thou seek Him with all thy heart and with all thy soul." Deut. 4:29. God desires earnestness in our seeking of Him, or we will not find Him.

Verse 7. "Way," "thoughts." God counsels the wicked to forsake his "way," that is, his manner of life. A man's "way" and "thoughts" are closely connected. The first is the effect, the second is the cause. Before a man does anything, he thinks. A criminal will plan his course of action before he commits a crime. The impure man will let his thoughts dwell on sin before he finally transgresses in act. All sin exists first in the mind, hence any real cure for sin must include a renewing of the mind. We are therefore told to be transformed by the renewing of the mind (Rom. 12:2), so that we will no longer be enemies in the mind

(Col. 1:21), but have the same mind that Jesus had (Phil. 2:5), in which the law is written (Heb. 8:10; 10:16).

"He will abundantly pardon." When God forgives, He forgets. There is no holding back, no reserve. It may be hard for us to forget some things, but may not the reason be that we secretly wish to remember?

Verse 8. God's thoughts toward us are thoughts of peace. He wishes for us a happy future, and is planning for it, and that in spite of the fact that mankind has crucified His only begotten Son. If we would occupy our thoughts in planning some happiness for those who have injured us, may it not be that we should forget our revengefulness? Why should we be secretly glad when some misfortune happens to one who has opposed us? Why should we ever be vindictive? Surely, we trust, and hope, and *know*, that God is not like that. Then why should we be?

Verses 10, 11. The rain and the snow do not return until they have accomplished God's purpose. So also the word. It shall not return unto God void. "It shall accomplish that which I please." We are at times too anxious about God's work. The seed lies buried under a heavy layer of snow. We want to remove the icy blanket, and expose the seed to the wind and sun so it can grow, not considering that God knows what He is doing. In time — in God's time — He removes the blanket, and the promise of harvest appears.

Verse 12. "Go out with joy." We are to rejoice always. We are to be cheerful, even when we give. 2 Cor. 9:7. God wants us to go out with joy, whether it be in the colporteur work, in visiting the sick, in Harvest Ingathering, in Big Week, or in any missionary effort. And our cheerfulness is to be so contagious that even nature will rejoice with us.

Verse 13. Thorns and briers. Some people are so much like thorns and briers that "they cannot be taken with hands; but the man that shall touch them must be fenced with iron and the staff of a spear." 2 Sam. 23:6, 7. David doubtless spoke from experience. But even for such there is hope. God can change them into fruitful trees, and thus they may become monuments of His grace.

CHAPTER III

Blessings to Jew and Gentile; Blind Watchmen

Lesson Scripture: Isaiah 56

Isaiah 56: 1-8. Blessings to Jew and Gentile.

Verses 1, 2. The Lord is speaking: Keep the law and do righteousness, for deliverance is near, and My righteousness is about to be revealed. That man is blessed, whoever he may be, who does this, and does not give up: who keeps the Sabbath and does not profane it, and who also keeps his hand from doing evil.

Verses 3-5. Let not the foreigner who has joined himself to the Lord say: God will surely separate me from His people; and let not the eunuch say: I am a barren tree. For the Lord has promised: the eunuchs that keep My Sabbaths, and do the things that please Me, and hold fast My covenant, to them will I give a name that is better than of sons and daughters, I will give them a monument in My house and within My walls, and an everlasting name which shall not be cut off.

Verses 6-8. The foreigner also, who joins himself to the Lord to worship and love His name and be His servant, every one that keeps the Sabbath holy, and holds fast to My covenant, will I bring to My holy mountain, and he shall rejoice in My sanctuary of prayer. There shall be no difference between the proselyte and the chosen people, but their offerings and sacrifices shall be alike accepted upon My altar; for My house shall be called a house of prayer for all peoples. For the Lord God who will gather scattered Israel will also gather many others that are not of Israel, besides those that are gathered to Him.

Verses 9-12. Blind watchmen.

Verses 9, 10. Let all the beasts of the field and forest come to devour the defenseless flock: for their spiritual leaders are blind and ignorant. They are not watching the flock, but are like dumb dogs that cannot bark. They are lazy, loving to lie down and dream and slumber.

Verses 11, 12. At the same time they are greedy dogs that are never satisfied and shepherds that entirely fail to comprehend the situation. They all pursue their own selfish way, and without exception are looking for gain for themselves. They also enjoy surfeiting, and one says: I will provide the wine, and we will drink ourselves drunk. And to-morrow we will do the same, and worse.

Notes

After the introduction in verses 1 and 2, exhorting to righteousness as exhibited in law keeping and the observance of the Sabbath, the main subject of the first part of the chapter is introduced, namely, the relation of strangers and eunuchs to the promises and rewards of Israel. If a foreigner joined himself to Israel, what would be his status? God had given some very explicit directions concerning the Moabites and Ammonites; and the Edomites and Egyptians were also under restrictions. Deut. 23: 3-8. Did these restrictions still hold?

The eunuchs also were proscribed from the congregation of the Lord. Deut. 23: 1, 2. Was that prohibition still in effect? In the different captivities to which Israel was subjected, many of the young men were made eunuchs, as otherwise they would not be permitted to serve in any capacity in the king's court or harem. Were such to be excluded from the covenant? These were weighty questions, and needed to be answered. Prophecy had definitely stated that some of the sons of Hezekiah should be "eunuchs in the palace of the king of Babylon." Isa. 39: 7. Would such be "cut off" from "the congregation of the Lord"? Deut. 23: 1. The answer is given in the following verses.

Verse 1. "Keep ye judgment," rather "keep ye law and observe righteousness," George Rawlinson's "Isaiah." Moffatt translates: "Hold to religion and do what is right."

"Justice" should be translated "righteousness," as in the A. R. V. It is, in fact, the same word that is translated "righteousness" in the latter part of the verse. Of these two words, both of which should be translated "righteousness," Skinner in the Cambridge Bible says: "In the first case, righteousness means conformity to the law of God (cf. 58: 2); in the second it is, as often, equivalent to salvation." A paraphrase of the verse might read: "Keep the law and do what is right, for the Lord will soon come and His righteousness is about to be revealed." It is an exhortation to keep the commandments of God in view of the fact that the Lord is soon to come and that His righteousness will then be revealed.

Verse 2. "Man." The Hebrew uses at least five different words for "man." The first "man" in this verse is derived from a word denoting that which is frail, incurable, mortal. The second "man" is from a different word, and denotes that which is healthy, red, ruddy, used of Adam in the beginning. The blessing pronounced is for all, whoever they may be and wherever found.

It is interesting to note the prominent place here given to Sabbath keeping. The first verse exhorts men to keep the law. This verse points out a special part of that law, and pronounces a blessing upon those who keep it. That this does not refer to the Jews only is clear from the expressions "man" and "son of man," including as they do all mankind.

The reason for selecting the Sabbath commandment as worthy of a special blessing, is thus given by the Bible Commentary: "The Sabbath was a memorial of the six days of *creation* (Ex. 20: 11; 31: 17); of the *redemption* out of Egypt (Deut. 5: 15); of God's continual *sanctification* of His people (Ex. 31: 13): so that, by its means, they dwelt in the presence of the Creator, Redeemer, and Sanctifier."

"Layeth hold on it," rather "holds to it;" that is, does not give up, but holds on.

Verse 3. "The son of the stranger"—"foreigner," A. R. V. "Joined himself to the Lord" here means conversion and union with the people of God.

"Hath utterly separated," "will surely separate," R. V.

"Eunuchs" are such as either by nature or castration are rendered incapable of becoming the head of a family. In the Bible the word is sometimes translated "officer" or "chamberlain." Eunuchs usually had charge of the king's harem, and were also intrusted with the education of the young princes. Their position was often one of great influence and importance, but they were also the objects of contempt by other men.

Even as the women of Israel considered barrenness a calamity and a curse, so the question would naturally arise as to eunuchs. Their family would die out when they died. Would they have any part in Israel, or would their name forever be forgotten?

Verse 4. This verse contains the conditions upon which the eunuchs may have a place among God's people. These conditions are three: Keeping the Sabbath; choosing the things that please God; holding fast to the covenant.

Verse 5. "In My house," in the temple.
"Within My walls," inside the city.
"A place," a monument, or as the American Revised Version has it, a memorial. Absalom, when he thought he should die childless, erected such a monument to himself. 2 Sam. 18:18.
"A name," "an everlasting name." The eunuchs might rightly expect that as the family died out, their name would soon be forgotten. God now promises them an everlasting name. Even the largest earthly family might conceivably die out, as has often happened. God's promise is better "than of sons and of daughters."

Verse 6. Five things are here predicated of the strangers or foreigners: "Join themselves," conversion; "love the name," love to be the motive power, not fear, or hope of gain; "servants," service, not agreement to a creed merely, but working for souls; "the Sabbath," reverence, obedience; "taketh hold of My covenant," with both hands, and holds on, never giving up.

Verse 7. "My holy mountain," Jerusalem. "My house of prayer," the temple. 1 Kings 8:29-53.
"Burnt offerings and sacrifices." These would be accepted from the strangers as well as from the Jews.
"A house of prayer for all people;" rather "peoples," that is, nationalities. Matt. 21:13; Mark 11:17; Luke 19:46.

Verse 8. "The outcasts," literally "the dispersed."
"Gather others," same as "other sheep" in John 10:16. This is a promise of the ingathering of the Gentiles. (See also John 11:52.)

Verse 9. "Beasts of the field." The prophet here turns from the promises of God to conditions as they actually were. The beasts that should devour were the enemies of Israel. Eze. 34:7-10. These should come because Israel had neglected to observe the things mentioned in the previous verses.

Verse 10. "His watchmen are blind." When blind men are set as watchmen, calamity may be expected.
"Blind," "ignorant," "dumb," "sleeping," "lying down," "loving to slumber." What a list of shortcomings for the watchmen! A blind watchman is certainly at a disadvantage. If in addition to being blind he is also ignorant so he would not recognize danger though he should see it; if he were unable to "bark," if he in fact were "dreaming" or talking in his sleep, as is here the meaning of the word "sleeping," and if he loved to do all this, what hope would there be for those who depended on him for protection?

Verse 11. "Greedy dogs." The watchmen not only neglect

their duty shamelessly, but are greedy, never having enough. The picture is not a pleasant one, but true. When the shepherds look "every one for his gain," the sheep must suffer.

Verse 12. This verse presents the climax in the indictment of the watchmen. They are not only blind, ignorant, lazy, and greedy, but here the sins of drunkenness and gluttony are added. "We will fill ourselves with strong drink," in the original a very coarse expression, suggesting the hog. "Let's swill our fill," very aptly and truly Moffatt translates.

Lessons for To-day

Verse 1. The exhortation to keep "judgment and do justice" is based on the nearness of Jehovah's salvation. Note the word "for." We are always to do right, but here a special reason is introduced: the Lord is near. We are to keep the law and observe righteousness, and this so much the more as the Saviour's coming is at hand. We may therefore confidently apply the principles of this chapter to our own time.

Verse 2. A special blessing is here pronounced upon Sabbath keepers. Were there not some special significance attached to the keeping of the Sabbath, we would not expect to see the Sabbath commandment stressed above the rest. In view of the fact that these verses find a special application at the time when God's salvation is near, and in view of the further fact that there is now a controversy as to the keeping of the Sabbath, it is very comforting indeed to know that while the world desecrates God's own day and uses terms of reproach to designate those who revere it, God definitely places Himself on the side of those who keep it and blesses them.

Let none, however, fail to note the second requisite for having a part in the blessing. We must keep our "hand from doing any evil." Evil is sin. We are not to sin. But the expression is still stronger. It is not merely "evil," but "any evil." That takes in every kind of sin, and demands holiness.

It is evil to speak or think ill of the brethren. It is evil to be unsympathetic and harsh. It is evil to leave debts unpaid. It is evil to be careless, rash, impatient, covetous, unclean. Even as a cleverly executed counterfeit is more dangerous than a crude imitation, so may a Saturday keeper do untold harm if his home life and general reputation are not above reproach. True Sabbath keeping involves holiness, and will effect a most careful observance of all the commandments.

Verse 3. National lines are obliterated in Christ. There are no inferior or superior nations, nor are any " foreigners." Castes exist no more, nor any aristocracy. Character alone counts.

Nor are physical defects a barrier. The maimed, the halt, and the blind are given a special invitation. Luke 14:21. Inherited, arbitrary, or acquired disabilities are no disbarment to the kingdom. Celibacy may not be a special virtue, but if done " for the kingdom of heaven's sake," at least no odium attaches to it. Matt. 19:12.

Verse 4. " The things that please Me." Among the things that please God are " loving-kindness, judgment, and righteousness." " In these things I delight." Jer. 9:24. The original word for " delight " is the same as for " please " in Isaiah.

Verse 5. " A place and a name." What will men in this world not do to obtain a place of prominence and a name for themselves? Many have sold soul and body to obtain these. Men erect imposing structures dedicated to prominent individuals, and some even place their own names on buildings to commemorate themselves. God's people are promised an " everlasting name," " written in heaven." Luke 10:20. And this promise is given on the usual conditions of obedience as outlined in Isaiah 56:4.

Verse 6. It should be noted that those " that join themselves to the Lord," do so " to serve," " to love," etc. Some join the church, and do little after they have joined. But those that join the Lord as well as the church do so " to serve." How many in your church have really " joined the Lord " ? Every one who has done so, also serves. He who does not serve may indeed have joined the church, but he has not joined the Lord. Apply this test to yourself, not to others.

Verse 7. A " house of prayer." The church building is not a place in which to buy and sell; it is not a place of entertainment nor a lunch room; it is not a place for visiting or criticism or discussion. It is first of all a place of prayer. Measure your church by that standard. Do you make your church a place of prayer? How long since you prayed in it, not audibly, but in your heart? Settle it for yourself that henceforth the church shall be a place of prayer for *you*. If all do this, it will be a place of quietness, of rest, of worshipful attitude, of reverence.

" Accepted." God does not refuse the smallest gift nor the most imperfect prayer. As we accept with appreciation the smallest flower, even though wilted, from the hand of a little child, so

God accepts our gifts. It is not the intrinsic value that counts, but the love that prompts the gift.

Verse 8. "Gather others." Our eyes and mind must ever be on others. Some of those "others" may be in our own family, some beyond the sea. They must all be gathered.

Verses 10-12. All need to be very careful lest they condemn in others what they allow in themselves. While these verses undoubtedly find their fulfillment in the watchmen and shepherds of the popular churches, we must not lose sight of the fact that many even of these are honest in heart, and that there must be no wholesale condemnation. We are rapidly coming to the time when the full force of the message of the third angel may be sounded. But even as Christ did not deliver His scathing rebukes until the last few months of His ministry, so the denunciatory parts of the third angel's message will not be fully preached until all things are ripe. Also, God's people must themselves be clear so that no accusing finger can be pointed at them when the message rings out. This presupposes holiness. The Sabbath and true holiness will thus condemn the world.

CHAPTER IV

The Righteous and the Wicked in the Day of Trouble

Lesson Scripture: Isaiah 57

Isaiah 57: 1, 2. The righteous removed.

Good men die and no one cares, and men of piety are removed, none seeming to comprehend that they are called away before the evil breaks. They at last obtain peace, resting in their beds, whoever has walked uprightly.

Verses 3-13. The works of evil-doers.

Verses 3, 4. But as for you, draw near, sons of a sorceress, offspring of an adulterer and a harlot. At whom is your derisive mirth aimed? At whom do you make faces and put out the tongue? Are you not children of transgression and the seed of liars?

Verses 4-6. You inflame your passions under every tree, you sacrifice your children in the valleys and in the clefts of the rock. To the smooth stones you have offered drink offerings and meat offerings, and they are your portion. Should I be pleased with such, and not punish? Upon a high and lofty mountain you have made your bed and have gone there to sacrifice.

Verses 8-10. Also behind the doors and the posts you have set up your foul symbols. You have loved others besides Me, and made a covenant with them. You have anointed yourself for Moloch, and have debased yourself to hell. You have worn yourself out, yet you did not give up, but revived a little and went on again.

Verses 11-13. Of whom have you been afraid, so that you thought it expedient to lie? I have said nothing to you, so you have not been afraid of Me. Now, however, I will expose you, and it will not be to your credit. When you cry, let your abominable idols deliver you. But a wind will blow them away, in fact, only a breath is needed. But those that trust in Me shall inherit the land and possess My holy mountain.

The Righteous and the Wicked in the Day of Trouble

Verses 14-21. God comforts His people.

Verses 14-16. Prepare the way, remove all stumblingblocks. For thus says the high and lofty One, whose name is Holy, and who inhabits eternity: I dwell in the high and holy place, and also with him who is contrite and humble, to revive the spirit of the humble and the heart of the contrite. I will not always be angry, else both spirit and soul should fail before Me.

Verses 17-19. I was indeed angry at Israel's covetousness, and smote him and hid Myself, while he willfully went on his way. But now I will heal him, lead him, and comfort him. I will give peace to him that is afar off, as well as to him that is near, says God, and I will heal him.

Verses 20, 21. But the wicked are like the restless sea, which casts up mire and dirt. To them there is no peace.

Notes

Verse 1. This verse is closely connected in thought with the last verses of the previous chapter. The watchmen are interested only in their own gain; they eat and drink to excess, and are not caring that the righteous perish and that pious men are taken away.

"Taken away from the evil to come." Another translation is permissible: "Taken away through wickedness," A. R. V., margin. The latter would seem to indicate that their death was not natural, but was brought about by wicked men. Both may be true. God will take some away before the evil comes, and it may also be that some will die the death of the martyr rather than do evil.

Verse 2. "Enter into peace," "rest in their beds." The grave is here meant. Evidently those here spoken of had a turbulent time while living. Perhaps persecution confronted them. Now they rest from their labors. Rev. 14:13. "Each one walking," rather "each one that walked."

Verse 3. "Sorceress." The same word is translated "soothsayer" in Isaiah 2:6, and "observed times" in 2 Chronicles 33:6. The people addressed are such as are "nursed in witchcraft and superstition."

Verse 4. "Sport yourselves," to make fun of, to deride, to mock.

"Wide mouth," "draw out the tongue," gestures of mockery and contempt.

"Children of transgression," rather "children of apostasy."

"Seed of falsehood." John 8:44.

Verse 5. "Enflaming yourselves." This is a reference to the licentious acts which were practised under the guise of religion, and to which Paul refers in Romans 1:22-32. Aside from the most debasing forms of immorality, this worship also included the slaying of children. These were at times put alive into leather bags, then thrown from a great height to the ground, breaking every bone in the body. At other times they were sacrificed directly to Moloch by being burned alive in the outstretched arms of the fire god. 2 Kings 16:3, 4; 2 Chron. 28:3, 4; Jer. 19:5.

Verse 6. "Smooth stones," probably stones worshiped as gods. "They are thy lot." The stones, not the Lord, would be their lot. Having chosen stones to be their god, stones should be their portion. "Should I receive comfort in these?" rather, as in the American Revised Version, "Shall I be appeased for these things?" that is, shall I let sin go unpunished?

Verse 7. "Set thy bed." The image here used is suggested by the frequent comparison of idolatry to adultery. God being the husband of His people (Isa. 54:5), to go after other gods is spiritual adultery. Hosea 2:2.

"Lofty and high mountain." Hills and high mountains were specially dedicated to idolatrous worship. (See Deut. 12:2; I Kings 14:23, etc.) They constituted the "high places" so frequently mentioned.

Verse 8. "Behind the doors." Israel was anciently commanded to write portions of God's word "upon the posts of thy house, and on thy gates." Deut. 6:9; 11:20. Some have thought that this verse has reference to this custom, and that instead of writing on the front of the door, they wrote on the back so it could not be seen. The reading will hardly bear this meaning, however. "Remembrance" should be translated "memorial," as in the American Revised Version, and must have reference to some heathen emblem or symbol, perhaps one of the common household gods. There may be a reference to this custom in Ezekiel 16:17.

"Enlarged thy bed," multiplied thy idolatries. (See 2 Kings 16:3, 4, 10; 21:3-7.)

"Made a covenant," not with God, but with sin.

Verse 9. "The king," literally Moloch. Moloch was a heathen god whose worship had been introduced into Israel. He was probably the most cruel of all gods, and his worship demanded the sacrifice of little children. These were placed in the outstretched arms of the god, and a fire was lighted beneath. This was causing the children to "pass through the fire." 2 Kings 16:3. Moloch, or the king, we take here to be symbolic of Satan, and to go "to the king" to be parallel to the expression in the latter part of the verse to debase oneself "even unto hell." There is nothing in religion that can conceivably be lower than Moloch worship, with its filthy, degrading rites and cruel child sacrifices.

Verse 10. "The greatness of thy way," rather "the length of thy way;" that is, it is a long and dreary path "even unto hell." The verse presents the thought that at times Israel would become weary of their much sin, yet would not give up, but would find "life," would revive again and go on sinning.

It is the common experience of mankind to tire of sin, and yet to go on in it. "Thou wast not grieved." They were not truly repentant. "Grieved" is literally "sick," and a common expression may here well express the meaning: they were not sick of their sin.

Verse 11. "Thou hast lied." Children will sometimes tell a falsehood for fear of punishment. God had held His peace and Israel did not fear Him, hence there was not even the excuse of fear for dealing faithlessly.

Verse 12. "I will declare thy righteousness." Probably an ironic expression. Moffatt translates: "I will expose your doings, this 'religion' of yours!"

Verse 13. "Thy companies"—"rabble of idols," A. R. V., margin.

"Vanity," rather "breath." Israel trusted in idols whom the wind, or even a breath, could carry away.

Verse 14. The image of a highway is the same as in chapter 40:3 and 62:10.

Verse 15. "Inhabiteth eternity," a profound expression, beyond man's comprehension.

Verse 16. "The spirit," "the souls." These words are the same as those used in the creation of man, and denote that if God held us to strict account, none could stand before Him, all would fail.

Verse 17. Covetousness was a besetting sin in Israel. (See Jer. 6:13; Eze. 33:31; Isa. 3:14, 15, etc.) It made God "wroth," but heedlessly Israel "went on frowardly in the way of his heart."

Verse 18. How wonderful is God's mercy! When it might be expected that God would punish, He says He will "heal," "lead him also, and restore comforts unto him."

Verse 19. "Fruit of the lips," thanksgiving and praise. Heb. 13:15; Hosea 14:2.

Lessons for To-day

Verse 1. "Blessed are the dead which die in the Lord from henceforth." Rev. 14:13. If this verse had not been written, some might think that a curse rests upon those who die and do not live to see the Lord come. "Blessed are the dead." They are "taken away from the evil to come," they "rest from their labors," yet "their works do follow them." It is a blessed thing to be translated without seeing death. When we consider, however, all that God's people must pass through before the Lord comes, including the time of Jacob's trouble, it may be well for us to leave the future in the hand of the Lord. If He sees best for us to live, let us thank Him for it. If otherwise, let us say, His will be done. God knows how much we can endure. He knows what is best, hence "whether we live therefore, or die, we are the Lord's." Rom. 14:8.

Verse 2. If the righteous go directly to heaven at death, it would be a strange description of the bliss of the redeemed to say that "they rest in their beds." Isa. 57:2. If, on the other hand, all sleep until the morn of the resurrection, how appropriate as well as comforting to know that after earth's toil and distress they have entered "into peace," that they "rest in their beds."

Verse 4. "Against whom do ye sport yourselves?" Mockery, derisive mirth, is not at any time a very acceptable diversion. It is a low type of "fun," and only a peculiarly adapted mind can find any satisfaction in it. When directed against those who honestly worship their Creator, He counts it as done against Him. Isa. 37:23. It is well for God's people to abstain from mockery, ridicule, and unkind allusions, even against our opponents and those whom we know to be mistaken.

Verse 5. "Slaying the children." We are horrified when we learn that Israel of old actually practiced "the abominations of the heathen," and offered up their own children in sacrifice to the gods. What shall we then say of modern parents who do the same thing, perhaps in a more refined way, but with the same result? Mothers will dress their children in a way that constitutes them an acceptable offering upon the altar of fashion; they will feed them to satisfy the god of appetite; they will educate them according to the demands of the god of Ekron; they will permit them to have part in all the pleasures and follies of a degenerate age; and when they go wrong, wonder what causes them to do so. The "slaughter of the innocents" is not a past event merely. In civilized lands millions of unborn children are crying out for life, but never see it, being sacrificed upon the altar of lust and convenience, a custom not much superior to that of untutored savages killing their weak and unwanted children.

Verse 6. " Smooth stones . . . are thy lot." As we sow, so we reap. If we worship stones, stones we get. If we worship God, God will be our portion.

Verse 8. " Behind the doors." Many things are hid " behind the doors." Israel hid their idols there, thinking they would not so readily be seen. Many now think that they can do things behind their doors that they could not do openly. But it is worth noting that God knows what goes on. The quarrels in the home; the outbursts of temper; the lack of family and private worship; the difference in home conduct as compared with public conduct; the faultfinding and criticism indulged in; the lack of love and courtesy and forbearance,— all are noted and recorded. Nothing goes on behind the doors of which God is ignorant.

Verse 9. " Thou wentest to the king, . . . and didst debase thyself even unto hell." High position in society is no assurance of right conduct. Kings do wrong, as well as common people. And the higher the position and the clearer the knowledge, the greater is the corresponding responsibility. If climbing up in society means a giving up or a lowering of true standards, the gain is a loss.

Verse 10. " Thou art wearied." Men will weary of sin and still continue in it. And often the reason for continuance is their inability to quit. Men may deplore their use of some drug, may know the evil it is causing, may even desire to discontinue its use, but find themselves unable to do so. They discover that they need a power greater than themselves to break with evil, and they are unwilling to accept the deliverance which God alone can give. And thus they remain slaves to sin, weary of themselves, yet continuing without hope of release. And this has reference to small sins as well as great. Sin's nature is the same, in whatever form it shows itself.

Verse 11. " Thou hast lied." How like the statement: " Thou art the man." God requires truthfulness in all respects. Lies may be acted as well as spoken. They vitally affect character. If we are in " the truth," we will speak the truth. There must be found no guile in the mouth of any believer.

" Hast not remembered Me." It is well to remember God when we are in trouble. Yet it is too bad to remember Him only when we have some pain or misfortune, and so realize our need of His help. If we had an earthly friend whom we neglected when all went well and whom we recognized only when we needed money or help of some kind, we would soon see, or be made to see, the inconsistency of our course. Why, then, should we treat God as we do?

Verse 13. In this verse God says in effect that men who have put their trust in a "rabble of idols" had better call upon them when they get into trouble. This is fair. There is no justice in our doing all manner of wicked things, ruining ourselves body, soul, and spirit, and then expect God to help us out of our difficulty. And yet that is the very thing God will do for us if we ask Him. This is more than justice; it is mercy. But should not every sense of gratitude demand that, having been thus helped, we should "sin no more"?

Verse 14. "The stumblingblock." The preacher who speaks on the wonderful work the Sabbath school is doing, but is not himself present in class; the teacher who talks of sacrificing for missions while decked with rings and useless adornments; the superintendent or elder who dwells on the law of God and the necessity of obedience while he is a law unto himself with reference to order, goals, punctuality, liberality in giving, and co-operation; the person who reports having studied the lesson every day during the week and yet is unable to answer a question; the families who expect to go to heaven together, but in the church service sit far apart,— all these might do well to consider the influence of their example.

Verse 15. "A contrite and humble spirit." How different from a haughty and rebellious attitude! God dwells with the one, not with the other.

Verse 17. Covetousness is idolatry. Col. 3:5. Some sins make God weary; some make Him sad; some make Him angry. Covetousness is among the latter. It is one of the "respectable" sins for which members are not removed from the church roll. Yet it causes God to hide Himself, it makes Him wroth. It is the root of many other sins. It dries up the springs of mercy and compassion. It shrivels the soul, hardens the heart, and petrifies the affections. It withholds tithe from the treasury, funds from missions, the bread of life from starving souls. It affects the individual himself, and also poor souls on the other side of the earth. Of all sins, its influence is most widely felt. We need to pray God to deliver us from its fearful ravages, and to ask Him for help to have every vestige of it removed from our heart.

Verse 18. Covetousness is such a heinous sin that we might expect God to turn in disgust from any one afflicted with it. But not so. God's love extends even to a covetous person. He "will heal him," yes, He "will lead him also."

Verses 19-21. "Peace, peace." "There is no peace." Troubled, buffeted, perplexed, God's people may yet have peace. A paradox indeed. Prosperous, no financial worries, abundant pleasures, yet a gnawing conscience and no real peace, is the lot of many in the world. Better is a little with contentment and the peace of God, than riches and a seared conscience.

CHAPTER V

True Fasting; The Sabbath Restored

Lesson Scripture: Isaiah 58

Isaiah 58: 1-7. True fasting.

Verses 1, 2. Cry aloud, spare not, let your voice sound aloud like a trumpet; show My people wherein they have transgressed, and reveal to Jacob's house their sins. Yet they inquire of Me daily, and take delight in a knowledge of My ways. As a people that have done righteousness and have not forsaken the law of their God, they ask of Me concerning ordinances of righteousness, and they delight to draw near to God.

Verses 3-5. Why have we fasted, they say, and Thou dost not see it? Why have we afflicted our souls, and Thou dost not notice it? Behold, in the day of fasting you carry on your business and oppress all your laborers. Your fasting makes you quarrelsome and contentious, so that it even leads to smiting with godless fists. Your fasting is not such as to cause your prayers to be heard in heaven. Do you think that I take any delight in such a fast? To afflict the soul for a day? to droop one's head like a bulrush, and lie in sackcloth and ashes? Do you call that a fast and a day of acceptance to the Lord?

Verses 6, 7. Is not this the fast that I desire: to loose men from unjust and oppressive chains, to untie the bands of violence, to liberate those that are crushed, and to break every yoke? Is it not to share your bread with the hungry, to bring the poor and homeless to your house, to clothe the naked when you see them, and not to hide yourself from your own flesh?

Verses 8-12. Blessings of true fasting.

Verses 8, 9. Then shall light come to you as the dawn, and healing proceed rapidly. Your righteousness shall go before you, and God's glory shall compass you. When you call on the Lord, He will answer; and when you cry, He will say, Here am I.

Verses 9-12. If you will do away with all oppression, with pointing the finger of scorn and with speaking of evil; if you will bestow on the hungry that which your own soul desires, and relieve the afflicted one, then shall light come to you in darkness, and your gloom shall be as the noonday. And the Lord will guide you continually, and satisfy your soul even in dry places. He will renew your strength, and you shall be as a well-watered garden, as a fountain whose water does not disappoint. And your sons shall rebuild the old waste places, the foundations of olden times they shall raise again; and you shall be called, The repairer of the breach, The restorer of paths to dwell in.

Verses 13, 14. True Sabbath keeping.

If you turn away your foot from the Sabbath, from seeking pleasure on My holy day; if you call the Sabbath a delight, the holy of the Lord, honorable, and shall honor it by not following your usual pursuits, nor finding your own pleasure, nor speaking idle words, then you will have your delight in the Lord, and I will cause you to ride upon the high places of the earth, and let you enjoy the heritage of your father Jacob. The mouth of the Lord has spoken this.

Notes

This chapter is of the highest importance, as it deals not so much with the sins of the world as with those of God's people. " The prophet is addressing Sabbath keepers, not sinners, not unbelievers."—" *Testimonies,*" *Vol. II, p. 36.*

While a false prophet will prophesy smooth things, it is the function of a true prophet to " declare unto Jacob his transgression, and to Israel his sin." Micah 3:8. This the prophet does in this chapter. It should be borne in mind, however, that no one will derive any benefit from the study who applies the counsels and rebukes to some one else. It is easy to see the application of a rebuke to another person or to a denomination. The person who reads this chapter and does not become sufficiently aware of his own shortcomings to refrain from condemning any one else, has read in vain. He needs to pray for the heavenly eyesalve, that he may get a correct view of himself.

The only fast known to the law was that of the day of atonement. (Lev. 16:29, where the phrase " afflict your souls " refers to fasting. Later on other fast days were appointed, but as mentioned above, the fast of the day of atonement was the only one recognized by the law.) This is interesting in view of the fact that the whole chapter has a special application to this time, and that we are now living in the antitypical day of atonement.

38 Isaiah, the Gospel Prophet

Verse 2. "Seek Me," rather "inquire of Me," the word used in consulting a prophet. Eze. 20:1.

"Ordinance of their God," the "law of God."

"Ordinances of justice," rather "ordinances of righteousness, that is, directions as to how righteousness is to be achieved."— *Cambridge Bible*.

Verse 3. Israel thought that God ought to take notice of their fasting and commend them for it.

"Find pleasure," rather "business." The word originally meant pleasure as in our version. Later on it took on an additional meaning, as in Isaiah 44:28, where God says of Cyrus that he "shall perform all My pleasure," that is, do what God "has in mind." The same word is translated "purpose" in Ecclesiastes 8:6, and "matter" in Ecclesiastes 5:8, in which latter case Young gives "business" as the first meaning. We might therefore translate: "In the day of fasting you carry on your business." Moffatt translates: "On fast days you find time for your business."

"Exact all your labors"—"oppress all your laborers," A. R. V., margin.

Verse 4. "Ye fast for strife and debate," or contention. Fasting instead of drawing Israel nearer to God made them fretful and quarrelsome, so that smiting "with the fist" was resorted to.

The latter part of the verse may be paraphrased to read: Your present mode of fasting will not cause your prayers to be heard in heaven.

Verse 5. God here condemns the kind of fasting that is merely negative. It is not enough to abstain from food. That may only make a person irritable and quarrelsome. True fasting is more than that. It is not to go with bowed head, or to lie down in sackcloth and ashes. That is not fasting, nor will any one because of this be accepted by the Lord.

Verses 6, 7. What, then, is fasting? It is abstinence from every form of evil (verse 6), and it is the doing of positive good (verse 7).

Four things are mentioned in verse 6 as constituting a fast acceptable to God:

Loose the chains that bind men unjustly.

"Untie the knots of hard bargains," Septuagint.

Let the "broken" go free — those whose liberty had been forfeited to their creditors. Neh. 5:5-12.

"Break every yoke."

Four things also are mentioned in verse 7:

"Deal thy bread to the hungry." Do not merely abstain from eating. Feed the hungry. If at times you go hungry that others may eat, *that* is fasting.

"Cast out," homeless. Give them a home.

"The naked." Cover him.

"Hide not thyself." Go not by on the other side, be not ashamed of your religion.

Verse 8. The results of true fasting affect both body and soul. The promises in this verse are most precious:

"Break forth as the morning," as the dawn.

"Thine health," rather "healing."

"Rereward." "The glory of God shall compass thee," Septuagint.

Verse 9. "Take away . . . the yoke," all oppression.

"Putting forth of the finger." A gesture of contempt, pointing the finger in scorn.

"Speaking vanity," rather "speaking evil."

Verse 10. "Draw out thy soul to the hungry." "If thou give bread to the hungry from thy heart," Septuagint.

Verse 11. "Make fat thy bones"—"strengthen thy bones," Leeser's Jewish Version. The meaning is probably that God will renew their strength.

"Whose waters fail not," literally "deceive not," do not disappoint.

Verse 12. "They that shall be of thee," strictly, "some of thee." An unusual phrase. The Jewish Version reads: "They that spring from thee." "That belong to thee," Kay. "Thy sons," Kent.

"Old waste places." "Foundations of many generations." The picture here presented is that of a foundation, a wall, many generations old, which has fallen into ruin. There is a large breach in the wall also, and there is need of some to repair the breach.

Verse 13. "Turn away thy foot." Do not trample upon. The Sabbath is "hallowed ground, from which the busy foot is to be kept back."

"Pleasure." (See verse 3.)

"Sabbath a delight," not a yoke.

"Honor Him," rather "honor it," the Sabbath.

"Thine own ways." "Not doing thy usual pursuits," Leeser.

"Thine own words," rather "idle words."

Verse 14. "Ride upon the high places of the earth." "Bring thee up to the good places," that is, God will reward with "high places" those that are faithful.

"The heritage of Jacob." Render: "Thou shalt enjoy the heritage of Jacob." Jacob's heritage is the whole earth. Gen. 28:14. But it includes more. It includes eternal life, God Himself. Deut. 30:20; Jer. 10:16.

Lessons for To-day

Verse 1. "Spare not." A prophet's work is not an easy one. Sin must be rebuked. There must be no favorites. The human tendency is to spare. But the message is plain: "Spare not." Let all therefore receive with humility the messages that have come to this people.

Verse 2. Note the good things God has to say of those He is about to chastise:
"They seek Me daily."
"Delight to know My ways."
"Forsook not the ordinance [law] of their God."
"Ask of Me the ordinances of justice [righteousness]."
"Take delight in approaching to God."

Verse 3. One difficulty seems to be that they expect a reward for their goodness as though they had earned something. They have fasted, but God apparently takes no notice. While we may rejoice in the things God has prepared for them that love Him, we must not hold the view that heaven is a kind of payment for work well done. Salvation with all that pertains to it is a free gift. A good deed loses its virtue if it is done with the hope that it will be noticed of men and rewarded. " When thou fastest, anoint thine head, and wash thy face; that thou appear not unto men to fast." "Hypocrites, of a sad countenance, . . . disfigure their faces, that they may appear unto men to fast." Matt. 6:17, 18, 16.

Verse 4. God hates injustice and oppression of all kinds. Sharp deals are no part of Christianity. Strife and debate are not Christian virtues. All these hinder prayers.

Verse 5. To appear very religious, to fast and mourn to be seen of man, does not commend one to God.

Verse 6. This verse brings to view the fact that we are not to sit still and afflict our souls when there is work to be done. As long as there are wrongs to be righted, as long as there are those who are oppressed and ground down by poverty, as long as there are people hungry, naked, sick, and homeless, God is much more pleased that we do what we can to help them, than He would be were we to bow our head like a bulrush, and spread sackcloth and ashes under us. Christ and His disciples were so busy doing good that "they had no leisure so much as to eat." Mark 6:31. That is fasting.

Verse 7. Personal missionary work is needed to keep alive in us the true object of religion. It is well that we give of our means; it is better that we give ourselves. It is well to give means to lead ten souls to Christ, but that does not substitute for the joy of personally leading one soul to the Master.

This verse brings to view the fact that home missionary work — helping those who need help — is a part of Christianity and acceptable to God. To feed the hungry and clothe the naked for Christ's sake is real religion.

Verse 8. Note the four words in this verse that describe the results of giving ourselves to the work of God as here outlined: light, health, righteousness, glory. We need all four. May it not be that we should seek them in the way of God's appointment?

Verse 9. "Then." There are certain conditions for answered prayer. God has here mentioned some of them. Our religion must be practical. It must show itself in good deeds and correct life. Only then can we expect God's blessing and answered prayers.

Verse 10. "Draw out thy soul to the hungry." It is not enough to feed the hungry as a bone is thrown to a dog. "Draw out thy soul."

Christian benevolence must be grounded in sympathy and love, not merely in duty. The "milk of human kindness" is a necessary ingredient in all acceptable service. Our hearts must be drawn out to the unfortunate and unprivileged; there must be no patronizing, no condescension, no sense of superiority, no "holier than thou" feeling.

Verse 11. What blessed promises! The Lord will "guide," "satisfy," "make fat."

Verse 12. A most important work is given this people. The breach in the wall must be repaired. There is a gap that must be closed. As in a besieged city the attack of the enemy is made where the breach is in the wall, so with reference to the law of God. The enemy has torn down the Sabbath. A gap has been made in the law. The enemy is attacking. God is seeking "for a man among them, that should make up the hedge, and stand in the gap." Eze. 22:30. The call has come to this people to stand in the gap, to repair the breach. Will we do it?

Verse 13. The Sabbath is a privilege, not a task; a blessing, not a curse; a delight, not a burden. It is hallowed ground, and we need to remember not to trespass on its sacred precincts. Its edges must be guarded lest they become frayed. Its purpose must ever be kept in view, or the day will degenerate into one of mere idleness. We should have in mind that "the Sabbath was made for man," so that Pharisaical strictness will not rob the day of its beauty; and we must equally watch any looseness in its observance that tends to make it a holiday rather than a holy day. Christ went about doing good, even on the Sabbath day. Mark 3: 1-6. We may well follow His example.

Verse 14. "Delight thyself in the Lord." Christians are not to be gloomy, nor is religion to be made a task. There is indeed an abundance of work to be done, but it must all be a labor of love; and that is never hard. If we do what God says; if we keep the Sabbath as He wants it kept; if we help the unfortunate and needy, and bring light and cheer to the downcast and sorrowing; if we ourselves have unbroken communion with God, we will enjoy our religion rather than endure it. God wants His people to have a delightful time. He wants the Sabbath to be a delight. He wants us to delight ourselves in the Lord. God's will, His testimonies, His law — all should be a delight to us. Ps. 40:8; 119:24; 1:2. Our eating should be a delight, and even our giving should be with cheerfulness. Isa. 55:2; 2 Cor. 9:7. In fact, when we reach God's ideal for us in living and giving, "nations shall call you happy, for you shall be a land of delight." Mal. 3:12, A. R. V.

"High places," "heritage of Jacob." God will prosper His people. To ride on the high places of the earth, to surmount obstacles, is to enjoy the heritage of Jacob. (Read Deut. 32:9-14.)

CHAPTER VI

A Redeemer Promised to a Penitent People

Lesson Scripture: Isaiah 59

Isaiah 59: 1-8. Sin and its results.

Verses 1-3. Behold, the Lord's hand is not shortened, that it cannot save, nor His ear so dull that it cannot hear. It is your iniquities that have been separating you from your God, and it is your sins that have caused His face to be hidden from you, so that He will not hear. Your hands are defiled with blood, and your fingers with iniquity; your lips speak lies, your tongue utters perverseness.

Verses 4-8. No one calls in righteousness, and no one pleads in truthfulness. All rely on pretense and speak lies, they conceive mischief and bring forth iniquity. They hatch adders' eggs and weave spiders' webs. Whoever eats their eggs dies, and if one is broken, out comes a viper. Their webs will not serve for garments, nor can one cover himself with what they make. Their works are works of iniquity, and violence is in their hands. Their feet run after evil, and they are quick to shed innocent blood. Their thoughts are thoughts of evil, desolation and ruin are in their ways. The way of peace they do not know, and there is no justice in what they do. They have taken a crooked course, and whoever follows them shall not know peace.

Verses 9-15. The result of sin.

Verses 9-11. Therefore is justice far from us, and righteousness does not overtake us. We look for light, but all is dark; for brightness, but all is perplexity. We grope along the wall like the blind; we feel our way as the sightless; we stumble at noon as if it were twilight; we are like dead men in darkness. We growl like bears, we mourn like doves; we look for justice, but there is none; for salvation, but it is far from us.

Verses 12-15. Our transgressions are many before Thee, and our sins testify against us. Our transgressions are ever in our minds, and we know our iniquities: transgressing and denying the Lord and deserting Him, speaking perverseness and rebellion, conceiving lies in the heart, and uttering them. Justice has been driven back, and righteousness stands afar off; for truth stumbles in the street, and uprightness cannot enter. Truth is missing, and he that departs from evil becomes a prey.

Verses 15-21. A Redeemer promised.

Verses 15-19. The Lord saw it, and it was evil in His eyes that there was no justice. He saw that there was no man, and was astonished that there was no intercessor. Therefore His own arm brought salvation unto Him, and His righteousness sustained Him. Righteousness He took for an armor, and salvation for a helmet upon His head; vengeance He took for a garment, and clad Himself with zeal for a cloak. According to their deserts He will repay, wrath to His adversaries, recompence to His enemies; the islands also will He recompence. Those from the west shall fear the name of the Lord, and those from the east shall see His glory. When the adversary shall come in like a flood, the Spirit of the Lord shall lift up a standard against him.

Verses 20, 21. A Redeemer will come to Zion, and shall turn ungodliness away from Jacob. This is My covenant with them, says the Lord: My Spirit which I have put in your mouth shall not depart out of your mouth or out of the mouth of your seed, or your seed's seed from henceforth and forever.

Notes

"Show My people their transgression, and the house of Jacob their sins," the prophet was told in the previous chapter. This is done in the present chapter, and the picture is not a pleasant one.

Verse 1. "The Lord's hand is not shortened," that is, God is as able to help as ever, He has lost none of His power.

Verse 2. "Your iniquities have separated." The word for "separated" is the same as that used in Genesis 1:6, 7, where it is translated "divided." In Exodus 26:33 it is used in reference to the veil. As there is a definite division between the waters above the firmament from those below, and as the veil in the tabernacle hid God's presence, so sin divides and separates the soul from God.

Verse 3. Note "hands," "fingers," "lips," "tongue."

Verse 4. "None calleth," etc.; rather "no one calls in righteousness and no one pleads in truthfulness." · The words "calls"

A Redeemer Promised to a Penitent People

and "pleads" are legal terms, the first meaning "to sue," as in legal procedure. The Lord is pointing out the sins of the people, and after saying in verse 3 that they are unreliable and untruthful, He now says that even in their lawsuits, when under oath, they subvert the ends of justice by falsifying and injustice.

Verse 5. "They hatch cockatrice' eggs." The people give themselves to hatching up wicked schemes as evil and pernicious as the eggs of poisonous serpents. Whoever "eateth of their eggs dieth," that is, whoever falls in with and is in favor of their evil purposes, will reap the sure result.

Verse 6. "Spider's web." As an ostrich buries his head in the sand and thinks he is hid, so these clothe themselves in a garment of spider's web and think they are covered. Men will do wicked things, and then present some flimsy excuse, thinking to deceive some. But "their webs" will not serve for "garments," nor cover their nakedness. "All things are naked and opened unto the eyes of Him with whom we have to do." Heb. 4: 13.

Verse 7. "Their feet, . . . their thoughts." In both doing and thinking they are evil. Gen. 6: 5.

Verse 8. "There is no judgment on their goings;" rather "there is no justice in what they do."

Verse 9. In verses 1-8 God has been speaking through the prophet. Now the people speak. They are no longer boastful, but admit the truthfulness of the accusations made against them.

For "judgment" and "justice" read "justice" and "righteousness," as in the American Revised Version. Note "therefore." Israel had sinned and done all that they were charged with. It was because of their sins, not because God's hand was shortened, that these calamities had overtaken them.

Verse 10. "We are in desolate places as dead men." Leeser's Jewish Version reads: "We are in complete darkness like the dead."

Verse 11. "We roar," rather "we growl."

The growling denotes discontent, impatience. The moaning denotes despondency. These two characteristics are native to the soul divorced from God.

Verse 12. Note "transgressions," "sins," "iniquities;" the same trinity of evils for which the high priest ministered on the day of atonement. Lev. 16: 21.

Note also the statements concerning these evils: they "are multiplied;" "testify against us;" "are with us;" "we know them." There is a sermon in those four phrases.

Verse 13. The people are still speaking. They are enumerating the sins of which they know themselves guilty. "As for our iniquities," they have just said, "we know them." Here they are: "Transgressing," willful sin.
"Lying against the Lord," not being honest with God.
"Departing away," backsliding, loss of first love.
"Oppression," iniquity, injustice, cruelty.
"Revolt," insubordinate, disloyal, rebellious.
"Conceiving falsehoods," thinking up and planning evil.
"Uttering falsehoods," bearing false witness against any one.

Verses 14, 15. A true description of the administration of justice in Isaiah's time. The application to this time is too obvious to require emphasis.

"Truth is fallen," rather "truth is missing," it is not there.

"It displeased Him;" the original is stronger, "it was evil in His eyes."

The first clause of verse 15 belongs to the preceding verses 8 to 14. The second clause of verse 15 belongs to the following section. The division should be in the middle of the verse, as in the American Revised Version.

Verse 16. "Wondered," rather "was astonished." (See the almost parallel passage in chapter 63:5, "no intercessor.") Moses and Aaron "stood between the dead and the living." Num. 16:48. Phinehas also averted further evil by his act. Numbers 25. God used Elijah on Mt. Carmel. 1 Kings 18. In the crisis here brought to view, God finds no man. Eze. 22:30. So He Himself interposes.

Verse 17. God used Cyrus to punish wicked nations. Isa. 45: 1-4. In like manner God uses one king or nation to punish another. 2 Kings 24:2. In this case, however, God Himself appears. It should be noted that while God puts on the garments of vengeance, He also has on the breastplate of righteousness and the helmet of salvation.

Verse 18. "According to their deeds." God will repay "every man according as his work shall be." Rev. 22:12. While God will "repay fury to His adversaries," He will not unjustly punish any. He still has on the breastplate of righteousness as well as the helmet or salvation. The day of salvation is not yet past; mercy still pleads; and whosoever will may come.

Verse 19. "So shall they fear the name of the Lord." "When Thy judgments are in the earth, the inhabitants of the world will learn righteousness." Isa. 26:9. But this can be only while probation lingers. When that ceases, he that is unjust must so remain. There will then remain "no more sacrifice for sins" (Heb. 10:26), no pardon for the transgressor.

Verse 20. Some will "turn from transgression," and to them "the Redeemer" will come.

Verse 21. A precious promise that henceforth God's Spirit shall never leave His people.

Lessons for To-day

Verses 1, 2. The Lord's hand is never shortened so that it cannot save. If God therefore has the power to save and help us and does not do so, it is because our sins hinder Him from doing what He otherwise might do. We should search our hearts carefully to see if we are really willing to be saved from sin, for we cannot be saved in sin.

Sin means separation — separation from God and man. The criminal is separated from society and put in prison. The moral leper separates himself from all clean-minded and worth-while associates. The disreputable and dishonest, even if not caught in the process of law, are shunned by upright citizens. Illicit love affairs, intemperance, cruelty, will cause separation in the home. Unguarded words will part the dearest friends. Always sin means separation from that which is good. And at last it will mean eternal separation from loved ones, from life, from God.

Verse 3. Sin penetrates to all parts of the body. We need to pray God to cleanse our hands, fingers, lips, and tongue.

Verse 4. "Speak lies." The opposite of truth God calls a lie, not a misstatement, or an exaggeration, or a fib, but a plain lie. Even a conventional falsehood merits God's denunciation.

Verses 5, 6. Evil men never weary of hatching up wicked schemes nor of trying to cover their tracks. The illustrations used in these verses are most apt.

"Hatch cockatrice's eggs." There is not much difference in the outward appearance of an egg between the first and the last day of incubation. *But something is going on on the inside.* So with men's schemes. They are hatched in the dark, and to outward appearances not much is transpiring. But the outcome is a viper.

We cannot but believe that many advocates of religious legislation, which at last will issue in persecution, are honest at heart, and do not know what is going on on the inside. They do not know that they are helping to hatch a viper. But they should not be permitted to remain in ignorance. They should be told what is involved.

This is part of our work, and an important part. We are not merely to try to save ourselves, but to try to save others from having a part in the nefarious work of compelling the conscience.

Verse 7. "Run," "haste." Men interested in such work brook no delay, but are rushing headlong into evil. Hence our work must also be done speedily.

Verse 8. "Crooked paths." Very few paths in this world are straight. The one who starts a path makes a little turn here and there, and all who follow him do likewise.

So also in spiritual matters. Some one is following you. See to it that your path is straight.

Verses 9, 10. "We wait for light." Only as we live up to the light we have, does new light come. Refusal to walk in the light brings darkness.

Verse 11. "We growl," "we mourn." A Christian should neither growl nor mourn. There are times when everything seems to go wrong, and patience is at a low ebb. Those are the times when real Christianity is needed. There are times when despondency and discouragement set in, when we mourn like doves. At that time "count your many blessings." A growling, dissatisfied Christian! There is no such being. A person may indeed be both growling and dissatisfied, but these characteristics are not Christian virtues. To be "cross as a bear" is a sin to be repented of. No wonder that "salvation is far off" when such humors are indulged in.

Verse 12. "Our sins testify against us." Sin is not our friend. We may like sin, but sin has no friendship for us. It will ruin any one who embraces it, and will testify against him. It has no honor, not a single redeeming virtue. Even wicked companions may at times evince some sense of duty and obligation, but sin will strangle its dearest friend and mock its dying victim. It will reduce its most beautiful devotee to a gaunt, disease-wrecked specter, and torture the conscience with remorse greater than a thousand hell fires. It has no pity, no bowels of compassion. The greater one's love for it, the greater the pain and misery it will inflict. "Ye that love the Lord, hate evil." Ps. 97: 10. That is our only hope.

"Our iniquities, we know them." An honest confession. There are few indeed who do not know wherein they come short. Some may not think that the particular sins they do are of great conse-

A Redeemer Promised to a Penitent People

quence, though they know that there are a few small matters in which they fail. Good, let them acknowledge their "small" sins, and then ask God to throw His own searchlight on these "small" sins and reveal their true nature. They will be found to be virulent disease germs, insidious cancer, ready to spread through the body unless checked immediately. Small they may be, but so are germs. "Kill sin, or it will kill you."

Verse 13. Lying is mentioned twice in this list of sins: lying against God and against men. Ananias lied " unto God." Acts 5: 4. That did not pay. Neither does lying unto men. "Whosoever loveth and maketh a lie" shall not "enter in through the gates into the city." Rev. 22: 14, 15.

Verse 15. "He that departeth from evil maketh himself a prey." How true that is! Advantage is often taken of one who desires to be true and do right. A person must have both eyes open, or he is likely to pay dearly.

"It displeased Him." We sometimes think that God does not care what happens in this world. Note that God is displeased with evil. Circumstances may require that God wait, even as men must do at times, until the situation is ripe. But God is displeased, and the reckoning day will come.

Verses 16-18. God clothes Himself with His own attributes and advances to set things right. Had there been a man, God would have let the man do the work. But there was none, so He does it Himself. This reveals one of God's working principles. He will use one man or nation to help or correct or punish another. When that cannot be done, God will step in.

Verse 19. When the enemy comes in "like a flood," God will send help. This is a most precious promise.

Verse 20. " The Redeemer shall come to Zion." This is not the coming in the clouds, but coming to the church. And when He comes, He will do the work mentioned in Malachi 3: 1-3.

CHAPTER VII

The Final Triumph of the Righteous

Lesson Scripture: Isaiah 60

Isaiah 60: 1-3. The Light has come.

Arise, be enlightened, for your light cometh, and the glory of the Lord is risen upon you. For, behold, darkness shall cover the earth, and gross darkness the people: but upon you shall the Lord arise, and His glory shall be seen over you. And Gentiles shall come to your light, and kings to the brightness of your rising.

Verses 4-9. The ingathering of the Gentiles.

Lift up your eyes and look around: they gather themselves together and come to you. Your sons come from far away, and your daughters shall be carried in the arms. You shall see it and be radiant, and your heart shall thrill and be enlarged; because the multitude of the sea shall be turned to you, and the wealth of the Gentiles shall come to you. Trains of camels shall come to you, the young camels from Midian and Ephah, and also those from Sheba; they shall bring gold and frankincense, and shall proclaim the praises of the Lord.

All Kedar's flocks shall be gathered to you, and the rains of Nebaioth shall serve you. They shall ascend the altar willingly, and My beautiful house shall be glorified. Who are these that fly as a cloud, and as a dove to their windows? Surely the isles shall wait for Me, and the ships of Tarshish first, to bring your sons from far away with all their silver and gold for the name of the Lord your God and for the Holy One of Israel who has beautified you.

Verses 10-14. The prosperity of Zion.

Foreigners shall build up your walls and kings shall minister to you; for in My wrath I smote you, but in My favor I have had compassion on you. Your gates shall be open continually, they shall not be closed day or night, that the riches of the Gentiles may be brought in and their kings led captive. For that nation and kingdom that will not serve you shall perish: such a nation shall be utterly destroyed. Lebanon's glorious cedars shall be yours, the fir tree, the pine, and the box tree also to beautify the place of My sanctuary, and I will make the place of My feet glorious. The sons of them that scorned and despised you shall come bending to you, they shall bow low before you, and they shall call you " The city of the Lord, The Zion of the Holy One of Israel.

Verses 15-22. The glory of the righteous.

Instead of being forsaken and hated so that no one passed through, I will make you an eternal excellency, a joy of many generations. You shall suck milk from the Gentiles, even from royal breasts, and come to know that the Lord is your Saviour and the Mighty One in Jacob your Redeemer.

Instead of brass I will set gold, silver instead of iron, brass instead of wood, iron instead of stones; I will make your officers peace, and your rulers righteousness. There shall be no more violence in the land, nor destruction and disasters within your borders, your walls shall be called Salvation and your gates Praise. The sun shall no more be your light by day, nor the moon by night: the Lord shall be your everlasting light, and your God your glory. Your sun shall no more go down, and your moon no more wane: the Lord shall be your everlasting light, and your days of sorrow shall be ended.

Your people shall be righteous, every one; they shall own the land forever; they are My planting, the work of My hands, an honor to Me. The little one shall become a thousand and the small one a strong nation. I, the Lord, will hasten it in its time.

Notes

Verses 1, 2. We are not told until we reach verse 14 who is addressed in these verses. There we find it is " The city of the Lord." The picture is a beautiful one: a city glittering in the first rays of the early morning sun. All the rest of the earth lies in thick darkness, there is only one point of light, and that point is the " Zion of the Holy One of Israel." God's people are enjoying the sunshine of His presence, and that in the hour of the world's darkness.

" But the Lord shall arise upon thee." The emphasis is upon " thee," and hence this phrase might better be translated: " But upon thee shall the Lord arise."

"His glory shall be seen," rather "shall show itself."

Verse 3. "Gentiles," here as in other places the American Revised Version translates "nations."

Verse 4. "Nursed at thy side," a picture drawn from the Eastern custom of carrying children on the back or more commonly on the hip.

Verse 5. "Flow together," literally "be lightened." The American Revised Version translates: "Then thou shalt see and be radiant, and thy heart shall thrill and be enlarged." Moffatt translates: "With radiant face you see them, your heart a-thrill and throbbing."

"The abundance of the sea." "Abundance" is sometimes translated "multitude," but in later usage has acquired the meaning of "wealth." The wealth of the sea would thus mean the wealth of maritime nations.

"The forces of the Gentiles," rather "the riches of the nations."

Verse 6. "Multitude of camels." This verse speaks of the riches that shall come to God's people. Midian, Ephah, Sheba, as well as Kedar and Nebaioth in the next verse, were all descendants of Abraham. Gen. 25:2-4, 13.

Verse 7. "Come up with acceptance." Paul doubtless had this verse in mind when he wrote Romans 12:1.

Verse 9. "Ships of Tarshish first to bring thy sons from far." These were merchant ships. God takes notice of them, however, only because they bring His "sons from far."

Verse 10. "Sons of strangers," aliens, foreigners.

"Kings." Many are the kings that have ministered to God's people, some willingly, others unwillingly. Note Cyrus (Isa. 45: 1-3); Artaxerxes (Ezra 7:11-26); Nebuchadnezzar (Dan. 2: 46-49; 3:26-30); Darius (Dan. 6:18-28); and many others in both ancient and modern times.

Verse 11. "The forces of the Gentiles," same as verse 5.

"That their kings may be brought"—"their kings led captive," A. R. V. Instead of kings' subduing God's people, they themselves shall be conquered by the gospel.

Verse 13. Lebanon was covered with forests of fir, pine, and box trees, while the hills around Jerusalem were barren. The promise is here that these barren hills should be beautified with stately forest trees, as was Lebanon. The spiritual meaning is that the graces of the Spirit should abound in and around the holy city.

Verse 14. "The sons also." Many nations have at different times oppressed and persecuted Israel. Among these are Egypt,

The Final Triumph of the Righteous

Assyria, Babylon, Rome, and the small heathen nations of Palestine and Syria. From all these shall come some who will worship the true God.

Verse 15. "Forsaken and hated." This verse brings to view the change that will come in the status of God's people. Too often they are hated here. That, however, shall be changed, and they shall become "an eternal excellency, a joy of many generations."

Verse 16. "Suck the milk of the Gentiles." This statement recognizes the right of God's people to obtain favors of the Gentiles, that is, from unbelievers. Note the decree of Artaxerxes in Ezra 7: 21-23.

Verse 17. Gold is more precious than brass, even as silver is more precious than iron. The thought is that God will ennoble and purify His people and make them more valuable.

Peace and righteousness shall be the governing powers. Instead of "exactors" the Septuagint has "overseers."

Verse 18. This carries the thought forward to the new earth, to the time when sin shall be no more; when there shall be no more crime, war, or violence; no storms and disasters that bring desolation and destruction.

Verse 19. Compare Revelation 21: 23. The meaning is not that the sun and moon shall cease to exist, but rather that the glory of the Lord shall be so much greater that these will be pale in comparison.

Verse 20. The Septuagint translates: "The sun shall no more set, nor shall the moon be eclipsed."

Verse 21. "Thy people also shall be all righteous." This is a most important statement. It explains why the days of mourning mentioned in the previous verse are ended. When sin is no more, sorrow and sickness will also cease.

"Inherit the land," rather "inherit the earth."

Verse 22. God's "little flock" (Luke 12: 32) will become "a great multitude." Rev. 7: 9.

Lessons for To-day

Verse 1. "Arise, be enlightened, for thy light cometh," reads the original. Not all to whom light comes are enlightened. The truth for this time may be preached in a neighborhood, and but few accept it. The light has come to them, but few are enlightened. The command here is to accept the light as it is revealed. Our duty toward light is twofold: First, accept and act upon any light given us of God; second, communicate that light to others.

Isaiah, the Gospel Prophet

"The glory of the Lord is risen upon thee." God's glory is His character. Ex. 33: 18-22; 34: 6, 7. This glory is here spoken of as having "risen upon thee." That is, God's glory, His character, shall be communicated to His people. When they thus have come into possession of the virtues constituting God's character, as revealed in Exodus 34: 6, 7, when they have the Father's name in their foreheads (Rev. 14: 1), they can but shine.

It is noteworthy that God's people are not to shine because of their own brilliancy or wisdom, or their profound knowledge of Scripture or science, but because of their character. Any virtue, however good it may be in itself, ceases to be of value when it is paraded.

Verse 2. Darkness now covers the earth and gross darkness the people. This darkness, however, is not intellectual, but spiritual. There never was a more enlightened age than this. Knowledge has been increased on every hand. Dan. 12: 4. But men are in fearful darkness as to spiritual values. Right and wrong are confused. Good is called evil, and evil good. It is in such a time as this that God's people are to arise and shine.

"Thee" occurs two times in the verse, and should be emphasized.

Verse 3. "Thy light." When God's glory, His character, so takes possession of us that we are transformed thereby, men will see it and be attracted. That, indeed, is God's intention and purpose. He is anxious to demonstrate what He can do for us. When men see and accept the light and are changed by it, others are attracted by the miracle wrought, and led to follow their example. Great care, however, must be taken to let the light *so* shine that the glory is not given to man, but to God. Matt. 5: 16.

There is no reason to believe that the message will be confined to the lowly only. God loves the common people, but He is interested in the souls of all. We take the promise in this verse literally, that the message will be preached to those in higher position, and that even kings will come to the light.

Verses 4-8. These verses bring to view a large ingathering of souls from all over the earth. From verse 5 it would appear that this large increase is a matter of surprise and joy to God's people. Apparently they have not been looking for such large numbers to join them, and their hearts shall "thrill and be enlarged" at what they see. This, of course, is nothing but the loud cry of the third angel. What a wonderful time it will be when "the abundance of the sea"— the multitudes of people — and "the wealth of the nations" shall come to God's people! No wonder their hearts shall rejoice.

We would be inclined to refer all these statements to the new-earth state were it not for the fact that this ingathering takes place when darkness covers the earth and gross darkness the people, and that these are converted because of the glory that comes to God's people. Were it simply the great meeting after the resurrection, the multitudes would be spoken of as raised from the dead, not as converted because of the light that comes to God's people, nor would it be stated that they brought their gold and their silver with them, as in verse 9. The mind of the prophet indeed projects itself forward to the earth made new, as evidenced in other verses in the chapter, but the verses under consideration seem to have a distinct application to the time mentioned in Revelation 18: 1, when the earth is lightened with the glory of the third angel's message.

Verse 9. "The isles shall wait for Me." Some of them are still waiting. Long ago we might have sent the light and the truth to them. But we have been negligent. How much longer must some of them wait? Mere emotional responsiveness does not constitute Christianity. Aspen leaves are greatly moved and agitated by even a small wind, but night finds them in the same place as the morning. Movement without progress is useless. Religion to be effective must issue in Christian service. To rejoice in this blessed truth is good. To cause that rejoicing to take practical form in sending the light to others is better. The isles should not have to wait much longer.

"Their silver and their gold with them." True conversion affects both life and possessions. We show our appreciation of the blessings of religion to the extent that we are willing to share them with others. A religion which does not cause a man to sacrifice, has not accomplished its purpose in the individual.

To bring "their silver and their gold with them" is one evidence of conversion.

Verse 10. "Strangers shall build up thy walls." This conveys the same thought as is contained in verse 5, "the wealth of the Gentiles," margin. God's people will apparently receive help from those not of Israel. To some this may seem strange, yet when we consider that the Lord is God of all and that all belongs to Him, may it not be fitting to ask those whom God has intrusted with means to recognize His ownership by giving a part of their possessions to help worthy causes? And may not this asking bring definitely before such their responsibility to God, and perhaps cause them to recognize God's claims on them as well as on what they possess? Considered in this light, we become messengers of God when we call upon those not of our faith for help in our missionary enterprises, announcing to them that God still recognizes them as His stewards, and our visit thus becomes a direct appeal to them to accept and acknowledge the God who has blessed and prospered them.

Verse 11. "Open continually." There should be no cessation in God's work. The gates must be open continually. Day and night we must be willing to do our part. Hours do not count, nor do days. The true minister of God will not spare himself any more than Christ did. "In the morning sow thy seed, and in the evening withhold not thine hand." Eccl. 11:6. And as with the minister, so with the laity. All must be ready at all times to do their part.

"Kings may be brought." The truth must be preached to all, high and low. The highways as well as the byways must be worked. Where are the workers prepared or preparing to work for the so-called privileged classes? There are hundreds of thousands in the professional callings for whom definite work must be planned. There is an ever-increasing number now mounting to the million, in the colleges and universities of the world who must be reached. There are the rich and the nobility among whom are honest hearts. Some of these will be saved. Let us not omit from our plans these neglected classes. Even some "kings may be brought."

Verse 12. As with nations and kingdoms, so with individuals. Those that will not serve the Lord "shall perish." This should spur us on to do all we can while we have the opportunity.

Verse 13. Spiritually applied, this verse means that men of standing, of influence, shall be brought under the influence of the gospel and become an honor to the truth.

Verse 14. Do not become discouraged even though immediate success is not apparent. Some that have formerly despised the message will yet accept it, and "bow themselves down at the soles of thy feet." Labor on in faith. God still lives.

Verse 16. "The Mighty One of Jacob" is our Saviour and Redeemer. Recall the checkered career of Jacob. He was saved in spite of his many mistakes and shortcomings. We are not unlike Jacob in many respects. We need the same help and the same God. Jacob overcame and became Israel. We need "the Mighty One of Jacob" to make us Israel.

Verse 17. God will ennoble, purify, and elevate us. He will take that which is of lesser worth and enhance its value. Talents put to use improve. They may be as brass, but God will make them as gold. Count the many blessings that have come to you because of the truth. What has the acceptance of the message done for you? Where would you have been and what would you be had not the light come to you? Then consider others you may know for whom the truth has wrought wonders.

Verse 19. "Thy God thy glory." Our message is: "Fear God, and give glory to Him." Puny man often accepts and even invites praise that belongs to God only. Of this and of such we must beware. Let God be our only glory.

Verse 20. "Mourning shall be ended." Happy day, whether it be mourning over the loss of some loved one, or mourning over our own or others' sins.

Verse 21. "All righteous." This is the goal which we must never lose sight of. God's people must and will be all righteous.

CHAPTER VIII

Builders of the Old Waste Places

Lesson Scripture: Isaiah 61

Isaiah 61: 1-3. The mission of Christ.

The Spirit of the Lord Jehovah is upon Me; because He has anointed Me. He has sent Me to preach glad tidings to the poor, to heal the broken-hearted, to proclaim liberty to the captives, and the recovery of sight to the blind; to proclaim the year of Jehovah's favor and the day of vengeance of our God; to comfort all that mourn; that there should be given to them in Zion coronets for ashes, the oil of joy for mourning; the garment of glory for the spirit of heaviness; and they shall be called sturdy oaks of righteousness, planted by the Lord for His own glory.

Verses 4-9. Builders of the old waste places.

They shall build the old waste places, they shall restore what has long lain desolate, they shall repair the ruined cities that have been desolate for many generations. Strangers shall stand and feed your flocks, and foreigners shall be your plowmen and vinedressers. But you shall be called the priests of the Lord, the ministers of God. You shall enjoy the wealth of the Gentiles, and their glory shall become yours. For the shame that you have endured, you shall have double reward; and as for the disgrace you have endured, joy shall now be your portion. In your own land you shall receive double, and everlasting joy shall be yours. For I, the Lord, love justice; I hate robbery with injustice. I will faithfully reward you, and I will make an everlasting covenant with you. Your sons shall be favorably known among the nations, and your offspring among the peoples; all that see them shall take notice of them that they are a seed blessed of God.

Verses 10, 11. Righteousness shall spring forth.

I will greatly rejoice in Jehovah, my soul shall be joyful in my God; for He has clothed me with the garment of salvation and covered me with the robe of righteousness, even as a bridegroom decks himself with garlands and as a bride adorns herself with jewels. For as the earth brings forth her buds, and as the seeds spring up in the garden, so the Lord will cause righteousness and praise to spring up before all the nations.

Notes

Verses 1-3 present in a very definite way the mission of Christ on earth. In the first recorded sermon of Jesus in His home town, He quoted Isaiah 61: 1 and part of verse 2. He evidently used the Septuagint Version, as Luke 4: 18 most nearly conforms to that.

Verse 1. "He has anointed Me." God anointed Christ. "God, thy God, hath anointed Thee." Ps. 45: 7. "God anointed Jesus of Nazareth with the Holy Ghost." Acts 10: 38. At His baptism the heavens were rent (Mark 1: 10, margin), and the Spirit descended on Him in token of His acceptance as the beloved Son in whom God was well pleased.

"The meek." The Septuagint, as well as the American Revised Version, margin, and also Luke 4: 18 has "poor" instead of "meek."

"Opening of the prison." The Septuagint as well as Luke has "the recovering of sight to the blind."

Verse 2. "The acceptable year," rather "the year of Jehovah's favor."

Verse 3. "Beauty for ashes," rather a "coronet" or "crown for ashes." Ashes were a sign of mourning and were put on the head. Now God will substitute a crown for ashes.

"Trees of righteousness," rather "oaks," sturdy trees.

It may be well to summarize what these verses contain as to the mission and work of Christ. As Christ quotes them in His first sermon giving an outline of His ministry, they become of great interest to all.

1. To preach good tidings. This is nothing but the gospel, including such glad news as free pardon for all sins, atonement, deliverance from the dominion of sin, a Comforter, peace and joy in believing.

2. Healing the broken-hearted. By broken-hearted is here meant, not so much those who are despondent because of some great sorrow or calamity that has befallen them or some dear one, as broken-hearted because of sin. The word has a religious significance. The thought is the same as that expressed in Ezekiel 9: 4, where some are spoken of "that sigh and that cry" for the sins committed in the land. True and earnest sorrow for sin will cause one to become broken-hearted over one's condition. Such Christ came to heal.

3. Liberty to the captives. The captives, of course, are the servants of sin, such as are bound by evil habits or inherited traits. Christ came to deliver "from the bondage of corruption" and introduce "into the glorious liberty of the children of God." Rom. 8:21.

4. Light to the blind. While on earth Christ opened the eyes of the blind, restoring to them their sight. Matt. 9:30; Luke 7:21; John 9:7. A larger work, however, is here undoubtedly meant. Men's spiritual eyesight had become dimmed. They called evil good and good evil. Isa. 5:20. They needed to have the eyes of their understanding opened, that they might discern the light, have their darkness dispelled, and that moral distinctions might not be confused.

5. The year of Jehovah's favor. The year of Jehovah's favor is this year, the time of acceptance is now. "Behold, now is the accepted time; behold, now is the day of salvation." 2 Cor. 6:2. This message calls attention to the fact that in spite of the past, God stands ready to forgive, and that He will do so *now*. It might be noted in passing that there is a manifest reference in verses 1-? to the year of jubilee. The phrase "proclaim liberty" in the first verse is a technical one, and the same words are used as of the jubilee year in Leviticus 25:10.

6. The day of vengeance. Christ omitted this phrase from His first sermon. (See Luke 4:18.) The time had not yet come for that announcement to be made at that place. At the close of His ministry, however, He spoke freely of the day of vengeance. Luke 21:22.

7. Comfort all that mourn. "Blessed are they that mourn: for they shall be comforted." Matt. 5:4. Three times in His ministry Christ came face to face with actual death, and each time He restored the dead to life. Mark 5:22-42; Luke 7:12-15; John 11:32-44. His life was one of comfort and consolation.

8. A crown for ashes. If Christ had His way with humanity, there would be no sorrow or death. Instead of the ashes of mourning, of dead hopes, of blasted ambitions, there would be garlands of joy, coronets of glory, crowns of rejoicing. This also carries us forward to the time when the saints shall receive the "crown of righteousness, which the Lord, the righteous Judge, shall give" to all them that love His glorious appearing. 2 Tim. 4:8. This was a definite part of the work which Christ came to do. Thus the "crown for ashes" has reference both to this life and to the one to come. *Here* it means joy instead of mourning, praise instead

of a heavy and depressed spirit; and *there* it means the fulfilling of every worthy ambition, the obtaining of all that the renewed heart desires.

9. Oaks of righteousness. Oaks stand both for that which has growth and at the same time is solid and substantial. God's people are not to be as a reed shaken with the wind. Matt. 11:7. Christ came to do solid work. The righteousness which He imparts is of the lasting kind.

10. That the Lord might be glorified, Christ came to glorify the Father. John 17:4. The whole plan of salvation will glorify the Godhead. As a result of the work of Christ, God will stand justified in creation and vindicated in His dealings with men and angels. This is the final and great object of Christ's coming to earth.

Verse 4. "The old wastes." The same words are here used as in Isaiah 58:12, and the application is the same. "This prophecy also applies in our time. The breach was made in the law of God when the Sabbath was changed by the Roman power. But the time has come for that divine institution to be restored. The breach is to be repaired, and the foundation of many generations to be raised up."—"*The Great Controversy,*" *p. 453.* "The prophet here describes a people who, in a time of general departure from truth and righteousness, are seeking to restore the principles that are the foundation of the kingdom of God. They are repairers of a breach that has been made in God's law,— the wall that He has placed around His chosen ones for their protection, and obedience to whose precepts of justice, truth, and purity, is to be their perpetual safeguard."—"*Prophets and Kings,*" *pp. 677, 678.*

Verses 5, 6. These verses speak of the time when God's people shall give themselves entirely to the work of ministering to a needy world.

"In their glory shall ye boast." The thought is here one of exchange. Israel ministers to the Gentiles, and in exchange the Gentiles give of their possessions. The sentence might be translated: "In their glory shall ye succeed," R. V., margin. The Gentiles gloried in their riches and fame, and to these God's people shall succeed.

Verse 7. This verse presents the same principle as Revelation 18:6. Where there has been much sin, there will be double punishment. Where there has been suffering because of the truth, there will be double reward.

Verse 8. For "judgment" read "justice." The Septuagint has "injustice" instead of "burnt offering," while the American Revised Version has "iniquity."

"I will direct." The thought here has reference to the recompense or reward which will be in accordance with "truth." It gives the idea of exact regard to merit. The passage may be translated: "I will give them their recompense faithfully."

Verse 9. "Shall be known," rather "shall be illustrious," or "renowned."

Lessons for To-day

The ten points under "Notes," verses 1-3, all contain lessons for to-day. We have the same work to do that Christ did. "As Thou hast sent Me into the world, even so have I also sent them into the world." John 17:18. As these verses constitute Christ's text for His first sermon in which He outlined the work He had come to do, they should receive special consideration by the people of God at this time. Review therefore the ten points under verses 1-3 in "Notes," and make application of them to yourself and your work.

Verse 1. From the very beginning of His ministry Christ did His work under the guidance of the Spirit. "The Spirit of the Lord God is upon Me." When we are under the direction of the Spirit, we can do acceptable work. It takes a Spirit-filled man to bind up the broken-hearted and heal the wounds sin has made.

"The Lord hath anointed Me to preach." Men may ordain, but only he who has been anointed by the Lord to preach is a preacher indeed. That anointing includes the one in Revelation 3:18 as well as the experience of Isaiah 6. Only he who has had his eyes anointed so that he sees his own frailty and weakness, and who has had the live coal applied to his lips and been cleansed, can rightly deal with souls whose eternal welfare hangs in the balance.

Verse 2. The gospel is essentially a message of comfort. "Blessed are they that mourn; for they shall be comforted." Matt. 5:4. Our religion should never take on a harsh, forbidding aspect. Even when Christ denounced the Pharisees in unmeasured terms, tears were in His voice.

Verse 3. "That He might be glorified." We should do all we do to the glory of God. Any practice, any pleasure, any association, that does not tend to that end should be carefully avoided.

Verse 4. "They shall build." Our work must ever be constructive. Others may tear down, we should build up. To save a soul in the church who has lost the way is just as important as to save a soul in heathen lands. Destructive criticism is just as bad as higher criticism. We should condemn the one as quickly as the other.

"They shall build, . . . they shall raise up, . . . they shall repair." This is not a new work or a new message, but rather the reviving of old truths. It is well to have this in mind when accused of preaching new doctrine.

Verses 5, 6. It is not wrong to accept help from those not of our faith. It is not wrong to ask them to assist in the work we are doing.

Verse 7. God notices every unkind word, every slight, every reproach. He keeps tally, and the reward will show how faithful God has been. Let us see to it that we are not guilty of unkind words, or slights, or reproaches.

"Everlasting joy." That means no sorrow, no heartaches, no regrets. It is far more than we have deserved or are even capable of comprehending.

Verse 8. "I love justice." "I hate robbery." God hates everything that has any taint of injustice in it. This must include all sharp deals, all petty disputes, all bickerings. We should be glad that we have a God who hates all such things. We also should hate them.

Verse 9. When we learn to hate every form of injustice, when we become scrupulously honest in all our dealings, and when the whole church becomes such, may we not expect that it will be "known among the Gentiles"? God will yet have a people to whom He can point with pride. There will be at least a hundred and forty-four thousand in whose mouth there will be no guile and who will be without fault even before the throne of God. Rev. 14: 5.

Verse 10. This verse brings to view the blessed state of the church after she is clothed with the garments of salvation and has put on the robe of Christ's righteousness. Note: "*He* hath clothed me," "*He* hath covered me." There is no praise for man in this; it is wholly God's work.

Verse 11. Neither righteousness nor praise can or should be forced. Let the seed be planted, and in due time it will spring forth and bear fruit. So with righteousness and so with praise. Plant the seed of the word in the heart, and it not only will but must spring forth. Righteousness springs from the life within planted by the Lord, and is not something forced or arbitrary. Praise comes spontaneously from the lips of the one whose life Christ fills, and is not merely to be grudgingly given at some prayer meeting after much urging.

CHAPTER IX

The Holy People: The Lord's Redeemed

Lesson Scripture: Isaiah 62

Isaiah 62: 1-5. God's Holy People.

For Zion's sake I will not hold My peace, and for Jerusalem's sake I will not rest, till her righteousness go forth as brightness, and her salvation as a blazing torch. And the nations shall see her righteousness and kings her glory; and she shall be called by a new name, a name determined by the Lord.

She shall be a crown of beauty in the hand of the Lord, and a royal diadem in the hand of her God. Her name shall no more be Forsaken, nor shall her land be called Desolate; but she shall be called Hephzibah, and the land Beulah; for the Lord's delight is in her, and the land shall be married. For as a young man marries a maiden, so shall her sons marry her; and as a bridegroom rejoices over the bride, so shall the Lord rejoice over her.

Verses 6-9. God's care for Jerusalem.

I have set watchmen upon your walls, O Jerusalem, which shall never hold their peace, day or night. You that are the Lord's remembrancers, take no rest, and give the Lord no rest until He make Jerusalem a praise in the earth. The Lord has sworn by His right hand, and by the strength of His arm, Surely I will no more allow your enemies to eat your corn, nor shall the foreigners drink the wine for which you have labored: but they that have gathered the corn shall eat it, and praise the Lord; and they that have gathered the grapes shall drink the wine in the courts of My sanctuary.

Verses 10-12. The Lord's redeemed.

Go through, go through the gates, prepare the way of the people. Cast up, cast up the highway, and gather out the stones; lift up an ensign for the peoples. Behold, the Lord has proclaimed to the end of the earth, Tell the daughter of Zion: Behold, your salvation cometh; behold, His reward is with Him and His recompense before Him. Men shall call them The holy people, The redeemed of the Lord. And you shall be called Sought out, A city not forsaken.

Notes

Verse 1. Zion and Jerusalem are emblematic of the church. Strictly speaking, Zion is the mountain on which Jerusalem stands, and Jerusalem is the city. Both here denote the people of God.

"I will not rest." God is speaking. He has determined that the righteousness of His people shall become evident, and He will not rest until it is accomplished. The words indicate not only determination, but also that there has been delay, that now the crisis has come, and that God is tremendously in earnest to see the work finished. God intends to exhibit His people to the world. He wants to demonstrate what can be done in human flesh; and He will not rest satisfied until His people reflect His image fully. When that is done, the earth will be lightened with the glory of God. Rev. 18:1.

Verse 2. "A new name," indicative of the new experience they have passed through. We are not told what that new name is, though verse 12 suggests that it might be "The holy people."

Verse 3. A crown is ordinarily placed on the head. Here it is pictured as being held in the hand of the Lord, that others might see and admire it. The crown that will eventually be given to God's people is "the crown of righteousness" which the Lord shall give "unto all them also that love His appearing." 2 Tim. 4:8.

Verse 4. This verse suggests that God's people have been considered forsaken of the Lord and desolate. The experience is mentioned in chapter 54:7, 8: "For a small moment have I forsaken thee," "in a little wrath I hid My face from thee for a moment."

"Hephzibah" means "My delight is in her." "Beulah" means "married."

Verse 5. "Thy sons marry thee." While the metaphor here employed may seem harsh, there is no doubt as to the meaning. Two pictures are employed. In the first God's people are spoken of as a young man marrying a virgin. In the second picture they are the bride, and God is the bridegroom. In either case the illustration is clear.

Verse 6. "Watchmen." These are the ministers of God who, as faithful watchers on the wall, are responsible for the safety of the people.

"Ye that make mention," "ye that are the Lord's remembrancers," margin.

"Keep not silence," "take no rest," that is, never cease to watch.

Verse 7. "And give Him no rest." This should be connected with the previous statement so as to read: "Take no rest, and give Him no rest."

Verses 8, 9. "Sworn by His right hand." A strong expression. This oath is in response to the plea of the "remembrancers" who have given Him no rest nor taken any themselves until He should make Jerusalem "a praise in the earth." This has reference to God's purpose as expressed in the first verses of the chapter, that the righteousness and salvation of the church shall go forth as a "lamp that burneth." God has determined to have a holy people, and now He swears by His right hand that nothing shall stand in the way of its accomplishment, but that they shall come into possession of that which is theirs rightfully.

Verse 10. "Prepare ye the way of the people." In Isaiah 40:3 similar language is used, but there the way is to be prepared for the Lord, while here the way is to be made ready for the people.

Verse 11. "End of the world," rather "end of the earth," A. R. V.

"Behold, thy salvation cometh." Salvation is here personified, and might be translated Saviour.

"His work," rather "His recompense."

Verse 12. Note the four names given in this verse.

Lessons for To-day

Verse 1 brings to view God's anxiety for His church. He will give Himself neither peace nor rest until His people shine forth in their righteousness even as a blazing torch. This anxiety we should share. It is in us that this righteousness is to be revealed. God is waiting to impart it. He is so much in earnest that He will not rest until it is accomplished; so if we do not possess it, it must be entirely our fault. Would it not therefore be well for us to co-operate with God in every way, that His will may be revealed in us? This brings before us the whole question of righteousness by faith, for the want of which many churches are dying. It is high time that we make earnest work of our salvation. There is no time to spare. Right now take an inventory of yourself and your progress toward the kingdom. Become as much in earnest as God, and give yourself no rest until you have obtained that righteousness which God stands ready not only to impute but to impart.

Verse 2. " The Gentiles shall see." Our religion should so affect us that other people will notice it. We need not go around and parade our goodness. Rather, if we really are Christians, our light will so shine that it cannot be hid, but men will see it. Matt. 5: 14-16.

" Thou shalt be called by a new name." They will not give themselves another name, but because of the change that has come to them, men will call them by a new name. This is significant. There is a world of difference between calling yourself holy and having others recognize that you have been with and learned of Jesus.

Verse 4. " No more to be termed Forsaken." " Forsaken " is a terrible word when applied to our relationship to men, and much more so to God. Contrariwise, not to be forsaken, stands for companionship, friendship, love. Here is a beautiful promise from God that we shall not be forsaken. God may chastise, He may reprove, but He will not forsake. This should give courage and strength, even in the darkest hour.

Verse 5. We are admonished not to lose our first love. Rev. 2: 4. In this verse God tells us that He has not left His first love, but that " as the bridegroom rejoices over the bride," so God rejoices over us. If God has not lost His first love, but loves us with the intensity here portrayed, should not we reciprocate, and love Him who first loved us and does so still?

Verse 6. The Lord's remembrancers. What a beautiful designation for those that remember the Lord and His memorial! The question should come home to each soul with great force, if he really remembers the Lord in all his conversations and dealings, so that God may justly call him one of His remembrancers? Some would perhaps deserve to be called forgetters rather than remembrancers.

" Keep not silence," or " take no rest." This has specific reference to prayer. We are to pray without ceasing, though it should be remembered that this has reference to more than the spoken prayer. Let each one examine himself. What is your habitual attitude of mind? Do thoughts of God and prayer recur to you again and again during the day, or do prayer and God come to your mind only when the stated hour arrives? Are there problems confronting you on which your mind constantly dwells and which preclude thoughts of God and heaven, or is your mind so habituated that it will naturally and easily come back to spiritual things the moment there is an opportunity for it? Prayer is more than words — it is life; it is more than bended knees — it is a bent of mind; it is more than speaking to God — it is communion with God.

Verse 7. "Make Jerusalem a praise in the earth." In the fulfillment of this prayer we can co-operate. The church can never become a praise in the earth as long as there are unconverted members in it whose tongue is not truthful, whose words are sharp and critical, whose business deals are questionable, whose debts remain unpaid, whose family is uncouth and unkempt, whose pride causes aloofness, whose covetousness depletes the mission funds, whose meddlesomeness stirs up strife.

Verse 10. "Prepare ye the way of the people." Some people make it very hard for others to be Christians. They put stumbling-blocks in the way, and take delight in annoying. God here counsels all to help prepare the way, rather than make it hard. Gather up the stones, cast up the highway, lift up a standard. Of how much help could we not be to one another if we really desired! How often we could smooth the way rather than obstruct it! A kind word, a helpful hand, a smile of approval — how blessed they are at times!

Verse 11. "Behold, thy salvation cometh." This is the advent message. The Lord is coming. His reward is with Him, and also His recompense. We must never lose sight of our specific message, nor must we lose the advent spirit. While we are to occupy until He comes, we must not become so engrossed in occupying that we forget that the Lord really is coming and coming soon. That must be the keynote of every message. And our lives must harmonize with the message.

Verse 12. This verse should cause serious reflections in the hearts of all. If men will call God's people a holy people, it must be because the members are holy. Do I belong to God's people? Am I holy? If not, when do I expect to be? What is there yet in my life that must be changed? Am I more interested in seeing that others are corrected than I am in correcting my own faults and habits? What changes must be wrought in my life and the life of the other members of the church, before men will begin to speak of us as "the holy people"? Whatever those changes are, they must be made before we can belong to "the holy people," or God will have to remove us.

CHAPTER X

Afflicted for His People's Sake

Lesson Scripture: Isaiah 63

Isaiah 63: 1-6. The day of vengeance.

Who is this that comes from Edom, with crimsoned garments from Bozrah? Who is this with glorious apparel, striding in His strength? I that speak in righteousness, mighty to save.

Why are your garments red, like the garments of those that tread in the wine vat?

I have trodden the wine press alone, and of the peoples there was none with Me; so I trod them in My anger, and tramped them in My fury; their lifeblood is sprinkled upon My garments, and has stained all my raiment. For the day of vengeance was in My heart, and the year of redemption is come. I looked for help, and there was none, and I wondered that there was none to aid; therefore My own arm brought salvation to Me, and My wrath upheld Me. And I trod the peoples down in My anger, and made them drunk in My wrath, and I poured out their lifeblood on the earth.

Verses 7-9. A Redeemer.

I will mention the loving-kindnesses of the Lord, and His praises, according to all that He has bestowed on us, and the great goodness which He has shown toward the house of Israel, according to His mercies and according to the multitude of His loving-kindnesses. For He said: Surely, they are My own people, children that will not deal falsely. So He was their Saviour. In all their afflictions He was afflicted, and the Angel of His presence saved them. In His love and in His pity He redeemed them, and He bare them and carried them all the days of old.

Verses 10-14. The people rebel.

But they rebelled and grieved His Holy Spirit. Therefore He turned and became their enemy, and fought against them. Then Israel remembered the days of old, Moses and his people, saying, Where is He that brought them up out of the sea with the shepherds of the flock; where is He that put His Holy Spirit within them? that caused His glorious arm to go at the right hand of Moses? that divided the waters before them to make Himself an everlasting name? that led them through the deep as a horse in the wilderness, so that they did not stumble as the cattle that go down into the valley? The Spirit of the Lord caused them to rest. Thus Thou didst lead Thy people to make for Thyself a glorious name.

Verses 15-19. A prayer.

Look down from heaven, from the habitation of Thy holiness and glory: where are Thy zeal and Thy mighty acts? the yearning of Thy heart and Thy compassions are restrained toward me. Thou art our Father, though Abraham does not know us and Israel does not acknowledge us. Thou, O Lord, art our Father; our Redeemer from of old is Thy name. Why, O Lord, dost Thou leave us to wander from Thy ways and harden our hearts from Thy fear? Return for Thy servants' sake, for the sake of the tribes of Thine inheritance. Thy holy people have possessed it but a little while, our adversaries have trodden down Thy sanctuary. We are become as they over whom Thou never barest rule, as they that were not called by Thy name.

Notes

The last part of the preceding chapter speaks of "the holy people, the redeemed of the Lord." The first section of this chapter concerns those that have rejected the Lord. To them the day of vengeance has come. The picture is not a pleasant one to look at, but it is true. It is God's "strange work."

Verse 1. "Edom" is another name for Esau. Gen. 25:30. "Bozrah" was one of the cities of Edom. The Edomites were avowed enemies of Israel, though Esau and Jacob were twin brothers. (See Num. 20:14-21; Eze. 25:12; 35:5; Gen. 27:41.) The punishment spoken of in the verses of this section is not meted out on the heathen, but on those who are closely related to Israel — such as have sold their birthright for a mess of pottage, such as have known the truth and fallen away and joined the persecutors of God's people. This view makes the wrath of God more understandable.

"Dyed garments," rather "crimson" or "bright-colored" garments.

"Traveling in the greatness of His strength." The picture here is of a warrior marching rapidly, bending forward in his haste;

hence the passage might be translated "striding in his strength."

Verse 2. Anciently the juice of the grape was trodden out by the feet of men. A large vat contained the grapes, and men would walk around in it, crushing the grapes with their feet. Naturally their garments would be splashed with the juice. This is the picture here presented. (See Gen. 49:11.)

Verse 3. "The Desire of Ages" refers the first part of this verse to the experience of Christ in the garden of Gethsemane. Christ passed through the agony alone, no one being with Him to comfort or sustain Him. The disciples were sleeping (Matt. 26:36-46) while Christ battled with the powers of darkness. Three times the Master prayed, and three times His humanity shrank from the last crowning sacrifice. Then He made the decision and accepted the baptism of blood. "Having made the decision, He fell dying to the ground from which He had partially risen. Where now were His disciples, to place their hands tenderly beneath the head of their fainting Master, and bathe that brow, marred indeed more than the sons of men? The Saviour trod the wine press alone, and of the people there was none with Him."—"*The Desire of Ages,*" *p. 693.*

Accepting this interpretation, we are called upon to explain why it appears in the midst of a description of the punishment which God will mete out to His enemies. Why should God speak of Edom and Bozrah as being punished, and then inject the thought that He Himself has suffered? We offer the following as the most reasonable explanation:

It is a strange act for God to punish. Isa. 28:21. There must be some good reason for His being so severe as these verses indicate. What may this reason be? Christ in the garden and on the cross, suffering for the sin of the world, emblematic of all the suffering and agony which have been brought on mankind because of transgression, is the answer and the reason. Sin crucified Christ, sin brought the blooddrops to His brow, sin caused Him to cry out in agony, and this sin not committed by the heathen alone, but by these who are near of kin. Far greater than the sin of a heathen is the sin of one who knows or has known the truth. In the midst of this description of the punishment of Edom is the picture of Christ's suffering. This we believe to be the reason and the explanation for its appearance in this particular place.

Verse 4. Note again the difference between the *day* of vengeance and the *year* of redemption. God's mercy is more enduring than His wrath.

Verse 6. For "bring down their strength" read as in the A. R. V., "poured out their lifeblood."

Verse 7. Isaiah delights in contrasts. After describing the fearful punishment on Esau, or Edom, he now turns to picture the wonderful loving-kindness of the Lord toward Israel. Neither Esau nor Jacob was very good or praiseworthy. Esau became Edom, and the first six verses of this chapter describe his end. Jacob became Israel, and the present verses picture his blessed destiny. Twin brothers, that started life on even terms, what a tragic difference in final results!

Verse 8. Jacob was not above sharp dealing. His very name means "a supplanter." He lied. Gen. 27: 18-29. But God looked beyond the present transgression, and saw that Jacob at heart meant to do right. So He expressed confidence in him, that he really would not deal falsely if he understood what it meant. "Surely, he will not lie," God said. And so God became his Saviour, and his name was changed to Israel. And so with all Israel. We are all Jacobs by nature. God bears with us, expresses confidence in us, and becomes our Saviour.

Verse 9. "In all their affliction He was afflicted." The affliction of Israel began in Egypt. Gen. 15: 13. This verse brings to view the wonderful and blessed thought of God suffering with His people. "I know their sorrows." Ex. 3: 7.

Verse 10. Israel did not always listen to God's counsel. They rebelled, and God turned to be their enemy. (See Judges 2: 15; Isa. 29: 2, 3.)

Verse 11. "He remembered." "He" has here reference to God. When God turned to be their enemy, the people suddenly remembered how God of old had fought for His people and not against them, and they ask: Where is the God of Moses?

"The sea," the Red Sea.

"Shepherd," "shepherds," margin; a reference to Moses and Aaron.

Verse 14. "As a beast goeth down into the valley." This phrase should be connected with verse 13, and a new sentence and verse begin with "the Spirit of the Lord."

Verse 15. "Where is Thy zeal?" The verse is a prayer to God for help. Has God forgotten His people? Has God, who so wonderfully helped Israel of old, now left them to their own devices? "Where is Thy zeal and Thy strength?" they ask, as if to stir up God to consider their need.

"The sounding of Thy bowels," a Hebrew expression denoting compassion.

Afflicted for His People's Sake

Verse 16. For "doubtless" read "for." This constitutes their reason and ground of appeal to God. He is their Father, hence He would have compassion on them. Abraham could not help, nor Israel. God was their only hope.

Verse 17. "Why hast Thou made us to err?" This is not a charge against God that He has caused them to sin, but rather a wish that God might have used even harsher punishment to bring them back to their senses. It might be paraphrased: "When you saw us go astray, why did you not use harsher measures to bring us back? Your goodness has had the effect of hardening our hearts."

Verse 18. "A little while." God's people had had possession of the land but a short while, comparatively speaking, when this was written. Though about five hundred years had elapsed since Israel took possession, it should be remembered that for a long while they had occupied only a small portion of the land which God intended they should have. God had promised it to them for an everlasting inheritance, hence it might truly be said that they had had it only "a little while."

Verse 19. The American Revised Version reads: "We are become as they over whom Thou never barest rule, as they that were not called by Thy name."

Lessons for To-day

Verses 1-6. These verses should bring serious thoughts to every soul. There is no more dreadful picture in all the Bible than this section presents. The figure of God's striding forth to tread the wine press of His wrath is an awful one. Yet it is true. Esau had all the opportunity that any one could have to know right from wrong. He willfully chose wrong, and became a persecutor of the true people of God.

We conceive that there are none upon whom God's wrath will be visited more completely than upon those who have known the truth, are closely related to it, as it were, and yet turn from it to become persecutors of those that do right. Even as it is a blessed thing to accept the truth, so it is a fearful thing to reject it. And rejection need not include all truth. To reject a part may be just as fatal as to reject the whole. So all should beware.

Verse 7. "I will mention the loving-kindnesses of the Lord." It is well to mention these. God has done so many things for us, that our mouths should be filled with praise for Him. "Loving-kindnesses." What a wealth of meaning in that word! The Lord is not merely kind, but His kindness is lovingly administrated.

Note the three "according to's" in this verse. Does the Lord bless us every moment of the day? If so, we should praise Him continually, for our praise should be "according to" His great goodness and mercy toward us.

Verse 8. "Surely they . . . will not lie." God expresses confidence in His people. They may be weak, but He will not discourage them by suggesting that they will probably not hold out. "They will not lie," He says, and the very confidence expressed in the words are as a bracing tonic to help them.

This principle is a good one in child training as well as in many other phases of life. It is good for new converts to know that God and men have confidence in them. It is good for sinners to know that though they may have failed many times, God has not given them up, but expects them to make good, and expresses His confidence that they will do so. A little more faith and confidence in our brethren in the church may help some discouraged soul. But above all, let every one remember that though men may have lost all faith in us, God has not. Let that be as an anchor to the soul.

Verse 9. "He was afflicted." One of the most blessed revelations of the Scriptures is the one that God is not a God far off, but is near to each one, and is vitally concerned in all that affects us. God is more than a God and Creator to be worshiped. He is a Father to be loved and counseled with in all the affairs of life. He weeps with those that weep, and rejoices with those that rejoice. When any suffer, He suffers with them. God's love and interest in man could hardly be more beautifully expressed than in the words: "In all their affliction He was afflicted." This portrays God's oneness with man, His identification with suffering humanity.

Verse 10. "Vexed His Holy Spirit." To vex is to irritate or grieve by small annoyances. Many times we vex the Spirit by our rebellious attitude. While vexing the Spirit is not the same as sinning against the Spirit, nevertheless it is a serious thing to vex God. It may not be sin against the Holy Ghost to refuse to have a part in the different activities of the church, but it must vex God to have us continually take a complaining or indifferent attitude to that which may mean the salvation of souls. It must vex God to have some take a self-righteous attitude or reveal a critical spirit, when God is perfectly well acquainted with their own shortcomings. We need to guard ourselves well lest we vex God with our pettiness and meanness.

"Turned to be their enemy." This statement should cause all to pause and consider. It is possible for us so to conduct ourselves that God will turn against us. Dreadful possibility! May God save us from that! And yet, continually vexing the Spirit will bring such a result.

Verse 11. "Then he remembered." When we are tempted to become discouraged, it is well for us to recount God's mercies, to remember all the blessings we ourselves have received, as well as God's dealing with His people in general. This always has a tendency to strengthen faith.

Verse 13. "Led them through the deep." God may at times lead His people into difficult places, but it is well to remember that He also leads them out. God "led them through," not merely into. With God we can confidently walk not merely into but "through the valley of the shadow of death."

Verse 16. We cannot expect any help from Abraham or Israel. We cannot expect any help from the best creed or the most accomplished minister. We cannot even expect help from our own good works or the faithful performance of church regulations. God only can help. But He *can*.

Verse 17. We are sometimes tempted to think that God uses harsh measures. Yet were we able to see the end from the beginning, we would not ask God to be more lenient. He permits calamities or reverses to come, and we think we are passing through hard experiences. God, however, has all weighed in the balances of the sanctuary. He knows just what we need. Did we know all, we would not wish to change God's plan.

CHAPTER XI

A Prayer for the Revealing of God's Power

Lesson Scripture: Isaiah 64

Isaiah 64: 1-4. A prayer for God's presence.

O that Thou wouldst rend the heavens, that Thou wouldst come down, that the mountains might quake at Thy presence, as when fire kindles the brushwood and the fire causes the water to boil, to make Thy name known to Thine adversaries! When Thou didst terrible things, unlooked-for things, Thou camest down, and the mountains trembled at Thy presence. For since of old men have not heard, have not perceived by the ear, no eye has seen, O God, beside Thee, what has been prepared for him that is waiting for the Lord.

Verses 5-12. A confession.

Thou meetest him that joyfully does right, those that remember Thy ways. Behold, Thou hast been angry, and we have continued to sin. Had we remained in the right way, we would now be saved; but we are all become as one that is unclean, and all our righteousnesses are as a polluted garment; we all do fade as a leaf, and our iniquities like the wind take us away. And there is none that calls on Thy name, none that stirs up himself to take hold of Thee. Thou hast hid Thy face from us, and hast consumed us because of our iniquities. But now, O Lord, Thou art our Father; we are the clay, Thou art the potter; and we are all the work of Thine hand. Be not very angry with us, O Lord, nor remember our iniquity forever; look down in mercy upon us, for we are Thy people. Thy holy cities are a wilderness, Zion also is a wilderness, and Jerusalem is desolate. Our holy and beautiful house where our fathers praised Thee is burned with fire, and all our pleasant places are laid waste. Wilt Thou refrain Thyself for these things, O Lord? wilt Thou hold Thy peace, and afflict us very sore?

Notes

Verse 1. "Rend the heavens." As a garment is rent. Isa. 36: 22. The same word is used in Mark 1: 10 and Matthew 27: 51.

"Might flow down," rather "quake."

Verse 2. "Melting." This Hebrew word occurs here only, and should be translated "brushwood," as in most translations.

"To make Thy name known." This refers to the statement in verse 1 concerning the coming of the Lord, and should therefore be read together: "O that Thou wouldst rend the heavens, that Thou wouldst come down . . . to make Thy name known," etc.

"That the nations may tremble." A parallel expression to "that the mountains might quake," in verse 1.

Verse 3. "Terrible things." (See Ex. 34: 10; 2 Sam. 7: 23.)

"Which we looked not for." Both God's mercy and His judgments transcend our expectations. (See Isa. 28: 21; 1 Cor. 2: 9.)

"The mountains flowed down." Same as in verse 1.

Verse 4. Compare this verse with 1 Corinthians 2: 9.

"Since the beginning," rather "from of old."

"O God, beside Thee." Some translate: "Neither has the eye seen a God beside Thee who does such great things for them that wait for Him." The Authorized Version is to be preferred as being most in harmony with 1 Corinthians 2: 9.

Verse 5. "Thou meetest him," as the angels of God met Jacob. Gen. 32: 1.

"In those is continuance." The reading here is rather obscure. We would paraphrase: "Behold, Thou hast been angry with us, yet we continued in sin. Had we continually followed the Lord, we should now be saved."

Verse 6. "An unclean thing," rather "as one unclean," a leper, who was to be excluded from the congregation. Lev. 13: 44-46.

"Filthy rags," literally "a polluted garment."

"Fade as a leaf," "withered."

"Have taken us away." The picture here is of a leaf, faded and withered, which the wind tears away from the tree. Thus our iniquities hurry us on to destruction.

Verse 7. "Hid Thy face," literally "made secret." This is because of "our iniquities."

Verse 8. This verse reveals a willingness to be molded as God sees fit. Stubbornness and self-will are no longer evident.

Verse 9. "Be not wroth or very sore." The thought is: Do not be overly severe with us. We have deserved punishment, but do not utterly discourage us.

Verse 11. "Pleasant things." Same as "goodly vessels." 2 Chron. 36: 19.

Verse 12. "Wilt Thou refrain Thyself?" Will God restrain Himself and do nothing when the enemy thus devastates the holy cities and lays waste the "pleasant things"?

Lessons for To-day

Verse 1. God dwells "in the thick darkness." 2 Chron. 6:1. "Think clouds are a covering to Him." Job 22:14. This verse is a prayer for God to reveal Himself.

Such a prayer should be very carefully considered before it is uttered. Are we ready for a revelation of God? Could we stand the glory of God's presence, or would we be consumed? Many prayers are not intelligently offered. We pray for that which may be our own destruction. While God indeed will accept our intention and the motive which prompts our prayers rather than their wording, why not learn to pray intelligently and in harmony with God's expressed will? If the disciples felt the need of learning to pray, may we not confidently take the same attitude? Luke 11:1. It may sound very beautiful for us to ask the Lord to "rend the heavens." It is doubtful if we would care to have Him do so.

Verse 2. "To make Thy name known to Thine adversaries." The purpose of having God "rend the heavens" was to impress the enemies of God, to make them "tremble."

We sometimes think that God ought to reveal Himself more directly when His enemies blaspheme Him. God could do so if He wished, and at times does it. But it would not be best for God to do so continually. That would put fear into men, and cause them to yield outward reverence, not of their own choice, but because of the results that would follow should they disobey. Thus God's whole plan to have men serve Him because they love Him would fail. We need not pray to have God rain fire on His enemies or ours. In His own time God will vindicate Himself and His people.

Verse 3. "Which we looked not for." A great many things will happen which we have not looked for. Some will be saved to whom we did not concede a chance to enter the pearly gates, and some may be lost whom we thought were sure of heaven. Both God's mercy and His severity transcend our anticipations.

Also God's methods may be such as we do not expect. We would like to have God rend the heavens and show His power, when He pleases to work in more quiet ways. Light is better than lightning, wind than whirlwind, and a still small voice than an earthquake. "The Lord knoweth how." 2 Peter 2:9.

Verse 4. God's mercy will exceed all expectations. The imagination cannot conceive of anything that reality will not surpass. What is in store for God's people, eternity only will reveal.

And even in the life to come there may be some things which many "looked not for." This will perhaps be true especially of those who in past ages were reared in churches which did not have the light that now shines in regard to the future life; but even with all the light which God's people now have, there will be many surprises in store. Note the following, taken from the last chapter in the book "Education:"

"Heaven is a school; its field of study, the universe; its teacher, the Infinite One. A branch of this school was established in Eden; and, the plan of redemption accomplished, education will again be taken up in the Eden school.

"'Eye hath not seen, nor ear heard, neither have entered into the heart of man, the things which God hath prepared for them that love Him.' Only through His word can a knowledge of these things be gained; and even this affords but a partial revelation." —*Page 301.*

"There, when the veil that darkens our vision shall be removed, and our eyes shall behold that world of beauty of which we now catch glimpses through the microscope; when we look on the glories of the heavens, now scanned afar through the telescope; when, the blight of sin removed, the whole earth shall appear 'in the beauty of the Lord our God,' what a field will be open to our study! There the student of science may read the records of creation, and discern no reminders of the law of evil. He may listen to the music of nature's voices, and detect no note of wailing or undertone of sorrow. In all created things he may trace one handwriting,— in the vast universe behold 'God's name writ large,' and not in earth or sea or sky one sign of ill remaining."—*Page 303.*

"There will be open to the student history of infinite scope and of wealth inexpressible. Here, from the vantage-ground of God's word, the student is afforded a view of the vast field of history, and may gain some knowledge of the principles that govern the course of human events. But his vision is still clouded, and his knowledge incomplete. Not until he stands in the light of eternity will he see all things clearly.

"Then will be opened before him the course of the great conflict that had its birth before time began, and that ends only when time shall cease. The history of the inception of sin; of fatal falsehood in its crooked working; of truth that, swerving not from its own straight lines, has met and conquered error,— all will be made manifest. The veil that interposes between the visible and the invisible world will be drawn aside, and wonderful things will be revealed."—*Page 304.*

"Every redeemed one will understand the ministry of angels in his own life. The angel who was his guardian from his earliest moment; the angel who watched his steps, and covered his head in the day of peril; the angel who was with him in the valley of the shadow of death, who marked his resting place, who was the first to greet him in the resurrection morning,— what will it be to hold converse with him, and to learn the history of divine interposition in the individual life, of heavenly co-operation in every work for humanity!

"All the perplexities of life's experience will then be made plain. Where to us have appeared only confusion and disappointment, broken purposes and thwarted plans, will be seen a grand, over-ruling, victorious purpose, a divine harmony."—*Page 305.*

"There will be music there, and song, such music and song as, save in the visions of God, no moral ear has heard or mind conceived. . . .

"There every power will be developed, every capability increased. The grandest enterprises will be carried forward, the loftiest aspirations will be reached, the highest ambitions realized. And still there will arise new heights to surmount, new wonders to admire, now truths to comprehend, fresh objects to call forth the powers of body and mind and soul.

"All the treasures of the universe will be open to the study of God's children. With unutterable delight we shall enter into the joy and the wisdom of unfallen beings. We shall share the treasures gained through ages upon ages spent in contemplation of God's handiwork. And the years of eternity, as they roll, will continue to bring more glorious revelations. 'Exceeding abundant above all that we ask or think' will be, forever and forever, the impartation of the gifts of God."—*Page 307.*

"Prepared for him that waiteth for Him." In a special way they that wait for Him, the remnant church, will have a part in the glories to come.

Verse 5. "Thou meetest him." Hardly more gracious words could be conceived of. God will meet any one, however far away he may be, if he will but turn around and face his Maker. But God cannot meet any one who turns himself away from Him. If a man turns away from God, there can be no meeting.

"We have sinned," or rather "continued to sin." In spite of

our own resolutions and the knowledge of the wrath of God, we continue to do what we ought not. Had we done right and improved our opportunities, we might ere this have been in the kingdom. How much longer will God have to wait before we, by full submission to Him, "make an end of sins"? Dan. 9:24.

Verse 6. "An unclean one," a leper. This is how God looks at sin. "He shall dwell alone; without the camp shall his habitation be." "He shall put a covering upon his upper lip, and shall cry, Unclean, unclean." Lev. 13:46, 45. Let this picture impress itself indelibly upon the mind. "Dwell alone," "without the camp," "Unclean, unclean." And that is not speaking of the leper in a far-off country, but of respectable sinners here at home. That is how God looks at sin in *me*. "God be merciful to me, a sinner."

"Filthy rags." That is how "our righteousness" is spoken of. Now count up what you consider *your* righteousness. Are you prompt in tithe paying, faithful in church attendance, scrupulous in Sabbath observance? Are you a good provider or an efficient housekeeper, correct in conduct and careful in your associations, cultured, refined, educated, liberal? All these are good traits, and not to be despised. But are you trusting in these for salvation? Are you a little proud of your good record? Without Christ all these avail nothing. As compared with the garment of Christ's righteousness, they are but as filthy rags. So do not display them. Keep yourself and all you do in the background, and let Christ stand forth, living His own life in you. (See Gal. 2:20.)

Verse 7. How few there are that stir up themselves? Events of supreme importance are taking place all about us, and we are not stirred. It seems necessary to send messengers to stir up the people, even our own, when the times themselves should cause us to be profoundly stirred. How can God speak more plainly than He has done in flood and disaster, in war and pestilence, in gracious outpourings of His Spirit, and in His opening providences? What more can God do to stir us? If the things now happening do not arouse us, will Gabriel's trumpet do so?

Verse 8. Are we ready to let God mold our lives? Have not our lives been "marred in the hands of the potter" because of our willfulness and perverseness? What mercy and love are revealed in the words of God, that after we had thus ruined ourselves, He made us again! (See Jer. 18:4.) Let all take hope. Our lives may have been marred, but God can restore the broken vessel. He "made it again." Instead of throwing it away, He put it on the wheel once more.

82   *Isaiah, the Gospel Prophet*

Verse 9. God will not deal with us more harshly than the case demands. Not one needless blow will be struck, not one unnecessary wound inflicted.

Verses 10-12. Disaster may come, will come. Whether men build on sand or on rock, the floods will come, the rains descend, and the winds blow. Matt. 7:24-27. The question is one of foundation. Can we stand? Are we built on the solid rock?

CHAPTER XII

A People Prepared for a New Heaven and a New Earth

Lesson Scripture: Isaiah 65

Isaiah 65: 1-7. A rebellious people.

I have let Myself be inquired of by them that asked not for Me, I am found of them that did not seek Me. I said, Behold Me, behold Me, to a nation that did not call on My name. I have spread out My hands all day to a rebellious people, which walk after their own thoughts in a way that is not good, a people that provoke Me to My face continually, sacrificing in gardens and burning incense on bricks, that sit in the graves and lodge in the vaults, that eat swine's flesh, and have a broth of abominable things in their vessels; that say, Stand by yourself, I am holier than you. Such are a smoke in My nose, a fire that burns all day. Behold, it is written before Me, I will not keep silence, but will recompense into their bosom your own iniquities and the iniquities of your fathers together, which have burned incense upon the mountains and defied Me upon the hills. Therefore I will measure their reward into their bosom.

Verses 8-12. The righteous spared, the wicked judged.

Thus says the Lord, As the new wine is found in the cluster, and one says, Do not destroy it, for there is a blessing in it, so will I do for My servants' sake, so as not to destroy them all. I will bring forth a seed out of Jacob, and out of Judah an inheritor of My mountains; and My chosen shall inherit it, and My servants shall dwell there. And Sharon shall be a pasture for their flocks, and the valley of Achor a place for herds to lie down in, for My people that have sought me.

But as for you who have forsaken the Lord and forgotten My holy mountain, that spread a table for Fortune and mingled wine to Destiny, I will destine you to the sword, and you shall all bow down to the slaughter; because when I called, you did not answer, and when I spoke, you did not hear; but you did evil in My sight, and chose that which does not please Me.

84   Isaiah, the Gospel Prophet

Verses 13-16. The difference between those who serve God and those who do not.

Therefore thus says the Lord God, Behold, My servants shall eat, but you shall be hungry; My servants shall drink, but you shall be thirsty; My servants shall rejoice, but you shall be ashamed; My servants shall sing, but you shall cry for sorrow of heart and shall wail for breaking of spirit. And your name shall be used as an oath by My chosen; for the Lord shall slay you, and He will call His servants by another name, so that he who blesses himself in the earth shall bless himself in the God of truth, and he that swears in the earth shall swear by the God of truth, because the former troubles are forgotten, and because they are hid from Mine eyes.

Verses 17-25. The new heavens and the new earth.

Behold I create new heavens and a new earth, and the former things shall not be remembered or come into mind. Be glad and rejoice forever in what I now create, for I create Jerusalem a rejoicing, and her people a joy. I will Myself rejoice in Jerusalem and joy in My people, and the voice of weeping or of crying shall no more be heard in her. No babe shall die there in infancy, nor any old man who has not lived out the years of his life; for the youth shall die a hundred years old, and the sinner being a hundred years old shall be accursed. They shall build houses, and live in them; they shall plant vineyards, and eat the fruit of them. They shall not build, and another inhabit; and they shall not plant, and another eat; for as the days of a tree are the days of My people, and My chosen shall wear out the work of their hands. They shall not labor in vain, nor bring forth children to die suddenly; for they are the seed of the blessed of the Lord, and their offspring with them. And it shall be that before they call I will answer, and while they are yet speaking I will hear. The wolf and the lamb shall feed together, and the lion shall eat straw like the ox, and dust shall be the serpents' food. They shall not hurt or destroy in all My holy mountain, says the Lord.

Notes

Verse 1. This verse has reference to the Gentiles. Paul so applies it in Romans 10:20. The exhortation, "Behold Me," is a call to the Gentiles to study God's ways, His character.

Verse 2. "Rebellious people." These were the Jews; and by extension any who while professing to obey God are in reality serving themselves.

A People Prepared for a New Heaven and a New Earth

Verse 3. "To My face." Much of their heathen worship was carried on in connection with the temple service and as a part of it. They mixed their own detestable customs with God's ordinances. Other forms of idolatry required gardens and groves for their performance. All of it provoked God. The Septuagint translates: They "burn incense on bricks to devils which exist not."

This verse brings to view a kind of nature worship especially repugnant to God. It was probably of Syrian origin and of the grossest and most debasing character, such as cannot be described, but is hinted at in the first chapter of Romans. Sensuality and beastiality were its distinguishing marks, while at the same time the groves where the rites were performed were rendered most attractive and alluring by works of art, statues, fountains, shrines, temples, as well as by music, processions, dances, shows. They were a kind of popular amusement parks, in beauty, however, far exceeding the tawdry, cheap amusement parks of to-day.

Verse 4. "Remain among the graves," rather "sit in the graves." The graves were chambers hewn out of the rocks, into which one could enter as into a room. To sit in them doubtless has reference to the custom of obtaining oracles from the dead, a kind of necromancy, which we nowadays would class under the head of spiritism.

"Monuments," rather "vaults" or "crypts," subterranean caves used as a kind of chapel. The Septuagint reads: "They lie down to sleep in the tombs and in the caves for the sake of dreams." Having had festivities and a kind of worship in these crypts, they would lie down to sleep. The dreams of the night were then thought to have special significance.

"Swine's flesh," "broth." Unclean food. Lev. 11:7.

Verse 5. "Holier than thou." Initiation into the heathen mysteries was supposed to confer a special kind of holiness. The man who had performed all the purification rites of pagan mysteries, even though saturated with sin, considered himself holier than one who in humility had gone to the temple to obtain forgiveness. Thus does sin deceive.

"A smoke in My nose," an expression of disapproval, of serious displeasure.

Verse 7. "Measure their former work," rather "measure their reward." The thought is that God will measure out to each his reward according to his work.

Verse 8. "Destroy it not." God always has a care for His own. God will punish, but whenever there is worth of any kind, God will refrain.

Verses 9, 10. God will save "a seed." This seed shall be a holy seed who shall inherit "My mountains." This is the remnant.

Verse 11. For "troop" and "number," read "Gad" and "Meni," as in the margin. These were Syrian gods supposed to preside over fortune and destiny. To "prepare a table" for the god of fortune was simply a way of imploring fortune to smile on them, a kind of superstitious worship.

Verse 15. "Your name for a curse." In pronouncing a curse a Jew would say: "God make thee like Zedekiah and like Ahab," or some other name that stood for misfortune or calamity. (See Jer 29:22.) This statement is a reference to that custom.

"The Lord shall slay thee." The wicked Jews shall be rejected. "Another name," a new name. Isa. 62:2.

Verse 17. "The former." This word being in the plural in Hebrew probably has reference to "former troubles," as in the preceding verse. This view is strengthened by the statement in the next verse, "But be ye glad." They shall not remember their troubles, but be glad.

Verse 20. "An infant of days," an infant who lives only a few days.

"The child," rather "the youth." "Men before the flood lived many hundreds of years, and when one hundred years old, were considered but youths."—"*Spiritual Gifts,*" *Vol. IV, p. 156.*

This verse refers to the time when the resurrection of the wicked takes place, and those who lived before the flood and those who lived after shall be raised together.

Verse 21. As it was in Eden before sin entered, so it shall be in the earth made new when sin shall be no more. We shall there live the Eden life and both build and plant.

Verse 22. "As the days of a tree." The tree is the longest lived thing on earth. The prophet here uses that which the people understood to describe long life. Some understand this to refer to the tree of life. (See Rev. 22:2.)

Lessons for To-day

Verse 1. The Jews were sure they were God's chosen people, and they were. That, however, did not insure salvation to the individual Jew. That depended on his personal relation to God. We can all profit by their experience. Our only hope is in personal union with Christ.

Verses 2-5: "After their own thoughts." How often a certain course seems good to us! We have thought the matter through, and are persuaded "after our own thoughts." It may be well to be more distrustful of self, and rather seek to know God's will.

The second verse brings to view a "rebellious people" who walk in a way that is not good, though to them it seems the right way. They provoke God and engage in wrong kinds of worship (verse 3); their eating and drinking is not in harmony with God's word (verse 4); yet they claim to be holier than other people (verse 5). Such are a smoke in God's nose, and He holds them in abhorrence.

We can find many people to whom this may apply, and we are sure that those who think lightly of God's requirements as to correct worship, and who go so far as to reject God's definition of the clean and the unclean, will not escape condemnation. Yet it may be well to apply these verses, as well as all other scriptures, to our own personal experience, as far as it may be needed.

Are we ever rebellious? Do we think there are too many "calls," too many campaigns, too much required of us? Do we ever walk after our "own thoughts"? Do we ever provoke God? Do we ever visit places where Christians do not belong, and thus "burn incense" to other gods than the Creator? Are we as careful in eating and drinking as we should be or as we once were? Do we ever take a "holier than thou" attitude? While we do not hold that these verses refer to "the remnant,"— quite the contrary is the case,— we never lose anything by making a personal survey of our standing before God.

Verse 8. God will not "destroy them all." We are apt at times to indulge in wholesale condemnation. We may speak harshly of this or that nation or denomination, condemning all alike. God does not do that. He always has the individual in mind, and wherever any good is found He recognizes it. We should do likewise.

Verse 11. Games of fortune, of chance, of destiny, have always been popular. To carry a rabbit's foot in the pocket, to hang a horseshoe over the door, to avoid the number thirteen, to consider some days lucky and others unlucky, are remnants of old superstitions. We have yet many of them. Let each dig down in his own mind and life, and rid himself of all superstitious ideas, none of which have any basis in fact, and all of which are harmful and detrimental to spiritual growth.

Verse 15. "Your name for a curse." Why should we not all so conduct ourselves that our names would be associated in memory with something good rather than evil? Some schoolmates are remembered because we know they cheated in examinations. The names of others call to mind some noble deed performed. Benedict Arnold did many noble things in life, yet he is remembered chiefly as a traitor. Abraham Lincoln was not perfect, yet he stands forth as the great Emancipator. It is possible for us to leave a fragrance of blessing connected with our name, rather than a curse.

Verse 16. "Former troubles." What a blessing it would be if even now we could forget our former troubles! There are enough of them. If we cared to keep them in mind, there would be sufficient to make us miserable the rest of our lives. Former troubles! How often they are rehashed! Troubles in the church! There are enough of them as you think of the past. They would make a long and interesting list. But let them be. Do not disturb them. Let the "former troubles" rest.

Nor are you to conjure up troubles that have not as yet arrived. They will come soon enough. Let them also be. Live in the present.

Verse 17. "New heavens and a new earth." This is good and wonderful, but not sufficient, unless there also are new people with new hearts and new minds, new ambitions, new desires, new tempers, new experience.

Verse 19. No weeping! Blessed state! This earth has enough of sorrow. In the new earth there will be no sorrow or any individual that will cause sorrow.

Verses 21-23. What a contrast to this life! We shall both build and plant, and have the reward of our labor. It is not always so here. Note, however, that each will get what he plants, not what some one else plants. That means reward according as our work shall be. No one will live off some one else. The kind of house you build, that is the kind you will live in. And that has an application now. While the houses in the new earth are literal and there will be real vineyards, we may also make an application right here and now. The kind of character you develop here, is the kind you will have there. What you make of yourself here, is a sure foreshadowing of what you will be hereafter. If that is so, you should make of yourself an agreeable companion. You will have to enjoy or endure your own company for a long while. Have you learned to live with yourself? or are you miserable when you are alone? Is your joy dependent upon circumstances and associations, or do you have sources of joy independent of environment?

We will indeed not be hermits in the new earth, why should we make ourselves so here? Rather, God has created us to be sociable beings. But it should be noted that our capacity for enjoyment will be proportionate to our preparation here for the life to come. As we plant, so we will eat; as we build, so we will live. And in a spiritual sense we do the planting and building here.

"Long enjoy the work of their hands." Do you take pride in your work? Do you appreciate a piece of work well done? Or is your work only drudgery? Do you consider it a task or a challenge? In this distinction lies much of life's pain or pleasure.

CHAPTER XIII

The Ingathering From the Gentiles; Worship in the New Earth

Lesson Scripture: Isaiah 66

Isaiah 66: 1-4. The ungodly rebuked.

Thus says the Lord, Heaven is My throne, and the earth is My footstool: what kind of house will you build Me, and what kind of place is My resting place? For I have made all these things, and caused them to come into being: but to this man will I look, to him that is poor and of a contrite spirit, and who trembles at My word. He that kills an ox, also sacrifices human lives; he that sacrifices a lamb, does it as though he broke a dog's neck; he that offers an oblation, does it as if he offered swine's blood; he that burns incense, also blesses idols. As they have chosen their own ways and delight in their abominations, I also will choose their delusions, and bring their fears upon them; because when I called, none answered; when I spoke, none heard; but they did that which was evil in My eyes, and chose that in which I was not pleased.

Verses 5-9. The increase of Zion.

All that tremble at the word of the Lord, hear: Your brethren that hate you. that have cast you out for My name's sake, have said, Let the Lord show Himself glorious, that we may see your joy. But they shall be ashamed. A voice of tumult from the city, a voice from the temple, a voice of the Lord rendering recompense to His enemies. Before Zion travailed, she gave birth; before her pain came, she bore a son. Who has ever heard of such a thing or seen the like? Shall a land be born in a day, shall a nation be born in a moment? As soon as Zion travailed, she brought forth her children. Shall I bring to the hour of birth, and not cause to be born? says the Lord; shall I close the womb when the time has come? says your God.

Verses 10-14. Jerusalem's glory.

Rejoice with Jerusalem, and be glad, all that love her; rejoice with her, all that mourn for her, that you may suck and be satisfied with the milk of her consolations, that you may drain to your delight her ample mother-bosom. For thus says the Lord, I will extend peace to her like a river, and the glory of nations like an overflowing stream; then shall you suck, and be carried upon the side and dandled upon the knees. I will comfort you as one whom his mother comforts, and you shall be comforted in Jerusalem. And when you shall see this, you shall rejoice, and your bones shall flourish like the tender grass; and God's hand shall be known toward His servants, but His indignation toward His enemies.

Verses 15-18. The judgment of the Lord.

The Lord will come with fire, and His chariots shall be like the whirlwind, to render His anger with fury and His rebuke with flames of fire. For with fire and with sword will the Lord execute judgment upon all flesh; and many are they that shall be slain. They that sanctify themselves and purify themselves in the gardens, following their leader, who eat swine's flesh and abominable things and mice, shall be consumed together, says the Lord. For I know their works and their thoughts. The time shall come when I will gather all nations and tongues, and they shall come and see My glory.

Verses 19-24. The remnant.

I will set a sign among them, and I will send the remnant to the Gentiles, to the four corners of the earth, to those who have not heard of My fame and have not seen My glory. And they shall declare My glory among the nations. And they shall bring all your brethren back as an offering to the Lord from all nations, they shall bring them in all manner of conveyances to My holy mountain Jerusalem, even as the children of Israel bring an offering in a clean vessel into the house of God. And I will take some of them to be priests and Levites, says the Lord. As the new heavens and the new earth which I will make shall remain, says the Lord, so shall your seed and your name remain. And it shall come to pass that from one new moon to another, and from one Sabbath to another, all flesh shall come and worship before Me, says the Lord. And they shall go out and look on the dead bodies of the men that have transgressed against Me: for their worm shall not die, neither shall their fire be quenched, and they shall be an abhorring unto all flesh.

Notes

Verse 1. "Where is the house?" rather "what manner of house?" As the heavens are God's throne and the earth His footstool, the house that man can build for God can bear no comparison to what God could do for Himself.

Verse 2. Is it therefore a house only that God is interested in? No, He would rather dwell with him who is poor and of a contrite heart, than in the most beautiful building.

Verse 3. Israel had a magnificent temple. To that they brought their offerings. But they had completely lost all sense of the meaning of these offerings. While the reading of verse 3 is not very clear, it might be paraphrased: One will kill a man, and think no more of it than if he killed an ox; he will kill a lamb as a sacrifice, but it means no more to him than if he were breaking the neck of a dog; he will offer an oblation to the Lord, but to him it is as swine's blood; he will burn incense to God and to idols at the same time. The verse brings clearly to view the thought that Israel had missed entirely the meaning of God's service, and made no difference between the holy and the profane.

"Yea, they have chosen," rather "as they have chosen." This should be put with the next verse to read: "As they have chosen, . . . I also will choose their delusions." (See 2 Thess. 2:11.)

Verse 5. The brethren who passed through the 1844 movement found this verse very precious. They had been both hated and cast out. They claimed the promise of this verse, that the Lord would yet reveal Himself and vindicate them, and in this they shall not be ashamed.

Verse 6. This verse comes as an announcement of the punishment threatened in preceding verses. Josephus, in his "Wars of the Jews," tells of one Jesus, the son of Ananus, who four years before the destruction of Jerusalem in 70 A. D., walked the streets of Jerusalem and the courts of the temple, crying constantly day and night: "A voice from the east, a voice from the west, a voice from the four winds, a voice against Jerusalem and the holy house, a voice against the bridegrooms and the brides, a voice against this whole people!"— *Book 6, Chap. 5, par. 3.* Dr. Kay sees in this a fulfillment of this verse.

Verses 7-9. These verses are of course to be spiritually understood. Zion is travailing. The church is in the birth throes. A whole nation is to be born. The time is ripe for a mighty movement, in which thousands will be converted in a day. And "as soon as Zion travailed, she brought forth her children;" that is, as soon as God's people became thoroughly in earnest, as soon as there was real travail for sinners, the work was done.

Verse 11. This verse refers to the babes in Christ, those newly come to the faith. They shall " be satisfied " and " delighted."

Verse 12. Peace " like a river." God's people have had trouble enough. Now peace, ever widening, ever increasing, shall be theirs.

Verse 14. " The hand of the Lord shall be known." We hold that the verses of this chapter, specially from verse 5 on, have their application in a specific sense to the advent movement. God will wonderfully bless His people; the loud cry will issue in a lightening of the earth with the glory of God; thousands will be converted in a day; it will seem as if a whole people had come suddenly into existence, and " the hand of the Lord shall be known." " When ye see this, your heart shall rejoice, and your bones shall flourish like an herb."

Verse 15. " The Lord will come." What a definiteness to that message! He may seem to delay, but He " will come."

Verse 16. " By fire and by His sword." The Lord will plead, He will execute judgment. This verse shows that the events mentioned in these verses are in close connection with the coming of the Lord.

Verse 17. " They that sanctify themselves." This has reference to the practice of false religions, specially such as Baal worship.

" Behind one tree," margin " one after another." The reading here justifies the translation: " following the leader," though the phrase is a difficult one and much disputed. The thought seems to be that as they go into the gardens for the purpose of purification in their heathenish rites, they are led by " one in their midst," and him they follow.

" Swine's flesh." God is not pleased with those that eat swine's flesh and abominable things. As this has specific reference to this time, it should cause all to consider this question seriously.

Verses 19-21. " I will set a sign." We are not told here what the sign is. The whole context leads us to believe, however, that we are not far wrong in considering the sign mentioned in Ezekiel 20: 12, 20, the Sabbath, as the sign here meant. God will " gather all nations and tongues," and among them He will set " a sign." Then He will send " the remnant," those that escape, to the four ends of the earth, to those that have not heard of God. The result of this foreign missionary movement will be that " out of all nations" will be brought brethren who shall bring "an offering in a clean vessel into the house of the Lord." And some of these shall become "priests" and "Levites."

Who cannot see in this a wonderful prophecy of the work now going on in the world, the finishing of the work of the first, second, and third angels' messages?

"From one new moon to another." As the tree of life bears fruit every month (Rev. 22:2), and as we are to come together every month, may we draw the conclusion that every month will be a special season of united worship, at which time we shall sit down together with Abraham, Isaac, and Jacob, and partake with all the redeemed of the fruit of the tree of life, rejoicing in our deliverance from sin, and from its awful consequences — separation from God, and from the life that He alone can give?

"One Sabbath to another." No one will be absent. "All flesh" shall come up to worship.

Verse 24. "Carcasses," dead bodies. No immortal souls, no eternal torment, just "dead bodies."

"Their worm shall not die, neither shall their fire be quenched." This does not speak of the soul, but of the total destruction of the bodies. The soul is not even mentioned. It would seem strange indeed, if the soul at this time were in torment, that God should fail to mention it, but instead call attention to "dead bodies." The soul would seem so much more important.

This refers to the last act of dissolution, to the final extinction of sin and sinners. When the worm and the fire have done their work, there is nothing left."

Lessons for To-day

Verses 1, 2. "A contrite spirit." God is not so much interested in outward display, or rich adornment of persons or places, as in purity of heart and humility of spirit.

"Trembleth at My word." Not in slavish fear, but rather in harmonious response, as one string answers to another when a corresponding note is struck.

Verse 3. Are we as reverent as we should be? Or do we perform some acts of devotion as a matter of routine rather than of worship? Do we rush into God's presence and out again as though He were a common person? Do we reverently kneel when prayer is offered, our whole attention riveted on the petitions uttered; or do our minds wander, our fingers leaf a book or hymnal, our eyes transgress in looking about, perhaps even a whispered word being uttered? Do we throw our offering in the collection plate as if we were giving it to a beggar? Do we reverence the ministry of the word as we should? Any act of worship, however good and praiseworthy in itself, loses all value if not performed with due appreciation and reverence.

Verses 3, 4. "They have chosen," "I will choose." What a fearful thing if delusion should at last overtake us! If we will now choose what God wants us to, we need not fear later.

Verse 5. While this verse found a fulfillment in 1844, it may yet find another fulfillment. It is well to know that we are on the Lord's side.

Verse 8. "As soon as Zion travailed." Why are we not more in earnest? We know the truth, and we also know that as soon as we really become in earnest, God will work mightily for His people. The end of all things is at hand. Let us do our part. God stands ready to do His.

Verse 9. God will not only "bring to the birth," but He "will cause to bring forth." All the work that has been done by this people to bring to men a knowledge of the truth will not be wasted. There will appear results. For years we have been sowing. The harvest will come. A nation will be born "at once."

Verse 11. "Be satisfied," "be delighted." We should be both, as far as what God has done for us is concerned. We should not, however, be satisfied with our present achievements, but ever press on.

Verse 14. The time shall come, and that soon, when God will reveal Himself and His hand "be known toward His servants, and His indignation toward His enemies." Do we see in the events happening in and out of the church "the hand of God"? He is shaping events, and it is for us to co-operate with Him.

Verse 15. "Anger with fury." A dread combination of words. Yet this is what God will be to His enemies. Should we not do all we can to cause some of these enemies to become friends of the Lord? If they but knew Him, they would love Him.

Verse 16. "By fire and by His sword." The Lord even now uses these weapons to call men's attention to Him. Are we so interpreting these events that they become messages of mercy?

Verse 17. "Sanctify themselves." Some sanctify themselves, others permit the Lord to do this work for them. While the wording here may not be stressed too much, we are sure that there is no effective way of either sanctifying or purifying ourselves. Education, culture, refinement, respectability, will not do it. The Lord only is sufficient.

"Swine's flesh." Why will men continue to eat that which is not best? It would seem that even those who believe all restrictions removed regarding eating and drinking, would consider the effect that wrong eating has on the human system. Few would consider eating mice and abominable things, yet God here classes them together with swine's flesh. Touch not, taste not, handle not.

Verses 19-21. The prophecy in these verses should cause the heart of all to leap for joy. While some will eat abominable things and pay no heed to God's requirements, there is another class to whom God gives a sign. These will hasten to earth's remotest bounds, and proclaim the message, and souls will be saved from among all nations and tongues. And some of these God will make priests and Levites, that is, He will give them prominent positions in His work.

"They shall declare My glory among the Gentiles." God's glory is His character as revealed in the law. This will be preached to all nations and kindreds and tongues and peoples. What a wonderful movement, and what a wonderful privilege to be permitted to have a part in it!

Verse 23. We do not appreciate as we should the privilege of meeting with those of like faith. It is, or should be, a foretaste of heaven. What will it be, then, when from one new moon to another and from one Sabbath to another we shall meet with the saints of all ages and hold communion with them!

"There we shall know even as also we are known. There the loves and sympathies that God has planted in the soul will find truest and sweetest exercise. The pure communion with holy beings, the harmonious social life with the blessed angels and with the faithful ones of all ages, the sacred fellowship that binds together 'the whole family in heaven and earth,'— all are among the experience of the hereafter."—"*Education,*" *p. 306.*

SABBATH SCHOOL LESSON
QUARTERLY

SENIOR DIVISION
First Quarter, 1929

Lessons from
The BOOK of ISAIAH

Thirteenth Sabbath Offering, March 30, 1929
Catholic Europe

Entered as second-class matter October 13, 1904, at the Post Office in Mountain View, Cal., under the Act of Congress of March 3, 1879. Acceptance for mailing at special rate of postage provided for in section 1103, Act of October 3, 1917, and authorized September 18, 1918.

PACIFIC PRESS PUB. ASSN. (A Corporation of S. D. A.)

No. 135   MOUNTAIN VIEW, CAL., JANUARY, 1929   20c A YEAR

Isaiah, The Gospel Prophet
Volume III
By M. L. Andreasen

THIS is the third and last of a series of practical Sabbath school lesson helps on the book of Isaiah. This pamphlet is intended for use in connection with the lessons for the first quarter of 1929.

Many thousands of copies of Volumes I and II have been sold, and those who have enjoyed the use of these helpful comments on the Sabbath school lessons will be anxious to secure Volume III. The information this little book contains is of interest to every member of the Senior and Youth's divisions, and of vital importance to every teacher.

If you have not already secured your copy, place your order immediately so you will not miss the help it will give you. Price, 25 cents; Canada, 30 cents. Order from your Book and Bible House.

The Next Thirteenth Sabbath Offering
L. L. CAVINESS
[Sabbath School Secretary of the European Division]

THE fields which are looking for an overflow offering on Sabbath, March 30, have more than one third of the entire population of Europe. The total appropriations voted for last year for all these countries amounted to a little over $180,000, or about one dollar per thousand population. We feel certain that our faithful Sabbath school members will give generously on the next thirteenth Sabbath that the third angel's message may go rapidly to the Roman Catholic lands of Europe.

Table (Round figures are given.)

	Population	Members
Latin Union		
Italy	42,000,000	420
France	40,500,000	1,300
Belgium	8,000,000	430
Iberian Union		
Spain	23,000,000	300
Portugal	6,000,000	250
Polish Union	30,000,000	2,300
Czecho-Slovakian Union	14,000,000	2,300
Hungarian Union	8,000,000	1,700
Austrian Conference	6,700,000	1,000
Totals	178,200,000	10,000

LESSON 1

THE GOD OF COMFORT

January 5, 1929

LESSON SCRIPTURE: Isaiah 54.
MEMORY VERSE: Isa. 54:10.

INTRODUCTION

This first part of the lesson deals with the relation of God to His church under the symbol of husband and wife. This idea forms the basis of many references in both the Old and the New Testament. Jer. 3:14; 31:32; 2 Cor. 11:2; Eph. 5:23-32. The Song of Solomon is founded on this conception. To be untrue to God is called adultery. Eze. 23:37. Hence we need not apply these lessons to Israel only. They have an application now.

The second part of the lesson deals with God's protecting care over His people. He created the smith who is forging the weapon with intent to torture God's people. In other words, God knows. He is responsible. Trust Him, and all will be well. "No weapon that is formed against thee shall prosper." That is our heritage.

THE LESSON

1. **Why is the barren told to break forth into singing? Isa. 54:1.**

NOTE.—Israel is told to sing because the desolate has more children than the married wife. This, of course, is to be spiritually understood. Paul, quoting this verse in Galatians 4:27, refers to the story of Hagar and Sarah. Sarah was desolate. She had no children, and there was no hope of any. Hagar had a son, Ishmael. Abraham thought that Ishmael might be the promised child, but God said, "My covenant will I establish with Isaac, which Sarah shall bear." "She shall be a mother of nations; kings of people shall be of her." Gen. 17:21, 16. That both Gentiles and Jews who surrender to Christ are included as the spiritual children of Abraham and Sarah is made clear by a comparison with Galatians 3:7, 16, 14.

This has reference to a great ingathering of souls for Christ, and how God will greatly bless and prosper the work of the gospel in the last day when He finishes His work in the earth.

2. **What should be done to make room for this gospel ingathering? Verse 2.**

NOTE.—The prophet is here looking forward to the time when the gospel shall be preached to the ends of the earth. (See "Prophets and Kings," page 374, par. 1.)

"Enlarge the place of thy tent." The work in the foreign fields must be ever extended. "Lengthen thy cords, and strengthen thy stakes." At the same time, the work at home must be strengthened.

3. **What does God say shall take place on the right hand and on the left? What shall the seed inherit? What change shall come to the desolate cities? Verse 3.**

NOTE.—"Thou shalt break forth," or "Thou shalt increase." It is because of the great increase that shall come to God's people that plans for enlargements are to be made.

"On the right hand and on the left"—on all sides. (See Gen. 28:14.)

"Inherit the Gentiles." Isaiah here looks away from the conception which the Jews of his day had, that only Jews could be saved. The redeemed will be saved from all nations, and the Gentiles will be among them.

"Desolate cities." Cities without godly inhabitants will hear the message, and many living in them will accept it. God thinks of and plans for the cities. Jonah 1:2; 3:2; 4:10, 11.

4. What encouraging message does God send? What shall be forgotten? Verse 4.

NOTE.—"Fear not." The preceding verses have mentioned the enlargement that shall come to God's people. They shall inherit the Gentiles and spread forth right and left. Does this seem too much? Fear not. They shall not be ashamed. The Lord is with His people. Their plans may seem ambitious and incapable of fulfillment, but the living God never fails.

"The shame of thy youth." "The reproach of thy widowhood." Israel again and again had left the Lord, her lawful husband, and gone after other lovers. Hosea 2:13. Hence the Lord considered the vow broken, and did not regard Israel. Hosea 2:2. But these sad experiences will be forgotten when God again returns to Israel.

5. How is the Lord spoken of in relation to the church? By what other three names is He called? Verse 5.

NOTE.—"Thy Maker is thine husband." This explains the statements in verses 1 and 4 concerning the "married wife" and "widowhood." That is, God is the husband of the church. This, of course, has specific reference to Christ. Eph. 5:32.

6. How had the Lord called Israel? Verse 6.

NOTE.—The American Revised Version has "wife" instead of "woman." The thought seems to be that although the church has left her Lord, God calls her back again, once more to resume her place as wife.

7. What had God done for a small moment? What does He say He will do? Verse 7.

NOTE.—Because of their sins, God had forsaken His people, for "a small moment." When this was written, the ten tribes had been carried into captivity a few years previously, 721 B. C. (See 2 Kings 17:6, 18.) But though in captivity, Israel was not forsaken, for God's mercy was still extended to them.

8. What had God done "in a little wrath"? What will He now do? Verse 8.

9. To what is this likened? What had God sworn? What does He now swear? Verse 9.

[4]

NOTE.—God here likens the carrying of the ten tribes into captivity to the time of Noah. Sin brought the Flood, and so sin had brought this calamity. God had promised not to send another flood on the earth, and here He promises not again to be wroth with His people, nor rebuke them. Some have thought that God has not kept this promise. Did He not more than a hundred years later permit Judah to be carried into captivity in the time of Daniel? And did He not finally in A. D. 70 reject the whole Jewish nation?

Note this: The captivity of the ten tribes in 721 B. C. was final. There was no return. The captivity in the time of Daniel was not final. There was a return. God rejected the Jewish nation and permitted Jerusalem to be destroyed in A. D. 70; but before that time, He had already established His New Testament church composed of such as should be saved in Israel, together with the Gentiles, and this constituted the true church, the continuation of the church of Isaiah's day. Hence God has kept His promise. The rejection of the nation did not mean the rejection of individuals.

10. What beautiful promise is given to God's people? Verse 10.

11. What promises does God give the afflicted? Verses 11, 12.

12. By whom shall the children be taught? What great blessing is promised them? Verse 13.

NOTE.—In John 6:45 Christ quotes this text. (See also 1 Thess. 4:9.)

"Great shall be the peace." In a world of tumult, God's people will have peace. Serene, confident, unperturbed, God's own will pass through the perils of the last days. (See John 14:27; Ps. 119:165.)

13. In what shall God's people be established? From what shall they be far removed? Verse 14.

14. What will be the fate of the enemies of God's people? Verse 15.

NOTE.—"Not by Me." Should thy enemies unite and attack thee, it is none of My doings, hence it shall not prosper.

15. Who has created the smith and the waster? Verse 16.

NOTE.—God's people need not fear any danger. The furnace may be heated seven times hotter than usual, but God has created both the fireman and the fuel he uses. These are in God's hands.

16. What shall not prosper against God's people? What shall be condemned? What is said to be their heritage? Of whom is their righteousness? Verse 17.

"If those to whom God's money has been intrusted will be faithful in bringing the means lent them to the Lord's treasury, His work will make rapid advancement. Many souls will be won to the cause of truth, and the day of Christ's coming will be hastened."—"Testimonies," Vol. 9, p. 58.

LESSON 2

GOD'S CALL TO RETURN; THE WORD THAT TRANSFORMS

January 12, 1929

LESSON SCRIPTURE: Isaiah 55.
MEMORY VERSE: Isa. 55:6, 7.

INTRODUCTION

Salvation is freely offered to all, but it becomes available only to those who enter into covenant relation with God.

While God thus extends mercy to all, the door will not always be open. God may be found now, later it may be too late. Therefore, seek Him now.

THE LESSON

1. **Who is invited to drink of the water of life? What are they to buy? How much does it cost? Isa. 55:1.**

NOTE.—"Every one that thirsteth." The condition for receiving the blessings of God is not riches, for you may come without money. It is not condition, or rank, or learning. It is simply your need. Are you thirsty? Then come.

Thirst is perhaps the greatest and most compelling of physical desires. A man who is hungry will, after a while, quietly lie down and die; the thirsty man will spend himself in mad strivings. His whole nature is burning up. He must have water. This strong desire is compared to spiritual thirst. David uses the same figure. Ps. 42:1, 2; 63:1. (See also John 4:13, 14.)

The water signifies:
Christ.—"Patriarchs and Prophets," p. 413.
The Word.—"Steps to Christ," p. 93.
Emblem of divine grace.—"Patriarchs and Prophets," p. 412.
Spiritual life.—"The Desire of Ages," p. 190.
Wine and milk are used as figures.

2. **What important question is asked concerning the spending of money? What similar question is asked concerning labor? What advice is given? Verse 2.**

NOTE.—Spending money uselessly is sin. In this day when there are people suffering for the necessities of life, when there is an even greater spiritual need, we must be careful in the expenditure of every penny. "Money is a trust from God. It is not ours to expend for the gratification of pride or ambition. In the hands of God's children it is food for the hungry, and clothing for the naked. It is a defense to the oppressed, a means of health to the sick, a means of preaching the gospel to the poor. You could bring happiness to many hearts by using wisely the means that is now spent for show. Consider the life of Christ. Study His character, and be partakers with Him in His self-denial."—"The Ministry of Healing," p. 287.

[6]

"Eat ye that which is good." "God demands that the appetites be cleansed, and that self-denial be practiced in regard to those things which are not good. This is a work that will have to be done before His people can stand before Him a perfected people."—"Testimonies," Vol. 9, pp. 153, 154.

Applying this text to spiritual matters, there is no better spiritual food than the word of God. On that we should feed morning, noon, and night. Any substitution will prove disastrous. It is the bread,—the very staff,—of life.

3. What invitation does the Lord give? What will He make with us? Verse 3.

NOTE.—"An everlasting covenant." This covenant of grace was first made in Eden. Gen. 3:15. It was renewed to Abraham. Gen. 22:18; 26:4, 5; 17:7. It was ratified by Christ on the cross. (See "Patriarchs and Prophets," pp. 370, 371.) And "in the last days of this earth's history, God's covenant with His commandment-keeping people is to be renewed."—"Prophets and Kings," p. 299.

"The sure mercies of David." These mercies are the precious promises given to David, including the promise of the Saviour through David's line. Ps. 89:1-5; 2 Sam. 23:5.

4. Who is the leader and commander mentioned in verse 4?

NOTE.—What is said here seems to have a very definite reference to Christ, who is called David in Jeremiah 30:9 and Ezekiel 34:23, 24. Christ is also the Son of David. Hence commentators rightly apply these verses to Christ. Matt. 21:9, Luke 1:32.

Christ is also a witness. John 18:37.

5. Whom shall He call? What shall nations do? Verse 5.

NOTE.—The thought in this verse is that Christ shall call nations with whom He had not hitherto made any covenant, that is, the Gentiles. These would be drawn to Him because God would glorify His Son. In the death and resurrection of Christ, God did glorify the Son. John 17:1; Acts 3:13-15.

6. What are men called upon to do? Verse 6.

NOTE.—The day will come when some shall seek, but shall not find. Amos 8:11, 12.

7. What must the wicked and the unrighteous forsake? How will God treat the sinner if he returns? Verse 7.

8. What does God say of His thoughts and ways? Verses 8, 9. (See Jer. 29:11.)

9. What is said of the rain and snow which come down from heaven? What is said of His word? How will it not return? What will it accomplish? In what will it prosper? Verses 10, 11.

NOTE.—"It shall prosper." "The work of the sower is a work of faith. The mystery of the germination and growth of the seed he can not understand; but he has confidence in the agencies by which God causes vegetation to flourish. He casts away the seed, expecting to gather it manyfold in an abundant harvest. So parents and teachers are to labor, expecting a harvest from the seed they sow."—"Education," p. 105.

10. In what spirit are we to go forth in seed sowing? How is nature said to rejoice? Verse 12.

NOTE.—The word "for" connects this verse with the preceding one. God will do His part. He will send rain and snow, but man must also do his part. We must do the planting; God will give the increase.

11. What transformation shall take place? What shall this be to the Lord? Verse 13.

NOTE.—Briers and thorns represent evil. Micah 7:4. By contrast, the fir and myrtle would represent righteousness.

"A name." "An everlasting sign." To turn briers and thorns, spiritually speaking, into beautiful and useful fir and myrtle, is a memorial to God's praise.

LESSON 3

BLESSINGS TO JEW AND GENTILE; BLIND WATCHMEN

January 19, 1929

LESSON SCRIPTURE: Isaiah 56.
MEMORY VERSE: Isa. 56:2.

INTRODUCTION

This chapter is divided into two distinct parts. Verses 1-8 deal with the promises of God to all who do His will. Lest some should think that they themselves are left out, the strangers and the eunuchs are especially mentioned. The Sabbath is vital to His covenant. The keeping of the Sabbath in verses 2, 4, and 6, is shown to be one of the conditions of receiving God's blessings. These promises and conditions apply to all other peoples as well as to the Jews.

Verses 9-12 state the condition of the blind watchmen. While we need to be careful in any local application of these statements, we must not forget that this is God's view of the situation. We need to pray God to make us faithful watchmen on the walls of Zion, and that we be not charged with surfeiting or drunkenness. We should be wholly clear ourselves of that which we condemn in others.

THE LESSON

1. What are we told to keep and to do? What is near, and what is about to be revealed? Isa. 56:1.

NOTE.—"Keep ye judgment, and do justice," might well be translated, "Keep ye law, and do righteousness."—Pulpit Commentary. This has a special application to this time. It has always been the duty of God's children to keep His law.

2. What is said of the man that keeps the Sabbath and refrains from evil? Verse 2.

[8]

NOTE.—This blessing is not for the Jews only, but for "man" and the "son of man." Neither is the blessing for the one who only once does it, but to him who "layeth hold on it;" "holds to it," as Moffatt translates the text.

"Keepeth the Sabbath." How much that includes! It requires nothing less than holiness. "No other institution which was committed to the Jews tended so fully to distinguish them from surrounding nations as did the Sabbath. . . . To keep the Sabbath holy, men must themselves be holy. Through faith they must become partakers of the righteousness of Christ."—"The Desire of Ages," p. 283.

3. What should the son of a stranger or the eunuch not say? Verse 3. Verse 3.

NOTE.—"Many from among the sons of the strangers were to learn to love Him as their Creator and their Redeemer; they were to begin the observance of His holy Sabbath day as a memorial of His creative power; and when He should make 'bare His holy arm in the eyes of all the nations,' to deliver His people from captivity, 'all the ends of the earth' should see the salvation of God. Many of these converts from heathenism would wish to unite themselves fully with the Israelites, and accompany them on the return journey to Judea. None of these were to say, 'The Lord hath utterly separated me from His people;' for the word of God through His prophet to those who should yield themselves to Him and observe His law, was that they should thenceforth be numbered among spiritual Israel—His church on earth."—"Prophets and Kings," p. 372.

"Eunuch." As the eunuch could not become the head of a family in Israel, he might fear that he could have no share in the hopes of Israel. God here allays the fear that any physical disability will keep a man out of heaven.

4. What three things are mentioned of the eunuchs whom the Lord addresses? Verse 4.

NOTE.—"Keep My Sabbaths." Of all the Ten Commandments, the fourth is the one chosen as the test and condition of one of the most beautiful promises either in the Old or the New Testament, as mentioned in the next verse.

"Choose the things that please Me." Christ pleased not Himself. We are not to please ourselves. In eating or drinking, in dress or adornment, in association or friendship, in the thousand decisions that come to us daily, the question should always be: What will please Him?

"Take hold of My covenant." The thought here is not merely to "take hold of," but to hold fast, not to give up.

5. What two things will God give to them? How is the name further designated? Verse 5.

NOTE.—"A place." This place will be "in Mine house and within My walls." While this special promise is given to the eunuchs, we may believe God is no respecter of persons. The same promise applies to all. The eunuchs to whom these promises were especially given, would have no sons or daughters. God, therefore, promises them something better. God will more than restore and make up for anything of which we may in this life be deprived. Eph. 3:20.

"An everlasting name." Some names will be blotted out. Some will remain. Rev. 3:5.

6. What do the strangers do that join themselves to the Lord? Verse 6.

NOTE.—"Serve Him." To join ourselves to the Lord means more than to subscribe to a creed. It means service.

To love the name of the Lord is to love all that name stands for.

"His servants" means worshipers. It includes the act of worshiping as also the mode and form.

"Keepeth the Sabbath." This is included in true worship. Whoever "join themselves to the Lord" will be Sabbath keepers. It should be noted that God here again selects the fourth commandment out of all the ten as the test commandment.

"Taketh hold of My covenant." He that "holdeth fast" the covenant will ever experience the blessing of forgiveness of sin and the renewing grace of God, and will be in harmony with God's law.

7. Where will God bring the strangers? Where shall they be made joyful? What will God accept from them? What shall God's house be called? Verse 7.

NOTE.—"My holy mountain," Jerusalem, or the church of Christ. Also symbolic of the new earth. Isa. 11:9; 65:25.

"House of prayer," the temple. ("The Desire of Ages," p. 27.) After "My house" had become "your house" (Matt. 21:13; 23:38); that is, after God had rejected the temple and its services, any place where God's people assemble is a place of prayer. Acts 12:5, 12; 16:13.

"An house of prayer." Prayer is more than asking for things. Prayer is communion. God's house is a "house of prayer for all people." That is, all are invited to come and pray, not for themselves alone, but for their neighbors here at home as well as in far-off fields. Thus in a double sense God's house is a "house of prayer for all people."

8. How does the Lord speak of Himself? What does He say of the ingathering of the Gentiles? Verse 8.

9. What is said to the beasts of the field and of the forest? Verse 9.

NOTE.—Verse 9 begins a new section. The wild beasts are the enemies of God's people, who are coming to devour the flock because the shepherds are asleep. (See Eze. 34:7-10.)

10. How are the watchmen described? Verse 10.

11. What further is said of them? Of what are they incapable? Which way do they look? For what reason? Verse 11.

12. What do they say? With what will they be filled? What is said of to-morrow? Verse 12.

NOTE.—It would be unjust as well as untrue to make a general application of these verses. There are many honest souls, priests as well as people, who are living up to all the light they have. These God will lead into still greater light. But there are also those to whom these verses refer in all their force.

[10]

LESSON 4

THE RIGHTEOUS AND THE WICKED IN THE DAY OF TROUBLE

January 26, 1929

LESSON SCRIPTURE: Isaiah 57.
MEMORY VERSE: Isa. 57:15.

INTRODUCTION

Verses 1 and 2 we have always and rightly applied to the time just before the beginning of the plagues. God will cause some to sleep that He may deliver them from the evil to come.

Verses 3-13 speak of the condition of the wicked at the same time. They make "sport" of God's true children, they go into depths of sin and degradation. They weary of their own wickedness, yet they do not repent.

In that time of peril, God will not forsake His own. He will dwell with the contrite and humble, and revive them. He will give them peace. The wicked, on the other hand, will continue to throw up "mire and dirt." For them there is no peace.

THE LESSON

1. After describing the unfaithful watchmen, what is said of the righteous? What happens to merciful men? What is not considered? Isa. 57:1.

NOTE.—"Taken away from the evil to come." Josiah was promised that he would be taken away before the evil should come. 2 Kings 22:20. So with these. At the time when the Sabbath is the test, when the watchmen are sleeping, when the day of trouble is approaching, some will be "taken away from the evil to come."

2. Into what shall they enter? How shall they rest? How have they walked? Verse 2.

NOTE.—"Into peace." "Blessed are the dead which die in the Lord from henceforth." Rev. 14:13. They rest while the world goes on. The last struggle is in progress. The two-horned beast of Revelation 13 is publishing his decree that whoever will not worship the image of the beast shall be killed. Rev. 13:15. God's people are entering into the time of Jacob's trouble. It is a terrific final struggle. During this time, some of God's people have entered "into peace." "Rest in their beds."

"Each one walking," rather "each one that walked," referring to those who have entered into peace.

3. What is said of the wickedness of evil men at this time? Verses 3-10.

NOTE.—The following suggestions are offered concerning the meaning of these verses:

Verses 3-10 are in sharp contrast with that which precedes them. God has been speaking of the righteous. Now He turns to the scoffers that "sport" themselves. It is evidently the few righteous that still live among them who are the object of this mocking. Even as Ishmael mocked Isaac (Gen. 21:9), and as there shall come mockers in the last days (2 Peter 3:3), so these mock. To make "a wide mouth," to "draw out the tongue," are childish gestures, an evidence of a complete lack of decency and self-respect.

This description definitely points out who are meant in the following verses. They are the "children of transgression," that debase themselves "even unto hell." Verses 4, 9.

4. What does God say further of these wicked ones? What has God done? Verse 11.

NOTE.—"Thou hast lied." God here asks of whom these people are afraid that they should think it necessary to lie. It can not be that they are afraid of God, for they do not believe in Him. The thought of lying to God is there also. Some of these people of rebellion profess to be God's children—their very profession is a lie.

5. What will God declare? Of what profit shall it be? Verse 12.

6. How does God contrast putting trust in companions with putting trust in Him? Verse 13.

NOTE.—Trust is the characteristic Old Testament word for the New Testament words "faith," "belief." It occurs one hundred fifty-two times in the Old Testament, and is the rendering of Hebrew words signifying to take refuge, as in Ruth 2:12; to lean on, Psalm 56:3; to stay upon, Job 35:14.

7. What shall be said? Verse 14.

NOTE.—"It shall be said," American Revised Version, margin.

"Cast ye up." That is, make a highway by heaping up material for it, and take all obstructions out of the way. (See Isa. 62:10.)

8. Who is the speaker of these words? Where is His habitation? What name is given Him? Where does He dwell? With whom also will He make His abode? For what purpose? Verse 15.

NOTE.—"High and lofty One." The same as "high and lifted up" in Isaiah 6:1. "Inhabiteth eternity." Lives forever, enthroned forever.

"Holy." Even as God is love, so also He is holy. That, in fact, is His name. Holiness includes all the characteristics of God.

"I saw then what faint views some have of the holiness of God, and how much they take His holy and reverend name in vain, without realizing that it is God, the great and terrible God, of whom they are speaking. . . .

"I also saw that many do not realize what they must be in order to live in the sight of the Lord without a high priest in the sanctuary, through the time of trouble. Those who receive the seal of the living God, and are protected in the time of trouble, must reflect the image of Jesus fully."—"Early Writings," pp. 70, 71.

9. What will God not do? What reason is given for this? Verse 16.

NOTE.—God will not keep His anger forever. Ps. 103:9. If God did so, no one could stand before Him. God's actions are based on His mercy. If God should hold all to strict accountability, none could stand. Ps. 130:3.

10. **Why was God wroth? What did He do? What did the people do? Verse 17.**

NOTE.—Covetousness is idolatry. Col. 3:5. "The greatest sin which now exists in the church is covetousness."—"Testimonies," Vol. 1, p. 194.

"The law of tithing was founded upon an enduring principle, and was designed to be a blessing to man. The system of benevolence was arranged to prevent that great evil, covetousness. Christ saw that in the prosecution of business the love of riches would be the greatest cause of rooting true godliness out of the heart. He saw that the love of money would freeze deep and hard into men's souls, stopping the flow of generous impulses, and closing their senses to the wants of the suffering and the afflicted. . . . Covetousness is one of the most common and popular sins of the last days, and has a paralyzing influence upon the soul."—"Testimonies," Vol. 3, p. 547.

"Smote him." Covetousness is here selected as the typical sin. For this God was "wroth, and smote him." For example, see Acts 5:1-11.

"I hid me." It is sin that separates from God. Isa. 59:2.

"He went on." Israel did not heed. "He went on" in his own way. How true that is of many professed Christians to-day!

11. **What has God seen? What will He do? What more will God do? Verse 18.**

NOTE.—"I have seen." God is fully aware of conditions. "Will heal him." He will heal the contrite ones. What a wonderful God is ours! He knows our way, that we have gone astray. Yet He does not leave us to ourselves.

"I will lead him." Even though we have gone our own way, God does not forsake us. He will still lead us. Though many have gone their own way, God does not forsake them, but leads them until they are brought back to Him!

"Restore comforts." There is no real comfort in sin; but there is wonderful comfort in the knowledge of sin forgiven.

12. **What does God create? What message is to be brought to him that is afar off and to him that is near? Verse 19.**

NOTE.—"The fruit of the lips" means praise and thanksgiving. Heb. 13:15.

"Peace, peace." At the birth of Christ the angels sang, "Peace, good will toward men." Luke 2:14. At the close of His ministry, Christ said, "Peace I leave with you, My peace I give unto you." John 14:27; 16:33.

13. **To what are the wicked likened? Verse 20.**

14. **For whom is there no peace? Verse 21:**

NOTE.—The wicked may engage in amusements and entertainments to divert the mind, but true, enduring peace is found only in Christ, and is not theirs.

LESSON 5

TRUE FASTING; THE SABBATH RESTORED

February 2, 1929

LESSON SCRIPTURE: Isaiah 58.
MEMORY VERSE: Isa. 58: 13, 14.

INTRODUCTION

"What saith the Lord in the fifty-eighth chapter of Isaiah? The whole chapter is of the highest importance."—"Testimonies," Vol. 8, p. 159.

This chapter is directed to God's people. "It is not the wicked world, but those whom the Lord designates as 'My people,' that are to be reproved for their transgressions."—"The Great Controversy," p. 452. "The prophet is addressing Sabbath keepers, not sinners, not unbelievers."—"Testimonies," Vol. 2, p. 36.

"The fifty-eighth chapter of Isaiah is a prescription for maladies of the body and of the soul. If we desire health and the true joy of life, we must put into practice the rules given in this scripture."—"The Ministry of Healing," p. 256.

THE LESSON

1. **How is the prophet told to make this announcement? How should he lift up his voice? Who are to have their sins pointed out? Isa. 58:1.**

NOTE.—"Spare not." Do not smooth matters over. Tell the truth. "Transgression." Sin is sin; righteousness is righteousness. The trumpet note of warning must be sounded. We are living in a fearfully wicked age. The worship of God will become corrupted unless there are wide-awake men at every post of duty. It is no time now for any to be absorbed in selfish ease. Not one of the words which God has spoken must be allowed to fall to the ground."—"Testimonies," Vol. 4, p. 517.

2. **How regularly do His people seek Him? In what do they delight? What have they not forsaken? For what do they ask? In what, further, do they take delight? Verse 2.**

NOTE.—"Daily." It is possible, then, to seek the Lord daily, to have family worship and private devotions, and yet not be right with God. What an alarming and heart-searching thought!

These people delight to know God's ways. They are eager to know the divine will, as eager as if they were in reality a people that practiced righteousness. They are not conscious hypocrites—quite the reverse. But they seem to lack a proper appreciation of what constitutes true religion.

"The ordinance of their God," the law.

3. **What complaint do they bring against God? Of what do they say He takes no notice? What answer does God give? Verse 3.**

NOTE.—Having fasted, these people expect God to take heed and give them due credit, or reward. Now they complain that God appar-

[14]

ently has not seen them. They are willing to conform to all the requirements of religion, but they want recognition for it, they want pay.

Real fasting presupposes such a seeking of God that worldly things will be forgotten. True fasting permits of no other "business" than that of seeking God. Merely to be hungry is not to fast.

4. **For what purpose do they fast? How does God say they do not fast? Verse 4.**

NOTE.—Fasting should humble the spirit and produce kindness and love in the heart for others. The fasting here spoken of produced irritation and ill feeling, even to the point of angry debate and "smiting."

"Ye fast not this day so as to make your voice to be heard on high," American Revised Version. Their fast was not such that God could hear them.

5. **What questions does God ask? Verse 5.**

NOTE.—God disapproves of the kind of fasting here mentioned. "Jesus said, 'When thou fastest, anoint thine head, and wash thy face; that thou appear not unto men to fast, but unto thy Father which is in secret.' Whatever is done to the glory of God is to be done with cheerfulness, not with sadness and gloom. There is nothing gloomy in the religion of Jesus."—"Thoughts from the Mount of Blessing," p. 131. (See also Matt. 6:16-18.)

6. **What four things are mentioned as being included in true fasting? Verse 6.**

NOTE.—"Loose the bands of wickedness;" to free from unjust and oppressive obligations.

"Undo the heavy burdens;" literally, to untie the bands of the yoke.

"Let the oppressed go free;" literally the "broken." Probably such as through debt had forfeited their liberty. (See Neh. 5:8.)

"Break every yoke." This includes all that hinders in any way. Every yoke that holds you must be broken. Every sin must be put aside.

7. **What are we to do for the hungry? For the poor? For the naked? From whom must we not hide? Verse 7.**

NOTE.—Read "Testimonies," Vol. 2, pp. 32-35.

"In all our work, the principle of unselfishness revealed in Christ's life is to be carried out. Upon the walls of our homes, the pictures, the furnishings, we are to read, 'Bring the poor that are cast out to thy house.' On our wardrobes we are to see written, as with the finger of God, 'Clothe the naked.' In the dining room, on the table laden with abundant food, we should see traced, 'Is it not to deal thy bread to the hungry?' "—"The Ministry of Healing," p. 206.

8. **What will come to those who do God's will? What is said of their health? What will go before them? What will be their rereward? Verse 8.**

NOTE.—"Righteousness shall go before." A life dedicated to doing good can not be hid under a bushel. The fame of it will spread far and wide and "go before." So also in regard to the life to come. Any good done will go before and come up before God as a sweet savor. (See Acts 10:4.)

"Glory of the Lord." Rereward means rear guard. As the pillar of cloud and of fire was a protection to Israel, so God's people now are promised God's glory as their protection. (See Ex. 14:19-25.)

9. What shall be the experience of those who fast according to God's conditions? What three things, however, must be taken away? Verse 9.

NOTE.—"Take away . . . the yoke," referred to in verse 6.
"Putting forth of the finger," a gesture of contempt.
"Speaking vanity," speaking evil.

10. What other two conditions are mentioned? What promises are given? Verse 10.

11. What beautiful promise of guidance is given? How will the Lord satisfy His own? What will they be like? Verse 11.

NOTE.—If we satisfy the afflicted soul, God will satisfy our soul. "A watered garden." "A spring of water." When the drought comes, the test comes. In the dark days of life true Christianity reveals itself. It is for that specific time that these promises hold.

12. What will happen to the old waste places? What will be raised up? What will they who do this be called? Verse 12.

NOTE.—"This prophecy also applies in our time. The breach was made in the law of God when the Sabbath was changed by the Romish power. But the time has come for that divine institution to be restored. The breach is to be repaired, and the foundation of many generations to be raised up."—"The Great Controversy," p. 453.

"The prophet here describes a people who, in a time of general departure from truth and righteousness, are seeking to restore the principles that are the foundation of the kingdom of God. They are repairers of a breach that has been made in God's law,—the wall that He has placed around His chosen ones for their protection, and obedience to whose precepts of justice, truth, and purity, is to be their perpetual safeguard."—"Prophets and Kings," pp. 677, 678.

13. From what are we to turn away our foot? What may we not do on the holy day? What three descriptive words are used of the Sabbath? Whom are we to honor? In what three ways may that be done? Verse 13.

NOTE.—"When the Sabbath commences we should place a guard upon ourselves, upon our acts and our words, lest we rob God by appropriating to our own use that time which is strictly the Lord's. We should not do ourselves, nor suffer our children to do, any manner of our own work for a livelihood, or anything which could have been done on the six working days. Friday is the day of preparation. Time can then be devoted to making the necessary preparation for the Sabbath, and to thinking and conversing about it. Nothing which will in the sight of Heaven be regarded as a violation of the holy Sabbath should be left unsaid or undone, to be said or done upon the Sabbath.

"God requires not only that we refrain from physical labor upon the Sabbath, but that the mind be disciplined to dwell upon sacred themes. The fourth commandment is virtually transgressed by conversing upon worldly things, or by engaging in light and trifling conversation. Talking upon anything or everything which may come into the mind, is speaking our own words. Every deviation from right brings us into bondage and condemnation."—"Testimonies," Vol. 2, pp. 702, 703.

Religion, Sabbath keeping, all spiritual exercises, should be considered a privilege rather than a yoke. Only thus considered can they ever be a delight.

14. What should come as a result of true Sabbath keeping? What promises are given? Who has said this? Verse 14.

NOTE.—"High places of the earth," that is, "I will carry thee triumphantly over all obstacles."—Cambridge Bible.

"Feed thee," cause thee to enjoy.

LESSON 6
A REDEEMER PROMISED TO A PENITENT PEOPLE
February 9, 1929

LESSON SCRIPTURE: Isaiah 59.
MEMORY VERSE: Isa. 59:1, 2.

INTRODUCTION

This chapter is a continuation of the preceding one. It reveals the reason for the Lord's not hearing or answering the prayers of the people. The people seem aware of their real condition, for in Isaiah 59:12 they admit that their iniquities are known to them, and that their sins testify against them.

The first fifteen verses of this chapter present a picture of terrible backsliding. A profession of Christianity has been used as a cloak for evil. Churchgoers have had a form of godliness without the power thereof. They admit that they have been neither truthful nor just, that they have made crooked paths, and, as the result, have stumbled like blind men. The situation is not hopeless, however, for the Lord Himself will gird up His loins like a man of war and deliver His people.

The lesson is clear. Sin will cause God to hide His face from us; but in turning from our iniquities, God will cause the Redeemer to come to Zion.

THE LESSON

1. What is said of the Lord's power to save and of His ability to hear? Isa. 59:1.

NOTE.—This verse is God's answer to the complaint made in the preceding chapter that God had not heard the requests of His people though they had fasted and afflicted their souls.

2. What has caused separation between God and His people? Why has God hidden His face? Verse 2; Deut. 31:17.

3. What has been defiled with blood and with iniquity? What is said of the lips and tongue? Isa. 59:3; 1:15.

4. For what do the people not call or plead? In what do they trust? What do they speak? What do they conceive and bring forth? Isa. 59:4.

5. What two illustrations are used? What happens if the egg is eaten, and what if it is crushed? Verse 5.

NOTE.—A cockatrice, the same as adder or basilisk, is a venomous serpent. A double image is here used, that of a cockatrice and a spider. The hatching of a cockatrice's eggs doubtless refers to the hatching of schemes by wicked men. These schemes take time for development, and all that is involved in them may not at once be apparent. Many plans look innocent and do not seem fraught with danger, but there is death in them. Of such are all attempts at religious legislation. Ostensibly innocent and said to be for the good of the people, there is seen but the hatching of cockatrice's eggs. Whoever eats of the eggs, that is, are in favor of and fall in with such schemes, will reap the sure result.

"That which is crushed." Some of the schemes will not materialize, but will be crushed. Opposition will develop. And it is at such a time that the real nature of the scheme will be revealed. It will break out "into a viper." Men will then show the spirit that animates them. As the figure of the cockatrice brings out the deadly nature of the schemes laid by wicked men, so that of the spider reveals the futility.

6. What shall the webs not become? With what are they unable to cover themselves? What are their works said to be? What is in their hands? Verse 6.

NOTE.—A spider's web is designed to catch unwary insects. But here an additional application is made of the figure. While evil men are hatching out deep-laid schemes, presented under the figure of cockatrice's eggs, they are trying to cover their real intention in a garment composed of spider's web. But who can shield himself in such a garment? Men may think they can hide themselves and their schemes, but to God they appear as clothed in a garment of spider's web. God knows their secret machinations, and so do His people. When wicked men are trying secretly to hatch a viper, and think that no one knows what they are doing, somebody will step on the egg and reveal what is inside before the scheme is fully hatched. An example of this is Haman's attempt on the life of God's people, as revealed in the book of Esther.

7. To what do their feet run? For what purpose do they make haste? What is said of their thoughts and of their paths? Verse 7.

8. Of what are they ignorant? What is not found in their goings? What do those not know who walk in crooked paths? Verse 8.

9. What is said of judgment and justice? For what do they wait? What is the result? Verse 9.

NOTE.—Thus far in the chapter God has spoken. Now the people speak. Verses 9-14. Instead of proclaiming their own righteousness as in chapter 58:3, they admit that the accusations against them are justified.

"Therefore," that is, because of the sins mentioned in verses 1-8.

"Judgment," "justice." The American Revised Version has "justice" and "righteousness."

"Wait for light." It is useless for anyone to wait for light so long as he has pleasure in iniquity.

10. What comparison is made with the blind? When do they stumble? To what are they likened? Verse 10.

11. What two illustrations are here used? For what two things are they said to look? Verse 11.

12. What has been multiplied? What is done by our sins? What is said of our iniquities and transgressions? Verse 12.

NOTE.—"Our sins testify." What a tremendous statement! Sin does not exist apart from personality. It exists only as it is committed by, and belongs to, some one. Lies, envy, vice, impurity, hatred, greed, pride. What a company! How repulsive! Yet these are the companions we choose; and after we have played with them, entertained them, loved them, they turn around and testify against us. It is not the sins of which we are unaware that will condemn us. It is the sins we know. We do not need more light, but more life, more power.

13. Name the seven sins mentioned in this verse. Verse 13.

14. What is said of judgment and justice? What has happened to truth? What can equity not do? Verse 14.

NOTE.—"Courts of justice are corrupt. Rulers are actuated by desire for gain, and love of sensual pleasure. Intemperance has beclouded the faculties of many, so that Satan has almost complete control of them. Jurists are perverted, bribed, deluded. Drunkenness and revelry, passion, envy, dishonesty of every sort, are represented among those who administer the laws. 'Justice standeth afar off: for truth is fallen in the street, and equity can not enter.' "—"The Great Controversy," p. 586.

15. What becomes of truth? Who makes himself a prey? How does this affect the Lord? Verse 15.

16. Why did the Lord wonder? What did His arm bring? What sustained Him? Verse 16.

NOTE.—"No man." (See Jer. 5:1.)

"No intercessor," such as Moses and Aaron. Num. 16:47, 48.

Though God found "no man" worthy of the name, yet He did not fail, but brought salvation and righteousness.

17. What did the Lord put on as breastplate and helmet? What was His garment and cloak? Verse 17.

NOTE.—God is here spoken of as a warrior going forth to battle for His people. He is arming Himself with His own attributes,—righteousness, salvation, vengeance, and zeal.

18. **According to what will God recompense His enemies? Verse 18.**
NOTE.—"According to their deeds." This is just. Rev. 22:12. The judgment here mentioned is not that of the last day, but rather such judgment as God metes out in this life to individuals and nations who transgress. The captivity of the children of Israel and the fall of Nineveh and Babylon are of this kind. This becomes clear from a study of the following verse.

19. **What is the effect of God's judgments? What will God do when the enemy comes in like a flood? Verse 19.**
NOTE.—"So," because of this. The result of God's punishing is that men will fear the Lord. That, however, is not the case in the last judgment, for that punishment is final, and will not result in men's fearing the Lord. Hence we conclude that this is not the judgment of the last day.
Read "The Great Controversy," p. 600, first paragraph.

20. **To whom shall the Redeemer come? Verse 20.**
NOTE.—God shall come in "fury to His adversaries," verse 18, but as a Redeemer to all that turn from transgression.

21. **With whom is the covenant? What is said of God's Spirit and of His word? Verse 21.**
NOTE.—"Thee" refers to the Redeemer of verse 20. The seed is the spiritual seed. Isa. 53:10.
"My Spirit," "My words." The Spirit is in the word. John 6:63. And that word is not to depart from our mouths "from henceforth and forever."

LESSON 7
THE FINAL TRIUMPH OF THE RIGHTEOUS
February 16, 1929

LESSON SCRIPTURE: Isaiah 60.
MEMORY VERSE: Isa. 60:21.

INTRODUCTION

This chapter deals with the glorious finishing of the work, and with the new earth state. "This message will close with power and strength far exceeding the midnight cry."—"Early Writings," p. 278.

Here is brought to view the great ingathering of souls, and how God will move upon men to support the work. Let our faith grasp these promises, and they are ours.

THE LESSON

1. **What are God's people bidden to do? Why? Isa. 60:1.**
NOTE.—"The words of Christ through the gospel prophet, which are but reëchoed in the Sermon on the Mount, are for us in this last generation: 'Arise, shine; for thy light is come, and the glory of the Lord is risen upon thee.'"—"Thoughts from the Mount of Blessing," p. 70.

[20]

"The world to-day is in crying need of a revelation of Christ Jesus in the person of His saints."—"Testimonies to Ministers," p. 458.

2. **What shall cover the earth and the people? In contrast to this, what shall be the experience of God's people? Verse 2.**

NOTE.—It is a strange contrast we see in the world to-day. On the one hand there is a wonderful advance in all kinds of worldly learning. Men delve into the secrets of nature and bring forth marvelous things. At the same time there is a lamentable lack of true knowledge. The fear of the Lord is the beginning of wisdom, and this fear men do not have. Hence it is that the world has much power, but little light; much learning but little wisdom. The world, in spite of its boasted progress, lies in darkness. But God's children are privileged to arise and shine. Read "Christ's Object Lessons," p. 41 , paragraph 3; new edition, p. 424.

3. **Who shall come to the light? What prominent persons are mentioned? Verse 3.**

NOTE.—"To those who go out to meet the Bridegroom is this message given."—"Christ's Object Lessons," p. 420. There is no doubt that these verses found their fulfillment at the first coming of Christ, and they will be fulfilled again at His second coming. We shall yet see a large ingathering of souls, and, according to prophecy, some of these will come from among the great of earth.

4. **What will they see as they lift up their eyes? Who comes from far and near? Verse 4.**

5. **What will happen when they see this? Who will be converted, and who will come? Verse 5.**

NOTE.—"The forces of the Gentiles," or "the wealth of the nations," as the American Revised Version gives it. While we may not look forward to a golden age here on earth, but rather to opposition and persecution, yet we may believe that God will grant His people favor for a little while before the storm breaks, and that these verses will find an application and fulfillment.

"The great work of the gospel is not to close with less manifestation of the power of God than marked its opening. The prophecies which were fulfilled in the outpouring of the former rain at the opening of the gospel, are again to be fulfilled in the latter rain at its close."—"The Great Controversy," pp. 611, 612.

The 1844 movement and the Reformation were mighty movements, "but these are to be far exceeded by the mighty movement under the last warning of the third angel."—Id., p. 611.

Read "The Great Controversy," pp. 611, 612.

6. **From what places are they said to come? What will they bring? Verse 6.**

NOTE.—The Ishmaelites to whom Joseph was sold were Midianites. Gen. 37:25, 36. The Ephahs were one of the tribes of Midian. Gen. 25:4. Sheba was a country of Arabia. The conversion of such self-seeking and roving tribes would constitute a supreme exhibition of the mighty power of God.

"Gold and incense." Gold denotes wealth, and incense, worship.

7. What should come up with acceptance upon the altar? Verse 7.

NOTE.—"With acceptance." The thought is taken from the sacrificial offerings of the Jews. Some offerings were called acceptance offerings because the Lord accepted them as a recognition of consecration on the part of the offerer. (See Lev. 1:4.) Of that nature were the burnt offerings which denoted full and complete dedication to God. These were brought to the altar and completely consumed upon it, thus indicating that the Lord was well pleased. Lev. 1:1-9; see also Judges 13:19-23. "That he may be accepted before Jehovah" is the American Revised Version rendering of the latter part of Leviticus 1:3. Kedar and Nebaioth are Arab tribes.

8. What questions are now asked? Verse 8.

NOTE.—"A cloud." Those that will be gathered in under the preaching of the gospel are here spoken of as being so many that they look like a cloud.

"Doves to their windows." As doves wend their way homeward to their accustomed window, so weary souls are turning to their God.

9. What are the isles said to do? What do the ships of Tarshish bring? For whom are their gifts? Verse 9.

NOTE.—"Tarshish," in Spain, was considered very remote in the days of Isaiah. It was in the west end of the Mediterranean Sea, far removed from Judea. Even from these outlying places should souls come, bringing gifts with them.

10. Who will build up the walls? Who shall be ministers? What has God done in wrath? What in favor? Verse 10.

11. What is said of the gates? What will be brought? Verse 11.

NOTE.—"These prophecies of a great spiritual awakening in a time of gross darkness, are to-day meeting fulfillment in the advancing lines of mission stations that are reaching out into the benighted regions of earth. The groups of missionaries in heathen lands have been likened by the prophet to ensigns set up for the guidance of those who are looking for the light of truth."—"Prophets and Kings," pp. 375, 376.

12. What will be the experience of nations that will not serve God's people? Verse 12.

NOTE.—Barnes gives the following explanation of this verse: "The idea is, that no nation can flourish that does not obey the law of God, or where the worship of the true God is not maintained. History is full of affecting illustrations of this. The ancient republics and kingdoms fell because they had not the true religion. The kingdoms of Babylon, Assyria, Macedonia, and Egypt; the Roman Empire, and all the ancient monarchies and republics, soon fell to ruin because they had not the salutary restraints of the true religion, and lacked the protection of the true God. France cast off the government of God in the Revolution, and was drenched in blood. It is a maxim of universal truth, that the nation which does not admit the influence of the laws and the government of God must be destroyed."

13. How is the glorious state of the church further emphasized? Verse 13.

14. What will they do who have afflicted and despised God's people? By what names will they be called? Verse 14.

NOTE.—This verse contains a promise like that in Revelation 3:9.

15. How have God's people been considered? What will God make them? Verse 15.

16. What symbol is here used to show how God provides for His own? What shall the church know? Verse 16.

NOTE.—As a child receives nourishment from its mother, so the church is here pictured as being supported by the Gentiles, even by kings. All wealth belongs to the Lord, and He will see to it that the abundance of the Gentiles shall be used for the furtherance of the gospel.

17. What change will be brought about? What will the officer and exacter be? Verse 17.

NOTE.—The thought here is that God will ennoble and elevate that which is of less worth. Souls whose value in their unsaved state may be likened to wood, iron, and brass, will God increase in value to brass, silver, and gold respectively. How often we see that! God will take an uncouth, backward boy and change him into an efficient soul saver or competent administrator.

"Officers peace." This phrase may be rendered: "I will appoint peace as thy government and righteousness as thy ruler." This and the following verses speak of the ideal condition of the church.

18. What will no more be heard in the land? What will the walls and the gates be called? Verse 18.

19. What is said of the sun and moon? Who shall be our light and glory? Verse 19; Rev. 21:23; 22:5.

20. What will the sun and the moon not do? What will the Lord be? What shall be ended? Isa. 60:20.

NOTE.—"In the city of God 'there shall be no night.' . . . The light of the sun will be superseded by a radiance which is not painfully dazzling, yet which immeasurably surpasses the brightness of our noontide. The glory of God and the Lamb floods the holy city with unfading light. The redeemed walk in the sunless glory of perpetual day." —"The Great Controversy," p. 676.

Read "The Ministry of Healing," pp. 504, 506.

21. What shall "a little one" become? What will the Lord do in His time? Verse 22.

NOTE.—Compare Luke 12:32 with Revelation 7:9 to see how the "little flock" becomes a "great multitude." In His own good time the Lord will hasten it. Rom. 9:28.

"The words of the living God are the highest of all education."— "Testimonies," Vol. 8, p. 308.

LESSON 8

BUILDERS OF THE OLD WASTE PLACES

February 23, 1929

LESSON SCRIPTURE: Isaiah 61.
MEMORY VERSE: Isa. 61:1.

INTRODUCTION

The first sermon Christ preached in His home town had for its text Isaiah 61:1. Never should it be forgotten that our mission is the same as Christ's. We are sent in His stead. John 17:18. 2 Cor. 5:20.

Study with care the work outlined for Christ in the first three verses. That work is our work. It is a work of healing, of comfort, of good cheer. It will take us to the broken-hearted, the captives, the mourners. It will cause us to "build the old wastes." The work will be so evidently blessed of the Lord that men will recognize it, the riches of the Gentiles shall come, and the message itself shall develop a people clad in the garments of Christ's righteousness.

THE LESSON

1. On what occasion did Jesus quote Isaiah 61:1 and part of verse 2? To whom did He apply these words? Luke 4:16-20.

NOTE.—"Jesus stood before the people as a living expositor of the prophecies concerning Himself. Explaining the words He had read, He spoke of the Messiah as a reliever of the oppressed, a liberator of captives, a healer of the afflicted, restoring sight to the blind, and revealing to the world the light of truth. His impressive manner and the wonderful import of His words thrilled the hearers with a power they had never felt before."—"The Desire of Ages," p. 237.

2. What did Christ say was upon Him? For what purpose was He anointed? Isa. 61:1, first part.

NOTE.—Jesus was anointed with the Holy Spirit and power. Acts 10:38. In the Old Testament the priests were anointed, and also the kings. Ex. 29:5-7; 1 Sam. 9:15, 16. It was a sign of appointment to high office, and denoted consecration and dedication to it.

"Anointed Me to preach." There is no higher office than that of the gospel minister. It was to this Jesus was anointed, and the qualifications for the anointing are given in Psalm 45:7 and Hebrews 1:9. Christ loved righteousness and hated iniquity, therefore, God anointed Him.

3. Whom should Christ bind up? To whom should liberty be proclaimed? For whom shall the prison be opened? Isa. 61:1, last part.

NOTE.—"The broken-hearted." As the Samaritans bound up the wounds of the man that fell among thieves (Luke 10:34), so Christ was to bind up the broken-hearted, to comfort, to heal the sorrowing and distressed. In this work we are to follow Him.

"Proclaim liberty." The only true liberty is freedom from sin. John 8:32, 36; Rom. 6:18.

[24]

"Them that are bound." Men are bound by sin and unbelief, by the customs and traditions of men. The worst prison is that which we make for ourselves, the worst blindness is willful blindness. But Christ came to open the prison, to give sight to the blind. Luke 4:18.

4. What year and day did Christ come to proclaim? Who shall be comforted? Isa. 61:2.

NOTE.—"Acceptable year." "The year of Jehovah's favor." American Revised Version. It may be well to contrast the year of Jehovah's favor with the day of vengeance. Even as the year is much longer than the day, so God's mercy is much more abundant than His wrath.

"When Jesus in the synagogue read from the prophecy, He stopped short of the final specification concerning the Messiah's work. Having read the words, 'To proclaim the acceptable year of the Lord,' He omitted the phrase, 'and the day of vengeance of our God.' This was just as much truth as was the first of the prophecy, and by His silence Jesus did not deny the truth. But this last expression was that upon which His hearers delighted to dwell, and which they were desirous of fulfilling. They denounced judgments against the heathen, not discerning that their own guilt was even greater than that of others. They themselves were in deepest need of the mercy they were so ready to deny to the heathen."—"The Desire of Ages," p. 240.

5. What three things will God exchange for them that mourn in Zion? Verse 3, first part.

NOTE.—This is a message of courage for those who are downcast and disheartened, for those who "mourn in Zion." This mourning is the same as the sighing mentioned in Ezekiel 9:4. It is a mourning for sin, not necessarily the sins of others, but their own. Read "The Desire of Ages," p. 300.

6. What will they be called? Why? Verse 3, last part.

NOTE.—"Trees of righteousness," literally "oaks" or "terebinths." "They shall be sturdy oaks of goodness," Moffatt translates it. The same figure is used in Jeremiah 17:8.

"That He might be glorified." God is to be glorified in His saints. He wants to reveal His character in us. His meekness, His humility, His self-control and purity should be our standard of conduct.

7. What shall God's people do? What shall they repair? How long have they been desolate? Verse 4.

NOTE.—Read this verse in connection with Isaiah 58:12, and the note under Question 12, Lesson 5.

8. What shall strangers and aliens do? Verse 5.

NOTE.—This work will become so all-important to many that they will let the Gentiles feed their flocks, while they go to feed the spiritually hungry world.

9. What will God's people be named? What will they be called? What will they eat? In whose glory will they boast? Verse 6.

NOTE.—"Priests." God's original intention was that His people should be priests. Ex. 19:6. Because of sin, Israel lost that privilege, and it was given to one of the tribes only. Ex. 28:1. In the New Testament this privilege is restored. 1 Peter 2:9.

"Ministers." A minister is a servant. As Christ our Lord we are to be among men as "he that serveth." Luke 22:27.

"Riches of the Gentiles." Read note under Question 16, Lesson 7.

"In their glory." "To their glory shall ye succeed," American Revised Version, margin. The Gentiles glory in their riches. But the time shall come when God's people shall succeed them and inherit even the riches of the Gentiles.

10. **For what shall they have double? In what will they rejoice? What shall come to them? Verse 7.**

NOTE.—The sense of this verse is that even as God's people have suffered, so shall a double portion of joy be theirs. For an application of this principle to the ungodly, see Revelation 18:6.

11. **What does the Lord love? What does He hate? What will God direct? What is said of the covenant? Verse 8.**

NOTE.—"Love judgment," "hate robbery." The Septuagint reads, "Love righteousness, and hate robberies of injustice."

"Their work." This is a definite promise of the Lord's direction. The American Revised Version reads: "I will give them their recompense in truth," that is, wherein they have been robbed I will see to it that they are recompensed justly.

12. **Where shall their seed be known? What shall all acknowledge? Verse 9.**

13. **In whom does the prophet say he will rejoice and be joyful? What reasons are given for this rejoicing? Verse 10.**

NOTE.—"Garments of salvation," "robe of righteousness." The covenant which God makes with His people (verse 8) includes the promise of forgiveness of sins and their covering with the garment of salvation. As the father, in the parable of the prodigal son, threw his robe over his son, so God throws His robe of righteousness over repentant sinners. This is what is called imputed righteousness.

"Whatever may have been your past experience, however discouraging your present circumstances, if you will come to Jesus just as you are, weak, helpless, and despairing, our compassionate Saviour will meet you a great way off, and will throw about you His arms of love and His robe of righteousness. He presents us to the Father clothed in the white raiment of His own character. He pleads before God in our behalf, saying: I have taken the sinner's place. Look not upon this wayward child, but look on Me. Does Satan plead loudly against our souls, accusing of sin, and claiming us as his prey, the blood of Christ pleads with greater power."—"Thoughts from the Mount of Blessing," p. 21.

"Bridegroom," "bride." (See Rev. 19:7, 8.)

14. **What comparison does the Lord here make between the garden which "causeth the things that are sown in it to spring forth" and His righteousness? Verse 11.**

NOTE.—Read "The Acts of the Apostles," p. 560.

LESSON 9

THE HOLY PEOPLE; THE LORD'S REDEEMED
March 2, 1929

LESSON SCRIPTURE: Isaiah 62.
MEMORY VERSE: Isa. 62:6.

INTRODUCTION

This chapter brings to view the high position to which God calls His people in Christ Jesus. Before the end comes, God will have a holy people, whose righteousness will be evident to all men, Gentiles and kings alike. God Himself will find joy in them. They will be His crown of glory and royal diadem. They will be a praying people, faithful watchmen on the walls of Zion.

We shall miss the lesson of this chapter if we apply it only to other times and peoples. We shall also miss it if we apply the lesson to a people rather than to ourselves individually. God will not merely have a holy people, He wants me to be holy. Personal sanctification is the aim of the truth.

THE LESSON

1. **For whose sake does God say He will not rest or hold His peace? How will righteousness and salvation go forth? Isa. 62:1.**

NOTE.—Zion and Jerusalem stand for God's people.

"Righteousness," "salvation." God is here revealed as having purposed to present His people before the world in the garment of righteousness and salvation, and that He will not rest until it is accomplished. It is not that God will reveal **Himself** directly, but that He will reveal His people to the world.

2. **What will the Gentiles and kings see? By what will God's people be called? Who decides upon this new name? Verse 2.**

NOTE.—"A new name." After Jacob had wrestled all night with the Angel, his old name no longer fitted him. He had passed through a new experience, and he was a changed man. So his name was changed because he was changed. Gen. 32:28. In like manner here. God's people will have an entirely new experience, and their new name will indicate that change. Rev. 2:17.

3. **What two things are God's people said to be in the hand of the Lord? Verse 3.**

NOTE.—"Crown of glory." "Royal diadem." As a person might hold an object of beauty in his hand for others to admire, so the Lord is here shown exhibiting His people to the world. They are to Him a crown of glory and a royal diadem.

These verses have a present application, and they will see their fulfillment in this generation; therefore, a great work lies before us. It concerns first and chiefly our own relation to God. If we are to be exhibited to the world as the handiwork of God, we should be greatly concerned about our progress in holiness.

Read "Testimonies," Vol. 2, p. 355.

[27]

4. What will God's people no more be termed? What will the land not be called? What names will be given to the people and the land? Why? What is said of the land? Verse 4.

NOTE.—"Hephzi-bah" means "delight," and "Beulah" means "married." (See margin.) This figure recalls Isaiah 54:1, where it denotes the fruitfulness, the increase that shall come in souls saved.

5. What illustration is here used? How will God rejoice? Verse 5.

NOTE.—Two figures are here used. First, God's people, under a symbol of sons, are married to the land, the virgin; second, God, as the bridegroom, is married to the bride, His people.

In Revelation the New Jerusalem in which are God's people is spoken of as coming down from heaven as the bride, and Christ is the bridegroom. Rev. 21:9, 10. So in like manner the figure is here used.

6. Whom has God set upon the walls? What shall they never do? Verse 6, first part.

NOTE.—"The watchmen anciently placed upon the walls of Jerusalem and other cities, occupied a most responsible position. Upon their faithfulness depended the safety of all within those cities. When danger was apprehended, they were not to keep silent day or night. Every few moments they were required to call to one another, to see if all were awake, and no harm had come to any. Sentinels were stationed upon some eminence overlooking the important posts to be guarded, and the cry of warning or of good cheer was sounded from them. This was borne from one to another, each repeating the words, till it went the entire rounds of the city.

"These watchmen represent the ministry, upon whose fidelity depends the salvation of souls. The stewards of the mysteries of God should stand as watchmen upon the walls of Zion; and if they see the sword coming, they should sound the note of warning. If they are sleepy sentinels, and their spiritual senses are so benumbed that they see and realize no danger, and the people perish, God will require their blood at the watchmen's hands."—"Testimonies," Vol. 4, pp. 402, 403.

• 7. What are those not to do who make mention of the Lord? Verse 6, last part.

NOTE.—"The Lord's remembrancers," margin. A strange expression, yet an appropriate one. In these last days when the whole world is prone to forget His law and His memorial, "the Lord's remembrancers" are admonished not to keep silence.

8. What are they told not to give the Lord? Until what time? Verse 7.

NOTE.—"Give Him no rest." This is said as an encouragement to prayer, to "pray without ceasing." 1 Thess. 5:17.

"Let all who are afflicted or unjustly used, cry to God. Turn away from those whose hearts are as steel, and make your requests known to your Maker. Never is one repulsed who comes to Him with a contrite heart. Not one sincere prayer is lost. Amid the anthems of the celestial choir, God hears the cries of the weakest human being. We pour out our heart's desire in our closets, we breathe a prayer as we walk by

[28]

the way, and our words reach the throne of the Monarch of the universe. They may be inaudible to any human ear, but they can not die away into silence, nor can they be lost through the activities of business that are going on. Nothing can drown the soul's desire. It rises above the din of the street, above the confusion of the multitude, to the heavenly courts. It is God to whom we are speaking, and our prayer is heard."—"Christ's Object Lessons," p. 174.

A similar lesson is taught by the parable of the importunate friend. Luke 11:5-8.

9. By what has the Lord sworn? What has He sworn? Verse 8.

10. What shall they do who have gathered the corn and the wine and have brought it together? Verse 9.

11. What command is given? For whom is the way to be prepared? What is to be done to the highway and the stones? What is to be lifted up? Verse 10.

NOTE.—"Go through the gates." Spread out. Proclaim the message beyond your own gates. "Prepare ye the way." Do everything in your power to help those in need. Remove every hindrance. "Lift up a standard." "The commandments of God, and the faith of Jesus" is such a standard. Rev. 14:12.

12. What message has God proclaimed to those living in the end of the world? What is said of His reward and work? Verse 11.

NOTE.—"Thy salvation cometh." This is the message of the second advent, and it is to be sounded to the ends of the earth. It will be accompanied with a judgment message, for "His reward is with Him." Rev. 22:12.

"His work," recompense, margin. Christ comes both with a reward and a recompense.

13. By what four names will the people be called? Verse 12.

LESSON 10
AFFLICTED FOR HIS PEOPLE'S SAKE
March 9, 1929

LESSON SCRIPTURE: Isaiah 63.
MEMORY VERSE: Isa. 63:9.

INTRODUCTION

Isaiah 63:1-6 presents a dreadful description of God's wrath; but these verses also hold a peculiar beauty and fascination. A view is given of God's going forth in fury to trample the people in His wrath. Their blood is sprinkled upon His garments, which are crimson, as are the garments of one who treads the winefat. In the midst of this description is the statement of Christ's treading the wine press alone. This may at first seem irrelevant and contradictory to the rest of the section. How can one be reconciled with the other? May it not be that as God is considering the effect of sin, the suffering and misery that it has caused both on earth and in heaven, culminating in the terrible struggle of the Son of God with powers of darkness in Gethsemane and Golgotha, forsaken and alone—that this thought makes it possible for Him to execute the final punishment for sin which is a strange work for God to do? Isa. 28:21.

The next section, verses 7-14, tells of God's goodness and mercy, of His participation in Israel's afflictions, and also of Israel's rebellion against God and His Holy Spirit.

Verses 15-19 are a prayer, some passages of which, in particular verse 15, are of surpassing beauty.

THE LESSON

1. After the words of comfort in the last of the preceding chapter, what question is asked? What is said of the garment? How does He travel? What answer is given? What is further said of His apparel? Isa. 63:1, 2.

NOTE.—"Edom" means red, and was the name given to Esau. Gen. 25:30. Bozrah was a city of Edom. The Edomites were the enemies of Israel. They tried to hinder Israel from entering the Promised Land. Num. 20:14-21. They were always ready to join the opposers of God's people. Eze. 25:12. They seemed to have the same spirit as Esau when he sought to slay his brother. Gen. 27:41.

Esau and Jacob were not only brothers, but twin brothers. This relationship should have caused them to draw close together; but, instead of this, Edom hated Jacob with a "perpetual hatred." Eze. 35:5. This scripture applies to all who partake of the spirit of Esau. These may be very closely related to Israel, but they are not of Israel. They may be twin brothers, but this only makes their sin more heinous. And now judgment is poured out upon the persecutors of Israel. God is shown in this verse as returning from Edom, having executed vengeance.

2. What does Christ say He has trodden? How does He speak of the day of vengeance? Verses 3, 4.

NOTE.—In the Garden of Gethsemane Christ was longing for human sympathy and help. But no help was near. The disciples were sleeping. Christ was alone with the powers of darkness. Three times the Master prayed, and three times His humanity shrank from the last crowning sacrifice. Then He made the decision and accepted the baptism of blood. "Having made the decision, He fell dying to the ground from which He had partially risen. Where now were His disciples, to place their hands tenderly beneath the head of their fainting Master, and bathe that brow, marred indeed more than the sons of men? The Saviour trod the wine press alone, and of the people there was none with Him."—"The Desire of Ages," p. 693.

When God at last executes vengeance on those that have disobeyed Him and persecuted the saints, He knows just what He is doing. He has trod the wine press Himself. He knows what it is to suffer. There was no one near to comfort Him. And the punishment meted out to the transgressors, great though it be, does not begin to compare with the agony He Himself passed through.

[30]

3. Why did God wonder? What brought salvation? How does God again speak of the punishment of evildoers? Verses 5, 6.

4. With what words does the prophet now turn from the contemplation of punishment? Verse 7.

NOTE.—The wrath of God has been dwelt on in the preceding section, and in contrast with this the prophet now calls attention to God's loving-kindness, goodness, and mercy. It would be well if we more often would think of God's goodness and how much we have to be thankful for. "Nothing tends more to promote health of body and of soul than does a spirit of gratitude and praise. It is a positive duty to resist melancholy, discontented thoughts and feelings,—as much a duty as it is to pray. If we are heaven bound, how can we go as a band of mourners, groaning and complaining all along the way to our Father's house?"—"The Ministry of Healing," p. 251.

5. How does God express His confidence in His children? What did He become? Verse 8.

NOTE.—"My people." God identifies Himself with His people as in the beginning. Ex. 3:7. (See also Hosea 11:1.)

"Children that will not lie," that can be depended on. The meaning is, that surely they will be faithful and not fall away. This expresses God's confidence in His people. Even though God knew from the beginning that some would fail, He deals with His children on the basis of confidence.

6. When Israel was afflicted, who also was afflicted? Who saved them? Because of what did He redeem them? What did God do all the days of old? Verse 9.

NOTE.—"Few give thought to the suffering that sin has caused our Creator. All heaven suffered in Christ's agony; but that suffering did not begin or end with His manifestation in humanity. The cross is a revelation to our dull senses of the pain that, from its very inception, sin has brought to the heart of God. Every departure from the right, every deed of cruelty, every failure of humanity to reach His ideal, brings grief to Him. When there came upon Israel the calamities that were the sure result of separation from God,—subjugation by their enemies, cruelty, and death,—it is said that 'His soul was grieved for the misery of Israel.' 'In all their affliction He was afflicted; . . . and He bare them, and carried them all the days of old.' "—"Education." p. 263.

7. What did Israel do? Whom did they vex? How did God then turn, and what did He do? Verse 10.

NOTE.—"They rebelled." In the worship of the golden calf, Exodus 32; at Meribah, Numbers 20; at Shittim, Numbers 25; in Samuel's time, 1 Sam. 8:5, 19, 20.

"Their enemy." (See Lam. 2:3-5; Jer. 30:14.)

8. What did the people then remember? What did they say? What question is asked concerning the Holy Spirit? Verse 11.

NOTE.—When the Lord had left Israel because of their sin, they remembered how God of old had been merciful to Israel in spite of their shortcomings, and asked: Where is God that brought His people through the Red Sea? Where is He that gave them His Holy Spirit? Jeremiah complains that the people do not remember. Jer. 2:6.

"Shepherd." Margin, "shepherds," probably Moses and Aaron, as in Psalm 77:20.

9. **How did God lead the people? What was divided? How did that affect God's name? Verse 12.**

NOTE.—It was one of the purposes of the miracles and wonders wrought in Egypt for the deliverance of Israel that God's name might be declared throughout the earth.

10. **By what illustration does God show how He leads the people? Verse 13.**

11. **Who caused Israel to rest? What is repeated concerning God's name? Verse 14.**

12. **How does the prophet, speaking for Israel, word his prayer for God's attention and help? Verse 15.**

NOTE.—This verse contains one of the most beautiful prayers in all Scripture. The prophet remembers what God has done in former days, how He led Israel and saved them. Can not God do the same now? God had then helped Israel for His name's sake. His name's honor is at stake now as much as then.

13. **By what endearing name is God called? What is said of Abraham and Israel? What two names for God are now used? Verse 16.**

NOTE.—"Doubtless," rather, "for," as in American Revised Version. "Abraham," "Israel." The Jews were proud of being the children of Abraham. Some of them trusted in that relationship even more than they did in God. John 8:39. In this verse the prophet expresses his supreme confidence in the Lord.

14. **With what does the prophet now charge God? What prayer does he offer? Verse 17.**

15. **By what term are God's people here described? How long had they been in possession of the Promised Land? What had happened to the sanctuary? Verse 18.**

NOTE.—"A little while." This was probably written about the year 700 B. C., when Israel had been in the land more than five hundred years. Yet it should be noted that they had not had possession of it that long. From the very beginning, the Canaanitish tribes had disputed Israel's advance, and for a long time God's people held but a small part of the country. Peaceful possession had hardly been theirs at any time. Twenty years before this was written, ten of the tribes had been carried into captivity. In the light of God's promise of an inheritance they had possessed the land but a little while.

16. **Into what strange condition had Israel fallen? Verse 19, A. R. V.**

NOTE.—The word "Thine" is supplied. The American Revised Version reads, "We are become as they over whom Thou never barest rule, as they that were not called by Thy name."

[32]

LESSON 11

A PRAYER FOR THE REVEALING OF GOD'S POWER

March 16, 1929

LESSON SCRIPTURE: Isaiah 64.
MEMORY VERSE: Isa. 64:4.

INTRODUCTION

This chapter deals with events that took place about 698 B. C. In 721 B. C., the ten tribes of Israel had been taken into captivity, and colonists had been brought over from Babylon to take the place of the Israelites who had been deported. That was the end of the northern kingdom. Judah had escaped at that time, but in 701 B. C. Sennacherib, king of Assyria, came westward on a tour of conquest, and Judah did not escape. Hezekiah stripped the gold from the doors of the temple and from the pillars to satisfy the Assyrian king. But he was not satisfied. He overran Judah, captured many towns, and carried more than 200,000 of Judah's population into captivity. It was in a crisis such as this that the prayer which constitutes this lesson was made. And God heard the prayers of His people, and saved them.

The first part of the prayer expresses the wish that God would come down and show His power in some mighty way. If He would only reveal Himself as at Mount Sinai, surely the people would tremble. We sometimes hear the same thought expressed now, that if God would only speak from heaven and proclaim that the seventh day is the Sabbath, all would be convinced and keep it. A paraphrase of Christ's words would fit here: "They have Moses and the prophets; let them hear them." "If they hear not Moses and the prophets, neither will they be persuaded, though God should speak from heaven." Luke 16:29, 31.

THE LESSON

1. **What does the prophet now pray that God would do? Isa. 64:1.**

NOTE.—This is a continuation of the prayer begun in the fifteenth verse of the last chapter.

"Rend the heavens." God had hid Himself from Israel. They could not pierce through to His dwelling place. Now they ask God to rend the heavens, to come down and show Himself. The expression "rend the heavens" is a very strong one, showing the intense desire of Israel to have God's presence with them again.

"The mountains." When God spoke the Ten Commandments, "the mountains melted from before the Lord." Judges 5:5. Israel is now asking for a like manifestation.

2. **What illustration is used? What would this make known? What effect would God's presence have on the nations? Verse 2.**

NOTE.—When Micah saw the Lord come "forth out of His place," the mountains melted and the valleys became as wax. Micah 1:3, 4.

[33]

The mountains represent that which is most solid here on earth. When they melt and flow down, well might men tremble at His presence.

"Make Thy name known." Israel wanted a demonstration of God's power. It looked to them as though God had forsaken His people. O that God in this critical hour would "rend the heavens"! they prayed.

"The depths of the earth are the Lord's arsenal, whence were drawn weapons to be employed in the destruction of the old world. Waters gushing from the earth united with the waters from heaven to accomplish the work of desolation. Since the Flood, fire as well as water has been God's agent to destroy very wicked cities. These judgments are sent, that those who lightly regard God's law and trample upon His authority, may be led to tremble before His power, and to confess His just sovereignty. As men have beheld burning mountains pouring forth fire and flames, and torrents of melted ore, drying up rivers, overwhelming populous cities, and everywhere spreading ruin and desolation, the stoutest heart has been filled with terror, and infidels and blasphemers have been constrained to acknowledge the infinite power of God."—"Patriarchs and Prophets," p. 109.

3. What is God said to have done? Verse 3.

NOTE.—"Terrible things." This is one of the phrases used in the Bible to describe the mighty and wonderful acts of God in connection with the Exodus. Deut. 10:21; 2 Sam. 7:23; Ps. 106:22.

4. What has not been seen or perceived from the beginning of the world? Verse 4.

NOTE.—"The Ministry of Healing," page 425, quotes the American Revised Version which reads: "Neither hath the eye seen a God besides Thee, who worketh for him that waiteth for Him." God is the only God who works for those who wait for Him. All other gods must be carried about.

5. Whom does God meet? Why is God wroth? Verse 5.

NOTE.—The picture brings to mind the Father with outstretched arms meeting and welcoming the returning son. This meeting refers not only to the world to come, wonderful as that will be. Right here and now God will meet every honest soul, and conduct him through the trials and pitfalls of life to everlasting habitations.

"We have sinned." This confession is at the basis of all true Christian progress.

6. What are we all said to be? What is our righteousness? What is the experience of all? What have our iniquities done? Verse 6.

NOTE.—"An unclean thing." (See Isa. 1:6.)

"Filthy rags." Not merely rags, but filthy rags. Our upright conduct, our good deeds done to be seen of men, our respectability, our correct outward deportment, our culture, refinement, education, our churchgoing and worship—all these, which in themselves are good and not to be condemned—merely constitute our own righteousness unless they are grounded in a deep sense of our unworthiness. Without Christ these seeming virtues are but as filthy rags.

"Fade as a leaf." This is the effect of sin. As the wind blows away the dead leaves, so shall those be that do iniquity.

7. What complaint does the prophet now bring? What has God done? Why? Verse 7.

NOTE.—"None that calleth upon Thy name, that stirreth up himself." This statement we may well apply to this time as well as to the time of Isaiah. It seems that every time God wants something done, it is necessary to send some one to stir up the people. Men are sleeping on the brink of eternity, and are not stirred by the events taking place right before them. And even God's people do not seem to be stirred as they should be.

"Hast consumed us." An expression which indicates not what had happened, but what would happen if they continued in sin.

8. What is God to His people? What are we? What is God? Whose work are we? Verse 8. (See also Isa. 29:16.)

9. What do the people ask the Lord not to remember? Verse 9; 43:25.

10. What have their holy cities and Jerusalem become? Isa. 64:10.

11. What is said of their holy and beautiful house, the temple? Verse 11.

12. What questions are now asked? Verse 12.

NOTE.—Will the Lord hold back any longer? The question demands the answer that the Lord will not delay any longer, that He will hear and help His people.

LESSON 12

A PEOPLE PREPARED FOR A NEW HEAVEN AND A NEW EARTH

March 23, 1929

LESSON SCRIPTURE: Isaiah 65.
MEMORY VERSE: Isa. 65:17, 18.

INTRODUCTION

Israel provoked God to anger by their "holier than thou" attitude. It was this same tendency that Christ so abhorred in the Pharisee. This chapter brings to view the rejection of the Jews and the acceptance of the Gentiles. Yet God will not reject all Israel. There is still a "seed in Jacob," that will be saved. For all who are eventually saved, God will create new heavens and a new earth. There all will be happiness and joy, no weeping or crying. Even the animal creation shall be at peace.

THE LESSON

1. **Of whom has God been sought and found? What did He say to them? Isa. 65:1.**

NOTE.—Paul, in Romans 10:20, applies this verse to the calling of the Gentiles.

"Behold Me." To behold God is to see His character, His love. To be convinced of God's goodness, all anyone needs is to behold Him.

2. **To whom does Paul apply Isaiah 65:2? Romans 10:21.**

NOTE.—Paul applies Isaiah 65:1 to the Gentiles, and verse 2 to the Jews.

3. **What does God say Israel had done? Isa. 65:3.**

4. **Where do some remain and lodge? What do they eat, and have in their vessels? Verse 4.**

NOTE.—"Among the graves," the rock tombs of Palestine.

"Monuments," "secret places," American Revised Version. Probably for purposes of divination.

"Swine's flesh," forbidden by God. Deut. 14:8.

5. **How did these Jews look upon themselves? How did God consider them? Verse 5.**

6. **What is written before God? What will God measure into their bosom? Verses 6, 7.**

7. **What illustration is used by the Lord to show that a seed of Jacob shall be saved? Verses 8-10.**

NOTE.—Israel may sin and do wickedly, but God will "not destroy them all." There is still a "seed" left; they shall inherit "My mountains," for they "have sought Me."

The Valley of Achor is a place for "herds to lie down in, for My people that have sought Me." (See Joshua 7:22-26.) The Valley of Achor means "the valley of troubling;" but later, the Lord, in His goodness toward Israel, says He will give us the Valley of Achor for a door of hope. Hosea 2:15. He lifts us out of our troubles, and this text to Israel makes it a place of peace and restfulness.

8. **What will happen to those that forget the "holy mountain," that is, forget God? Verses 11-15.**

NOTE.—Prepare a table for Gad and Meni. (See verse 11, margin.) These were Syrian gods. The Jews forgot the holy mountain, Jerusalem with its worship, and turned to strange gods. Therefore, God would punish them, "number you to the sword." The following verses describe the punishment. They shall hunger and thirst, they shall be ashamed and cry for sorrow of heart, and their very name shall be a curse.

9. **How shall a man bless himself? How shall he swear? What will be forgotten? What will God create? Verses 16, 17.**

10. **In what are we told to rejoice? What shall not be heard any more? Verses 18, 19.**

11. What shall no more be? When shall the child and the sinner die? Verse 20.

12. What will those do who build houses? Who will eat the fruit of the vineyards? Verse 21.

NOTE.—"In the earth made new, the redeemed will engage in the occupations and pleasures that brought happiness to Adam and Eve in the beginning. The Eden life will be lived, the life in garden and field."—"Prophets and Kings," p. 730.

13. What will not happen to those who build or plant? What will their days be like? What will they long enjoy? Verse 22.

NOTE.—"Days of a tree." The tree is the longest-lived living thing known. Hence the prophet uses that to illustrate long life.

"There every power will be developed, every capability increased. The grandest enterprises will be carried forward, the loftiest aspirations will be reached, the highest ambitions realized. And still there will appear new heights to surmount, new wonders to admire, new truths to comprehend, fresh objects of study to call forth the powers of body and mind and soul."—Id., p. 731.

14. What are the saved called? Who is with them? Verse 23.

15. How quickly will God answer? Verse 24.

16. What will be the conditions in the new earth? Verse 25.

NOTE.—"To us who are standing on the very verge of their fulfillment, of what deep moment, what living interest, are these delineations of the things to come,—events for which, since our first parents turned their steps from Eden, God's children have watched and waited, longed and prayed!

"Fellow pilgrim, we are still amid the shadows and turmoil of earthly activities; but soon our Saviour is to appear to bring deliverance and rest. Let us by faith behold the blessed hereafter, as pictured by the hand of God. He who died for the sins of the world, is opening wide the gates of Paradise to all who believe on Him. Soon the battle will have been fought, the victory won. Soon we shall see Him in whom our hopes of eternal life are centered. And in His presence the trials and sufferings of this life will seem as nothingness. The former things 'shall not be remembered, nor come into mind.'"—Id., pp. 731, 732.

THIRTEENTH SABBATH OFFERING—MARCH 30, 1929
Catholic Europe

LESSON 13

THE INGATHERING FROM THE GENTILES; WORSHIP IN THE NEW EARTH

March 30, 1929

LESSON SCRIPTURE: Isaiah 66.
MEMORY VERSE: Isa. 66:22.

INTRODUCTION

God is more interested in the spirit of the giver than in the value of the gift. The greatest offering may be an abomination if not accompanied by a contrite heart.

God will do a wonderful work in a short time. When God's people receive the latter rain, it is for service. Thousands will accept the truth in a day. It will look as though the work was done suddenly. Yet a long preparation went before. The seed has been sown and watered. Now it will suddenly blossom forth and bear fruit. The work will not have been done in vain. It may now seem as though very little fruit has come from a large sowing. But God who has brought "to the birth" will also "cause to bring forth." God's sign will be proclaimed by the remnant in the whole earth, and men from all nations will be brought as an offering to the Lord, many of whom will hold responsible positions.

Then will come the new earth. The righteous will worship the Lord, and the wicked be destroyed.

THE LESSON

1. Where are God's throne and His footstool? What questions are asked? Isa. 66:1.

NOTE.—"What manner of house will ye build unto Me? and what place shall be My rest?" American Revised Version. The contrast between the first part of the verse and the last is the same as in 1 Kings 8:27 and 2 Chronicles 2:6.

2. Who has made all things? To whom will God look? Verse 2.

3. By what four statements does God show that an offering brought to Him without a contrite spirit is not acceptable? What have they chosen, and in what do they delight? Verse 3.

NOTE.—The meaning seems to be, "He that offers an ox or any other sacrifice to Me, but does not have a contrite heart, is as little pleasing to Me as a murderer." (See Isa. 1:11.)

4. What will God choose? Why does He do this? Verse 4.

NOTE.—The time will come when God shall send strong delusions. 2 Thess. 2:11. These have chosen their own way (verse 3), and now God will choose their delusions.

5. What shall be said to those who tremble at His word? How will the Lord appear? Verse 5.

NOTE.—This word was very precious to the brethren who passed through the experience of 1844. They had been both hated and cast out. But the precious promise was theirs that the Lord would appear to their joy. (See "The Great Controversy," p. 372.)

[38]

6. How does the prophet express his astonishment? What questions does he ask? What took place as soon as Zion travailed? Verse 8.

Note.—Verses 6 and 7 form the introduction to the announcement given in verse 8. The work of the Lord has gone forward so rapidly that the prophet in astonishment asks if a nation can be born in one day? This, without doubt, refers to this time, after the events to which verse 5 has reference. God's people have been endued with power from on high, thousands are converted in a day, and it looks as though a whole nation were born in a day. This takes place "as soon as Zion travailed," that is, as soon as God's people really become deeply in earnest.

7. Who is to rejoice with Jerusalem? Verse 10.

8. What will God extend to His church? Verse 12.

9. How will Jerusalem be comforted? When His people see this, what will they do? What will come to God's enemies? Verses 13, 14.

10. How will the Lord come? What is said of His anger and rebuke? With what will the Lord plead? What is said of the slain? Verses 15, 16.

Note.—The slain mentioned in this text are the slain in the great battle of Armageddon, explained in Jeremiah 25:27-33.

11. Who will be consumed together? What does God know? Verses 17, 18.

12. What will God set among the nations? Where will God send the remnant? What will they declare? Verse 19.

Note.—"A sign." Eze. 20:12, 20.
"Those that escape," the remnant.
"Unto the nations." The nations here mentioned are representative of the nations of the earth. That is, the messengers shall go to the ends of the earth and declare God's glory.

13. What will they bring as an offering from all nations? What will the Lord take of them? Verses 20, 21.

Note.—This widespread missionary work will bring sheaves from all nations brought as an offering to God. Some of them God will use as priests and Levites.

14. How long will the seed and the name remain? Verse 22.

15. What will come to pass from one new moon to another, and from one Sabbath to another? Verse 23.

Note.—"The Sabbath was not for Israel merely, but for the world. It had been made known to man in Eden, and, like the other precepts of the Decalogue, it is of imperishable obligation. Of that law of which the fourth commandment forms a part, Christ declares, 'Till heaven and earth pass, one jot or one tittle shall in nowise pass from the law.' So long as the heavens and the earth endure, the Sabbath will continue as a sign of the Creator's power. And when Eden shall bloom on earth again, God's holy rest day will be honored by all beneath the sun. 'From one Sabbath to another' the inhabitants of the glorified new earth shall go up 'to worship before Me, saith the Lord.' "—"The Desire of Ages," p. 283.

AN APPEAL

I. H. EVANS

O men of God! These are the last, last hours;
  Before us, all the whitened harvest field,
Unreaped, untouched by sickles such as ours.
  This closing message will a harvest yield,
    If we, His messengers, in zeal proclaim
    The everlasting gospel in His name.

O men of God! Jesus our Priest awaits
  On high to close His ministry; to take
His crown as King of kings; to ope the gates
  Of heaven to all His ransomed ones; and shake
    The powers of heaven; to wake the sleeping dead;
    Receive His kingdom as its kingly Head.

O men of God! These are the last, last hours
  Of time. Eternity is drawing near.
A lost world's doom should wake our drowsy powers
  To deeds of valor in His name; and clear
    Our title to a starry crown to wear;
    Enjoy the mansions Jesus will prepare.

O men of God! These are the last, last hours
  When mercy waits the sinner. Shall we sleep
In ease till all is lost? Or pray for showers
  Of latter rain to fructify and keep
    Our labors strong in spirit, win the lost
    To love our Lord, regarding not the cost?

O men of God! These are the last, last hours
  When labors count and bring a rich reward.
In yonder lines of danger, heavenly powers
  Unfurl His blood-stained banner, us to guard!
    Who'll follow where the Master leads the way?
    Go, reap in every land, while lasts the day.

We'd love to have you download our catalog of
titles we publish at:

www.TEACHServices.com

or write or email us your thoughts,
reactions, or criticism about this
or any other book we publish at:

TEACH Services, Inc.
254 Donovan Road
Brushton, NY 12916

info@TEACHServices.com

or you may call us at:

518/358-3494

Produced in partnership with
LNFBooks.com

www.ingramcontent.com/pod-product-compliance
Lightning Source LLC
Chambersburg PA
CBHW070932230426
43666CB00011B/2412